The Cambridge Companion to the Musical

The Cambridge Companion to the Musical provides an accessible
introduction to one of the liveliest and most popular forms of
musical performance. Written by a team of specialists in the field of
musical theatre especially for students and theatregoers, it offers a
guide to the history and development of the musical in England and
America, including coverage of New York's Broadway and London's
West End traditions. Starting with the early history of the musical,
the volume comes right up to date. It examines the latest works and
innovations, and includes information on the singers, audience and
critical reception, and traditions. There is fresh coverage of the
American musical theatre in the eighteenth and nineteenth
centuries, the British musical theatre in the middle of the twentieth
century and the rock musical. The *Companion* contains an
extensive bibliography and photos from key productions.

William A. Everett is Assistant Professor of Musicology at the
University of Missouri–Kansas City Conservatory of Music. His
articles and reviews have appeared in a number of journals
including *American Music, Opera Quarterly* and the *Journal of the
American Viola Society*, and he is also the author of *British Piano
Trios, Quartets, and Quintets, 1850–1950: A Checklist* (2000).

Paul R. Laird is Associate Professor of Musicology in the
Department of Music and Dance, University of Kansas. He is the
author of *Towards a History of the Spanish Villancico* (1997) and
Leonard Bernstein: A Guide to Research (2002), and co-editor with
Craig H. Russell of *Res Musicae: Essays in Honor of James W. Pruett*
(2001).

Cambridge Companions to Music

Instruments

The Cambridge Companion to Brass Instruments
Edited by Trevor Herbert and John Wallace

The Cambridge Companion to the Cello
Edited by Robin Stowell

The Cambridge Companion to the Clarinet
Edited by Colin Lawson

The Cambridge Companion to the Guitar
Edited by Victor Anand Coelho

The Cambridge Companion to the Organ
Edited by Nicholas Thistlethwaite and Geoffrey Webber

The Cambridge Companion to the Piano
Edited by David Rowland

The Cambridge Companion to the Recorder
Edited by John Mansfield Thomson

The Cambridge Companion to the Saxophone
Edited by Richard Ingham

The Cambridge Companion to the Violin
Edited by Robin Stowell

Composers

The Cambridge Companion to Bach
Edited by John Butt

The Cambridge Companion to Bartok
Edited by Amanda Bayley

The Cambridge Companion to Berg
Edited by Anthony Pople

The Cambridge Companion to Beethoven
Edited by Glenn Stanley

The Cambridge Companion to Berlioz
Edited by Peter Bloom

The Cambridge Companion to Benjamin Britten
Edited by Mervyn Cooke

The Cambridge Companion to Brahms
Edited by Michael Musgrave

The Cambridge Companion to John Cage
Edited by David Nicholls

The Cambridge Companion to Chopin
Edited by Jim Samson

The Cambridge Companion to Debussy
Edited by Simon Trezise

The Cambridge Companion to the

MUSICAL

. . . .

EDITED BY
William A. Everett
University of Missouri–Kansas City

Paul R. Laird
University of Kansas

CAMBRIDGE
UNIVERSITY PRESS

PUBLISHED BY THE PRESS SYNDICATE OF THE UNIVERSITY OF CAMBRIDGE
The Pitt Building, Trumpington Street, Cambridge, United Kingdom

CAMBRIDGE UNIVERSITY PRESS
The Edinburgh Building, Cambridge CB2 2RU, UK
40 West 20th Street, New York, NY 10011-4211, USA
477 Williamstown Road, Port Melbourne, VIC 3207, Australia
Ruiz de Alarcón 13, 28014 Madrid, Spain
Dock House, The Waterfront, Cape Town 8001, South Africa

http://www.cambridge.org

© Cambridge University Press 2002

This book is in copyright. Subject to statutory exception
and to the provisions of relevant collective licensing agreements,
no reproduction of any part may take place without
the written permission of Cambridge University Press.

First published 2002

Printed in the United Kingdom at the University Press, Cambridge

Typeface Minion 10.75/14 pt   *System* LATEX 2_ε [TB]

A catalogue record for this book is available from the British Library

Library of Congress Cataloguing in Publication data

The Cambridge companion to the musical / edited by William A. Everett, Paul R. Laird.
     p.   cm. – (Cambridge companions to music)
Includes bibliographical references (p.) and index.
ISBN 0 521 79189 8 (hardback) – ISBN 0 521 79639 3 (paperback)
1. Musicals – History and criticism.   2. Musical theater – History.   I. Everett, William A., 1962–
II. Laird, Paul R.   III. Series.
ML2054 .C35   2002
782.1′4 – dc21   2002023788

ISBN 0 521 79189 8 hardback
ISBN 0 521 79639 3 paperback

Contents

Illustrations

1 John Durang in the character of Harlequin. Photo courtesy of York County Historical Society, Pennsylvania [6]

2 Editorial cartoon concerning the popularity of *The Merry Widow* from *The Evening American*, 1909. In public domain [36]

3 The original New York production of *The Student Prince* with Ilse Marvenga and the Male Chorus. Photo courtesy of Shubert Archive [52]

4 A production of *Show Boat*, c. 1938 at the St Louis Municipal Opera. Photo courtesy of the Municipal Theatre Association of St Louis [74]

5 Gertrude Lawrence with the doll that George Gershwin gave her to hold while singing 'Someone to Watch Over Me' in *Oh, Kay!*. Photo courtesy of New York Public Library, Billy Rose Theatre Collection [95]

6 Programme cover from original production of *Twenty to One* (12 November 1935, Coliseum). Photo from private programme collection of John Snelson [102]

7 Programme cover from the 1945 revival at the Victoria Palace of *Me and My Girl* (original premiere 16 December 1937, Victoria Palace). The design is the same as the original cover and Lupino Lane starred in both productions. Photo from private programme collection of John Snelson [109]

8 Programme cover from original production of *Bless the Bride* (26 April 1947, Adelphi Theatre). Photo from private programme collection of John Snelson [109]

9 Programme cover from original production of *Gay's the Word* (16 February 1951, Saville Theatre). Photo from private programme collection of John Snelson [109]

10 Programme cover from *Expresso Bongo* (23 April 1958, Saville Theatre). Photo from private programme collection of John Snelson [109]

11 Shirley Jones as Maria with the children in the 1977 production of *The Sound of Music* at the Starlight Theater, Kansas City, Missouri. Photo courtesy of Starlight Theater, Kansas City, Missouri [134]

12 Carol Channing in 1977 production of *Hello, Dolly!* at the Starlight Theater, Kansas City, Missouri. Photo courtesy of Starlight Theater, Kansas City, Missouri [160]

13 Lotte Lenya performing the song 'Pirate Jenny' with Leonard Bernstein conducting during concert production of *The Threepenny Opera* at Festival of the Creative Arts, Brandeis University, 1952. Photo courtesy of The Kurt Weill Foundation for Music [168]

14 Production of *Company* in 2001 at the Missouri Repertory Theatre. Photo courtesy of Missouri Repertory Theatre [185]

15 Ann Reinking, P. J. Mann, and Christine Colby Jacques in 'Stout-Hearted Men', a dance number from Bob Fosse's *Dancin'* in 1979. Photo courtesy of TimePix, Martha Swope Collection [204]

16 The original production of *Hair* in 1968. Photo by Dagmar [234]

Contributors

Geoffrey Block, Professor of Music History at the University of Puget Sound in Tacoma, Washington, is the author of *Charles Ives: A Bio-Bibliography* (1988), a Cambridge Music Handbook on Ives's *Concord Sonata* (1996) and *Enchanted Evenings: The Broadway Musical from "Show Boat" to Sondheim* (1997), the co-editor of *Charles Ives and the Classical Tradition* (1996), and the editor of *The Richard Rodgers Reader* (2002). He is now completing a book on Richard Rodgers's Broadway career for Yale University Press's 'Yale Broadway Masters', a new series for which he is General Editor.

William A. Everett teaches music history at the University of Missouri–Kansas City Conservatory of Music. Prior to his present appointment, he taught at Washburn University in Topeka, Kansas. He completed his Ph.D. in musicology at the University of Kansas. In addition to the musical theatre, his research interests include music and musical life in Croatia, Finland and Great Britain. He is the author of *British Piano Trios, Quartets, and Quintets, 1850–1950: A Checklist* (2000) and contributed to *The New Grove Dictionary of Music and Musicians,* 2nd edn. His articles have appeared in *American Music, Opera Quarterly* and elsewhere. He is currently working on a book on Sigmund Romberg for 'Yale Broadway Masters'. He was treasurer of the Society for American Music from 1996 to 2001.

John Graziano is Professor of Music at the City College and Graduate Center, City University of New York. His most recent publications include: articles on the early life and career of Sissieretta Jones, the "Black Patti"; Arthur Farewell's music for the Shakespeare Tercentenary; and a volume of chamber music for strings by the mid-nineteenth-century American composer, Charles Hommann. His article on Sissieretta Jones appeared in the *Journal of the American Musicological Society* and won the 2000 Irving Lowens Award from the Society for American Music.

Orly Leah Krasner received her Ph.D. in musicology from the City University of New York. She has taught at Franklin & Marshall College and Boston University, and is currently on the faculty of City College, CUNY. She was also visiting scholar at the Université de Rouen in France, where she taught a course on the Broadway musical. Dr. Krasner has lectured and written extensively about turn-of-the-century musical theatre, particularly *The Merry Widow* and Reginald de Koven. She prepared an edition of his *The Highwayman* for the series *Nineteenth-Century American Musical Theatre.* Her work has appeared in *Current Musicology, College Music Symposium, The New Grove Dictionary of Opera* and *The New Grove Dictionary of Music and Musicians,* 2nd edn.

Paul R. Laird is Associate Professor of Musicology at the University of Kansas, where he has taught since 1994. He is the author of *Towards A History of the Spanish Villancico* (1997) and *Leonard Bernstein: A Guide to Research* (2002). He is co-editor with Craig H. Russell of *Res Musicae: Essays in Honor of James W. Pruett* (2001). Laird is currently writing *The Baroque Cello Revival: An Oral History.* Laird's articles and reviews have appeared in *The New Grove Dictionary of Music and Musicians*, 2nd edn, *Revista de Musicología, Anuario musical, Early Music* and many other sources. He is also a Baroque cellist who directs the Instrumental Collegium Musicum at the University of Kansas.

Jim Lovensheimer attended the University of Cincinnati College – Conservatory of Music where he studied theatre performance. After working in the professional theatre as an actor, musical director, accompanist, and arranger, he returned to academia. In 1994, he graduated *summa cum laude* and Phi Beta Kappa from the University of Tennessee with a Bachelor of Music in music history. Continuing his studies in music history, Lovensheimer earned an MA at The Ohio State University with his thesis '*La grandmère amoureuse*: A Case Study in 18th-Century Parisian Operatic Parody'. He is currently finishing his Ph.D. at Ohio State with a dissertation on 'The Musicodramatic Evolution of Rodgers and Hammerstein's *South Pacific*' and recently joined the faculty at Vanderbilt University.

bruce d. mcclung is an associate professor of musicology at the University of Cincinnati College – Conservatory of Music. His articles on the music theatre works of Kurt Weill may be found in *A Stranger Here Myself: Kurt Weill Studien, Kurt Weill Newsletter, Pipers Enzyklopädie des Musiktheaters, The Playbill*, and *Theater*. He co-edited *Lady in the Dark: A Sourcebook* (Kurt Weill Foundation) and acted as music/text consultant for the first London production of *Lady in the Dark* (National Theater). He is editing *Lady in the Dark* for the *Kurt Weill Edition* and is the author of a forthcoming monograph, *American Dreams: Kurt Weill's Lady in the Dark*.

Paul Prece holds a BA from Catholic University, an MFA from Florida State University, and is working on his doctorate in Theory and Criticism at the University of Kansas. He is Professor and Chair of Theatre Department at Washburn University in Topeka, Kansas where he teaches performance, directing, dramatic literature and history. Prece has directed over 120 productions ranging from contemporary to classic, theatre for children and youth to musical theatre.

Katherine K. Preston is Associate Professor of Music and Chair of the Department of Music at the College of William and Mary in Williamsburg, Virginia. Her area of specialization is the history of music and musical culture in nineteenth-century America; she is particularly interested in performance and reception history of musical theatre. She is the author of *Opera on the Road: Traveling Opera Troupes in the United States, 1825–1860* (1993/2001) and editor of *Irish American Theater*, Volume X in the series *Nineteenth-Century American Musical Theatre* (1994). She is currently working on the reception history of English-language opera in the United States of the late nineteenth century.

Thomas L. Riis has served as Professor of Musicology and Director of the American Music Research Center at the University of Colorado at Boulder since 1992. His previous publications devoted to American musical theatre include the first complete edition of Will Marion Cook's 1902 musical comedy, *In Dahomey* and *Just Before Jazz: Black Musical Theater in New York, 1890 to 1915* which received an ASCAP-Deems Taylor Award in 1995. He lectures widely on African-American performers and their performances in the US and abroad, as well as many other topics in American popular and classical music. In 2001 he served as the Albert Seay Distinguished Visiting Professor at Colorado College. He is currently working on a monograph on Frank Loesser for 'Yale Broadway Masters' as well as a comprehensive textbook on the American musical theatre.

Ann Sears is Professor of Music and Chair of the Music Department at Wheaton College in Norton, Massachusetts, where she teaches piano and courses in European and American music history. An active solo and collaborative pianist, she appears on two compact discs: *Deep River: The Art Songs and Spirituals of Harry T. Burleigh*, and *Fiyer! A Century of African-American Song*. She has presented papers at meetings of the Society for American Music, the College Music Society, the International Society for the Study of European Ideas, and the American Matthay Association, and published in the *Sonneck Society Bulletin*; *American Music*; *The New Grove Dictionary of Music and Musicians*, 2nd edn; *International Dictionary of Black Composers*, *Reader's Guide to Music: History, Theory, Criticism*; *St. James Encyclopedia of Popular Culture*; *American Music Teacher*; *Black Music Research Journal*; and *Music Library Association Notes*.

John Snelson researches and writes on musical theatre, specialising in British repertory. He has contributed to *The New Grove Dictionary of Music and Musicians*, 2nd edn (for which he was also a commissioning editor), *The New Dictionary of National Biography* and *The Oxford Companion to Music*. His most recent project is a volume on Andrew Lloyd Webber for 'Yale Broadway Masters'.

Scott Warfield holds a Ph.D. from the University of North Carolina at Chapel Hill, where he wrote his dissertation on Richard Strauss's first tone poem, *Macbeth*. His articles and reviews have appeared in the *Richard Strauss-Blätter*, *Music Library Association Notes*, *Fontes Artis Musicae*, *Kurt Weill Newsletter* and elsewhere. He has been the chief programme annotator for the North Carolina Symphony since 1985, and he has written frequently for other ensembles. Since 2002, he has been on the faculty of University of Central Florida, previously he taught at Nebraska Wesleyan University, several colleges in North Carolina and Centre College in Danville, Kentucky.

Graham Wood is Assistant Professor of Music at Coker College in Hartsville, South Carolina. A native of England, he has a BA in music from the University of Newcastle, and an MA and Ph.D. in Musicology from the University of Minnesota. His doctoral dissertation, 'The Development of Song Forms in the Broadway and Hollywood Musicals of Richard Rodgers, 1919–1943' is an interdisciplinary study showing how the construction of songs, and in particular their chorus patterns, function in larger dramatic-narrative frameworks and also in broader cultural scenarios. In addition to teaching classes in music history and musical theatre, Wood is also active as a musical director conductor and French horn player.

Preface

In the four weeks that are needed you get about two hours of sleep a night. But it's fun. You can't really start doing the orchestration until the rehearsals begin, because until you know who the singers are going to be, you don't know which key to choose for each number. The American musical is a custom-made job.   KURT WEILL [1]

Those who love American and British musicals know how they are created. Whether first conceived for Broadway or for London's West End, successful musicals are monuments to collaboration between composer, lyricist, producer, director, choreographer, costume designer, lighting designer, orchestrator, dance arranger, actors and others. As Weill notes, basic issues are left unsettled shortly before a show goes into rehearsal. Any aspect of a show's content might change before opening night. In some shows, such as *Camelot* (1960), wholesale changes were made after opening night in New York.

Some theatrical figures make their reputations as 'play doctors', experts who come in at the last moment and make the best possible product out of existing material, finding that which will most please an audience. The goal of the frenetic activity that constitutes Weill's 'custom job' is to make a show entertaining. Those who enjoy a show tell friends about it, selling more tickets. Musicals are part of the so-called entertainment industry, ruled by a brutal bottom-line philosophy: the 'angels', or the show's financial backers, wish to have their investment returned, if possible with a profit.

Surely this is a crass way to begin a history of the musical in the English-speaking world, but it is where we must begin. Those who created this book, and many of its readers, think of the musical as art. In a good musical, a play, or 'book', combines with songs, dances and stagecraft to create a whole, artistic entity. In the insane weeks before a show opens, however, at least as important as artistic concerns is the need to entertain. Wonderful scenes, songs and dances are cut because they do not fit into the whole. No successful figure in the history of the musical worked for artistic reasons alone: a career is based on the ability to entertain. Artistic concerns are secondary and often only recognized later. Michael John LaChiusa, a composer and lyricist currently active on Broadway, recognizes this basic truth when naming models for his own work: 'we're free to borrow from both European operatic tradition and American musical tradition, toss out what we don't need and

---

[1] Weill spoke these words after the opening of *One Touch of Venus* (1943); quoted in Jürgen Schebera, *Kurt Weill: An Illustrated Life* (New Haven and London, 1995), p. 288.

invent whatever creature we want, whatever we choose. *And above all else, entertain.*[2]

These basic truths have existed for the entire period described in this book. Most musicals went through the crucible that Weill describes. Figures in the musical theatre often describe the agony of opening night, when, even with all of their experience, they really do not know whether a show will be a hit, a flop or something in between. Much of the history of the musical described here is made during the weeks before an opening night. At the premiere the creator finds out if the show works. These experiences unite each of the creators described in these pages from the eighteenth century to the present and give the theatre much of its breathless quality.

The history described in this book is built upon such commonalities of experience as they relate to what creators, actors, and audience feel as participants in live musical theatre. What brings people back to the musical theatre is the genre's magical ability to entertain and help one experience life afresh, if only for a moment. The possibility of such experience is almost an unwritten contract between a show's presenters and their audience. What we offer here is a history of that contract's consistent renewal and reinvention. The details of the contract differ in various types of musical theatre, including ballad operas, operas, minstrel shows, operettas, revues, musical comedies, more serious shows that some call musical plays, megamusicals, various types of song and/or dance compilations, and even revivals of earlier shows.

The relationship between drama and music in the musical theatre encompasses a broad range of approaches. The 'book musical', where a narrative libretto provides the plot, is perhaps the most common type of musical theatre on Broadway and in the West End. When creators divert from this 'standard' approach, it is viewed as a departure from the norm. Whereas book musicals emphasise the linear progression of time, non-book musicals tend to eschew it. This breadth of creative approaches is what makes the musical theatre such a fascinating genre and simultaneously such a difficult one to arrange into neat, definable sub-categories. Its very nature along with its potentially inexhaustible creative possibilities thankfully keep it from being too easily demarcated.

Weill's description of a musical as a 'custom job' implies a genre with a rich, diverse history. As Katherine Preston demonstrates in the first chapter, the history before 1900 goes beyond rich and diverse to the chaotic, and in some ways the musical theatre has never outgrown its messy adolescence. In the midst of such variety and confusion, it is our intention to try to bring a modicum of order and describe as many of those 'custom jobs' as possible,

---

[2] Michael John LaChiusa, 'I Sing of America's Mongrel Culture', *New York Times*, 14 November 1999.

placing each show in the incredibly rich tapestry that is the musical theatre in the United States and Great Britain.

This book is another monument to collaboration. We thank each of the writers who shared their knowledge and love of various topics in the chapters of this book and who responded without fail to our editorial requests. We would also like to thank Victoria Cooper and the staff at Cambridge University Press without whom this book would never have appeared. Thanks as well to the people and institutions who made illustrations available for use. We thank Jay Martin and Kathleen Roley for helping to compile the bibliography. We also thank our families and colleagues for putting up with us while bringing this book to fruition.

William A. Everett
Paul R. Laird

PART I

Adaptations and transformations: before 1940

1 American musical theatre before the twentieth century

KATHERINE K. PRESTON

The history of musical comedy begins in confusion.[1]   EDITH BORROFF

Most histories of American musical theatre give short shrift – at best – to the 'origin of the species', to use Edith Borroff's apt phrase. Despite lofty ambitions (titles that claim coverage 'from the beginning to the present'), most authors are content to offer a brief essay about the antecedents of musical comedy, usually including definitive identification of 'the first American musical' (*The Black Crook*, *Little Johnny Jones*, *Evangeline*, *Show Boat*, *The Beggar's Opera*, *The Wizard of the Nile* or any number of other works), before turning, with an almost discernible sigh of relief, to musical theatre of the twentieth century. The reasons for the brevity and for the disagreement on the 'first' musical become readily apparent as soon as one attempts to sort out the myriad different types of musical theatrical forms that materialised, metamorphosed, became popular, disappeared, re-emerged, and cross-fertilized prior to the twentieth century. To put it simply, for the scholar in search of a clear lineage to the forms of the twentieth century, musical theatre in the eighteenth – and even more so in the nineteenth – century was a tangled, chaotic mess. This was not the impression at the time, of course. To the contrary, a nineteenth-century American, especially the resident of a large city like New York, found musical theatrical life during the time to be gloriously rich, varied, and ever-changing; it was a world that was entertaining, interesting, exciting and innovative to an extent that should elicit a twinge of envy from the modern reader. But the job of the historian is to clarify and attempt to put into some kind of order the messiness of a bygone era. And the richness of that period makes the job both difficult and important.

What follows, then, is a carefully guided and succinct tour of the American musical-theatrical world of the eighteenth and nineteenth centuries. To some readers – especially those anxious to reach the more familiar terrain of the twentieth century – the description of musical life of the earlier eras will be a little puzzling, primarily because this essay will describe genres that have since been removed from the general category of 'musical theatre'. But the varied musical forms that Americans enjoyed in the late eighteenth and early nineteenth centuries (including opera, pantomime, melodrama, minstrelsy and dance) developed, changed and influenced each other to a remarkable degree. The wealth of earlier musical styles evolved into the wonderfully diverse, rich and confusing jumble that was the American musical-theatrical world of the last third of the nineteenth century, which many scholars agree was the birthplace of the twentieth-century musical. It is important, then, to examine the whole picture – albeit in summary fashion – in order to comprehend the foundations of this truly American musical form.

The eighteenth century

There is scattered evidence of theatrical activity in the American colonies in the seventeenth century, but the real history of musical theatre commences in the eighteenth. The first opera mounted in English-speaking America was the ballad opera *Flora, or, Hob in the Wall,* performed in Charleston, South Carolina in 1735; two weeks prior to that, the same theatre had offered a different work that was equally musical in nature: the pantomime *The Adventures of Harlequin and Scaramouche,* performed as an afterpiece.[2] From the 1730s until the Revolution, Americans – especially those living in the urban centres of the Northeast or the market towns of the rural Southeast – witnessed a constant stream of theatrical offerings imported from the British Isles. Many thespians of this period were associated with itinerant or 'strolling' companies, formed by players (frequently family members) who performed in return for shares of the box-office take. Women performers, in particular, were all but obliged by the mandates of society to tour with male family members, in order to preserve any semblance of reputation already made suspect by public performance. The first permanent such strolling troupe in the colonies was Lewis Hallam's Company of Comedians, which arrived from London in 1752, renamed itself the American Company, and gave its first performance in Williamsburg, Virginia.[3] This company and others like it travelled from town to town and city to city on regular circuits (primarily via horse-drawn vehicles) during the mid-eighteenth century; they eventually built theatres in larger towns from which they branched out – especially during the summer – to perform in smaller towns and villages located within a reasonable distance from the hub city. This *modus operandi* was similar to that in the British Isles, where London was the principal hub, cities like Manchester, Birmingham, Edinburgh and Dublin were smaller hubs, and other towns and villages were served by itinerant troupes that used theatres in the larger urban areas as seats of operation. To a great extent, then, strolling theatrical troupes active in America were transatlantic extensions of the provincial theatrical circuit of Great Britain; American theatres were essentially part of the London cultural sphere.

In 1774 professional theatrical activity in the colonies officially stopped (although dramatic performances continued, mostly under the guise of 'concerts'), when the Continental Congress passed a resolution that prohibited activities that were distracting to the Revolution. After the War, the banished strolling companies resumed activities. Hallam's troupe, now proudly called the Old American Company, returned from Jamaica in 1784, re-established its circuit and enjoyed a virtual monopoly until the early 1790s. During that decade American theatrical life underwent significant change, as urban areas in the new nation increased sufficiently in size to allow the establishment of permanent theatres with resident stock companies. Important theatres were built (especially in the 1790s) in New York, Philadelphia, Boston, Charleston, Baltimore and other cities on the East Coast. Resident stock companies, complete with orchestras and musical directors, were hired; their performances frequently included the assistance of 'gentlemen amateurs', which reflects a continuing – and growing – active interest in the theatre among American city-dwellers. Since theatres traditionally offered permanent work to musicians, this spate of theatre-building helped to attract to America a whole coterie of musicians from Europe. These musicians – most of whom arrived in the 1790s – included Alexander Reinagle (1756–1809), Rayner Taylor (1747–1825), Benjamin Carr (1768–1831) and James Hewitt (1770–1827) from Scotland and England, Victor Pelissier (c. 1740/50 – c. 1820) from France, and Gottlieb Graupner (1767–1836) from Germany.

The repertory of all theatres during this period relied heavily on music; the historian Julian Mates asserts that by the beginning of the nineteenth century fully half of the repertory on the American stage was musical in nature.[4] Every theatre had an orchestra, and a typical evening, in the words of William Brooks, consisted of 'an encyclopedia of entertainment, a potpourri of performance', much of which required orchestral accompaniment.[5] The evening's activity generally commenced with a short concert of 'waiting music' played by the orchestra, followed by first a prologue and then the principal dramatic work (the mainpiece), which – in turn – was followed by a shorter work, usually a farce or pantomime (the afterpiece). Between the mainpiece and the afterpiece, the orchestra would play several selections, and during both dramatic works the actors would interpolate songs or dances as *divertissements* or changes of pace. The evening's entertainment – which frequently lasted four or five hours – would conclude with diverse amusements such as singing, dancing, further works performed by the orchestra, or possibly a short epilogue; sometimes the choice of repertory was in response to requests from audience members.[6] Audience behaviour at

Plate 1   John Durang in the character of Harlequin

such entertainments was not unlike that typical of twentieth-century sport-ing events: members of the audience would come and go, eat and drink, talk among themselves, applaud wildly, heckle the actors mercilessly, or sing along with the performers. The 'dramatic' evening just described is one that featured a drama; when the mainpiece consisted instead of a ballad opera or a comic opera (both, on the American stage, essentially plays with songs), the percentage of music performed was even greater. It should be clear that during this period the terms 'theatre' and 'musical theatre' were essentially synonymous.

For the most part, the American theatre during the final decades of the eighteenth century remained firmly British in orientation: American theatres became important competitors with provincial English theatres for actors, actresses, and even pantomimists, most of whom were French (but who arrived via England).[7] Costumes and scenery were either imported outright or copied from productions in England, and theatrical repertory was also, by and large, from London – imported either as manuscripts, or as promptbooks or as published music in keyboard or vocal format.[8] One of the principal tasks for a theatre's musical director was the re-orchestration (frequently from keyboard reduction) of musical accompaniment to dramatic or operatic works; musical directors also composed new incidental music, and – increasingly – musical-theatrical works of their own. The most popular musical works performed on the American stage between 1790 and 1810, according to Susan Porter, included such standard London fare as the comic operas *The Poor Soldier* (1783) and *Rosina* (1782) by William Shield; *The Children in the Wood* (1793) and *The Mountaineers* (1793) by Samuel Arnold; and *No Song, No Supper* (1790) by Stephen Storace.[9] During the last decade of the eighteenth century, however, American theatre-goers could increasingly witness musical theatrical works written in America, usually by the recent musical immigrants mentioned above. These included such works as Victor Pelissier's *Edwin and Angelina* (1791), operas by James Hewitt (*Tammany; or, the Indian Chief*, 1794) and Benjamin Carr (*The Archers*, 1796), and music for pantomimes by composers such as Pelissier, Reinagle, Hewitt, and Taylor. Melodrama (introduced from France by way of England) also became part of the American theatrical repertory in the 1790s; it would become one of the dominant forms of musical theatre in the nineteenth century. The music from all of these shows increasingly permeated American society by means of sheet music; it was both imported and published by American firms, snapped up from music store shelves, and played on fortepianos in American parlours all over the country.

The nineteenth century: 1800–1840

By the first decades of the nineteenth century, theatrical production in the United States was accomplished almost exclusively by established theatres with resident stock companies. Itinerant theatrical troupes (like the earlier 'strolling' players) were still active in the less settled parts of the country (and would remain so, moving ever further west with the frontier); the 'star system', under which a visiting dramatic star (usually from England) would visit different theatres in turn, taking the starring roles of plays mounted by the stock companies, had just been introduced from Great Britain. For the most part, however, theatrical performances in Federal-period America were mounted by the stock companies of local theatres, with musical accompaniment by the theatres' orchestras. For repertory during this period, American theatres for the most part continued to rely on London for their material. With an ever-growing critical mass of skilled actors, playwrights and composers resident in the United States, however, these imported materials, more frequently than not, were extensively modified (mostly in subject matter) for American audiences.

Melodrama

Melodrama, which would (arguably) become the most important and popular dramatic and musical genre in America during the nineteenth century, emerged in full force during the first decades. Originally a French technique from the mid-eighteenth century, melodrama – the use in drama of short musical passages to heighten emotional affect, either in alternation with or underlying spoken dialogue – came to America, as had pantomime, from the British popular theatre.[10] The first melodrama presented in America was probably *Ariadne Abandoned by Theseus in the Isle of Naxos*, with music (now lost) by Victor Pelissier, performed in New York in 1797. Early melodramas used music quite sparingly; this, as we shall see, would change later in the century.

Few instrumental 'melos' (snippets of 'hurry music', 'music to express discontent or alarm', etc.) survive from before 1850; it was rare for such manuscripts to be published, and most perished in the fires that regularly consumed theatres in the nineteenth century. But specific directions indicated in prompt books, in conjunction with information from the few scores that do survive, suffice to provide a clear indication of the nature of melodrama. Two early works merit some mention. Victor Pelissier's complete orchestral score to William Dunlap's *The Voice of Nature* (1803) is the earliest extant musical score for a complete dramatic work written for the American theatre.[11] It includes several composed pieces (marches, a dance, choruses); musical cues in the first and third acts indicate clearly where the music is to be inserted.[12] Dunlap's score is actually a good illustration of contemporary *incidental* music, for – although sometimes referred to as such – *The Voice of Nature* is not technically a melodrama, since the music neither alternates with nor underlies spoken dialogue.[13] The first extant score to a melodrama that is closer to the mark (and the only extant American score for melodrama prior to 1850) is J. N. Barker and John Bray's *The Indian Princess, ou, La Belle Sauvage* (1808), which is identified on the title page of the published score as an 'operatic melo-drame'.[14] As a hybrid, *The Indian Princess* is more than 'a mixed drama of words and ten bars of music' (Dunlap's description of melodrama), for it has both vocal music (songs, glees and choruses) and passages of instrumental melodramatic music that underlie mimed dramatic action.[15] Music used to accompany action was borrowed from the world of pantomime; small dances and closed-form songs (usually seen at the beginnings of scenes) were traditions from *opéra-comique* and ballad opera.[16] Most of the melodramas popular on the American stage prior to 1850 were from London (or France via London); most probably had new music composed by American theatre composers, and none survives.[17]

One final insight into the popularity of early melodramas in America comes from an examination of the careers of French dancers who toured the United States during the period. One such is Madame Celeste Keppler Elliott (b. 1810), a French actress and dancer. Like other French dancers who visited during this period, Madame Celeste originally performed in 'ballets' (in her case, in New York after her arrival in 1827), but very quickly switched to melodramas such as *The French Spy; or, the Siege of Constantina* (with music by Daniel François-Esprit Auber), in part because of the popularity of the form, in part because the lead female role in the melodrama is mute (her spoken English was weak). Madame Celeste eventually used as performance vehicles some dozen mimed melodramatic works (including an adaptation of James Fenimore Cooper's *The Wept of Wish-Ton-Wish*); as a 'melodramatic artist' she mounted several lucrative tours of America from the late 1820s through the early 1840s.[18] Presumably the music to many of the works in which she and other dancers so successfully appeared was composed, as was normal, by musicians associated with American theatres. The performances of such dancers in both ballets and melodramatic works suggests a clear overlap between the two styles of dramatic art; Madame Celeste's remarkable success on the American stage, furthermore, is additional evidence of the popularity of melodrama.

Itinerant singers and vocal stars

In the 1810s a new kind of musical performer began making the rounds of theatres in the United States; they were the musical counterparts of the theatrical 'stars' who had begun to visit in the 1790s. These vocal stars began to arrive individually in 1817; they performed in concert and in operas with stock companies, all of which still included in their standard repertories English operatic works by such composers as Thomas Arne, Charles Dibdin, William Shield and Thomas Linley.[19] These early vocal stars were followed in the 1820s by a whole host of (mostly) British singers, who toured on the American theatrical circuit in the company of such British *theatrical* stars as Edmund Kean, William Charles Macready, Junius

Brutus Booth, Peter Richings, and Charles Kemble. The most important early vocal stars were Elizabeth Austin (toured 1827–35) and Joseph and Mary Anne Paton Wood (1833–36, second tour in the 1840s), who opened the floodgates for additional singers in the 1830s and early 1840s. Vocal stars who banded together into small 'vocal-star troupes' in the late 1830s included Jane Shirreff (1811–83), John Wilson (1801–49) and the husband-and-wife team of Anne (1809?–88) and Edward (Ned) (1809–52) Seguin, all of whom arrived in 1838. These singers toured up and down the East Coast, utilising the expanding steam (rail and water) transportation system to take them to large cities as well as to the smaller towns and hamlets in between. These (and many other) singers – whether touring alone or as duos or trios – became a regular part of American popular musical theatre; they electrified American audiences, who flocked to performances and who purchased reams of arias 'as sung by' the vocalists, whose images were engraved on sheet music covers. The singers took the starring roles in standard English comic operas such as those mentioned above, with stock company performers singing secondary roles and functioning as the chorus. They also introduced to American audiences more opera from the *bel canto* and French schools (in English adaptation), including works by Auber, Boieldieu, Rossini, Bellini and Mozart.[20] These translated operas fitted readily into an American theatrical repertory that already included English comic and ballad operas, pantomime and melodrama. But the introduction of the more difficult *bel canto* operas – made possible by the higher-calibre performances of the itinerant vocalists – thrilled American audiences of all economic classes; as a result, Americans developed an almost insatiable appetite for Italian operatic music. The enthusiastic reception of the newer operatic repertory opened the door both for larger English opera troupes (starting in the 1840s) and for foreign-language opera companies. The singing by the women vocal stars, in particular, spurred a fondness among Americans for 'bird-like' vocal gymnastics that would continue throughout the century.

In 1825 the Spanish tenor Manuel García (1775–1832) visited New York City with his family (including his daughter María Malibran), where they mounted the first American seasons of opera in Italian.[21] Two years later John Davis's French Opera Company of New Orleans embarked on an East Coast tour, the first of six annual tours (1827–33) during which they performed opera in French in various East coast cities.[22] Throughout the 1830s numerous itinerant Italian opera companies (mostly based in New York) attempted to capitalise on the growing American taste for this particular flavour of musical theatre; they met with varying degrees of success, but built the foundation for many more – and more successful – Italian opera troupes that would follow in the 1840s.[23] It is worth reminding the reader that during this period both English and foreign-language opera fitted easily into the American theatrical repertory. Opera had not yet been segregated from the regular theatre, nor did Americans readily make a distinction between 'theatre' and 'musical theatre'.

The nineteenth century: c. 1840–1865

By the 1840s the infrastructure to support the theatre in America was firmly in place. The increase in population in the country (fuelled, in part, by a phenomenal immigration rate) was such that there were now numerous towns and cities large enough to support at least one – and frequently more than one – theatre with a resident stock company. These theatres now hosted on a regular basis increasing numbers of theatrical and musical 'stars', who utilised the ever-expanding steam-powered (water and rail) transportation system.[24] The stock companies – with or without the 'stars' – performed repertory that continued to be heavily musical in nature. Added to the mix of visiting stars were specialised musical-theatrical performers who likewise traversed the theatrical circuit in ever-increasing numbers: blackface minstrel troupes; English, Italian and French opera companies; acrobats, dancers and pantomimists – each of these will be discussed below. The 'star' system would eventually destroy the stock company system (and the fault lines were already readily apparent during the 1850s and 1860s); it would be replaced – in the last decades of the century – by the combination system, of which these itinerant 'specialty' companies already proliferating in the 1840s and 1850s were forerunners. During the period 1840–65, however, the dominant *modus operandi* for theatrical production was still the local stock company, augmented by 'stars' and supplanted, for weeks at a time, by visiting troupes of minstrels, opera singers or specialty acts.[25]

The theatrical offerings available to American town- or city-dwellers in the 1840s and 1850s changed regularly – usually weekly or bi-weekly – and (by modern standards) varied wildly. To antebellum Americans, going to the theatre was the modern equivalent of going to the multiplex cinema, and the range of diversity represents a certain degree of catholicity of taste among the middle and upper middle classes. By the 1850s there were already apparent seeds of the breakdown in theatrical tastes that eventually would result in a more socially and economically stratified audience; during this period, however – especially in non-East Coast towns that supported fewer theatres – that stratification was not yet a *fait accompli*. Americans went to the theatre regularly and enjoyed a wide array of different kinds of entertainments, most of which could be considered, by the standards of later centuries, musical.

Stock company repertory: melodrama and plays with songs

Melodrama continued its dominance of the American theatrical repertory during this period. By the 1850s, the earlier technique of alternating speech and music had given way to more specialized use of music within the drama: to draw attention to – and heighten the emotional impact of – specific scenes or portions of scenes. As Shapiro points out, instrumental music was now used to heighten 'strong emotional moments of the play when speech was inadequate or even – as in a fight scene – realistically impossible'.[26] It was also during this period that the term melodrama came to refer not to a technique but rather to a particular kind of drama (whether or not it included music). This stereotype (of characters, clearly good or evil, involved in an action-filled plot where evil temporarily succeeds but is eventually defeated by good) is the popular definition of melodrama today (Snidely Whiplash and Dudley Do-Right of Rocky and Bullwinkle fame come immediately to mind); its dramatic style clearly provides much opportunity to use music to express emotion.

Few scores have been found for melodramatic pieces from this period, but those that are extant indicate that there were generally some thirty or forty 'melos' per drama, and that they were composed (not improvised) for full theatre orchestra. Evidence from promptbooks also suggests that the melodramatic music was used in tight coordination with scenic and lighting effects to create the heightened mood. Pantomimic techniques such as short snippets of 'hurry music' were employed regularly to underscore quick action or to indicate emotional agitation.[27] In its impact on audience members the music was probably similar to film scores today: extremely successful in terms of underscoring dramatic emotion, but almost completely unnoticed by most auditors.

By mid-century the use of instrumental music for melodramatic effect had become so accepted a theatrical practice that it was not uncommon for such music to be added to non-melodramatic plays. Dramatised versions of Harriet Beecher Stowe's *Uncle Tom's Cabin* are instructive. The novel, which became an immediate best-seller after its publication in 1852, was adapted to the stage within the year. Extant programmes, promptbooks and playbills suggest clearly that music was central to the performances. One published version includes some two dozen cues for instrumental music to undergird particularly emotional scenes (Eliza's escape, Simon Legree's whipping of Uncle Tom or Eva's assumption).[28] Stage productions also included hymns, minstrel tunes and sentimental songs; some were composed specifically for adaptations of the novel, others were simply popular songs interpolated into particular productions. This insertion of vocal music into stage productions was by no means unusual performance practice for the period and is further evidence of the important role of music in the American theatre at mid century.

Blackface minstrelsy

Blackface minstrelsy, the most important American musical-theatrical development of the antebellum period, would quickly come to rival melodrama in popularity. Ostensibly, the form burst upon the American theatrical scene in 1843, with the inaugural appearance of the Virginia Minstrels in New York City. In reality, the four performers who banded together to form the troupe simply codified performance traditions and techniques – including blackface – that had been seen on the American stage for decades; they also incorporated sensibilities, such as burlesque of the powerful, that had been part of western culture for centuries.[29]

The Virginia Minstrels' format quickly became the standard for other early minstrel troupes: four or six performers, all male and all in blackface, would stand on stage facing the audience in a line or a shallow semi-circle; 'Mr Bones' (who played a rhythmic 'instrument' fashioned from animal bones) and 'Mr Tambo' (who played a tambourine) would be on either end, with the 'Interlocutor' in the middle. The performance was divided into two halves, and included a wide variety of entertainment modes, including singing, skits, jokes, dancing and stand-up comedy; the first half focused on the stereotype of the urban dandy, the second portrayed plantation life. The minstrel songs and dances at first were inspired by the emerging fiddle-tune tradition, but quickly came to be influenced by other popular-song traditions, including sentimental songs, glees, and the four-part harmony of itinerant singing families.[30] Minstrelsy, at bottom, was a musical experience; excepting the skits and comedy routines, the entire performance was musical in nature, with song accompaniments and dances alike performed by the minstrel band, which consisted of fiddle, banjo, tambo and bones.

Blackface minstrel troupes quickly joined the other 'specialty' musical-theatre companies on the circuit in the 1840s and 1850s, attracting audiences of varied social and economic classes.[31] With the increased commercialisation of the form during the late 1840s, minstrel troupes became more streamlined and the format more formulaic. By the late 1850s the first section had become more of a song concert (of genteel and sentimental songs), and a middle section – called the 'olio' – had been added; this latter featured blackface songs and burlesque skits, mocking everything from Shakespeare, to singing families, to opera. The third and final part remained the core of the show, with its depictions of extended plantation scenes. The whole theatrical extravaganza ended with a finale called a 'walk-around', in which the entire company would parade around the stage, singing and accompanied by the minstrel band.[32] The increased commercialisation of the form is also evident in minstrels' exploitation of the growing technology of popular culture. Minstrels – like other contemporary theatrical companies – utilised the expanding American transportation network to travel all over the Eastern United States; they published song-books containing the words of their latest tunes, and sheet music of the sentimental ballads featured in their performances; they corresponded with musical or theatrical journals of national circulation, which published reports of their comings and goings; they advertised upcoming performances in local newspapers prior to arrival in town. Exploitation of such tools helped to create rapidly a large audience for this new musical-theatrical form.

To a great extent the minstrel show – which would continue to evolve and change after the Civil War – was a condensation of various elements of American popular musical theatre during the period. Essentially a variety show (a musical-theatrical form that would become increasingly popular), minstrelsy featured dancing, singing, and irreverence; undergirding it all was an emphasis on burlesque, which was an elemental aspect of nineteenth-century American humour.

Pantomime, ballet, spectacle and extravaganza

The pantomime tradition on the American stage had changed significantly by mid-century: the earlier English mode was replaced by a style of visual theatre best exemplified by the family of Gabriel Ravel – exponents of the 'French style' of pantomime, and entertainers *extraordinaires* during the 1840s and 1850s. The four Ravel brothers, who combined physical virtuosity and sophisticated stage machinery with the visual narrative of pantomime (all to musical accompaniment), arrived in America with their entourage in 1832 and toured all over the country (including California) before returning to France in 1858. (Some members of the family returned to the States in the 1860s.[33]) Nor were the Ravels the only performers in their genre; other troupes – both foreign and domestic – likewise traversed the American theatrical circuit at mid-century and dazzled their audiences with feats of physical prowess. A typical Ravel Family programme consisted of several parts: a pantomime, physical feats (tightrope tricks, balancing, military and sporting skills, and exhibitions of tableaux), and a ballet (e.g. the first act of a contemporary ballet, such as Paul Taglioni's *La sylphide*, including a *grand pas de deux*, a quickstep, a Grand Tableau and 'The Flight of the Sylphide').[34] The strength of the Ravel Company was its mixture of repertory: ballet, gymnastic skills and (most important) pantomime. The latter category – especially the combination of physical virtuosity, pantomimic narrative, and stage machinery and scenery – would evolve into a form that several decades later would be termed 'spectacle' or 'extravaganza'.

American theatre-goers during this period also witnessed many itinerant European dancers who were the successors to Madame Celeste. The Austrian ballerina Fanny Elssler (1810–84) was the most prominent visitor of the 1840s; she toured from 1840 to 1842 and provoked an outpouring of near-hysterical adulation from American audiences. Many individual dancers and entire troupes (such as the Rousset sisters, the Montplaisir Ballet Troupe, Natalie Fitzjames, the Ronzoni Ballet Company and others) toured the United States in the 1850s and 1860s; they frequently performed either as part of or in conjunction with opera troupes. Their repertories included *divertissements* or portions of nineteenth-century ballets such as *La sylphide* (music by Jean Schneitzhoeffer), *Le dieu et la bayadère* (Auber) and *La sonnambule* (Ferdinand Hérold).

Very little research has been conducted on companies like the Ravels or on ballet troupes that toured America in the nineteenth century; as a result, we have almost no knowledge of the music that accompanied these performances.[35] Both types of performers (and their music), however, were ubiquitous; as such, they must be included in a discussion of the antecedents of the modern musical. Furthermore, it should be clear that both 'pantomimic acrobats' and dancers had an important role in the formation of 'spectacle' and 'extravaganza', two closely related musical-theatrical forms that would become popular in the second half of the century. Another important proponent of American 'spectacle' and 'extravaganza' was Laura Keene, whose shows – which combined burlesque, music, ballet, transformation scenes, and spectacular scenery and costumes – were among the most popular theatrical works in New York during the 1860s.[36] All of these theatrical forms (burlesque, pantomime, ballet and drama), accompanied by music and augmented by lavish costumes and scenery, commingled and cross-fertilized during the second half of the century; all had a role in the eventual formation of the twentieth-century American musical.[37]

Burlesque

The American theatrical burlesque in the early and mid nineteenth century was a dramatic production of a satirical and humorous nature (the form would only later become a variety show with striptease as its major component). By the mid-nineteenth century, the form had adopted some of the characteristics of extravaganzas – in particular, whimsical humour presented in pun-filled verses full of double- and triple-entendres and oblique humorous word-play. Burlesques also began during this time to include a significant amount of music.[38] Poking fun at someone or something – whether German or Irish immigrants, the pretensions of the wealthy, African Americans, or the latest entertainer to catch the public's fancy – was so much a part of American humour in the nineteenth century that the popularity of a musical-theatrical form of this nature was inevitable. Hundreds of burlesques or burlesque-extravaganzas (mostly one-act farces or afterpieces) were written for the American stage in the 1840s and 1850s; as already mentioned, the technique was also employed by blackface minstrel troupes in the 'olio' sections of their performances.

In New York the burlesque was raised to new heights by the actor/manager William Mitchell at his Olympic Theatre starting in the late 1830s; Mitchell's competitor, the actor and playwright John Brougham (1810–80), followed Mitchell's successful example and wrote and acted in numerous burlesques from 1842 until 1879.[39] The best example of Brougham's burlesques (and one of the most popular of the century) was *Po-ca-hon-tas; or, the Gentle Savage* (1855), a parody on Indian plays that were currently the rage. The music, which occupies over a third of the show, was arranged by New York theatre composer James G. Maeder; it ranges from simple contrafacta (to the tunes of 'Rosin the Bow', 'Widow Machree' and 'The King of Cannibal Islands', all identified in the script) to complicated extended pieces constructed by patching together tunes from sources as widely divergent as 'Old Folks at Home' and 'Là ci darem la mano' from *Don Giovanni*. The long-lasting popularity of *Po-ca-hon-tas* would keep it – and its example as a successful merging of burlesque and music – before the American public for decades.[40] From the 1860s onwards, burlesques often functioned as the framework for elaborate spectacles and extravaganzas, the characteristics of which have already been discussed.

Opera: English, French and Italian

By the 1840s, the vocal stars that had been such an important part of the American stage had all but disappeared, replaced by English opera companies performing repertory that had become firmly established as popular theatre. The Seguin Opera Company, a troupe that was both wildly popular and enormously successful, had a virtual monopoly on English opera performance during the 1840s. They – like other English troupes that began to appear later in the decade – performed repertory that included works by British composers (Wallace, Balfe, Rooke) as well as translations of operas by French (Auber, Adam), German (Weber and Mozart) and Italian composers (Bellini, Donizetti, Mercadante, and Rossini). In the 1850s English opera began to be considered old-fashioned, as increasing numbers of large skilled Italian troupes performed on the American theatre circuit. Despite the competition, several English troupes – including the Pyne and Harrison, the Anna Bishop, and the Lyster and Durand English opera companies – managed to mount very successful tours in the United States and maintained a strong presence within the repertory of American popular theatre.

French opera during this period was firmly established in New Orleans, but was represented in the rest of the country primarily by the performance of translations of French repertory (by Auber, in particular), usually by English opera companies. In the 1840s and 1850s a handful of French opera companies – some from New Orleans and some from France – toured America, but the heyday of French opera would arrive only in the 1860s, with the influx of the operettas of Jacques Offenbach and companies to perform this repertory.[41]

The major thrust for operatic development during the middle decades of the century was in the arena of Italian-language opera. Various incarnations of the Havana Opera Company visited occasionally during the 1840s (performing in New Orleans, Pittsburgh and Cincinnati, and on the East Coast), and numerous transient New York-based Italian companies imported from Europe appeared and performed repertories of works by Rossini, Bellini, Donizetti and – increasingly – Verdi. The overall picture of Italian operatic activity in the 1840s and 1850s is one of growth: larger and more polished companies, more extensive itineraries and repertories, and more troupes. Furthermore, many of the imported Italian singers remained in America after the completion of their companies' tours; by the early 1850s there were enough Italian singers living in New York (and teaching music there) to make possible the formation of locally based Italian opera companies. Because of this development, impresarios such as Bernard Ullman, Max Maretzek, Maurice Strakosch and Max Strakosch could circumvent the logistical and financial difficulties inherent in recruiting an entire company from abroad and could now concentrate recruiting efforts (and funds) on big-name stars. As a result, impresarios could engage higher-calibre performers, which contributed to the established trend: heightened audience expectations and subsequent engagement of even more highly skilled musicians. The list of stellar singers who appeared in various companies in the States during the period includes some of the best vocalists of Europe: Marietta Alboni, Henriette Sontag, Teresa Parodi, Giovanni Matteo Mario, Giulia Grisi, Lorenzo Salvi and many others. It is important to reiterate that although Italian-language opera was beginning, by the 1850s, to become associated with the elite and wealthy, this change in the opera audience was still new and limited primarily to the East Coast. The appearance of an Italian opera company during the 1850s in a theatre in, say, St Louis or Cincinnati was regarded as a special event (similar to the visit of a major dramatic star); it was not yet regarded as an 'exclusive' engagement that appealed only to the elite or wealthy. Italian opera was still entertainment; as such, it was still a part of the constantly changing potpourri of American popular musical theatre at mid-century. Furthermore, music from the operatic stage, by this time, had completely infiltrated the American sound-scape, and many Americans attended operatic performances to hear music that was readily familiar. Americans danced to quadrilles and lanciers fashioned from tunes from the most popular continental operas; they heard brass bands playing these same tunes in open-air concerts; theatre orchestras performed operatic selections as entr'acte music or overtures; piano benches all over America overflowed with piano variations, arrangements of operatic 'gems' and sheet-music adaptations of the most popular arias. Musical theatre, then, was not limited to theatres; it permeated American life.

The nineteenth century: c. 1865–1900

The last third of the nineteenth century was a period during which musical theatrical forms on the American stage proliferated to the point of rank confusion. Most of the styles already discussed (burlesque, minstrelsy, opera, melodrama, pantomime, dance and plays with songs) continued to be performance vehicles, but these older styles mutated, expanded and cross-fertilised each other. Furthermore, new styles were introduced: operetta (including *opéra-bouffe*, Austrian and British operetta, and 'light operas' by American composers), farce-comedy, spectacle/extravaganza and the expansions of variety (including the early revue and the shows of Harrigan and Hart).

By this time many of the local stock companies of earlier decades had disappeared; most theatres now relied exclusively on the itinerant 'combination' companies that performed everything from drama and opera/operetta to variety and farce-comedy. Itinerant musical-theatrical companies now toured all over the United States, including – after the opening of the transcontinental railroad in 1869 – the interior of the far West. Although many of the theatrical innovations of this period can be covered by an examination of developments in New York City, this should not mislead the reader; travelling performers were able to exploit fully a well-developed transportation system that criss-crossed the United States and they took their performances to city and hamlet alike. During this period there also emerged the theatrical syndicate – a central managerial office (usually in New York or Chicago) that controlled both local theatres and the itinerant troupes that visited them.[42] This centralisation of control exemplifies another element of the coming-of-age of the theatrical business. Scheduling was much less haphazard; managers also exploited the national and local press for purposes of advertising and publicity and collaborated with publishing houses to ensure that 'hit' songs from popular shows would be readily available to consumers in sheet-music format.

Added to the rank confusion of musical-theatrical forms of the time was an imprecision of terminology that can drive a codifier mad: the same show might be called a 'farce-comedy', a 'revue', or an 'extravaganza'; many shows exhibited characteristics of numerous categories. The first use of the term 'musical comedy' dates from this period, but there is general disagreement upon which show, precisely, the name was first bestowed; some of the candidates include *The Pet of the Petticoats* (1866), *Evangeline* (1874) and

The Gaiety Girl (1894).[43] The American musical stage was beginning to come of age during this thirty-year period: metaphorically, it was a gangly and untidy adolescent experiencing a magnificent growth spurt; this diverse yet contradictory youngster would eventually mature into the twentieth-century American musical.

Spectacles, extravaganzas, and burlesques

During the post-Civil war period terms such as 'extravaganza', 'burlesque' and 'spectacle' were frequently used interchangeably or in combination. The theatrical works in this style were clearly based on forms that had been familiar to American theatre-goers for some years, but shows of this nature became more prominent and numerous during the last third of the century.

The Black Crook (1866), with music by Thomas Baker, is frequently cited as the first real precursor to the twentieth-century musical. A combination of many of the forms already discussed, the five-and-a-half-hour extravaganza (performed at Niblo's Gardens in New York City) included elements of melodrama and fantasy (inspired in part by Carl Maria von Weber's opera *Der Freischütz* and Goethe's *Faust*), ballet (performed by a troupe of one hundred French female dancers, in tights), spectacular scenery and costumes, and transformation scenes made possible by sophisticated stage machinery.[44] The play, although not particularly novel (it was constructed of many elements already familiar to American theatre-goers), became astonishingly popular, achieving a run of 474 performances over the course of sixteen months. It remained a mainstay of the American theatre until almost the end of the nineteenth century. In addition to the music written by Baker for the original production, there were many additional compositions written for interpolation later.[45]

The success of *The Black Crook* (coupled with the popularity of the Ravels' and Laura Keene's productions) inevitably resulted in a spate of additional extravaganzas and spectacles, including the unsuccessful sequel to *The Black Crook*, *The White Fawn* (1868). The two decades after the Civil War marked the height of popularity for American spectacle, which – as we have seen – combined elements from a variety of familiar theatrical forms and in which music played an important role as unifying accompaniment.[46] The burlesque-spectacles mounted by Lydia Thompson and her 'British blondes', who arrived from London in 1868, are good examples of this admixture of elements. Thompson first appeared in New York in a full-length burlesque, *Ixion, or the Man at the Wheel*, which boasted of a pun-heavy script, topical references to and burlesques upon contemporary events and people, *opéra-bouffe*-like songs, spectacle, transformation scenes, gags and dances.[47] Thompson and her troupe, furthermore, were responsible for injecting into burlesque the element of the 'girlie show' that eventually would become closely associated with the genre. This overt exploitation of stage women as the object of the male gaze represents an important development in the role of women performers on the musical stage; it would have major repercussions early in the twentieth century, in particular with the revue style developed by Florenz Ziegfeld.

Edward Everett Rice's *Evangeline; or the Belle of Acadie* (1874), to words by John Cheever Goodwin, is another excellent example of the cross-fertilization typical of late-century musical-theatrical forms: from spectacle it took elaborate costumes, sets and stage machinery (a spouting whale, a balloon trip to Arizona); from burlesque it borrowed a rhyming text full of puns and topical references, and ostensibly with a literary basis (it was originally a burlesque on Longfellow's poem, although Goodwin's version has little to do with its plot); from variety show and minstrelsy it took skits, gags and specialised 'acts'; from comic opera it borrowed spoken dialogue, a romantic plot, and a musical score of songs, dances, ensemble numbers and choruses.[48] There were also elements of melodrama and pantomime in the work, which was the only nineteenth-century musical production to rival the popularity of *The Black Crook*; it was mounted all over the country for the next thirty years.[49]

Three years after the premiere of *Evangeline*, there emerged another style of burlesque, called farce-comedy. *The Brook* (1877), created by Nate Salsbury and first performed by his troupe in St Louis, was a parody of musical-theatrical conventions, although it was not a burlesque in the standard definition of the form (Salsbury called it a 'laughable and mu-sical extravaganza').[50] *The Brook* featured music that was borrowed and arranged;[51] it was also a simple show with a small cast: it was neither an extravaganza nor a spectacle, and it required no chorus, ballet dancers, pantomime, transformation scenes, extravagant costumes or spectacular scenery. From the variety stage and the British music hall, *The Brook* incorporated the concept that a theatrical work could be casual and natural. The simplicity (and success) of *The Brook* guaranteed immediate imitations; farce-comedies remained popular in New York for only five years, but itinerant companies (called 'combinations') toured North America for the rest of the century.[52] The most popular successor to *The Brook* was *A Trip to Chinatown* by Charles H. Hoyt (music by Percy Gaunt); this show opened in 1890 and ran for a record 650 performances in its first engagement. Loosely constructed with an extremely thin plot (typical of a farce-comedy) and incorporating elements from vaudeville (such as specialty act appearances by artists like dancer Loie Fuller), the work featured a score that included some popular tunes that are still known today, e.g. 'The Bowery' and 'Reuben and Cynthia'.

Melodrama

By the last third of the century, the technique of using instrumental 'melos' as dramatic cues had become almost ubiquitous in musical-theatrical (and many dramatic) forms of all kinds. Melodrama itself also continued its domination of the American stage; the popularity of full-length melodramatic plays would not begin to wane until the twentieth century.[53] Continued popularity in the late nineteenth century was enhanced by the use of more elaborate scenery, better lighting and more sophisticated stage machinery to increase the sense of realism; the overlap with spectacle and extravaganza should be obvious.[54] The continued importance of music to melodramatic presentation – and hence the significance of melodrama as one of the precursors of the twentieth-century American musical – is sometimes ignored. As the theatre historian David Mayer points out, however, 'nowhere is the use of musical accompaniment more pervasive . . . from ten years before the start of the nineteenth century until well after the First World War, than in the melodrama'.[55]

Scores to melodramatic works are rare, even from the second half of the nineteenth century; there are perhaps a dozen known scores to such plays in the United States and some thirty in collections in Great Britain.[56] One of the most important examples of melodramatic music from this period is for the play *Monte Cristo* (1883), an adaptation by Charles Fechter of Alexandre Dumas's 1844 romance novel *Le Comte de Monte-Cristo*, first produced in the United States in 1870. The twenty-eight melos in the manuscript score, for the most part, are extremely brief, but this music was greatly augmented by overtures and entr'acte music, played before and between the acts. Some of the melos in *Monte Cristo* are used almost as leitmotifs, to indicate not only entrances and exits of important characters, but also to signify emotional and psychological developments in the *dramatis personae*. Other non-melo music used in melodramatic plays, however, did not differ significantly from interpolated songs and incidental music performed in many 'straight' dramatic plays of the period, indicating both the continued importance of music to most theatrical works and the ubiquitous overlap among different 'distinct' forms on the American stage in the late nineteenth century. The subsequent impact of these well-developed (and familiar) melodramatic musical techniques at the turn of the century was two-fold. On the one hand, the pervasive use of music for dramatic purposes clearly influenced those individuals who – consciously or unconsciously – were writing the works that would be the immediate precursors to the early musical. On the other hand, melodramatic music would inevitably influence the adaptation of similar melos for use in the early 'silent' cinema; the primary difference, of course, was that the musical accompaniment for film had to be continuous instead of intermittent.[57]

Minstrelsy; black musical theatre

By the final decades of the century the 'Golden Era' of blackface minstrelsy (1840s–70s) had almost run its course. During the 1870s minstrel troupes grew ever larger, sometimes including as many as thirty performers. Known as 'mastodon' or 'giant' minstrel troupes, these companies grew in order to compete with the burgeoning forms and styles of entertainment emerging during the period.[58] Minstrel troupes also began to employ other 'hooks': all-female minstrel troupes, all-black minstrel troupes. The first important example of the latter, called the Georgia Minstrels, appeared in 1865; this company (managed by a white man) was followed, in turn, by numerous other troupes, some of them managed by African Americans.[59]

The advent of black minstrel companies marked the beginning (in the final decades of the nineteenth century) of a great influx of African-American performers onto the American stage. Minstrelsy, minstrelsy-influenced vaudeville (or variety) and the craze for 'coon' songs all offered to African Americans entrée into a hitherto all-white world; Alfred Woll, in fact, notes that a majority of African-American actors enumerated in the 1890 census identified themselves as minstrels.[60] The Hyers Sisters represent the first attempt by blacks to produce dramatic shows with songs. The sisters' combination company produced musical plays starting in the late 1870s and lasting well into the 1880s.[61] The influx of African-Americans into the theatrical world led, inevitably, to the creation of black 'musicals'. *The Creole Burlesque Co.* (1890), produced for the burlesque stage, was very much a minstrel-flavoured entertainment. It was followed by *Octoroons* (1895), which included a hit Tin Pan Alley 'coon' song, 'No Coon Can Come Too Black for Me'.[62] Two shows of 1898 were closer to what we think of as 'musical comedy': *Clorindy, or the Origin of the Cakewalk* (Will Marion Cook) and *A Trip to Coontown* (Bob Cole) were both vaudeville-like – rather than book-like – musical theatrical works; the latter was the first musical written, directed and performed by black performers.[63]

Opera and operetta

During the last thirty years of the nineteenth century, foreign-language opera performance in America gradually became ever more closely associated both with the elite and with immigrant communities. In mainstream America, it was also gradually removed from the domain of the popular theatre, in part because of this increased sense of 'exclusivity', in part because of the tendency in the theatre towards the concept of 'niche marketing': as the American population grew, it became increasingly possible for theatres devoted to a particular repertory to be economically viable, especially in large cities. In the 1880s and 1890s theatres devoted primarily to the performance of opera, for the most part, were found in the larger American cities (New

York, Boston, Philadelphia, Washington DC, Chicago and San Francisco);
even many of these houses, however – such as Albaugh's Opera House in
Washington DC, the Academy of Music in Philadelphia and Crosby's Opera
House in Chicago – also hosted productions of musical comedy and operetta in addition to grand opera. It is also important to mention that opera
companies – even the New York Metropolitan (founded in 1883) – continued to travel throughout America for the remainder of the century and to
perform, for the most part, in normal theatres rather than in houses limited
to opera production. As a result, there persisted an ambiguity about the
place of foreign-language opera within the spectrum of American musical
theatre during the last decades of the century.

English-language opera continued to appeal to a broadly based musical
theatre audience during this period; its popularity would inevitably have
a major impact on the development of the twentieth-century American
musical. Much of the repertory consisted of translations of the Italian and
German operas that were increasingly associated with the upper classes;
this contributes (in retrospect) to the aforementioned sense of ambiguity in
relation to opera reception. English-language troupes continued to tour the
United States regularly in the 1870s and 1880s, headed by Italian-opera
impresarios and by prima donnas such as Caroline Richings (daughter
of the British actor Peter Richings mentioned earlier; active 1863–74),
Euphrosyne Parepa-Rosa (active in the US 1865–74), and Clara Louise
Kellogg (active in English opera 1873–77). These troupes performed English
translations of Italian and German operas as well as operas written in
English; many of them billed their productions as 'opera for the people',
clearly as an attempt to counter the growing perception of opera as an elite
pastime. Emma Abbott (active 1879–91), known as 'the people's prima
donna', headed a troupe that opened some thirty-five different opera
houses in the far West and introduced this musical-theatrical form to many
Americans; her sudden death (of pneumonia) while on tour in Utah provoked a national outpouring of grief from her supporters. Emma Juch,
a successful performer with Italian troupes, was also known as a crusader for English opera for 'regular' Americans. Dozens of other English-
language troupes were active in the United States during this period; they
performed a mixed repertory of operas and operettas by composers who
wrote in English (Balfe, Wallace, Benedict, Eichberg and Sullivan), French
(Auber, Meyerbeer, Lecocq, Thomas, Offenbach, Gounod, Planquette and
Bizet), Italian (Mozart, Bellini, Rossini, Donizetti, Verdi, Puccini, and [later]
Mascagni and Leoncavallo) and German (Mozart, Weber, Beethoven and
Wagner). The spectacularly *unsuccessful* American Opera Company, established by Jeanette Thurber in 1885 in an attempt to establish English opera
in America, should be noted, but its failure was anything but typical.

Many of the English-language companies were increasingly influenced by the growing American enthusiasm for operetta, and many operetta troupes also performed standard repertory. The Boston Ideals, for example – founded in 1879 to perform Gilbert and Sullivan operettas – regularly performed such typical fare as *The Bohemian Girl* (Balfe), *The Marriage of Figaro* (Mozart), *Fra Diavolo* (Auber), *Martha* (Flotow) and *L'Elisir d'amore* (Donizetti), in addition to 'lighter' operettas like *The Pirates of Penzance* and *Fatinitza*. Operetta had first been introduced to American audiences in the 1860s, in the form of the *opéras-bouffes* of Jacques Offenbach. *La Grande Duchesse de Gerolstein* was first performed in New York (in French) in 1867. Several troupes mounted this and other works in New York and elsewhere, with great success. The 1870s, in fact, were a heyday of *opéra-bouffe* production in the United States; performances of operettas by Offenbach, Lecocq, Audran, Hervé and Planquette – in English, French and German – were widespread.[64] As a result of the new-found craze for French opera, the number of French companies that toured widely in the United States increased during this time; these included the French Opera Company of New Orleans and troupes formed in support of the *opéra-bouffe* sopranos Marie Aimée and Lucille Tostée. Offenbach himself visited the United States in 1876 and conducted performances in Philadelphia and New York. As this repertory became more popular, an increasing number of troupes performed the *opéra-bouffe* repertory in English translation; this, paradoxically, led to a decrease in the popularity of these works, as more Americans understood and were offended by the double entendres and compromised sexual situations of the plots. German companies (notably in New York, Cincinnati, Chicago and Milwaukee) also performed translations of this repertory, but primarily for the large German immigrant populations of those cities. The French light opera repertory was augmented during the 1870s and 1880s by Viennese operettas, including works by Franz von Suppé (*Fatinitza*), Karl Millöcker (*The Black Hussar* and *The Beggar Student*) and Johann Strauss (*The Merry War* and *The Queen's Lace Handkerchief*).

The most successful operettas on the American stage during the last third of the nineteenth century were by W. S. Gilbert (1836–1911) and Arthur Sullivan (1842–1900). Scholars generally agree that the 1878 Boston premiere of *HMS Pinafore* marks a turning point in the history of American musical theatre.[65] Within a year the work had become the most frequently performed operetta in America, with more than ninety *Pinafore* companies touring the United States. In 1879 Gilbert, Sullivan and the company of Rupert d'Oyly Carte travelled to the United States to perform *Pinafore* and to mount the world premiere of *The Pirates of Penzance* (in order to secure the American copyright). Neither *Pirates* nor *The Mikado* (1885) achieved the popularity of *Pinafore*, but the level of performance of the D'Oyly Carte company greatly influenced American operetta and English opera companies, and the format of the Gilbert and Sullivan shows – the inoffensiveness of the humour (especially in comparison with burlesque, vaudeville or even *opéra-bouffe*), the witty satire at the expense of the British establishment, and Sullivan's skilful melodies – appealed mightily to American audiences. The shows would remain popular for the rest of the century. British operetta clearly had a profound impact on the future course of American musical comedy; Gerald Bordman, in fact, claims that *Pinafore* itself 'determined the course and shape of the popular lyric stage in England and America for the final quarter of the nineteenth century'.[66] Part of the astonishing success of *Pinafore* can be attributed to the operetta's unprecedented assimilation into American mass popular culture; a veritable mushroom-crop of amateur theatrical companies – devoted to the performance of *Pinafore* – sprang up all over America in the late 1870s and early 1880s.

American composers also found a voice in operetta, although most operetta and English opera companies preferred to perform European imports. Julius Eichberg's *Doctor of Alcantara*, which was premiered in Boston in 1862, was an attempt by that German immigrant to emulate the success of Offenbach. The show, which was referred to in the contemporary press as an 'opera', 'operetta', 'opera of the comic order', 'comic operetta', 'opera bouffa', and 'light operatic entertainment', entered the repertories of numerous troupes in the 1860s and 1870s and made Eichberg the most successful American operetta composer during the 1860s.[67] Other Americans followed in Eichberg's footsteps, including the opera impresario Maretzek (*Sleepy Hollow, or the Headless Horseman*, 1879) and J. S. Crossey (*The First Life Guards at Brighton*, 1879). Willard Spencer's *The Little Tycoon* (1886) was almost the only American comic opera to enjoy any popular success in the 1880s. John Philip Sousa, who wrote some fifteen operettas, was clearly influenced by the works of Gilbert and Sullivan, but suffered from inadequate librettos. Although his works held their own against foreign operettas in the late 1880s and early 1890s, his only true success was *El Capitan* (1896).[68] Ludwig Engländer (1853–1914) also enjoyed some success as a composer of comic operas, primarily in the 1890s. George Whitfield Chadwick, a more 'classical' composer, also tried his hand at the genre, with *Tabasco* (1894). Two late-century American composers of comic opera enjoyed greater success than the others. Reginald de Koven (1859–1920) wrote several operettas in the late 1880s, including *The Begum* (1887) (described as a cross between *La Grande Duchesse* and *The Mikado*).[69] De Koven relied heavily on Gilbert and Sullivan for his only major success, *Robin Hood*, premiered by the Bostonians (formerly the Boston Ideals) in 1890. Victor Herbert (1859–1924), who also wrote for the Bostonians (and for other English opera companies), was by far the most successful and skilled American comic opera composer

of the late nineteenth century. Most of his best known works – characterised by dramatic and memorable melodies and skilful orchestrations – are
twentieth-century works; several of his operettas, however, were premiered
in the 1890s, including *The Wizard of the Nile* (1895), *The Serenade* (1897)
and *The Fortune Teller* (1898).

Vaudeville and variety show

Variety shows came of age on the American stage during the final years
of the nineteenth century. Many concert saloons had begun offering 'light'
varied entertainment in the 1850s as inducement to drink; the amusement
was similar to that of the English music hall and included a bill of songs
(comic and sentimental), instrumental solos, comic skits, dancing, juggling
and acrobatics of various sorts. Americans, of course, were already readily
familiar with the format through minstrelsy. By the mid-1860s, concert saloons and their style of entertainment were common all over the country;
after the Civil War the format moved from saloons into theatres.[70] Variety
theatres became commonplace during the 1880s and 1890s; as such they –
like opera houses – are another example of the increasing numbers of theatres catering to specific audiences. For the most part variety entertainment
was considered disreputable (because of the association with saloons and
the prevalence of objectionable material). Managers of variety theatres or
'théâtres comiques' (including, most notably, Tony Pastor and B. F. Keith in
New York) attempted to attract family audiences by cleaning up the content of their shows, professionalising the performances, banning drink and
changing the name of the entertainment form to 'vaudeville', a term already
used in Europe for variety-like entertainment.[71] Playbills from American variety theatres from the last two decades of the century illustrate the diversity
of programming: an evening's entertainment might consist of a full-length
vaudeville show, burlesque skits, revues, magic shows and minstrelsy; most
of these performances were to musical accompaniment.[72] It is also during
this period that many variety entertainers began fruitful collaboration with
music publishers to 'plug' particular songs. This combination of musical
theatre and music publishing illustrates another aspect of an emerging music business that occurred during the early Tin Pan Alley era; it also suggests
the important role of musical theatre in that coming of age.

In the 1870s many variety shows – like minstrel shows – included extended comic skits. One variety performer who eventually transformed his
skits into something much closer to an extended musical-theatrical show
was the actor, lyricist and playwright Edward Harrigan (1844–1911), who
in 1871 teamed up with the actor Tony Hart (Anthony Cannon, 1855–91) to
form the variety team of Harrigan and Hart. In the same year Harrigan also
commenced a fruitful collaboration with the established theatre composer

Dave Braham (1834–1905); the partnership eventually produced a whole series of comical musical plays that relied heavily on burlesque and ethnic humour (caricaturing Irish and German immigrants as well as African Americans). The first version of *The Mulligan Guard*, from 1873, was a ten-minute sketch typical of variety-show fare: it contained three or four songs, dialogue, and 'gags and business'.[73] Encouraged, Harrigan and Braham continued to expand upon the theme; eventually the sketch evolved into a full-length play that, in turn, spawned an entire cycle of related 'Mulligan' musical plays that were performed (in New York and elsewhere) throughout the 1880s and into the 1890s.[74] The evolution of the Mulligan series is a perfect example of the transformations and cross-fertilizations characteristic of the American stage: a variety show song-and-dance routine developed into a full-length musical entertainment that incorporated elements of variety, burlesque, melodrama and minstrelsy. Furthermore, the growing importance of Dave Braham's music – the increased number of songs and the greater reliance on incidental music as dramatic cues (in the style of melodrama) – points clearly towards the close integration of music and drama that is the hallmark of the mature American musical comedy.[75]

In the 1890s variety continued to be popular on the American stage; many other individuals important to the development of American musical theatre cut their performance teeth in vaudeville. One of the most notable was George M. Cohan (1878–1942), whose play *Little Johnny Jones* (1904) is frequently cited as the first American musical. Cohan grew up a member of his family's itinerant vaudeville troupe ('The Four Cohans'). The company's first musical comedy, *The Governor's Son* (1901) – like Ned Harrigan's works of twenty years earlier – was an elaboration of a vaudeville sketch. This show was an immediate failure, but the dramatic and musical seeds were sown and would result, three years later, in Cohan's more integrated *Little Johnny Jones*.

Another style of entertainment that would have an impact on twentieth-century musical theatre also emerged in the 1890s on the vaudeville stage. 'Revues', a style of entertainment that had become popular in Paris, were introduced in New York in the early 1890s. The first successful American example of this genre, *The Passing Show* (1894, Ludwig Engländer), was called a 'topical extravaganza' and combined burlesque, satire, specialty acts, minstrelsy, dance, a scantily-clad female chorus and *tableaux vivants*; in essence it was a variety show in the best of the American tradition.[76] The revue as a form would have a profound impact on musical theatre of the early twentieth century; the 'follies' and 'scandals' of Florenz Ziegfeld and George White (for which composers such as Irving Berlin, George Gershwin and Cole Porter wrote music) were outgrowths of this Parisian style.

Conclusion

In the eighteenth and nineteenth centuries the theatrical realm was not so clearly separated from normal life as it is now; elements of the stage permeated American life during this period – especially the last several decades of the nineteenth century – to an extent almost unimaginable today. Americans were readily conversant with songs from theatrical venues as widely divergent as opera and variety show; their dance cards were full of music from the stage; they played arrangements of show tunes on their parlour pianos, mounted amateur productions of operettas and listened to concerts by the local brass band playing arrangements of music of operas, operettas and variety shows. Furthermore many Americans of varied social and economic standing attended musical-theatrical performances with a matter-of-fact regularity foreign to us today. The variety of musical-theatrical repertory available then is approximated two centuries later only in the largest of American cities, or in the local multiplex.

It is also impossible, for most of the nineteenth century, to view the repertory of 'musical theatre' as different and distinct from the repertory of the 'theatre'. It is true that by the final decades of the century the concept of the 'legitimate' stage – a style of drama that did *not* include music – had begun to emerge. But as the theatre historian David Mayer points out, this development – which modern theatre-goers take for granted as the natural order of things – was an aberration and clearly marked a change from long-standing tradition.[77] A thorough understanding of the antecedents of the American musical, then, must include an examination of a wide variety of different types of musical-theatrical styles and genres, including many that today are not included in the modern definition of 'musical theatre'.

Finally, it is important to realise that our modern preference for clear distinctions between musical-theatrical forms even in the twentieth century is sometimes artificial and counterproductive. Well into the twentieth century American 'musical theatre' continued to be varied and changeable, with a rich and valuable tradition of cross-fertilisation; as Joel Kaplan notes in his introduction to a study of the Edwardian theatre, it is precisely this 'interplay of forms or genres that seems, to late twentieth-century eyes, one of the most remarkable features of pre-[World War I] entertainment'.[78] It is clear that during at least the first third of the twentieth century composers and performers moved readily between variety, film musicals, burlesque, revues and book musicals. Recognition of this is essential in any attempt to understand the development of the American musical; it also illustrates a healthy continuation – into the twentieth century – of many of the musical-theatrical traditions of the nineteenth.

2 Birth pangs, growing pains and sibling rivalry: musical theatre in New York, 1900–1920

ORLY LEAH KRASNER

It has been a matter of regret with many music lovers that we have had so few really good comic operas during the past few years. . . . the so-called comic opera stage has degenerated hopelessly of late.[1]   MUSICAL AMERICA (1906)

Critics in every generation lament the dearth of good material on the Broadway musical stage, but these lines, published in *Musical America* in 1906, do not actually sound the death-knell of a genre. During the first two decades of the twentieth century producers, performers, librettists and composers grappled with the notion of a single genre that could combine the best of all worlds into a unified, coherent whole. The problem of varied and inconsistent terminology, implied in the phrase 'so-called comic opera', was a legacy from the nineteenth century that continued to plague critics in the early decades of the twentieth. Musically well-educated writers often adopted a highbrow stance and treated anything lighter than opera with disdain while other critics, reviewing the same work, might praise it as a cut above similar fare. Composers in the dawning century struggled with their inherited options trying to evolve a new and uniquely American art form: what we now blithely call the Broadway musical. Several things had to happen in order to establish the book show as the norm. Librettists had to create plots that jibed with the rhythms and concerns of contemporary experience; this eventually caused a shift from the politically tinged satires of Gilbert and Sullivan and Offenbach to the sentimental love stories of Victor Herbert and Sigmund Romberg. Composers had to discard or integrate remnants of hand-me-down imported musical vocabularies into a language that embraced American vernacular idioms in song and dance. 'Broadway' has always had room for multiple genres playing simultaneously – operetta and musical comedy, spectacle and revue, burlesque and vaudeville – although the specific characteristics, names and relative audience support for each continue to shift.

The first tremors of change could already be felt in 1903 when a critic for the *New York Times* pointed out that 'the name of comic opera, as well as the thing itself, has fallen into disfavor'.[2] From the audiences' vantagepoint, however, the scene was hardly so dire. Gustav Luders's *The Prince of Pilsen* had its New York debut on 17 March 1903 and became a perennial favourite (in London and Australia as well as in the United States). Victor Herbert's *Babes in Toyland* opened in the fall and played 192 performances before its road tour began. Later that year Herbert's *Babette* and Reginald de Koven's *The Red Feather* opened within a week of each other; for several seasons these two composers had works running in competition. Comic opera was not dead yet, but it was indeed changing.

Vaudevillian roots

In 1904, George M. Cohan (1878–1942) toddled towards the future with *Little Johnny Jones*, the show that often is credited with being the first American musical. Its brisk plot was inspired by the recent adventures of Tod Sloane, an American jockey who rode in the English Derby. Cohan wrote the book, lyrics and music, and also played the title character; Ethel Levy, Cohan's wife, co-starred. Although he had played violin in the pit orchestra for his family's vaudeville act as a child, Cohan was essentially an untrained musician. His vaudevillian roots nourished him in ways that set him apart from his more classically tutored contemporaries. Fast-paced dialogue, street-wise humour and the vernacular slant of his lyrics approximated the ordinary speech of his audiences at a time when other Broadway writers, still in thrall to the polysyllabic rhymes of W. S. Gilbert, often wrote grammatically awkward, inane texts filled with overblown imagery. Cohan's melodic writing was direct and uncomplicated; its simple harmonies and undemanding vocal ranges have made a number of his over 500 songs standards of the repertoire. Cohan wrote and occasionally starred in musical comedies until the 1920s.

Little Johnny Jones opened at the Liberty Theater on 7 November 1904. Its first Broadway run lasted only 52 performances, but Cohan continued to tinker with it during its road tour. When he brought it back to New York the following year, it amassed over 200 performances. The score contains two of Cohan's most memorable numbers: 'Give My Regards to Broadway' and 'Yankee Doodle Boy'.

Cohan was not the only vaudevillian to make the transition to the legitimate stage. In 1904, the famous partnership of Joseph Weber (1867–1942) and Lew Fields (1867–1941) disbanded. The pair had a long association both on stage and off. On stage, they were known as a Dutch-dialect duo whose sketches featured a thickly accented broad comedy. Off stage, they managed the Weber and Fields Music Hall. When their partnership dissolved after nearly thirty years together – they started to do their act together at about the age of ten – Weber continued to manage their theatre, mounting vaudevilles and burlesques. Fields hoped to move into a higher class of theatrical entertainment as a producer and actor.

Fields joined with the producer Fred Hamlin and the director Julian Mitchell to organise the Lew Fields Stock Company. Hamlin and Mitchell had been involved with two hits from 1903: *The Wizard of Oz* and *Babes in Toyland*. Mitchell's directorial career covered the full spectrum from Herbert's comic opera *The Fortune Teller* starring Alice Nielsen, to Ziegfeld's *Papa's Wife*, to spectacle-revues such as *Hoity-Toity, Twirly-Whirly* and *Whoop-de-Doo* at the Weber and Fields Music Hall. To his new venture, Fields brought the knowledge that rapid pacing, topical references, catchy tunes and visual splendour – both scenic and feminine – kept audiences engaged. Tired of his foreign-accented, low-comedy stage roles, Fields wanted to act in a vehicle that would 'reconcile the era's two most popular forms of stage entertainment, vaudeville and operetta'.[3] For the first production in the Lew Fields Theater, under construction by Oscar Hammerstein, Fields hired the composer Victor Herbert.

Victor Herbert

Dublin-born Victor Herbert (1859–1924) always took great pride in his Irish heritage, even though he was brought up and educated in Germany. He began his musical career as an orchestral cellist in Stuttgart. In 1886, he and his wife, the soprano Therese Foerster, left for New York and their new positions with the Metropolitan Opera House, she on stage and he in the orchestra pit. Herbert readily joined New York's musical life as solo cellist, orchestral conductor and bandmaster; he began his Broadway career in the 1890s, and remained close to it for the rest of his life.

Although the plots of his shows are extremely diverse, they all share happy endings and stereotypical characters. Herbert is usually discussed as a composer of operettas, but the scores of his works, like those of his contemporaries, carry a variety of genre designations. Many of Herbert's best numbers, unlike Cohan's, lie beyond the technical capabilities of amateur performers; his rich, dense harmonies support melodies that demand a wide and flexible range. In spite of its homegrown popularity, surprisingly little of Herbert's substantial *œuvre* travelled outside of the United States. By comparison, *The Belle of New York*, a now-forgotten work by Gustave Kerker (1857–1923), became a West End hit – it played nearly 700 performances at the Shaftesbury – and did well on tour in Australia, Hungary, Germany, Austria and France. Herbert also composed two cello concertos, the film score (now lost) to *The Fall of a Nation*, and two operas, *Natoma* (1911, starring Mary Garden) and the one-act *Madeleine* (1914).

For his Lew Fields show, Herbert worked with Glen MacDonough (1870–1924), an association that had already produced *Babes in Toyland*. On 5 December 1905, the Lew Fields Theater opened its doors for *It Happened in Nordland*; Cohan's *Little Johnny Jones* was playing a half of a block away.

It Happened in Nordland takes place in a fictitious Central European court. Queen Elsa, on the brink of an arranged marriage, has disappeared. Katherine Peepfogle (played by Marie Cahill), the new American diplomat, just happens to resemble the missing monarch. Katherine agrees to impersonate her and, as temporary queen, irons out the various wrinkles in the plot, one of which is the arrival of Katherine's long-lost brother, played by Lew Fields. Herbert's score, in addition to its lyrical waltzes, contained marches, ragtime and comic numbers (including a coon song routine) – enough stylistic variety to please any audience. The women were given plenty of opportunity to dance and look gorgeous in extravagant costumes.

Marie Cahill (1870–1933) could command star billing; her stage presence, similar to Marie Dressler and May Irwin, was plump, robust rather than pretty, and strong voiced – in essence, a 'coon shouter'. Backed by her husband and manager Daniel Arthur, Cahill insisted on diva treatment, which included the right to interpolate whatever material she chose. It was common at the time for stars to interpolate songs into a show, either to puff up the role or freshen a long-running vehicle. This was also a useful marketing trick since sheet music covers could then tout in bold letters 'as sung by so-and-so in such-and-such a production'. However, at a time when composers were striving to create ever greater coherency between song, dance and book, such extraneous material was clearly detrimental. Herbert, who was active in the political fight to establish suitable copyright protection for music, usually included a no-interpolation clause in his contracts, but inexplicably neglected to do so in his new one with Hamlin, Mitchell and Fields. Conflict was inevitable. Cahill, who had no understudy, threatened to quit if management refused to acquiesce to her dialogue changes. Herbert, who was also the conductor, refused to include her demanded musical interpolations; in an initial compromise, Herbert handed over his baton to the musical director for any added numbers. Then Hamlin, the producer, died just before the New York premiere, delaying the opening by a few days. The fateful showdown occurred during the last New York performance before the summer road tour. Cahill presented Fields with an ultimatum: either she or Herbert would appear in Boston, but not both. Fields backed composer over star, and Cahill was replaced.

It Happened in Nordland was musically strong enough to hold up without a star on tour, but when it returned to Broadway for a second season (still alongside *Little Johnny Jones*), Fields signed Blanche Ring

(1877–1961), another temperamental actress known for her interpolations. An ex-vaudevillian, Ring could not resist the habit of breaking character to address her fans from the stage. This was precisely the sort of behaviour that had driven Fields to leave vaudeville and he was not about to tolerate it from Ring. After another showdown, Ring quit, taking her costumes with her. A frantic call to the understudy ensued. When the curtain came up an hour later, a poised young Pauline Frederick – her three-octave soprano clearly superior to either of her predecessors' – delivered a performance that (foreshadowing *42nd Street*) launched her on a sturdy career. In spite of all the backstage whoop-de-doo, *It Happened in Nordland* garnered 154 performances in New York before its summer tour and another 100 after its autumnal return.

Herbert then scored two successive hits with *Mlle Modiste* and *The Red Mill*, both with librettos by Henry Blossom (1866–1919). *Mlle Modiste* starred Fritzi Scheff in the role of the milliner Fifi. The Viennese-born Scheff (1879–1954) had trained as an opera singer and performed at the Metropolitan Opera House before decamping to Broadway where she first appeared in the title role of Herbert's *Babette* (1903). Herbert's score for *Mlle Modiste* included the waltz 'Kiss Me Again', part of Fifi's first act tour de force 'If I Were on the Stage', and the bass-baritone standard, 'I Want What I Want When I Want It'. Scheff's career had its ups and downs, but she remained identified with her early triumph; she reprised the role of Fifi at the age of fifty, in 1929.

The Red Mill was an instant success after its premiere at the Knicker-bocker Theater on 24 September 1906; after 274 performances in New York, it continued to do good business on tour. Blossom's libretto contained all the requisite features of comic opera, but integrated them into a scenario far better than most. The low-comedy pair, Con Kidder and Kid Conner – played by the famed team of David Montgomery and Fred Stone – are Americans who arrive penniless in the Dutch town Katwyk-aan-Zee after touring the Continent. They lodge at an inn with a view of the old red mill. The inn-keeper's daughter, Tina, is the soubrette. The Burgomaster (comic authority figure) refuses to let his daughter Gretchen (soprano) marry the man of her choice, Captain Doris (*sic*) Van Damm (tenor). The plot complications allow Con and Kid to adopt various disguises, including Sherlock Holmes and Dr Watson. Ultimately, Gretchen and the Captain are united, because he is heir to a heretofore-undisclosed large fortune.

Herbert's score, labelled a 'Musical Play in Two Acts' contains some of his most enduring music, including 'Every Day Is Ladies' Day with Me' and the waltz 'The Streets of New York'. To characterise the Americans Kid and Con, Herbert invoked the popular rhythms of ragtime in numbers such as the duet 'Good-a-bye, John!' and the quartet 'Go While the Goin' is Good'.

Furthermore, Herbert gave the pair ample opportunity for stage business, such as the spirited, syncopated dance that concludes each of the three verses in the trio 'Whistle It'.

Reginald de Koven

Audiences who had already seen Herbert's newest works could compare them with plenty of others, including those by Reginald de Koven (1859–1920). For over a decade, Herbert and de Koven had works running simultaneously on Broadway. De Koven was born in Middletown, Connecticut, but was Oxford-educated and had studied music in Europe. A trio of English-inspired successes secured his reputation in the 1890s – *Robin Hood* (1891), *Rob Roy* (1894) and *The Highwayman* (1897), which was also the subject of a Weber and Fields burlesque, *The Wayhighman*. In addition to the roles of composer and conductor, de Koven was also a music critic and socialite. His many press statements made explicit his aim to elevate and improve audience taste through his music. Unfortunately, de Koven was not always able to sugarcoat his pill. His theatrical output, like Herbert's, ran the gamut of genres, but he became increasingly uncomfortable catering to the musical demands of the lower end. De Koven's works after 1900 met with a varied reception, and at the end of his career, he composed two operas, *The Canterbury Pilgrims* (1917) and *Rip Van Winkle* (1920), in an attempt to reach audiences whose vision of the theatre matched his own.

De Koven's *Happyland*, set in the congenial kingdom of Elysia, ran concurrently with Herbert's *It Happened in Nordland* and Cohan's *Little Johnny Jones* in 1905. King Ecstaticus, played by De Wolf Hopper (1858–1935) – one of the pre-eminent comic actors of the day – is bored by excessive happiness, so he orders everyone to get married. The work, produced by the Shubert brothers, struggled to achieve its 136 performances.

The Student King, labelled a 'Romantic light opera', opened on Christmas Day, 1906 and played alongside *The Red Mill*. In Prague at carnival time, Francis, a university student, is elected king for a day according to tradition. The Tyrolean princess Ilsa is promised to the real king, but, while disguised as Anne, falls in love with Francis. All is resolved when, using a favourite Gilbert-and-Sullivan ploy, Francis is revealed as the King of Bohemia's long-lost son. A similar story, the bittersweet product of nostalgic Ruritania, would eventually become one of Sigmund Romberg's crowning achievements, but de Koven's *Student King* was deposed after forty performances. The rousing student songs and large male choral ensembles at the heart of *The Student King* were something of a novelty, but its plot devices were familiar and audiences perceived its massive choral writing as being too operatic. The critic Rennold Wolf, writing in the *New York Telegraph*, suggested that perhaps this was the best that could be expected given the state of theatrical entertainments at the time.[4]

At this point in his career, de Koven may not have been the best that critics could expect from the theatre, but his works nevertheless exhibited a certain level of craftsmanship over uninspired material. Industry buzz and the word on the street, however, were beginning to hint at another imminent change. While Cohan's shows were establishing a taste for vigorous Americana, and de Koven and Herbert were making their first tenuous moves towards sentimental romances set in mythic European locales, Continental operetta was on the brink of entering a second golden age. Just as imported operettas by Johann Strauss and others transformed the American musical stage at the end of the nineteenth century, so, too, would these new imports revitalise it at the start of the twentieth.

The Merry Widow

On 30 December 1905, a Viennese audience at the Theater an der Wien attended the premiere of Franz Lehár's three-act operetta *Die lustige Witwe*.[5] Its libretto, written by Victor Léon and Leo Stein, was based on Henri Meilhac's four-act play, *L'attaché d'ambassade* (1861). The plot revolves around Hanna Glawari, a rich, young widow from Pontevedro – a transparent disguise for the Balkan Montenegro. Her countrymen fear that she will marry a foreigner while visiting Paris, thus withdrawing her millions from the national bank and bankrupting the country. The Pontevedran delegation to Paris hopes to convince her to marry a loyal countryman, Count Danilo, who prefers associating with Margot, Lolo, Dodo, Clo-Clo, Jou-Jou, and Frou-Frou – the *grisettes* at Maxim's. The flirtation between an amorous Frenchman and the 'highly respectable wife' of the Pontevedran ambassador provides a comic foil for the relationship between Danilo and Hanna.

Lehár exploited pseudo-Balkan, Parisian and Viennese colour for his score. Act II, for example, opens with a Pontevedran dance, followed by 'Vilja' – a counterfeit folk tale from the widow's homeland. Danilo's number in praise of Maxim's captures the sparkle of Parisian nightlife. Most important are the waltzes, which achieve a new prominence by assuming a psychological importance in portraying romance and sexual tension.[6] They are no longer just vocal numbers in triple metre labelled 'à la valse' – these waltzes are meant to be danced as well as sung, thus raising the choreography above mere spectacle and integrating dance into the book. At a remove of

Plate 2 Editorial cartoon concerning the popularity of *The Merry Widow* from *The Evening American*, 1909

nearly a century, Lehár's masterpiece may seem sentimental and nostalgic. In its day, it was daring and risqué.

By the end of the 1906–07 season, *Die lustige Witwe* was all the rage throughout the German-speaking theatrical world. Having seen the work during its first few months in Vienna, English-speaking impresarios made immediate plans to transport it. The translation by Basil Hood and with lyrics by Adrian Ross remained, for its day, remarkably faithful to the original. In its transformation from 'Witwe' to 'Widow', the locale was changed from Pontevedro to the equally fictional Marsovia, and some of the characters' names were altered, most notably Hanna to Sonia, Njegus to Nisch, and Baron Mirko Zeta to Popoff. Lehár's score was left virtually intact. When *The Merry Widow* opened at the Daly Theatre, London on 8 June 1907, no one anticipated that it would run for an unprecedented 778 performances; King Edward VII himself attended four of them.

On 21 October 1907, *The Merry Widow* finally waltzed into Broadway's New Amsterdam Theatre. Although the Marsovian millions were nightly made safe, real-life finances were precarious. Within days of the premiere, the Knickerbocker Trust Company closed its doors, precipitating a wave of bank closures. It was the third financial panic in fourteen years. But it was not the only hysteria sweeping the nation. 'Merry Widow Madness' had also begun.[7]

Savvy entrepreneurs quickly applied the words 'Merry Widow' to a wide range of products as a marketing gimmick. In particular, Ethel Jackson's broad-brimmed, feather-trimmed hat created a fashion furor. The *Oxford English Dictionary* credits the earliest written use of the phrase 'Merry Widow hat' to July 1908, but spoken usage would likely have predated the written.[8] Within months of the New York premiere, vendors peddled readily available sheet music on street corners for a nickel a copy.[9] Several touring companies further disseminated its waltzes throughout the country, and there were even competitions for the best Sonia–Danilo couple.[10] The ensuing social-dance craze would soon open the door for Vernon and Irene Castle, and later Fred and Adele Astaire, who were then children dancing in vaudeville.

As part of the hype preceding *The Merry Widow*'s arrival in New York, *Musical America* quoted an excerpt from the London *Daily Graphic* in which an unidentified critic declared that 'Musical comedy being dead... and comic opera not yet resuscitated... [*The Merry Widow* is] something between the two and partaking of the character of both.'[11] Terminological indecision was not unique to the American side of the Atlantic. What is particularly important here, however, is the shared perception of a moribund genre on the brink of revivification.

The New York reviews of Lehár's operetta were unanimously laudatory, but they also show distinct differences in tone. The extensive, but unsigned, opening night review in the *New York Sun* was probably written by W. J. Henderson (1855–1937), the musically literate, Princeton-educated son of a theatrical manager. He predicted that *The Merry Widow*

> will undoubtedly remain in West Forty-second street for many a long day to gladden the spirits of a town which has been bored to death with lamentable rot and debasing rubbish wearing the outward guise of 'comic opera'....
>
> Although it has been run through the sieve of honorable British censorship, all the bewitching diablerie of this operetta has not been eliminated, for the London book carpenter has done no serious wrong to the essentially Austrian comedy and the music of Franz Lehar remains

intact. The story is excellent comedy and there are scenes and incidents calling for the exhibition of genuine acting ability instead of for acrobatic buffoonery on the American plan. This is a great joy.

Henderson also rhapsodised about the 'expression' of the dances, particularly 'the irresistible seduction of the Viennese waltz, the dance of dances, that steals men's souls out by way of their toes'.[12]

The uncredited review in the *New York Times* was probably penned by Richard Aldrich (1863–1937), a Harvard graduate who had studied music with John Knowles Paine. Under the headline ' "The Merry Widow" Proves Captivating', Aldrich wrote that Ethel Jackson 'comprehends the verve and joy of the part, as well as its seductiveness. She makes the waltz the dramatic moment in the action, as it should be.'[13]

The curmudgeonly critic for the *New York Tribune*, however, was the noted champion of Wagner, Henry E. Krehbiel (1854–1923). His review, which appears between two columns of obituaries, is sedately headed 'Music. "The Merry Widow" '. With measured enthusiasm, Krehbiel proclaimed: 'At length a real operetta, one that does not filch the appellation, but fits it and fills it and does it credit'. He did not mention the work's seductiveness, but commented twice on its lack of vulgarity. As for the waltz, he conceded that it 'takes on the color of emotionality in the climax of the dramatic situation'.[14]

Perhaps the most patrician stance was taken by the *Musical Courier*. Unlike *Musical America*, it adopted the attitude of its cultivated readership, and there were neither preliminary publicity notices for *The Merry Widow* nor a formal review. On 30 October 1907, however, an item about Lehár with no headline was buried on page 22.

'The Merry Widow' ... by the way, in the first week of her visit to New York has danced herself deeply into the affections of the metropolitan public and bids fair to be welcome here for an unbroken run of two seasons at least ... It is admitted on every side that Lehar is not a genius like Strauss, Offenbach, Genée, Lecoq, Sullivan, Milloecker, etc., but nevertheless 'The Merry Widow' has been performed thousands of times everywhere in Europe. With no wish to detract in the slightest degree from the great charm of Lehar's popular work, nevertheless that great popularity demonstrates how poor was most of the light opera stuff which our transatlantic cousins had been getting – and exporting to us – for the past decade or so. Up to date, Lehar has made over $250,000 in royalties, which places him in the record ranks, together with the composers of 'Robin Hood' and 'The Belle of New York'.[15]

These other two record-holding composers were the German-born Gustave Kerker, whose *The Belle of New York* opened in 1897, and Reginald de Koven.

Having recently rejoined the staff of the *New York World*, de Koven attended the premiere of *The Merry Widow* and wrote that

> The dramatic purpose and coherency, the artistic sincerity...shown in
> 'The Merry Widow' last night, came like water in the desert after the
> tawdry musical inanities which have pervaded and infested Broadway for
> some years...[B]ook and music are welded together into an organic,
> artistic whole, and it is this artistic unity in purpose and dramatic
> treatment that is the controlling factor in the success which the opera has
> obtained the world over.[16]

His praise hardly seems self-interested, especially when Victor Herbert seconded this idea of renewal. *Musical America,* on 26 October 1907, ran a bold front-page headline: 'American Public's Taste is Improved.' Printed in slightly smaller type beneath it was: 'Victor Herbert Sees Good Signs in Success of "The Merry Widow" in New York.'[17]

Contemporary writers implied that Lehár's *Merry Widow* was raising audience standards when, in fact, they were only indulging America's historically conferred inferiority complex towards native creativity. Critics had for years been insinuating that American composers should strive to unify book and score into coherent structures that subjugated comedic elements to romance. The immediate popularity of *The Merry Widow* affirmed and validated these indigenous efforts. American operettas composed after Lehár's New York triumph were not substantially different from those that preceded it, but their creators gained cachet from the association. Just as the operettas of Strauss, and Gilbert and Sullivan, had invigorated the musical stage at the end of the nineteenth century by creating a touchstone against which American works might be judged, so too *The Merry Widow* revitalised American operetta by reinstating a foreign standard. Perhaps the best testament of *The Merry Widow*'s popularity were the burlesques that opened in its wake.

Burlesques, with their emphasis on broad comedy, are generally considered low-brow works, but even if there are clear distinctions along the continuum of genres, no such divisions can be made among audiences. A parody is funniest, and therefore most successful, in direct proportion to the audience's familiarity with the original being spoofed. Less than three months after *The Merry Widow* first appeared in New York, Lew Fields's former partner brought *The Merry Widow and the Devil* into Weber's Music Hall (2 January 1908). It lasted 156 performances and worked from a new script by the prolific George V. Hobart (1867–1926); the Lehár score was used by permission of Henry Savage.[18] Joe Weber appeared as Disch, the embassy's janitor, while Fonia was played by Lulu Glaser (1874–1958), best known for her starring role in Julian Edwards's *Dolly Varden* (1902).

The critic Acton Davies called Charlie Ross's performance as Prince Dandilo 'legitimate – in fact, it was too legitimate.'[19] This apparent blurring of boundaries bothered critics, including the one who wrote, 'A burlesque this transplanted "Merry Widow" can hardly be called, because there never was a musical comedy yet serious enough to offer the contrast needed for real burlesque.'[20]

Operetta after *The Merry Widow*

According to Charles Hamm,

> The immense popularity of European operetta resulted from its appeal to a number of different groups: recent immigrants from Europe and first- or second-generation Americans enjoying a fairytale view of their ancestral culture; the upwardly mobile, who wished to associate themselves with a more sophisticated form of musical theater than the minstrel show or vaudeville, but were unwilling or unable to derive pleasure from opera in foreign languages; and the urban middle class who responded to effective and well-crafted stage pieces produced by talented writers and composers.[21]

Tempted by the profitability of *The Merry Widow*, American producers imported more than twenty-five different operettas from Vienna and Berlin over the next decade. These often came by way of London, including Leo Fall's *The Dollar Princess* (1909), Oscar Straus's *The Chocolate Soldier* (1909) and Lehár's *The Count of Luxembourg* (1912). New American works continued to compete with the imports, and several of Herbert's later works have become repertory staples of today's light opera companies. *Naughty Marietta* (1910), for example, starred the Italian prima donna Emma Trentini (1878–1959). Composing for singers of operatic calibre led Herbert to create many of his finest numbers for this score, including the marching-song 'Tramp! Tramp! Tramp!', the waltz 'I'm Falling in Love With Someone', 'Italian Street Song' and the dreamy duet 'Ah! Sweet Mystery of Life'. In spite of its triumphant Broadway run, *Naughty Marietta* remained virtually unknown outside America until Jeanette MacDonald and Nelson Eddy's 1935 film version popularised it abroad. Herbert's 1913 *Sweethearts* had a silly plot reminiscent of the Savoy shows, but it did uniformly well on Broadway, on the road and in revivals; it, too, became an Eddy–MacDonald film.

The imminent upheavals of World War I prompted several European composers to emigrate to the United States, most notably Sigmund Romberg (1887–1951) and Rudolf Friml (1879–1972), both of whom continued to write operettas in the New World. Friml's first American work was *The Firefly* (1912). With a second vehicle for Emma Trentini in mind, Oscar

Hammerstein offered Otto Harbach's book to Victor Herbert, but when Herbert declined to work again with the temperamental Trentini, the task fell to Friml. *The Firefly* ran for 120 performances on Broadway and was produced throughout the United States; its substantial coverage in recording and radio ensured the composer's reputation in his new country. (Trentini was ultimately less fortunate. Having started her career in opera, she eventually worked her way down to vaudeville. In 1919, she appeared in the London revue *Whirlygig* and eventually retired to oblivion in her native land.)

At one and the same time, Lehár's *Merry Widow* crystallised two opposing trends. Producers who had once used skeletal plots as a framework on which to hang hit songs, revealing costumes and dazzling effects either moved towards better-integrated, symbiotic relationships or unabashedly did away with scenario in favour of scenery. Furthermore, with anti-German sentiment on the rise because of the war, many potentially profitable European works needed to have their books cooked into a dish more palatable to current American taste. Several composers who would become prominent in Broadway's next generation served their apprenticeship in this kitchen.

Follies and Scandals

Florenz Ziegfeld Jr (1867–1932) epitomised all that was luxurious and alluring on Broadway. His near-mythic career began with musical productions featuring his wife, the petite Polish-born, French-bred Anna Held (1873–1918). Several of Ziegfeld's early confections for her were adaptations of French works, such as *Papa's Wife* – an amalgam of Hervé's *La Femme à Papa* and *Mam'zelle Nitouche*. The composite *Papa's Wife* was nominally the work of Reginald de Koven (interpolations were plentiful!) and his long-time librettist Harry B. Smith (1861–1936), whose librettos served virtually every composer of the era, including Herbert, Kerker, Julian Edwards, Ludwig Engländer, Jerome Kern, Irving Berlin and Sigmund Romberg. *Papa's Wife* opened on 13 November 1899 and ran for 147 performances. Several of de Koven's numbers were topical songs using novelty to good theatrical advantage, such as 'The Automobile Song' celebrating the imported French vehicle in which Miss Held made her sensational entrance. Another opulent production used the same creative team to remake the French *Niniche* into *The Little Duchess*. It opened in New York on 14 October 1901 using its music to halo wasp-waisted women in chic couture. The score suffered so many successive interpolations that a programme for a performance a year after the opening warned audiences that due 'to the length of the performance the plot has been eliminated'.

In July 1907, Ziegfeld launched the first of a series of summertime diversions. The *Follies of 1907* boasted a bevy of 'Anna Held Girls' whose presence was supported by Harry B. Smith's book, Julian Mitchell's direction, and the financial clout of Klaw and Erlanger, the powerful and generally disliked Broadway producer syndicate. Over the next twenty years, Ziegfeld refined his presentation of feminine pulchritude, parading an average of sixty belles in each revue. He also had an eye for talent, and many legendary figures – Fanny Brice (1891–1951), Eddie Cantor (1892–1964), W. C. Fields (1879–1946) and Ed Wynn (1886–1966), among others – had their start under Ziegfeld's aegis. The 1910 edition, for example, featured three notable *Follies* first-timers who exemplify the ethnic humour endemic to the genre. Fanny Brice rendered Irving Berlin's unpublished (and now lost) Yiddish novelty song 'Good-bye Becky Cohen'. More importantly perhaps, Ziegfeld was willing to break the colour barrier for the sake of his show, and *The Follies of 1910* highlighted the black comedian Bert Williams (1874–1922), formerly part of a minstrel team with George Walker (d. 1911).

Ziegfeld's formula consisted of balancing comedy and songs with gorgeous girls in lavish and revealing costumes. As the popular ideal of feminine beauty shifted, partly in response to new celluloid images, Ziegfeld's girls grew slimmer, their skirts shorter and their skin barer – even to the point of allowing bare midriffs and some full nudity. In 1915, the art deco set designs of Joseph Urban upgraded the look of the shows and added a new dimension to their spectacular nature. It was also the year of W. C. Fields's *Follies* debut, and he would continue to appear in them until 1921. Ziegfeld produced his *Follies* until 1927, but they were not without competition from other regular series of revues.

From 1912 to 1924, the powerful Shubert brothers produced an annual series of *Passing Shows* that rarely surpassed Ziegfeld in either extravagance or artistry (even though their dance roster included Fred and Adele Astaire). The *George White Scandals* appeared regularly from 1919 to 1927, and sporadically thereafter until the final *Scandals 1939–40*. George White, a vaudeville dancer as a child, had been partnered with Ann Pennington in several *Follies* dance routines.

If Ziegfeld's series exemplified pre-war elegance and expansiveness, then White's *Scandals* harnessed the streamlined energy of the roaring twenties. White was attuned to the subtle changes in the post-*Merry Widow* dance craze, from the refined tango and maxixe to quick-stepping dances with gimmicky names like the turkey trot or grizzly bear. He envisaged a fast-paced show with harder colours (instead of nostalgic pastels) and edgier topical skits – a leaner post-war style suited to the age of Prohibition, gangsters and jazz. George Gershwin (1898–1937) composed the music for five of White's annuals, 1920–24, which included pop standards like 'I'll Build a Stairway to Paradise' and 'Somebody Loves Me'.

Irving Berlin

Establishing one's reputation as a songwriter was an important first step towards a life in the theatre, and Irving Berlin (1888–1989) was no exception. Berlin's early career consisted of interpolating songs – often ethnic novelty numbers – into the likes of Weber and Fields' shows and Ziegfeld's *Follies*. 'Alexander's Ragtime Band', published in 1911, brought him worldwide fame. Its popularity sealed the rhythms of ragtime into the American imagination, and Berlin used this to good advantage in his first full Broadway score, *Watch Your Step* (1914). Any weaknesses of plot were overshadowed by the fact that this was the first full-length book musical to have a score written entirely in the style of syncopated dance music.[22] *Watch Your Step* starred Vernon and Irene Castle, and was produced by C. B. Dillingham (1868–1934). It ran for 175 performances after opening on 8 December 1914 at the New Amsterdam Theatre and had a successful London run as well.

A sidelight of Berlin's early years was the 1916 revue *The Century Girl*, jointly produced by Dillingham and Ziegfeld. On the principle that two would be better than one, they asked the twenty-eight-year-old Berlin to share the score with the considerably more senior Victor Herbert. In no way collaborating, each composer worked independently, and a star-studded cast brought the whole to life against a dazzling set by Joseph Urban that included the trademark Ziegfeld staircase. A year later, Dillingham and Ziegfeld asked Herbert and Jerome Kern to team up with Bolton and Wodehouse for *Miss 1917*, a successor to *The Century Girl*. In spite of rave reviews for a cast that included Lew Fields and Irene Castle, and sets by Urban, *Miss 1917* folded after six weeks.

Given the length of his career, the number of song standards that emanated from Berlin's pen should hardly be surprising; several of them date from these early years. The short-lived, all-sailor vaudeville *Yip, Yip, Yaphank* (1918) included a *Follies* burlesque and left posterity the song 'Oh, How I Hate to Get Up in the Morning'. 'A Pretty Girl is Like a Melody' aptly hails from the *Ziegfeld Follies of 1919*.

In 1921, Berlin joined forces with the producer Sam H. Harris (1872–1941), who had recently ended his long alliance with George M. Cohan. Harris had produced *Little Johnny Jones* and many of Cohan's later pieces, including *The Little Millionaire* (1911) and the 1912 revival of *Forty-Five Minutes From Broadway* (1906). The new partnership resulted in the Music

Box Theatre, an intimate playhouse smaller than the venues currently hous-
ing the *Follies, Scandals,* or *Passing Shows.* Although there were only four
editions of the *Music Box Revues,* starting in the 1921–22 season, Gerald
Bordman referred to them as 'forty-carat flawless gems of the revue form'.[23]
The Music Box Revue of 1923–1924 included the song 'What'll I Do?'.

Jerome Kern

A similarly jewel-like venue also featured prominently in the early career of
Jerome Kern (1885–1945). Kern had a thorough Tin Pan Alley apprenticeship as a shipping clerk, song plugger and rehearsal pianist. He spent several
years working in London, and, like Berlin, was one of Broadway's busiest
interpolators before becoming a successful composer in his own right. Many
of his incidental songs found their way into European operettas revamped
for the London or Broadway stage, including Emmerich Kálmán's *The Gay
Hussars* (1909) and Leo Fall's *The Dollar Princess* (1909). Kern's first billing
as a show's principal composer (along with Frank Tours) was *La Belle Paree,*
which inaugurated the Shuberts' Winter Garden Theatre on 20 March 1911.
The show ran for 104 performances, largely on the strength of its debut
performer, Al Jolson (1886–1950).

The year 1915 was a busy and decisive one in Kern's career since it
marks his first joint effort with Guy Bolton (1884–1979). Along with lyricist
Harry B. Smith, the three wrote *Ninety in the Shade,* which starred Marie
Cahill in what would be her last Broadway role. The show was mounted
by Daniel V. Arthur, Cahill's husband and sole producer ever since her
unfortunate earlier *contretemps* with Victor Herbert. Although *Ninety in
the Shade* quickly folded (driving the Arthurs into bankruptcy and Marie
back to vaudeville), Kern salvaged most of his best numbers for later reuse,
often as interpolations into his own or others' shows. Bolton became one
of his most important collaborators, and with the fortuitous addition of
P. G. Wodehouse (1881–1975) as lyricist, the trio was poised to rescue and
redeem Broadway's smallest theatre.

The Princess Theatre was built at the edge of the theatre district in 1912
with a seating capacity of 299. When the one-act plays by up-and-coming
new dramatists for which the house was originally intended failed to attract
enough attention, management called in Elisabeth Marbury, the respected
theatrical agent, for advice. She suggested musicals. What followed would
be a series of shows synthesising the sophistication of European operetta
with the pacing and verve of Cohan's American musical style.

The 'Princess Shows' offered audiences a theatrical experience the polar
opposite of what Ziegfeld, Dillingham or White presented. The tiny house

provided an intimate setting for a necessarily elitist gathering since it had limited less-expensive balcony seating. The orchestra pit held fewer than a dozen players and the stage not many more. Bolton's stories relied on situational humour; audiences laughed not at the mistaken identities of the characters, but rather at the mistaken relationships between them – familiar upper-middle-class figures caught in everyday situations gone awry. Wodehouse's lyrics captured the flow of natural speech while still turning a neat phrase or inventive rhyme, and they allowed the characters such scope for change as is practicable within the genre. Kern suffused the whole with musical warmth, wit and panache.

The success of works like *Oh, Boy!* (1917), which ran for 463 performances, left Kern with ample time to compose songs for other projects, including the revamping of another import. Klaw and Erlanger produced *The Riviera Girl* in 1917, an adaptation of Kálmán's *Die Czárdásfürstin* by Bolton and Wodehouse with additional music by Jerome Kern. It closed after 78 performances. European operetta, in the decade before the war, spurred both action and reaction in American creativity but was slowly losing sway to the native product as the war drew to a close.

One work crowns Kern's career before *Show Boat*, bringing together the most important names of its time. *Sally* is essentially a Cinderella story of an orphaned dishwasher turned *Follies* star. Bolton wrote the book; Wodehouse was one of four lyricists. The score, including 'Look for the Silver Lining', was Kern's, but Victor Herbert contributed 'The Butterfly Ballet'. Ziegfeld dictated the production values for the show. Marilyn Miller, who starred in Ziegfeld's *Follies* in 1918 and 1919 (and, after his separation from Anna Held, in his heart, too), played the title role. *Sally* became one of the longest-running and highest-grossing shows of its day with 570 Broadway performances, 387 performances at the Winter Garden in London, substantial road tours in the United States and Australia, and several Hollywood film versions.

Conclusion

If one believes critics, Broadway at the threshold of the twentieth century provided yet one more example of the Dickensian 'best and worst of times'. At the distance of a century, musical theatre has proved to be a hardy organism. Some fruits withered on the vine, others were cross-pollinated, grew new roots and scattered the seeds that are flourishing today. If vaudeville has slipped into the realm of late-night television, burlesques can be found in *Forbidden Broadway*. Follies à la Ziegfeld may not be politically correct in to-day's society, but revues flourish in works like *Riverdance, Smokey Joe's Café* and *Songs for a New World* not to mention seasonal extravaganzas like the Radio City Music Hall Christmas shows. Contemporary production values take full advantage of modern technology to dazzle audiences with ever more spectacular effects. Using the *Merry Widow* to sell hats and cocktails is not all that dissimilar to the logos of today like the *Cats* eyes and the *Phantom*'s demi-mask. Shows travel in both directions across the Atlantic, and 'Broadway' no longer seems limited to New York. Composers and choreographers continue to adapt their styles to the current vernacular of their audiences, exploring rock, Latin and, increasingly, non-western idioms. With *Sweeney Todd* just as likely to show up in the opera house, writers continue to deliberate over the parameters of the genre while critics wonder pessimistically if this is as good as it gets. In the final analysis, however, these are all secondary considerations. Audiences know what they like.

3 Romance, nostalgia and nevermore: American and British operetta in the 1920s

WILLIAM A. EVERETT

Operettas from the 1920s, the titles of which evoke romantic images of times and places far away – not to mention the music and lyrics – enjoy a continued popularity that stems directly from their very nature of being 'old-fashioned'. Shows such as *The Student Prince, Rose-Marie* and *Bitter Sweet* are as nostalgic at the dawn of the twenty-first century as they were at the time of their creation. It is this very sense of sentiment and nevermore, deeply rooted in romantic innocence, that has been both the ultimate blessing and the paramount curse of the genre.

In nineteenth-century and early twentieth-century Vienna, operetta was envisaged as a popular form of entertainment set in some sort of fictionalised Ruritania – a Central European (usually Balkan) domain with nobles and peasants suspended in an eternal nineteenth century. Even the name 'Ruritania', the setting of Anthony Hope's 1894 novel *The Prisoner of Zenda*, evokes a sense of familiar exoticism.[1] Audiences adored such entertainments with plots in which characters interacted with each other in humorous and amorous ways while dressed in fanciful costumes amidst lavish sets. The action took place against a glorious musical score replete with waltzes, marches, and tour-de-force solos and duets.

This stylized version of Viennese operetta found tremendous favour with American audiences in the early years of the twentieth century, and nothing could match the success of Franz Lehár's *The Merry Widow* when its English-language version waltzed into New York in 1907.[2] Following on the heels of *The Merry Widow* were numerous shows hoping to achieve success in its wake: Oscar Straus's *A Waltz Dream* (1908) and *The Chocolate Soldier* (1909), Paul Rubens's *The Balkan Princess* (1911) – a London import – and Felix Albini's *Baron Trenck* (1912), to name but a few.

With the First World War, as would be expected, fondness for Central European operetta fell dramatically. English-speaking audiences did not want in their theatrical escapements to visit mythical Balkan kingdoms with overt German overtones. It would take time for audiences to want to return to Ruritania, and when they did, it could not be to its pre-war archetypes.

Musical styles could possibly be drawn upon, if done so in a nostalgic vein, but physical locales would have to be altered. Operetta, therefore, would have to be redefined on several levels if it was going to continue.

The influence of Tin Pan Alley and other forms of musical theatrical entertainments provided the catalyst through which such necessary transformations took place. In New York, the immigrant composers Rudolf Friml (1879–1972) and Sigmund Romberg (1887–1954) emerged as the leading composers of operetta during the 1920s. Two of the genre's defining works appeared in 1924, Friml's *Rose-Marie* (first performed 2 September) and Romberg's *The Student Prince in Heidelberg* (first performed 2 December). Friml, with his European training and concert career, provided contrast to Romberg, with his practical experience acquired in Viennese and New York theatres.

The success of the genre during the 1920s (and beyond, in various manifestations) was quite remarkable. Of the eleven longest-running musicals of the 1920s, six of them – just over half – were operettas by either Romberg or Friml.[3] Post-war audiences craved the escapist nature of the operetta. In many ways the genre represented the opulence of the era – wealth and splendour were clearly evident. This was the Gilded Age of F. Scott Fitzgerald's *The Great Gatsby* – a time when people had money and wanted to flaunt it. Here was a type of theatrical entertainment filled with characters of affluence, most of whom were European.

The escapist nature of the genre was an integral part. While musical comedies centred on contemporary characters (almost always New Yorkers) in comic situations, operettas by definition had to take place in some remote time and/or place. Because of the Great War, German and Ruritanian locales were not going to be the most logical settings for an operetta (although Romberg's *The Student Prince* was set in Germany and Coward's *Bitter Sweet* in Vienna). Other locales would have to be discovered against which sentimental tales could unfold, and American and French historical settings provided the solution.

Friml and Romberg: transforming operetta

Rudolf Friml, born in Prague, studied with Antonín Dvořák before moving to the US and settling in New York in 1906. He was active as a composer of piano music and as a concert pianist during these early years. In 1912 Friml benefited greatly from Victor Herbert's last-minute decision to break his contract to write *The Firefly*. Oscar Hammerstein suddenly found himself needing to find a new composer, and his gamble on the young Czech proved successful. Although the score sounds European, the operetta shares with Herbert's *Naughty Marietta* an American locale. In 1915 Friml created a

Viennese setting for *Katinka,* an operetta whose plot involved Russians, Americans and Arabians. His classical European training is clearly evident in these scores.

Sigmund Romberg, born in Nagykanizsa, Hungary, spent his youth in Beliŝće and Osijek, today in Croatia. It was there, while working at the local theatre, that he became entrenched in the world of musical theatre. He eventually made his way to Vienna to study civil engineering, but musical pursuits dominated his years in the capital of both the Austro-Hungarian Empire and the Operetta Kingdom. Romberg befriended people such as Victor Heuberger and Franz Lehár while working at the Theater an der Wien, a house known for its operetta productions.

Romberg arrived in New York City in 1909 and found work as a pianist in various restaurants. He formed and conducted a small orchestra at Bustanoby's, a venue frequented by the theatrical crowd, including the brothers J. J. and Lee Shubert. The Shuberts soon engaged Romberg to contribute to their revues, most notably *The Passing Show* series, and to adapt Central European operettas for American audiences.

Among the most important of these adaptations were *The Blue Paradise* (1915), from Edmund Eysler's *Ein Tag im Paradis* and the show that introduced Romberg's first hit waltz, 'Auf Wiedersehn'; *Maytime* (1917), based on Walter Kollo's *Wie Einst im Mai* and including the nostalgic waltz 'Will You Remember?'; and *Blossom Time* (1921), a fictionalised account of the life of Franz Schubert and a second-generation adaptation of Berté's *Das Dreimäderlhaus.* Romberg used several of Schubert's best-known melodies as the basis for this score, most notably 'Song of Love', a waltz derived from the second theme of the first movement of Schubert's Eighth Symphony. These adaptations were central to Romberg's development as a composer, for it was in them that he refined his skills as a creator with one foot in the European operetta tradition and the other on Broadway.

And so we arrive at the pivotal year of 1924, when two of the most important and most successful musicals of the decade appeared. *Rose-Marie,* with its Canadian Rockies setting, was one of the first operettas to have a North American backdrop while *The Student Prince* captured the charm and nostalgia of Ruritania. These were the two most frequently performed operettas of the decade in New York. (See Table 3.1.) Curiously, the triumph of these works and their settings was not followed by their composers, for Friml would choose France for his next two major works of the decade and Romberg would eventually voyage to North African and American realms.

Rose-Marie (music by Rudolf Friml and Herbert Stothart, book and lyrics by Oscar Hammerstein II and Otto Harbach) played for an impressive 557 performances in its initial New York run. In the operetta, the title character, part North American Indian, is a singer at Lady Jane's Hotel, a small lodge in

Table 3.1 *Numbers of performances of significant Friml and Romberg operettas in New York and London*

Much of the data in this table comes from Kurt Gänzl, *The Musical: A Concise History* (Boston, 1997), p. 196.

	New York	London
The Student Prince in Heidelberg (1924) (Romberg)	608	96
Rose-Marie (1924) (Friml)	557	851
Blossom Time (1921) (Romberg)	516	–
The Vagabond King (1925) (Friml)	511	480
The New Moon (1928) (Romberg)	509	148
The Desert Song (1926) (Romberg)	471	432
The Three Musketeers (1928) (Friml)	318	240
My Maryland (1927) (Romberg)	312	–

the Canadian Rockies. She loves Jim Kenyon, who is accused of murdering Black Eagle and goes into hiding in the Canadian woods. His accuser is Ed Hawley, who has his eye on Rose-Marie. It turns out that Wanda, Black Eagle's wife, was the killer, and Rose-Marie and Jim are reunited as the operetta ends.

A number of musical styles and influences are evident in *Rose-Marie*, including a concerted waltz ('The Door of My Dreams'), a rousing march ('The Mounties'), a Tin Pan Alley love song ('Rose-Marie'), Indianist numbers ('Indian Love Call' and 'Totem Tom Tom') and aspects of melodrama (Finaletto sequence in act 2). Friml followed his mentor Dvořák's instructions to American composers and created local colour through the inclusion of certain Indianist identifiers such as drone fifths, slithering chromaticism and a driving beat in the score.

In 'Indian Love Call' the chromaticism is especially evident in the opening phrase, and drone fifths appear in the accompaniment at the words 'When the lone lagoon stirs in the spring' and again at various points in the underscoring for 'That means I offer my love to you to be your own. If you refuse me, I will be blue and waiting all alone.' These Indianist identifiers add credence to the setting, but the techniques themselves would reappear in later, non-Indianist Friml scores.

In the woefully politically incorrect 'Totem Tom Tom', not only do Indianist musical clichés such as drone fifths and the incessant repetition of distinctive rhythmic motifs dominate the sound world, but the text promotes an image of Native Canadians as drunkards who only dance and sleep. Led by the murderess Wanda, the number was the show-stopping spectacle that preceded the first-act finale. Possibly the centrality of this musical number has prohibited *Rose-Marie* from enjoying a renewed popularity through revivals.

The primary march of the show, 'The Mounties', includes a middle section in the minor mode surrounded by assertive major-mode passages. The opening phrase, 'On thro' the hail', includes the stage direction that it is to be sung by 'Mounties off stage at great distance'. The middle section is a solo passage (with off-stage choral interjections) for Malone, leader of the Mounties, in which he warns of the impending arrival of the singing constabulary. The sense of foreboding is enhanced through the choice of the minor mode. The final section, returning to major, is a reprise of the opening passage, but scored as a solo for Malone with a continuation of the choral interjections from the middle section. This use of the minor mode in a march is not unique in Friml's work, for he would use the technique in 'Song of the Vagabonds' from *The Vagabond King*. Especially significant in the number is the careful attention to the spatial relationship between on-stage and off-stage voices. Malone, in addition to being a Mountie, is the suitor of the title character. His psychological allegiances are divided and this dichotomy is presented to the audience through the staging of the number. He is not completely at one with his male colleagues – his attentions lie elsewhere, namely with Rose-Marie.

Three months after the premiere of *Rose-Marie*, Romberg's first original operetta, *The Student Prince*, appeared on Broadway for 608 performances. All the elements of operetta were present in Dorothy Donnelly's book and lyrics, save for the happy ending. Karl Franz, prince of mythical Karlsberg, is in love with Kathie, the waitress at the Inn of the Golden Apples. A large male beer-drinking chorus was one of the highlights of the production. In a genre dominated by two principals who spend a great deal of the evening singing love songs, to have a male chorus at the centre of the musical focus (especially in the first act) was something quite novel. In contrast to *Rose-Marie*, the chorus was on stage for their numbers, not in the wings. The score was filled with nostalgic waltzes and marches – 'Golden Days', 'Deep in My Heart, Dear' and 'Students' Marching Song' – and of course the immortal concerted 'Serenade'.

Although *The Student Prince* was the longest-running musical in New York during the 1920s, it did not fare well in London – a musical which romanticised and even celebrated Germanness was not going to succeed in the decade following the First World War. Furthermore, the concept of college and university fraternities and male glee clubs, both epitomised through the significant role of the male chorus, were alien to the London public. By contrast, *Rose-Marie* was a tremendous hit in the West End with its impressive 851-performance run. *Rose-Marie* would continue its success by playing for 1,250 performances in Paris and eventually being staged in places as diverse as Berlin and Budapest, cities in the geographic heart of the Ruritanian sphere of influence.

Plate 3   The original New York production of *The Student Prince* with Ilse Marvenga and the Male Chorus

After the success of *The Student Prince*, it was to the 'real' Ruritania that Romberg would return the next year with *Princess Flavia* (1925; book and lyrics by Harry B. Smith), an adaptation of Anthony Hope's novel *The Prisoner of Zenda*. The operetta was supposed to capitalise on the popularity of *The Student Prince*, but as so often happens in such instances, the copy did not live up to the original. The beginning of the refrain to the primary love duet, 'I Dare Not Love You', bears an uncanny resemblance to the opening of the refrain in the song's parallel number in *The Student Prince*, 'Deep in My Heart, Dear'.

After *Princess Flavia*, Romberg left Ruritania and began exploring other exotic locales for his operettas. From North Africa to Civil War Maryland and eighteenth-century Louisiana, Romberg would apply his fundamentally Viennese aesthetic to stories set outside a mythical Central Europe. It was in these shows that Romberg effected the transformation of American operetta from a fundamentally Viennese genre to an American art form.

The Desert Song (1926; book by Otto Harbach, Oscar Hammerstein II and Frank Mandel, lyrics by Hammerstein) proved to be one of Romberg's greatest successes and is considered one of his outstanding achievements. Capitalising on the popularity of Rudolf Valentino, Lawrence of Arabia,

Beau Geste and the actual Riff Wars in North Africa, the libretto of *The Desert Song* included overt references to contemporary events and popular culture. The exoticism and intrigue of French Morocco replaced the nostalgia of Ruritania.

The story is one of dual identity: the Red Shadow (a.k.a. the awkward Pierre) helps the North African natives resist their French oppressors. Margot, daughter of the French governor, is in love with the mystique of the Red Shadow, and Pierre is in love with her. Not until the end of the operetta does Margot realise the dual identity of the person with whom she had been singing all evening. Like *Rose-Marie*, *The Desert Song* included a dancing villainess, Azuri. Azuri, though, is only a betrayer, not a murderess like her predecessor Wanda.

The score includes some of Romberg's most operatic music: 'The Desert Song', 'The Riff Song', 'The Sabre Song', 'One Alone' and 'Romance'. In the title waltz, the dual identity of Pierre is heard through the judicious use of major and minor modes. When Pierre is expressing his true feelings as a Frenchman, he sings in the major mode. When he is singing as the mysterious Red Shadow, his music is largely pentatonic and is harmonised in the minor. A similar duality is present in the concerted scene 'Eastern and Western Love' where the Red Shadow and Ali Ben Ali compare views on women – the Moroccan view, 'One Flower Grows Alone in Your Garden', is in the minor mode while the French view, 'One Alone', is in the major. Romberg, in this way, creates a general sense of the 'other' through his choice of mode. When compared with the Indianist elements in Friml's *Rose-Marie*, Romberg's musical depictions of exoticism may be less complicated but are equally effective.

Romberg continued his experiments with the physical setting of operetta during the following year (1927). *Cherry Blossoms*, *My Maryland*, *The Love Call* and *My Princess* are set in Japan, Maryland, Arizona and New York City. While *My Maryland* enjoyed a certain amount of success, the other shows did not. With the exception of *My Princess*, they all took place in locales other than New York City of the 1920s, adhering to the requisite precept of re-moteness in operetta, though Ruritania was now off-limits not only because of the First World War but also because of the failure of *Princess Flavia*.

My Maryland is a re-tooling of the Civil War legend of Barbara Fritchie. The principal march in the operetta, 'Your Land and My Land', includes a quotation from 'The Battle Hymn of the Republic' at the end of its refrain, an allusion to local colour. Its Viennese roots are evident in the romantic waltz that serves as the operetta's principal love duet, 'The Same Silver Moon'.

My Princess is central to this discussion because it was a dismal failure. It played for a mere twenty performances at New York's Shubert Theatre. Dorothy Donnelly's libretto took place in 1920s New York and concerned a society woman who wanted to marry an Italian prince. She found a person who she thought was a poor Italian immigrant and made him into her prince. Of course, it is ultimately revealed that he really was Italian royalty. All the elements of operetta were present – mistaken identity, royal and common interactions, glorious waltzes – but what was lacking was a remote sense of time and place. The story would have worked much better with a score in the style of musical comedy, on the models of the Gershwins, Rodgers and Hart, or Kern. The principal love waltz, 'Follow the Sun to the South', was too deeply rooted in Ruritania to be a convincing musical depiction of 1920s New York.

When *The New Moon* (1928; book by Hammerstein, Mandel, and Laurence Schwab, lyrics by Hammerstein) appeared in late 1927 at its Philadelphia tryout, Romberg had left contemporary New York for 1780s Louisiana, French according to the libretto but Spanish in historical reality. The operetta shared its setting with Victor Herbert's *Naughty Marietta* (1910), but also included parts that took place aboard the ship 'The New Moon' and on an island in the Caribbean, recalling Friml's *The Firefly*. The story of Robert Mission, an escaped French aristocrat who wanted to rid France of its monarchy, and Marianne Beaunoir, daughter of a Royalist landowner in Louisiana, provided the romantic backdrop against which the libretto would unfold. Romberg's score included the obligatory waltzes and marches, but his handling of musical material, including a rather sophisticated use of underscoring, is surely the influence of the previous year's *Show Boat*. As a matter of fact, after the initial tryout of *The New Moon*, work was suspended on the operetta so that Hammerstein could spend more time preparing *Show Boat*, another show that included shipboard scenes, for its release from dry dock.

Adhering to the operetta adage that men march and women waltz, Romberg created some of his most memorable music for *The New Moon*. The march 'Stouthearted Men' is one of Romberg's most famous numbers, as is Marianne's concerted waltz, 'One Kiss'. Although these songs are clearly rooted in Central European models, they utilise the verse–refrain form of Tin Pan Alley. Romberg, rather than evoking eighteenth-century Louisiana in his score, incorporated aspects of the Tin Pan Alley style that he had embraced in the 1910s. The operetta also contains such impressive musical numbers as the tango 'Softly, As in a Morning Sunrise', a gentle homage to Hispanic popular music, and the love duet 'Wanting You'.

In 'One Kiss', Marianne shares her plea for what she desires more than anything else. The verse begins with one of many historic inaccuracies in the show, 'In this year of seventeen ninety two'. The scene takes place *before* the 1789 French Revolution, an event central to the second act's plot. The alternative year is necessary because of the rhyme scheme:

> In this year of seventeen ninety two
> Our conventions have been thrown all askew

Romberg's triumvirate of internationally known operettas from the 1920s, *The Student Prince*, *The Desert Song* and *The New Moon*, all explore the issue of remoteness. A distant (i.e. non-American) locale appears in *The Desert Song*, although it is set in the present. Historicism provides the escapist element in *The New Moon*, while *The Student Prince* is remote in terms of both time and place. Romberg transformed the nature of dramatic distance in his work, demonstrating that *both* time and place do not have to be other than the present for success – one or the other will suffice as long as the score and libretto are demonstrably strong.

To return to Friml's career after *Rose-Marie*, *The Vagabond King* (1925) and *The Three Musketeers* (1928) depict different eras in French history. Friml's career in the 1920s basically circumvented many of the norms of Ruritanian operetta, although he did create glorious marches and waltzes. Perhaps it was the way in which Friml began his Broadway career that curtailed this obligation. As a replacement for Victor Herbert, Friml was coming from the British side of operetta, one *not* rooted in Ruritania. Furthermore, he did not have the direct contact with Viennese operetta that Romberg did. His more straightforward, musical comedy approach to characterisation allowed him the freedom to transfer a sense of place much more easily than Romberg's allegiance to Central Europe would allow him to do.

Friml was much more involved with current trends in art music culture during the 1920s than was Romberg. The Indianist movement was strongly afoot, and Friml paid allegiance to this trend in *Rose-Marie*, as discussed above. *The Vagabond King* and *The Three Musketeers*, by contrast, manifest the Francophilia of the 1920s. This was certainly in keeping with wider cultural and aesthetic issues of the decade. France and French culture were paramount. Glamour magazines promoted French style, and in classical music circles, composers such as Edgard Varèse and members of Les Six were held in very high regard.

The Vagabond King (1925; lyrics by Brian Hooker, book by Hooker, Russell Janney, and W. H. Post) played for an impressive 511 performances in its initial run. The libretto, based on the play *If I Were King* by Justin McCarthy, related a fictitious tale of the real François Villon, a fifteenth-century poet who becomes a pawn in King Louis XI's plan to play a joke on a lady in his court, Katherine de Vaucelles. The King dubs Villon king for a day, during which time he must woo Katherine or be beheaded. Villon succeeds in his romantic efforts. Meanwhile, the Duke of Burgundy invades Paris, and Villon must gather his fellow vagabonds to defeat the assailants. He accomplishes this feat as well, and as a reward, the King allows Villon to marry Katherine. In keeping with tradition, Friml created one of his most memorable marches, 'Song of the Vagabonds' – with its central section in the minor mode – for the show, as well as the sentimental numbers 'Only a Rose' and 'Love Me Tonight', the latter a waltz filled with the slithering chromaticism so characteristic of Friml.

The Three Musketeers (1927; lyrics by P. G. Wodehouse and Clifford Grey, book by William Anthony McGuire) took as its basis Alexandre Dumas's novel of swashbuckling adventure. The score included such arresting numbers as 'Ma Belle', 'One Kiss', 'My Dreams', 'My Sword and I' and 'March of the Musketeers'. The Queen's 'My Dreams' is a lilting duple-metre ballad in which the first note of each phrase begins one step lower than its predecessor, paralleling the character's descent into slumber.

American operetta, with its escapist romantic notions, came to an end with the 1929 Stock Market Crash and subsequent Great Depression. Audiences wanted to laugh, not cry, when they went to the theatre for entertainment. Furthermore, the costs of mounting operettas with their lavish sets, costumes and casts became prohibitive. Likewise, as a result of these factors, operetta in the Ruritanian guise and its American successor faded as far as new contributions to the genre were concerned. Road tours continued (sets already existed), films were waiting to be made and operetta would begin a new life as a somewhat clichéd theatrical manifestation of nostalgia, nevermore and old-fashionedness. Its overt sentimentality would both endear the genre to older generations of theatre and cinema audiences and subsequently cause it to become the subject of parody in many aspects of popular culture, as will be discussed below.

The British scene: from *Chu Chin Chow* to *Bitter Sweet*

With the arrival of the 1920s in London, two operettas whose lives began in the previous decade were still going strong: *Chu Chin Chow* and *The Maid of the Mountains*. The exotic nature of these works would set the stage for subsequent developments in the decade.

When *Chu Chin Chow* (1916; music by Frederick Norton, book and lyrics by Oscar Asche) first appeared at His Majesty's Theatre on 31 August 1916, Britain was in the midst of the Great War. Escapist theatrical entertainment was not only popular, it was necessary. The show was an Arabian Nights fantasy with spectacular sets and starred Jose Collins, one of the leading actresses of the time. Here was pure escapism, but not in a Ruritanian sense. It is all too obvious why British audiences did not want to venture into Ruritania, the created epitome of Central European culture, in 1916. The show played for an impressive 2,235 performances and closed on 22 July 1921, after playing for nearly five years.

The other big hit of the War, *The Maid of the Mountains* (1917; music by James Tate, lyrics by Harry Graham, book by Frederick Lonsdale), was also escapist in setting, the action taking place in the high mountains of a brigand land. The story told of Teresa, who is arrested by General Malona, the Governor of Santo. Malona has promised her release only if her lover, the outlaw Baldasarre, is captured. Complications ensue, Baldasarre is jailed, and Teresa succeeds in engineering her lover's release. Jose Collins, again the star, introduced the standard 'Love Will Find a Way' in the show. The operetta played for a total of 1,352 performances in its initial London run and enjoyed continued popularity as a vehicle for amateur operatic societies. The show transferred to New York (unlike *Chu Chin Chow*), where it opened at the Casino Theatre on 11 September 1918, and played for a disappointing thirty-seven performances.

Operetta did not enjoy the same sense of native popularity in Britain that it did in America during the 1920s. Much of this certainly had to do with the post-war sentiment towards things Central European. The original operettas that did appear were decidedly non-Ruritanian. *The Rose of Araby* (1920; music by Merlin Morgan, book by Harold Simpson) and *Cairo* (1920, New York; 1921, London; music by Percy Fletcher, mime by Oscar Asche) both capitalised upon the Arabian-nights exoticism of *Chu Chin Chow*. Their success and the accepted exoticism of North Africa certainly was at least partly responsible for the tremendous popularity of *The Desert Song* among British audiences.

Adaptations of German-language operettas were not completely un-known, however. *The Lady of the Rose* (1922, music by Jean Gilbert), an adaptation of *Die Frau im Hermelin,* played for nearly fifteen months, and *Lilac Time* (1922, music arranged by Heinrich Berté and G. H. Clutsam, book and lyrics by Adrian Ross), an adaptation of *Das Dreimäderlhaus,* enjoyed an eighteen-month run in London before entering the domain of touring productions and revivals. *Lilac Time* shared its source material with the Romberg–Donnelly *Blossom Time*, but the two shows are substantially different – *Lilac Time* is not a British version of the Romberg operetta.

As would happen again in the 1940s, American imports dominated much of the British musical scene. *Rose-Marie*, with 851 performances, *The Vagabond King*, with 480 performances, and *The Desert Song*, with 432 performances, found great favour among London audiences. Significantly, none of these works had Ruritanian settings – when *The Student Prince* appeared in London, as mentioned above, it played for a mere ninety-six performances.

True Ruritanian operetta, but with a decidedly modern twist, would appear at the end of the decade, however. *Bitter Sweet* (1929), with book, music and lyrics by Noël Coward (1899–1973), was its creator's first major musical triumph. Told in flashback, the story takes place in nineteenth-century Vienna, the bastion of Ruritanian sentimentality. The libretto concerns the life of Sarah, Marchioness of Shayne, previously known as Sari. Sari was to have married a socially appropriate young man but instead ran off with her music teacher, Carl Linden. After they married, Linden worked as a conductor in a Viennese café where she sang. A lustful soldier tries to seduce Sari, and Carl is killed trying to protect her honour. Although Sari becomes a successful singer and has numerous romantic liaisons that culminate in marriage to a British Marquis, it is her faithfulness to Carl that rules her heart. Her tale is both bitter and sweet, reflected in the two-word title of the show, *Bitter Sweet*. Coward's mastery of musical styles is clearly evident – the 1920s Charleston numbers are rooted in contemporary idioms while the Viennese waltzes such as 'Zigeuner' and 'I'll See You Again' capture the spirit of a time that exists only in sentimental remembrance.

Hollywood versions of operettas

With the advent and growth of the sound motion picture industry in the late 1920s, film versions of classic operettas formed a significant part of the Hollywood industry. Certainly the most famous adaptations are those that starred Jeanette MacDonald and Nelson Eddy, known as 'America's Singing Sweethearts' or 'The Beauty and the Baritone'. But films starring one or both of these stars were not the only ones to bring operettas to film-going audiences: opera stars such as Grace Moore and Lawrence Tibbett would sing on celluloid, as would Hollywood singing legends such as Gordon MacRae and Kathryn Grayson. While space does not permit a thorough investigation of each of the fourteen film adaptations of 1920s stage operettas, the fact that these films exist confirms the popularity of the genre. (See Table 3.2.) With the Great Depression, when producing stage spectacles became cost-prohibitive, the cinema became the medium through which operetta found new life.

The first operetta to receive a full-sound Hollywood treatment was *The Desert Song*. The 1929 Warner Brothers film starred John Boles and Carlotta King in the lead roles. A young Myrna Loy portrayed the exotic antagonist Azuri. The film remained faithful to the original stage version, and every scene in the film is underscored, the result of the 'silent' film era, where live musicians played throughout a film.

Table 3.2 *Film adaptations of 1920s operettas*

Bitter Sweet
1933, British and Dominion Film Corporation
Anna Neagle, Fernand Gravet

1940, MGM
Jeanette MacDonald, Nelson Eddy

The Desert Song
1929, Warner Brothers
John Boles, Carlotta King

1942, Warner Brothers
Dennis Morgan, Irene Manning

1953, Warner Brothers
Gordon MacRae, Kathryn Grayson

Maytime
1937, MGM
Jeanette MacDonald, Nelson Eddy

New Moon
1930, MGM
Lawrence Tibbett, Grace Moore

1940, MGM
Jeanette MacDonald, Nelson Eddy

Rose-Marie
1928 (silent), MGM
Joan Crawford

1936, MGM
Jeanette MacDonald, Nelson Eddy

1954, MGM
Ann Blyth, Fernando Lamas, Howard Keel

The Student Prince
1954, MGM
Ann Blyth, Edmund Purdom (dubbed by Mario Lanza)

The Vagabond King
1930, Paramount
Dennis King, Jeanette MacDonald

1956, Paramount
Oreste, Kathryn Grayson

Two other versions of *The Desert Song* exist: a 1943 version with Dennis Morgan and Irene Manning and a 1953 version starring Gordon MacRae and Kathryn Grayson. The plot for the 1943 version was altered to include Nazis in the North African desert, while the MacRae–Grayson rendition was closer to the original stageplay.

Whereas the 1929 film of *The Desert Song* remained quite true to the stage libretto, the 1930 film of *The New Moon*, called *New Moon*, did not. Starring renowned opera stars Grace Moore and Lawrence Tibbett, the film includes some of the finest singing of any Romberg score. Set on the Caspian Sea and the Russian frontier, the plot was completely rewritten. The musical score was also modified and included only the songs 'Wanting You', 'Lover Come Back to Me', 'One Kiss' and 'Stouthearted Men'. In an effort to create Russian atmosphere, a 'vulgar' gypsy song, 'The Farmer's Daughter', was added to the score and a balalaika appeared in the orchestration for 'Lover Come Back to Me'. The subsequent 1940 version with Jeanette MacDonald and Nelson Eddy would return to French New Orleans with a plot that resembled, but was not identical to, the original.

Treatments of *Rose-Marie* also varied considerably from the original. The 1936 Jeanette MacDonald–Nelson Eddy version was radically transformed to allow the stars to sing all the major songs. The lavish 'Totem Tom Tom' was maintained in all its splendour, as it was in the 1954 Technicolor version with Ann Blyth, Fernando Lamas and Howard Keel. The 1954 version was closer to Hammerstein's original plot concept than its predecessor.

It was the legendary team of Jeanette MacDonald and Nelson Eddy who more than any other performers epitomised the genre of the operetta film. In their eight films together, they not only provided countless audiences with hours of entertainment but also became models for aspiring young singers. Their collaborations included *Naughty Marietta* (1935), *Rose Marie* (1936), *Maytime* (1937), *The Girl of the Golden West* (1938, music by Romberg, lyrics by Gus Kahn), *Sweethearts* (1938, their first colour film), *The New Moon* (1940), *Bitter Sweet* (1940) and *I Married an Angel* (1942, music by Richard Rodgers, lyrics by Lorenz Hart). The duo epitomised the romantic lovers who, though adversities plague them either through their own doings or through those of others, always end up together at the end. MacDonald typically played the aristocrat who is placed in circumstances that are uncomfortable for a person of her upbringing. Eddy was often clad in a military uniform, a symbol of his masculinity.

In the MacDonald–Eddy films, songs were usurped from their original dramatic roles and became the means through which countless audience members in cinemas throughout the US were enraptured and entranced by the nostalgic and nevermore aesthetic of the genre. Plots were revised to allow MacDonald and Eddy to sing all the major musical numbers. Many aspiring singers during the era attended the cinema to see 'the Beauty and Baritone' and looked to them as role models for good singing.

The legacy of operetta

The 1920s American operetta influenced popular culture throughout the twentieth century. Through innumerable road tours, New York and London revivals and other productions (from high schools to professional opera companies and everything in between), the legacy of Ruritania continued to live on. Further popularity of the genre developed through film versions (discussed above) and its reputation is kept alive to this day through numerous references in popular culture both in the US and in Britain.

Operettas from the early decades of the twentieth century provide a tremendous source for imitation in either pastiche or parody. The continued popularity of the repertory allows this to happen, for if audiences did not understand the original reference, the derivative treatment would lose its meaning.

Operetta served as a direct model for several musical theatre works and numbers in the latter part of the century. 'One More Kiss' from Stephen Sondheim's *Follies* (1971) is a pastiche of a quintessential operetta waltz for coloratura soprano. Stephen Banfield suggests Romberg influences in two songs from the Disney animated film (and subsequent stage musical) *Beauty and the Beast* (1991; music by Alan Menken, lyrics by Howard Ashman). 'The Mob Song' is a cinematic recreation of Nelson Eddy's nocturnal march 'Stouthearted Men' in the 1940 film of *The New Moon*, while 'Gaston' is an homage to 'Drinking Song' from *The Student Prince*.[4]

Rose-Marie was the fundamental source material for the operetta parody *Little Mary Sunshine* (1959; music, lyrics and book by Rick Besoyan). Set in the Colorado Rockies, the plot concerns Mary Potts and Captain 'Big Jim' Warrington of the Forest Rangers. Their rapturous love duet is the 'Colorado Love Call', and other numbers in the show, such as 'Do You Ever Dream of Vienna?' and 'Naughty, Naughty Nancy', recall the quintessence of the genre. Besoyan created another operetta parody, *The Student Gypsy* (1963), this one set in Ruritanian climes. It lacked the success and popularity of *Little Mary Sunshine*, possibly because the American version of operetta was better known to audiences than the Ruritanian one.

In addition to its overall concept, *Rose-Marie* contained two specific numbers that live in parody: 'Indian Love Call' and 'The Mounties'. Among the most intriguing reappearances of 'Indian Love Call' is Slim Whitman's rendition that causes Martian heads to explode (literally) in the film *Mars Attacks!* (1996). The overt masculinity of Canadian Mounties promoted in 'The Mounties' is lampooned in Monty Python's 'The Lumberjack Song' – complete with the physical separation of the soloist and the chorus.

Other references to the genre include the insertion of 'Ah, Sweet Mystery of Life' from Victor Herbert's *Naughty Marietta* in Mel Brooks's film *Young Frankenstein* (1974). The song appears to great comic effect at several of the film's climactic moments. References to operetta are not limited to the entertainment industry, however, for Heidelberg College in Tifflin, Ohio has as its mascot none other than 'The Student Princes'.

Operetta is a genre whose legacy has endured well beyond the decade during which it was at its peak, the 1920s. It played an important role in the English-language musical theatre from mid-century onwards not only because of stage revivals, film versions and parodies but also because it provided the fundamental dramatic model for the musical plays of creators such as Rodgers and Hammerstein. It was the same Oscar Hammerstein II, after all, the wordsmith for shows such as *Rose-Marie, The Desert Song* and *The New Moon,* who crafted the texts for *Oklahoma!, South Pacific* and other classic shows in his collaboration with Richard Rodgers. (See Chapter 7.) The world of Ruritanian romance, whether in Central European climes or other remote locales ranging from then-contemporary French Morocco and Canada to historic France and French Louisiana, had great power for audiences in the 1920s. The opportunity to escape to a world filled with waltzes and marches provided a sentimental and nostalgic alternative to the modern, jazz-influenced world of musical comedy, the topic of chapter 5.

4 Images of African Americans: African-American musical theatre, *Show Boat* and *Porgy and Bess*

JOHN GRAZIANO

Soon after the end of slavery, African Americans formed musical troupes to sing, dance and act in a variety of shows. One of the first black companies was the Georgia Slave Troupe Minstrels, which was organised in April 1865 by a white manager, W. H. Lee. Another Georgia Minstrels company was organised in Indianapolis, under the management of a black performer, Charles B. Hicks; his company was to achieve fame as the foremost African-American minstrel troupe of the latter part of the nineteenth century. In these shows, African Americans followed the practice of established white troupes: they darkened their faces with burnt cork; staged burlesques on popular operas and operettas of the time, such as Jacques Offenbach's *The Grand Duchess of Gerolstein*; performed farces, such as *Mr Jinks*; pranced through eccentric and grotesque dances; and sang dialect, plantation and well-known minstrel songs both as solos and as ensemble pieces. The novelty of the black minstrel show was the race of the performers – the Georgia Minstrels, for example, advertised that in their shows the black performers were offering audiences a glimpse of 'genuine' plantation music and dance.[1]

Not all black troupes during the 1870s and 1880s, however, were of the burnt cork minstrel variety. The Hyers sisters, Anna Madah (1855–1920s) and Emma Louise (1857–99?), performed operatic excerpts, art and parlour songs, and jubilee songs and spirituals during their concert tours in the first half of the 1870s. From 1876 through 1883 the sisters performed as part of the 'Hyers Sisters Combination', managed by their father, Samuel B. Hyers.[2] Their repertory of musicals included *Out of Bondage*, written by the white playwright Joseph Bradford; *Urlina, the African Princess*, by E. S. Getchell; and a dramatisation of Harriet Beecher Stowe's *Uncle Tom's Cabin*. In the first of these shows, which is subtitled *Before and After the War*, the company demonstrates how life has changed for African-Americans after emancipation. In Act I, audiences see a Southern slave family at dinner, eating possum, drinking homemade whiskey and singing spirituals and plantation songs. The action of the second act takes place outside the cabin, with dancing and the singing of popular songs. As the act ends, Union troops arrive to battle the Southern soldiers. After the family is liberated, several former slaves decide to go North to seek their fortunes. Five years later, in Act III, the family is reunited in Boston. Uncle Eph and Aunt Naomi, who had elected to stay on their family farm, discover that the four young people who left the plantation are now professional vocalists, who live and work in a society that treats them as equals. During this final act, the sisters, along with their singing co-stars, John Luca and Wallace King, sang operatic excerpts by Verdi, Flotow and Balfe, among others.

Urlina, the African Princess, touched on a theme – life in Africa – that was to be reinvestigated by African Americans during the first decade of the twentieth century. Although the plot of *Urlina* is not concerned with African Americans who want to return to the lands of their birth, it does reflect nineteenth-century interest in the 'exotic', as seen in operas such as Giacomo Meyerbeer's *L'Africaine* (1864) and Léo Delibes's *Lakmé* (1883), and in operettas and comic operas that include James Barnes's *Chow Chow, or A Tale of Pekin* (1872) and Gilbert and Sullivan's *The Mikado* (1885). Advertised as an 'operatic bouffe extravaganza', the plot concerns a princess whose rights as successor to her father's throne have been usurped by another king. The latter's son, Prince Zurleska, falls in love with a picture of the princess, and decides to rescue her. After several attempts, the prince is successful in freeing Princess Urlina and overthrowing his father, the usurper. In their production of the musical, the Hyers sisters appeared in the two leading roles: Anna Madah, a soprano, played the Princess Urlina, while Emma Louise, a contralto, was the Prince. Others in the cast included a female impersonator, Willie Lyle, who played the maid, and the great comedian Billy Kersands (1842–1915), who was featured in several comic roles, including an Irish missionary, a pigtailed Puritan, and a Christian Chinaman. The production of *Urlina* was an important milestone for African-American performers, because it demonstrated that they could appear successfully on the stage in works that were devoid of the stereotypes of minstrelsy. Although there were broadly comic scenes in the musical, there were also serious moments that placed *Urlina* squarely in the tradition of the musical theatre. That tradition was virtually ignored in African-American theatre for the remainder of the nineteenth century.

The Hyers sisters' 1880 production of *Uncle Tom's Cabin* was also groundbreaking. Prior to their performances, the major roles in the dramatic versions of Stowe's anti-slavery novel were usually performed by white actors in blackface. In casting their show, the sisters chose white actors to play the white parts and black actors to play the black parts. As was the case with *Urlina*, the company appears to have preferred to offer a musical that did not rely solely on minstrel show stereotypes; rather, it portrayed blacks realistically on the American stage before mixed audiences.

During the 1880s, black minstrel shows, still tremendously popular with the public, were seen in large and small cities and towns across the United States as well as in England, Scotland and Wales. Several 'double' companies, with black and white performers, toured during the latter part of the 1880s and through much of the 1890s. In 1890 a new type of minstrel show was unveiled by Sam Lucas (1840–1916), another of the legendary African-American comedians who helped to shape black musical theatre, and Sam T. Jack, the white proprietor of several theatres in the Chicago area. Their extravaganza, the *Creole Burlesque Co.*, added women to the traditional all-male minstrel show. The show, in its first version, followed the usual tripartite format of the minstrel show. In the first part of the show, 'Tropical Revelries', the semicircle included women as well as men. The Interlocutor, who stood in the middle and attempted to bring order to the proceedings, was a woman in male attire, while Tambo and Bones were the usual male comedians and punsters. The company alternated with the featured singers, elocutionists, dancers and comedians in their solo turns. Following the opening chorus, there was a female 'conversationalist', a team of male punsters, who probably doubled as the endmen, and a sister act that specialised in 'sweet songs'. After the next song by the company, there were two more acts – a second conversationalist and a different pair of comedians. Two additional acts, with yet another conversationalist and a pair of 'courtiers', followed the third ensemble performance. The company then concluded that part of the programme. In the traditional minstrel show, the second part was called the 'olio'; it consisted of a series of solos by the stars of the troupe, and was usually followed by an afterpiece, which was a brief sketch that combined comedy, pathos, suspense, song and dance. In the *Creole* show, a burlesque, 'The Beauty of the Nile, or Doomed by Fire', began the second part. While there is no information concerning the plot of this burlesque, we can assume from the names of the characters in the programme that it was in the tradition of those brief song and dance sketches that were expected by knowledgeable minstrel show audiences. At the conclusion of the sketch, the *Creole* olio was seen; for the finale of the show, the women of the company were once again spotlighted in a 'Grand Amazonian March'. The *Creole Burlesque Co.* toured the country and was very successful with the public; during the summer of 1893, it was seen in Chicago at one of Jack's theatres not far from the Columbian Exposition, and continued touring in new 'editions' for several more seasons. While the format of *Creole Burlesque Co.* was clearly derived from the minstrel show, it transcended the limitations of the genre, allowing African-Americans to demonstrate a wide range of talents in many areas. It also provided employment and served as a training ground for a number of male and female performers who would be in the forefront of black musical theatre during the first decade of the twentieth century.

The success of the *Creole Burlesque Co.* led to the development of several competing shows. John W. Isham, who was an advance man for Sam Jack, formed his own company, the *Octoroons*, in 1895. While one can note that the format of the minstrel show is still underlying the show, there are significant differences as well. The minstrel show semicircle with Interlocutor, Tambo and Bones has disappeared, and the afterpiece now opens the show. The olio with star specialties still begins the second part of the show, but replacing the afterpiece is a musical extravaganza, '30 Minutes Around the Operas', in which the whole cast performs well-known excerpts from popular operas and operettas such as 'The Anvil Chorus'.

The opening sketch, 'The Blackville Derby', is set at a racetrack; the main characters are Lucky Bill, Good Thing Jackson, a Bookmaker and a variety of betting 'belles' and 'swells'. The plot is slim (as were the plots of most musicals of the time), and turns on an unlikely race between several horses and a mule, which the mule wins. Lucky Bill has beat the odds in all three races and has won enough money to invite all his friends to accompany him to Coney Island for the evening. As with most musicals, song and dance interrupt the plot. There is an opening chorus, a solo number, 'The Sporty Coon', for Lucky Bill at his first appearance, several special dances including 'The Milkmaid's Flirtations' and a Spanish ballet, songs for most of the remaining leads and a grand finale for the whole company.

In contrast to the musicals presented by the Hyers sisters, in which characters were seen to be moving upwards on the socio-economic-cultural ladder, Isham's show portrays the stereotype of the lazy, cunning, non-working black and his tough and possibly dishonest friends. Lucky Bill is a professional gambler who tells the crowd that he has been on a winning streak for several days; his invitation to the crowd to join him at Coney Island conjures up the image of a big spender who, when he is flush, will spend all the money he has. Bill is certainly not a member of the middle class who goes to church every week; when he comments on the possibility that his good luck won't last, he invites the crowd to come to see him baptised because he's going to join a church when his luck starts to go. Ike, the bully, is another representative of the lower class, and his entry in the race is the mule. In general, the characters in 'The Blackville Derby' do not represent African Americans at their best. They do not represent the hard-working upwardly-mobile 'New Negro'; instead the Bookmaker happily exclaims that he is as willing to take money from the ladies at the races as he would from their husbands. These are ladies of leisure, who are wealthy enough to gamble. No doubt these characterisations were frowned upon by church-going and intellectual African Americans, who saw this type of sketch as demeaning to the race.

Isham's *Octoroons* was a great success; not only did he launch a second touring company in the autumn of 1896, but he also formed a new company, *Oriental America*. Its opening sketch, 'Madame Toussante L'Ovature's Reception', takes place in a hotel on the south Florida coast. Here well-to-do African Americans are attending an anniversary party. Because of labour problems, Mr Waldorf, the proprietor of the hotel, has to ask his guests to cook and serve the tables. To mollify his guests, Waldorf provides some unusual entertainment: first, four Japanese maidens; second, the men of the Magnolia Golf Club and ladies of the Grove Lawn Tennis Club; and finally, the Twentieth Century Bicycle Maids, who wear bloomers when they cycle, and their 'dudes', who call themselves Manhattan sports. Waldorf's servant complains that this last group is not up to the standard of the establishment. This sketch, while still a farce, is clearly delineating a higher class of blacks; there are no gamblers, touts, bullies or bookmakers here. Indeed, these cultivated people, members of golf and lawn tennis clubs, are attending a society gathering, and if Waldorf has not got his party to go without a flaw, he and his guests represent an upwardly-mobile segment of African-American society that even frowned on women wearing bloomers in public. The music heard in these shows included ragtime songs, generally referred to at that time as 'coon' songs, as well as sentimental songs that audiences would have been familiar with from vaudeville, and descriptive songs (such as Dave Marion's 'Still the World Goes On'), which for many years had been featured in popular entertainments. Isham's companies were extremely popular with both black and white audiences. During 1897 and 1898, two of his three companies travelled all over the United States, while the third sailed for Great Britain, where it toured for a year.

Each season, Isham's touring shows opened with a new farce. During the 1897–98 season, the *Octoroons* company's sketch was 'Darktown Outing at Blackville Park', the following season 'A Tenderloin Coon', and in the 1899–1900 season '7–11–77'. While these shows were obviously popular with audiences, they were not generally booked into first-run theatres in the larger cities and they were performed before segregated audiences in many parts of the country. In addition to Isham's and Jack's companies, another important troupe was the *Black Patti's Troubadours* company, which toured the country from 1896 to 1915. For the first ten years, the *Troubadours* presentation was similar to *Octoroons* and *Oriental America*; each show opened with a one-act farce, followed by solo turns by the stars. It concluded with an appearance of Sissieretta Jones (1868–1933), the 'Black Patti', who sang opera and operetta selections with the entire company.

In the summer of 1898, however, a black show finally reached Broadway. *Clorindy, or the Origin of the Cakewalk*, with a script and lyrics by Paul Laurence Dunbar (1872–1906) and music by Will Marion Cook (1869–1944), was seen as part of a late evening entertainment on the roof garden of the Casino Theatre. Unlike the shows produced by Jack and Isham, which had eclectic scores with songs by both black and white composers, *Clorindy* was the first black show to have music by a single African-American composer. It was a stunning success; critics were enthusiastic in their praise for the novelty of the music and dancing, and audiences kept it running through most of the summer. Cook's music was primarily of the coon song variety, with titles such as 'Who Dat Say Chicken in Dis Crowd?' and 'Darktown Is Out Tonight'. Although *Clorindy* was probably conceived as a full-length show, when it finally reached Broadway as the finale of the late-night entertainment, most of Dunbar's script had been eliminated in favour of extended song and dance numbers that featured ragtime and eccentric dancing, with a cast headed by one of the leading African-American composer-performers, Ernest Hogan (1859–1909), who referred to himself as the 'unbleached American'.

Until the success of *Clorindy*, ragtime 'coon' songs had been heard primarily in vaudeville and in the few black shows that were produced by Jack and Isham. By 1898, they had been heard on Broadway in only a few shows; the white comedienne and 'coon shouter' May Irwin (1862–1938) had first featured several coon songs in her show *The Widow Jones* (1895) and the following year in *Courted into Court*. Thus, when *Clorindy* achieved its great public success, the difference to audiences was that these syncopated songs, and the dances associated with them, were once again being performed authentically by African-Americans. Ragtime had long been associated with establishments that catered to immoral pursuits; Scott Joplin and Eubie Blake both played rags in bordellos early in their careers. Over the next two decades, syncopated music was to become a mainstay of American popular song, but in 1898, it was still enough of a novelty and a representative of lower-class immorality to cause consternation among the general public. Compared to the patter, genteel and sentimental songs that were the basis of most Broadway shows prior to *Clorindy*, the new music was catchy and representative of the modern period. So too was the cakewalk, an African-American dance probably deriving from the plantation dance in antebellum America, where slaves held dance competitions. The popularity of the cakewalk with white audiences was so great that it appeared in most African-American shows for the next five years.

While *Clorindy* captivated audiences, another show, *A Trip to Coontown*, was touring the eastern seaboard without the same recognition, though it travelled for four seasons in various versions. This full evening's entertainment starred Robert (Bob) Cole (1868–1911) and Billy Johnson (1858–1916); the plot, derived in part from minstrelsy, followed a predictable pattern. A con man, Jim Flimflammer (played by Johnson) tries to take a $5,000 pension from an old man, Silas Green (played by Sam Lucas). Willie Wayside, a tramp (played by Cole), saves the pension for Green by exposing the Flimflammer's schemes. Here again, audiences saw some black stereotypes in the characters of Flimflammer and Green. Willie Wayside, however, occupies a rare place in these shows; he is selfless and honest and is looking to protect innocent gullible people from the schemes of crooks. Though the character of Wayside is sympathetic, Flimflammer is not. And more often than not, his type of unsavoury and dishonest character appeared in the musicals that followed.

The next major black musical seen on Broadway was *Sons of Ham* (1901), which starred the up-and-coming team of Bert Williams (1876–1922) and George Walker (1872–1911). By the time of their appearances on Broadway, Williams and Walker had perfected their act. Williams, who appeared in blackface, played the slow gullible type (later personified by Stepin Fetchit), a dupe for the shenanigans that ensued, while Walker played the dude (descended from minstrelsy's 'Zip Coon'), fast-talking and usually looking to enrich himself at another's expense. In *Sons of Ham*, they play Tobias Wormwood (Williams) and Harty Lafter (Walker), who go to the house of Hampton J. J. Flam, masquerading as his sons, whom he has not seen for six years. The old man is fooled by the imposters until the final minutes of the show when his real sons, Aniesta Babdola and Jeneriska Hassambad, known as Annie and Jennie, arrive to inform him that it was all a joke. Toby and Harty, in the interim, have taken two packages of clothes that were delivered to Ham's house, and have disguised themselves so others will not realise that they are impostors. While in disguise, Harty tells the assembled guests that Toby is the renowned Professor Skinnerbunch, 'a palmist, phrenologist, ocultist [*sic*], chropodist [*sic*], odontologist, dentist, florist, ahem-ist, mind reader, and fortune teller', who can tell the past, present, and future, as long as he is paid. Harty's introduction leads into a song, 'The Phrenologist Coon', which is sung by Bert Williams; his sly but knowing delivery was so well received that he recorded it for Victor soon after the show opened. As with all black shows of this period, scripts merely served as outlines for the actual performance, which changed according to the actors available during the tour. In the script for *Sons of Ham*, as in other African-American musicals of the time, minstrelsy and racial pride coexist uncomfortably. The names of the characters, such as Professor Skinnerbunch, Professor Nicholas Switchem (who has difficulty making up his mind) of Riske College, Willie Wataboy, Gabby Slangtry ('an advocate of Modern English'), Tobias Wormwood and Harty Lafter, recall the punning repartee associated with minstrelsy. Still, the young people who populate this show are college students who represent a new educated black America. Though Ham's sons, Jennie and Annie, are involved in high jinks to fool their father, he has worked hard to pay for their education, sending them to Riske Industrial School for six years. For black audiences at the turn of the twentieth century, the farce that parodied them and their ethnicity also painted a brighter future by demonstrating that they were becoming part of the educated middle class.

Williams and Walker's next show, *In Dahomey* (1902), was their first big hit.[3] After fifty-three performances on Broadway, it travelled to England, where it was well received by audiences and critics. As in *Sons of Ham*, there is an underlying reality beneath the clowning and pratfalls of the characters; in this show, it is the romance of returning to Africa, which was being hotly debated in the African-American community during the first decade of the twentieth century. Most of *In Dahomey* takes place in Florida, where Williams, as Shylock Homestead, and Walker, as Rareback Pinkerton, pretend to be detectives so they can hoodwink Cicero Lightfoot to collect a $500 reward and join the African Colonisation Society. When Lightfoot finds a pot of gold, however, he decides to take all his friends to Dahomey so they can see the homeland for themselves. The final act, mostly in pantomime with dance, begins with a jungle scene. As all the Americans arrive, they are expected to adapt to the strange customs of Dahomey. Eventually, they all decide to return to Florida and the 'good life'. Cook once again provided most of the score; significant among his songs in the show are the chorus 'Swing Along', which highlights black pride ('We'll a swing along, yes, a swing along An' a lif a' yo' heads up high, Wif' pride and gladness beamin' from yo' eye'), and 'On Emancipation Day', which celebrates post-Civil war festivities ('On Emancipation day, All you white folks clear de way, Brass ban' playin' sev'ral tunes, Darkies eyes look jes' lak moons, Marshall of de day a struttin' Lord but he is gay'). Although the show was generally viewed as a comedy, there were moments of seriousness where the characters spoke to blacks in the audience.

The African theme appears once again in Williams and Walker's next musical, *Abyssinia* (1906). Having won a lottery, Rastus Johnson (Walker) decides to take his relatives and a friend, Jasper Jenkins (Williams), to Europe. After some difficulties in France, the group goes to Abyssinia where they meet the Grand Emperor, Menelik. As in *Sons of Ham*, the use of an abbreviated name, in this case, 'Ras' for Rastus, leads the Americans into trouble. The Emperor believes that Ras is a prince, since 'Ras' in Abyssinian means 'prince'. As in their earlier play, mistaken identities lead to complications that are resolved at the last moment by the intervention of an Abyssinian princess. After the two friends are freed, they decide to return to America. Much of the play contrasts the cultural and social differences between Americans and

Abyssinians, with the Africans depicted as the more enlightened of the two. Cook once again wrote most of the score, though Bert Williams contributed several numbers, one of which, 'Nobody', was to become his signature song.

Contemporary with Williams and Walker's musicals were those of Cole and the Johnson brothers, James Weldon (1871–1938) and J. Rosamond (1873–1954). Their two shows, *The Shoo-Fly Regiment* (1907) and *The Red Moon* (1909), avoided many of the stereotypes noted above. In the former show, the plot revolves around a black regiment sent to the Philippines, where a Tuskegee Institute graduate, Hunter Wilson, leads his men in an attack on an enemy fortress. On his victorious return to the United States, his sweetheart, who had broken off their engagement, readily agrees to marry him. In the latter show, Cole and the Johnsons explore the interactions of African Americans and Amerindians. Minnehaha is the half-black, half-Indian daughter of Chief Low Dog, who abandoned her and her black mother when she was an infant. He suddenly returns after fifteen years to bring Minnehaha back to his reservation. She is rescued by Slim Brown and Plunk Green, her boyfriend, who, after some comic situations at the reservation, bring her back to Virginia, where they are married and Chief Low Dog is reunited with his wife. Rosamond Johnson's music for the show utilises native Indian tunes that he and Cole heard while travelling the vaudeville circuit through the western United States. Although a few of the songs are still reflective of the earlier ragtime genre, many are written as art-songs, similar to those written by Amy Beach, George W. Chadwick and Reginald de Koven, making *The Red Moon* more of an operetta than a musical comedy.

At the end of the decade, African-American musical theatre suffered a tremendous setback with the deaths of Hogan in 1909 and Walker and Cole in 1911. Bert Williams joined Ziegfeld's *Follies*,[4] where he became a regular headliner, and Johnson joined briefly with several other performers, but did not seem to find a partner who was equal to Cole. In 1915 he became the director of the Music School Settlement in Harlem, which was funded by the white philanthropist David Mannes.

During the second decade of the twentieth century, several younger performers continued to write musicals, but few of their efforts attracted mixed audiences to the same degree as the earlier shows. *Dr Beans from Boston* by Sherman H. Dudley (1873–1940) reverted to stereotypes. An ex-minstrel, Gymnasium Butts, who has taken the identity of Dr Beans, and his sidekick, Bill Simmons, purchase a drug store in which a love potion is stored. Butts gives it, in a large dose, to Susie Lee, to win her affection. The real Dr Beans arrives and is hit over the head by Butts; he loses his memory and Butts is able to conclude his scheme successfully. Another veteran of the stage, J. Leubrie Hill (1873–1916), who was a member of the Williams and

Walker repertory company, wrote and starred in *Darktown Follies* (1914), a revue that mirrored Ziegfeld's popular show. While the show did not succeed in drawing the large black audiences that Hill expected, the rights for several of the musical numbers, including 'Rock Me in the Cradle of Love' and 'At the Ball, That's All', were purchased by Ziegfeld for use in his *Follies* revue. The brothers J. Homer Tutt (1870s?–1930s?) and Salem Tutt Whitney (1869–1934) wrote numerous musicals during the decade. While most of their shows included slapstick, the characters they portrayed were usually representative of up-to-date African-American culture and devoid of caricature. In *How Newtown Prepared* (1916), for example, George Washington Bullion, played by Whitney, hears about the fight between Mexican troops and the Tenth Cavalry, which was a black unit. He takes his volunteer army to join the fight, but owing to a number of mishaps, his soldiers are captured by the Turks. Eventually the company is rescued by an American man-o'-war. In *The Children of the Sun* (1919), the Dean of Howard University finds an archaeological document that establishes the origins of the Negro race. After adventures in Japan, Persia, India and Egypt, Abe and Gabe Washington (played by the brothers) reach Ethiopia, which is the original site where the race began. To judge by the titles of the songs heard in these shows, they were a mixture of various genres that appeared in most musicals of the period. Because most of Tutt's songs were not published, they have probably not survived.

In 1921 *Shuffle Along* arrived on upper Broadway. It created a sensation with audiences and critics and ushered in a new period of black musicals on Broadway. The book of *Shuffle Along*, by Flournoy Miller (1887–1971) and Aubrey Lyles (1883–1932), was neither groundbreaking nor representative of the 'New Negro' position that was central to the writings of W. E. B. DuBois, Alain Locke and others. Rather, it was a continuation of the stereotypical representation of African Americans that had been seen twenty years earlier. Miller and Lyles had created the comic characters of Steve Jenkins and Sam Peck at the Pekin Theatre in Chicago more than a decade earlier. They had written a number of short and full-length skits around these characters, including 'The Mayor of Dixie', which were then refined over the years.

The plot of *Shuffle Along* relates the comic struggles of Jenkins and Peck to become mayor of the southern town of Jimtown. Through some dishonest dealings, which includes stealing money from the grocery store that they jointly own, Jenkins becomes mayor to the dismay of the honest candidate, Harry Walton, who can marry the daughter of the richest man in town only if he is elected. After the election, Jenkins goes back on his campaign promises, refusing to name Peck his Chief of Police. There is a boxing match – one of their famous set pieces – between the partners, which Peck wins. Jenkins appoints him and Peck quickly assumes authority and begins to arrest as many townspeople as the jail will hold. But a New York detective uncovers their misdeeds; Walton becomes the new mayor and is able to marry his sweetheart, and the partners are allowed to return to their grocery store without punishment.

While the plot did not demonstrate the kind of originality that would catch the attention of the public, the music and lyrics of Noble Sissle (1889–1975) and James Hubert 'Eubie' Blake (1883–1993) were first-rate, up-to-date, and varied enough to guarantee a long Broadway run.[5] There are more than twenty numbers in the show; they run the gamut from blues ('Gypsy Blues', 'Lowdown Blues' and 'Serenade Blues'), jazz ('I'm Just Simply Full of Jazz') and African-American songs ('Pickaninny Shoes', 'Old Black Joe and Uncle Tom', and 'If You've Never Been Vamped by a Brownskin') to ballads ('Everything Reminds Me of You' and 'Love Will Find a Way') and up-tempo numbers ('I'm Just Wild about Harry'). Although Sissle was a member of the cast, he appeared out of character towards the end of the show when he and Blake appeared on stage in tuxedos for 'A Few Minutes with Sissle and Blake', which recreated their vaudeville act. In this instance, they were following the example of Bob Cole and J. Rosamond Johnson, who had pioneered a high-class act almost two decades earlier.

The immense popularity of *Shuffle Along* kept it on Broadway for 504 performances. The book musicals that ensued were, for the most part, copies of Sissle and Blake's blockbuster; even revues, such as *From Dixie to Broadway* and the various editions of Lew Leslie's *Blackbirds*, which became increasingly popular during the decade, alternated antebellum plantation scenes with current social problems, such as rent parties.[6] Many shows also included cemetery scenes, with ghostly apparitions and stereotypical humour, and farcical scenes that satirised African-American social issues, such as weddings and gambling. Jungle scenes, which had been seen in *In Dahomey* and *Abyssinia*, became popular once again, with music and costumes that were much more suggestive than those seen in the earlier shows.[7]

The publication of Edna Ferber's *Show Boat* in 1926, both in serialized form and as a book, raised serious issues about relationships between the races. The mixed cast of characters were real people; there was no intended stereotyping of African Americans. The novel, which quickly became a best seller, traces the lives and fortunes of a riverboat family, their troupe of actors and their deck crew through several generations; Ferber addresses difficult social issues, such as 'passing' and miscegenation. A little more than one year later, in December 1927, a musical by Jerome Kern (1885–1946) and Oscar Hammerstein (1895–1960) based on the novel opened in New York City. Although Hammerstein changed some aspects of Ferber's novel, he retained these two issues that are so central to the plot.

Plate 4 A production of *Show Boat*, c. 1938 at the St Louis Municipal Opera with Minto Cato as Queenie, Kenneth Spencer as Joe, and the Jubilee Singers and Dahomey Dancers

Show Boat was not the first Broadway musical to employ a multiracial cast; several companies had mixed-cast productions of *Uncle Tom's Cabin*, and *The Southerners*, with music by Will Marion Cook, had a brief run in 1904. But the popularity of Hammerstein and Kern's musical brought these sensitive issues to the forefront of public attention. Instead of the caricatures that populated most black musicals of the Harlem Renaissance, Hammerstein offered a serious and sympathetic portrayal of African Americans. The problems faced by blacks during the last quarter of the nineteenth century is dealt with directly. Julie, one of the actresses in the troupe, is passing for white; Hammerstein and Kern give the first hint that something is amiss in a scene that is not part of the novel, when Queenie, the cook of the Cotton Blossom, comments that the song Julie is singing, 'Can't Help Lovin' Dat Man' is associated with black folks. A bit later, when Julie's true origins are discovered, she and her white husband, Frank, are forced to leave the show boat. Though *Show Boat* is a Broadway musical in the grand tradition, Hammerstein did not try to evade these issues. His forthrightness was a shock to audiences that were accustomed to lightweight plots that did not ask them to think.

Kern's music for the show is a pastiche. In addition to Julie's number, there is a spiritual, 'Misery', that is sung by the black chorus, and 'Ol' Man River', which is Kern's version of a work song. Ravenal and Julie, however, sing a Viennese waltz, 'Make Believe'. And because *Show Boat* is an epic, Kern composed music in a number of styles to represent different time periods – the 1880s, 1893 (at the time of the Columbian Exposition in Chicago), 1906 and 1927. For the New Year's Eve scene in the second act, Kern even uses well-known pieces of the 1880s and 90s, including 'After the Ball', an 1892 waltz-ballad by Charles K. Harris, John Philip Sousa's 'Washington Post March' (1889), Joseph Howard's 'Goodbye My Lady Love' (1904) and Kerry Mills 'At a Georgia Camp Meeting' (1897), to lend authenticity to the score. The success of *Show Boat*, however, did not lead others to write dramatic musicals. *Show Boat*'s serious treatment of social issues was not matched until *West Side Story*.

George (1898–1937) and Ira (1896–1983) Gershwin's opera, *Porgy and Bess*, provides a different view of African-Americans. Based on the novel and play *Porgy* by Dorothy (1890–1961) and [Edwin] DuBose (1885–1940) Heyward, the opera depicts the residents of Catfish Row, a tenement on the waterfront in Charleston, South Carolina. Heyward's depiction of the community focuses on its general despair and the violent nature of life there. His characters include a bully, Crown; his woman, Bess; a cripple, Porgy; a ne'er-do-well, Sportin' Life, who offers Bess some 'happy dust'; and the various residents of the tenement. Heyward opens the story with a scene of nightlife in Catfish Row; there is dancing, a mother sings a lullaby to her baby, and some of the men are playing a crap game. When Crown commits murder as a result of an argument at the crap game, the tone for the rest of the drama is set. Although the play as a whole tends towards melodrama and operatic exaggeration, Heywood attempted to provide realism through his use of local colour, such as a picnic on one of the Charleston area's well-known barrier islands, Kitiwah (or Kiawah), where Bess is confronted by Crown, who is hiding from the police. A hurricane provides a symbolic background for the confrontation scene over Bess between Porgy and Crown, while the frightened residents of Catfish Row sing spirituals to try to appease the fury of the storm.

In spite of his Charlestonian background and his knowledge of the Gullah language and tenement life, Heyward's depiction of African Americans has been controversial, with some critics asserting that he was dealing only with stereotypes and did not understand the black character. This negative appraisal of his work began soon after the play was seen on Broadway in 1927 and reached its zenith after the Civil Rights movement was established. Seen in the context of the 1920s, however, Heyward's serious attempt to delineate poor urban Southern black life was far removed from the efforts of black writers of musicals such as Miller and Lyles in their Broadway shows, or Billy King (1875–1936) in Chicago, whose stereotypical depictions included malapropisms, knockabout humour, and portrayals of cheating and other dishonest practices.

Gershwin's music for the drama is eclectic. There are hit songs, such as 'Summertime', 'Oh, I Got Plenty O' Nuttin'' and 'It Ain't Necessarily So'. There are also operatic ensembles that demand a style of singing usually not required in a Broadway musical. When Serena and the chorus sing 'My Man's Gone Now' in the second scene of Act I, the tessitura of the solo requires that Serena sings an octave and a fifth, from e′ to b″, a range that is suitable for an operatic singer but not for most Broadway performers. Gershwin's use of sung recitative as a replacement for spoken dialogue also separates his opera from the usual musical comedy. By Broadway standards, *Porgy and Bess* was not a great hit with the public; it closed after 124 performances. By operatic standards, however, it would have to be considered quite successful. The most notable American opera premiered at the Metropolitan during the 1930s, Deems Taylor's *Peter Ibbetson*, was given only sixteen performances over three seasons.

From its beginnings after emancipation, African-American musical theatre pursued two contradictory goals – to entertain and to enlighten. As a primary and necessary economic goal, it had to entertain audiences. Its dependence on white patronage may have imposed some of the stereotypes of minstrelsy on the scripts and music of most shows, though this cannot be stated unequivocally; at the same time, some show scripts included brief scenes or dialogue that, to those who were listening carefully, heralded the arrival of the African-American middle class, symbolized by the New Negro. While black minstrel stereotypes continued to be prominent during the Harlem Renaissance (and beyond), a few musicals attempted to portray African Americans with enlightened realism. Several Tutt and Whitney shows, as well as a few by other African-American authors, endeavour to address serious issues; among white-authored musicals, *Show Boat* falls into that category also. *Porgy and Bess* is likewise realistic – but only when viewed within the conventions of late nineteenth-century opera. It attempts, however, to offer a non-stereotypical view of African Americans, and, in doing so, joins the small group of musical works that present theatrically realistic characterisations of black people and their lives.

5 The melody (and the words) linger on: American musical comedies of the 1920s and 1930s

GEOFFREY BLOCK

Setting the stage

The period under surveillance in this chapter divides with discomforting accuracy into two vastly contrasting national moods. America in the 1920s, retrospectively tagged as the Jazz Age (from F. Scott Fitzgerald's 1931 essay, 'Echoes of the Jazz Age'), the Roaring Twenties or, more euphemistically, Prohibition, experienced a decade of unprecedented prosperity and self-confidence. Republican presidents, for whom the business of America was business, led the country. Immigration, which had in the previous generation brought the parents of future songwriters to America, came to a virtual halt, and isolationism reigned as the prevailing sentiment. Women voted for the first time in the election of 1920 and the Smart Set began to explore social freedoms as well, such as public smoking, reading sex and confession magazines, applying makeup, bobbing their hair and wearing short skirts. As further manifestation of what contemporary social historian Frederick Lewis Allen called 'a revolution in manners and morals', both men and women sharply increased their alcohol consumption, imbibing in thousands of newly sprouting metropolitan speakeasies in Prohibition America.[1] By the end of the decade radio became a family ritual, and sound films revolutionised an already popular entertainment and created new opportunities for musicals, both adapted from the stage and original. The twenties introduced an exceptional generation of American playwrights (Eugene O'Neill, Maxwell Anderson), novelists (Sinclair Lewis, Ernest Hemingway, Fitzgerald), classical composers (Edgard Varèse, Aaron Copland) and jazz artists (Louis Armstrong, Duke Ellington). It was also a period, not unlike the present, when a news event (e.g. the plight of Floyd Collins trapped in a Kentucky mine for a month in 1925 or Charles Lindbergh's transatlantic solo flight in 1927) could transfix and dominate national attention to the exclusion of all else.

In sharp contrast, the 1930s were marked by economic despair, disastrously high unemployment and a social unrest that fell dangerously close to cultivating the kind of political upheavals that demoralised much of Europe and the Far East. Broadway was not immune to the austere economic conditions that overshadowed the decade, conditions which prompted all of the songwriters featured in this chapter – with varying degrees of commitment and success – to heed the siren call of the more lucrative, if less artistically free, Hollywood film milieu. In contrast to the 1920s, where ten book shows ran for more than 500 performances on Broadway (including four musical comedies), in the 1930s only three book shows (all musical comedies) lasted more than 400 performances (*Of Thee I Sing*, *Anything Goes* and *DuBarry Was a Lady*). Nothing seemed to cure Broadway's woes, not even the repeal of Prohibition in 1933 or President Franklin D. Roosevelt's alphabet soup of social programmes. In the 1933–34 season only thirteen new musicals of any type appeared, and most of these failed. Two seasons later the total was reduced still further to twelve, five book shows and seven revues, and of these, only Richard Rodgers and Lorenz Hart's *On Your Toes* made a clear profit (although their *Jumbo* and Cole Porter's *Jubilee* were imaginative and musically rich, and George and Ira Gershwin's and Dorothy and DuBose Heyward's *Porgy and Bess* was soon recognised as one of America's great artistic treasures). For most of the first month that *I'd Rather Be Right* played (November 1937), Rodgers and Hart's only competition was their own *Babes in Arms*, which for a time during the previous July (of course, without air-conditioning) was the only show then running on Broadway. This relative inactivity presents a sober contrast to the largesse of the twenties, in which *No, No, Nanette* (Vincent Youmans, Irving Caesar and Otto Harbach), *Dearest Enemy* (Rodgers and Hart), *The Vagabond King* (Rudolf Friml and Brian Hooker) and *Sunny* (Jerome Kern and Oscar Hammerstein II) all had their debuts during one seven-day period in 1925. The 1927–28 season witnessed over fifty new musicals among a record-breaking total of possibly 270 theatrical offerings (264 according to *Variety*), most notably *Good News!*, *A Connecticut Yankee*, *Funny Face* and *Show Boat*, all of which arrived between September and December. (See Table 5.1.)

Musical comedies in the 1920s favoured topical subjects such as Cinderella stories in modern urban America (*Sally*) early in the decade, and later bootlegging (*Oh, Kay!*), the Florida land boom and land speculation (*Tip-Toes* and *The Cocoanuts*), the Lindbergh flight (*Rosalie*) and sports, the last most systematically in the B. G. DeSylva – Lew Brown–Ray Henderson trilogy that revolved around popular sports crazes: football (*Good News!*), boxing (*Hold Everything!*) and golf (*Follow Thru*). In the 1930s several musicals, for example, Porter's *Red, Hot and Blue!* and Rodgers and Hart's *On Your Toes* (both from 1936), and also Kern and Hammerstein's 1931 operetta, *The Cat and the Fiddle*, grappled with an alleged aesthetic gulf between popular and classical music, the former coming out ahead in each

Table 5.1 *Selected American and British musical comedies of the 1920s and 1930s*

	Kern	Gershwin (lyrics: I. Gershwin)	Porter	Rodgers (lyrics: L. Hart)	Others
1920	*The Night Boat* (313) (Caldwell) *Sally* (570) (Bolton; L: Grey, et al.)				
1921	*The Cabaret Girl* (361) (Grossmith, Wodehouse; L: Wodehouse) [London] *Good Morning Dearie* (347) (Caldwell)				*Shuffle Along* (504) (Miller, Lyles; L: Sissle; music: Blake)
1922					
1923	*The Beauty Prize* (213) (Grossmith, Wodehouse) [London] *The Stepping Stones* (241) (Burnside, Caldwell; L: Caldwell)				
1924	*Sitting Pretty* (95) (Bolton, Wodehouse; L: Wodehouse)	*Sweet: Little Devil* (120) (Mandel, Schwab, L: DeSylva) *Lady, Be Good!* (330) (Bolton, Thompson) *Primrose* (225) (Grossmith, Bolton. L: Carter) [London]			
1925	*Sunny* (517) (Harbach, Hammerstein)	*Tell Me More!* (100) (Thompson, Wells, L: DeSylva, I. Gershwin) *Tip-Toes* (194) (Bolton, Thompson)		*Dearest Enemy* (286) (Fields)	*No, No, Nanette* (321) Harbach, Mandel; L: Caesar; music: Youmans) *The Cocoanuts* (276) (Kaufman; L: Berlin; music: Berlin)

(cont.)

Table 5.1 (*cont.*)

	Kern	Gershwin (lyrics: I. Gershwin)	Porter	Rodgers (lyrics: L. Hart)	Others
1926	Criss-Cross (206) (Harbach, Caldwell)	Oh, Kay! (256) (Bolton, Wodehouse)		The Girl Friend (301) (Fields) Lido Lady (259) (Bolton, Kalmar, Ruby) [London] Peggy-Ann (333) (Fields) Betsy (39) (Caesar, Freeman)	
1927		Funny Face (244) (Thompson, Smith)		A Connecticut Yankee (418) (Fields)	Hit the Deck (352) (Fields; L: Grey, Robin; music: Youmans) Good News! (551) (Schwab, DeSylva; L: DeSylva, Brown; music: Henderson)
1928	Blue Eyes (276) (Bolton, John; L: John) [London]	Rosalie (335) (Wodehouse; music: Romberg, G. Gershwin) Treasure Girl (68) (Thompson, Lawrence)	Paris (195) (Brown)	She's My Baby (71) (Bolton, Kalmar, Ruby) Present Arms (155) (Fields) Chee-Chee (31) (Fields)	Hold Everything! (413) (DeSylva, McGowan; L: DeSylva, Brown; music: Henderson)
1929		Show Girl (111) (McGuire, L: Kahn, I. Gershwin)	Wake Up and Dream (263) (Hastings) Fifty Million Frenchmen (254) (Fields)	Spring Is Here (104) (Davis) Heads Up! (144) (McGowan, Smith)	Follow Thru (403) (Schwab, Mandel; L: DeSylva, Brown; music: Henderson)
1930		Strike Up the Band (191) (Ryskind) Girl Crazy (272) (Bolton, McGowan)	The New Yorkers (168) (Fields)	Simple Simon (135) (Wynn, Bolton) Ever Green (254) (Levy) [London]	Flying High (357) (McGowan, DeSylva, Brown; L: DeSylva, Brown; music: Henderson) Fine and Dandy (255) (Stewart; L: James; music: Swift)
1931		Of Thee I Sing (441) (Kaufman, Ryskind)		America's Sweet-heart (135) (Fields)	

Year					
1932			*Gay Divorce* (248) (Taylor)		*Face the Music* (165) (M. Hart; L: Berlin; music: Berlin) *Take a Chance* (243) (DeSylva, Schwab, Silvers; L: DeSylva; music: Whiting, Brown, Youmans)
1933	*Roberta* (295) (Harbach)	*Pardon My English* (46) (Fields) *Let 'Em Eat Cake* (90) (Kaufman, Ryskind)	*Nymph Errant* (154) (Brent) [London]		
1934	*Three Sisters* (72) (Hammerstein)		*Anything Goes* (420) (Lindsay, Crouse)		
1935			*Jubilee* (169) (M. Hart)	*Jumbo* (233) (Hecht, MacArthur)	
1936			*Red, Hot and Blue!* (183) (Lindsay, Crouse)	*On Your Toes* (315) (Rodgers, L. Hart, Abbott)	*Johnny Johnson* (68) (Green; music: Weill)
1937				*Babes in Arms* (289) (Rodgers, L. Hart) *I'd Rather Be Right* (290) (Kaufman, M. Hart)	*The Cradle Will Rock* (19) (Blitzstein) [1938: 104 perf.]
1938			*You Never Know* (78) (Leigh) *Leave It to Me!* (291) (B. & S. Spewack)	*I Married an Angel* (338) (Rodgers, L. Hart) *The Boys from Syracuse* (235) (Abbott)	*Knickerbocker Holiday* (168) (Anderson; music: Weill)
1939	*Very Warm for May* (59) (Hammerstein)		*DuBarry Was a Lady* (408) (Fields, DeSylva)	*Too Many Girls* (249) (Marion)	

Numbers in parenthesis refer to first-run performances. Unless otherwise indicated the names in parentheses refer to librettists and lyricists. L. = lyrics.

case. *Anything Goes* targeted celebrity criminals such as Baby Face Nelson and celebrity evangelists like Aimée Semple McPherson.

Political themes proliferated in the 1930s, affecting virtually everyone in addition to Kern and Hammerstein, who had daringly explored racial politics the previous decade in *Show Boat*. Between 1930 and 1933 the Gershwin brothers, along with George S. Kaufman and Morrie Ryskind, offered a political trilogy that satirised war in *Strike Up the Band*, the vapidity of political campaign themes (and nearly everything else) in *Of Thee I Sing*, and even political revolution in the latter's more acerbic sequel *Let' Em Eat Cake*. In *Face the Music* (February 1932) Irving Berlin, working with Moss Hart and Kaufman, satirised police corruption and eerily foreshadowed the scandals that would force New York City Mayor James Walker out of office a few months later. Rodgers and Hart made President Roosevelt the central character in *I'd Rather Be Right* (with a book by Kaufman and Hart), in which Roosevelt was impersonated by Broadway legend George M. Cohan in his last Broadway hurrah. The same year, 1937, Rodgers and Hart effectively spoofed socialism in the character Peter from *Babes in Arms*, a socialist who advocates money and property sharing until he acquires instant wealth. Porter's main contribution in this vein was *Leave It to Me* (1938; book by Bella and Samuel Spewack), the story of an ambassador to Russia abruptly recalled when he presents a plan for world peace. The first American musical comedies of Kurt Weill offered a satire on war in the parable about a pacifist during World War I, *Johnny Johnson* (1936; book and lyrics by Paul Green), and a play about the despot Governor Peter Stuyvesant in colonial New York in *Knickerbocker Holiday* (1938; book and lyrics by Maxwell Anderson), a parable that suggested the modern potential for similar abuses.[2] Marc Blitzstein created a musical that paralleled real-life union struggles amidst the larger theme of metaphorical prostitution and selling out in *The Cradle Will Rock*, which, when banned from its theatre for its uncompromising leftist leanings in June 1937, made front-page news in its own time and inspired a popular political movie in ours.[3] Two of the decade's most highly acclaimed revues, Irving Berlin and Moss Hart's *As Thousands Cheer* and Harold Rome's *Pins and Needles*, were also based on political themes, from the gently satirical (Rome's 'Doing the Reactionary') to the profoundly disturbing song about the lynching of African Americans (Berlin's 'Supper Time'). At the end of the decade, when war became an imminent reality, the political musical disappeared. Thus in 1939, two years after *I'd Rather Be Right*, Rodgers and Hart offered the college musical *Too Many Girls*; one year after *Leave It to Me* Porter wrote the apolitical *DuBarry Was a Lady*.

By 1920, America, in the aftermath of the Great War, indisputably a world political, economic and nascent cultural power, had long since begun extricating itself from the courtly muses of Europe to develop its own dramatic and musical identity. After two decades of American vernacular jingoism on the one hand (the musicals of Cohan) and musicals either imported directly from Europe or closely modelled on European products on the other (Franz Lehár's *The Merry Widow*, Victor Herbert's *Naughty Marietta*), a new generation had arrived. Several years before the new decade Berlin, Kern and Gershwin had each composed a major hit song, Berlin's Tin Pan Alley song 'Alexander's Ragtime Band' (1911), Kern's interpolation in *The Girl From Utah*, 'They Didn't Believe Me' (1914) and Gershwin's 'Swanee' (added for Al Jolson in the road tour of Sigmund Romberg's *Sinbad* in 1919). By 1920 Berlin, Kern and Gershwin had also composed Broadway scores of their own, Kern's *The Red Petticoat* (1912) and a series of historic and widely praised shows now known for the theatre, the Princess, that housed several of them, Berlin's 'ragtime' musical *Watch Your Step* (1914) and Gershwin's *La! La! Lucille* (1919). Porter saw his first Broadway musical, *See America First* (1916), quickly close, moved to Europe, and would not compose his next complete show for another twelve years. In 1919 Rodgers and Hart heard their first song, 'Any Old Place with You', interpolated in a Broadway show; the following year, the new team shared half a score of *Poor Little Ritz Girl* with the established prince of operetta, Sigmund Romberg.[4]

In 1924, the year Kern tried unsuccessfully to create an enlarged Princess-type show in the musically rich *Sitting Pretty* (with Princess collaborators Guy Bolton and P. G. Wodehouse), musical comedy seemed to change direction. Possible catalysts for this change, marked musically in the perceptible transition from ragtime to jazz, were the extended solo appearance of Armstrong in New York City with the Fletcher Henderson Orchestra and Gershwin's popular adaptation of jazz into the concert world in *Rhapsody in Blue*, both events occurring also in 1924. In musical comedy the change is readily apparent from even a superficial comparison between *Sitting Pretty* and *Lady, Be Good!*, the latter inaugurating, again in 1924, the collaboration of George and Ira Gershwin in a show that captured both the fashion and spirit of a new kind of jazz syncopation ('Fascinating Rhythm', 'Little Jazz Bird' and the title song), and contemporary dance rhythms such as the Charleston ('I'd Rather Charleston').

In the 1920s and 1930s distinctions between home-grown musicals, i.e. musical comedies, and musicals that conspicuously revealed their debt to European themes and styles, operettas, were sharper and more easily recognized than they would be in future generations. One such distinction is that American musical comedies, in addition to the romantic ballads common to both genres, also featured vernacularly inflected rhythms and melody. With increased frequency the duty of composing both types of songs were combined in a single composer and a single show (e.g. Kern's *Roberta* has the romantic 'Smoke Gets in Your Eyes' and the jazzy 'I'd be Hard to Handle'). By the end of the decade the decision to join the vernacular Gershwin (then, unlike the Rodgers of *Poor Little Ritz Girl*, at the height of his fame) with the Ruritanian Romberg in *Rosalie* (1928) was unusual. Musical comedies normally utilised contemporary American urban settings with matching dialogue and music (e.g. ragtime, blues, jazz and, after 1930, swing).[5] Operettas were customarily set in exotic locations or fabled early Americana and tended to emphasise the trappings of opera, including operatic voices, contrapuntal duets and choruses, and more elaborate and frequent sections with continuous music. Occasionally, perhaps most notably with *Show Boat*, a musical that successfully balances musical comedy and operetta, or musical comedies like *Of Thee I Sing* and *Let 'Em Eat Cake*, operetta characteristics gradually intruded on musical comedy turf sufficiently to pose a taxonomic challenge. Throughout the era the formats of both operettas and musical comedies called for spoken dialogue and occasional choruses mixed with solos and duets, the latter often harmonised in operettas.

The role stars played in the success of musical comedies of the 1920s and 30s is analogous to the fame and high salaries enjoyed by the film stars of today. In both eras certain performers consistently ensured box office success. The 1920s featured several stars, for example, Marilyn Miller, who possessed an invariable ability to entrance live audiences (*Sally*, *Sunny* and *Rosalie*). Her recordings do not reveal the secret to her strong stage persona and appeal. Fortunately, other stars, such as the ever-bumbling Victor Moore, first seen in Cohan musicals as early as 1906 (*Forty-Five Minutes from Broadway*) and in the 1920s and 30s most memorably in *Oh, Kay!* (1926), *Funny Face* (1927), *Of Thee I Sing* (1931), *Anything Goes* (1934) and *Leave It to Me!* (1938), can be enjoyed in at least one film musical, Berlin's *Top Hat* (1935).

Generations of movie audiences continue to appreciate the comic persona of Bert Lahr, the man for whom *Flying High* (1930) was designed, as the Cowardly Lion in *The Wizard of Oz*, a film musical released the same year Lahr sang 'Friendship' with Ethel Merman in *DuBarry Was a Lady* (1939). Merman, who went on to have some of her biggest successes after 1940 (*Annie Get Your Gun*, *Call Me Madam* and *Gypsy*), also starred in shows of the 1930s, such as *Girl Crazy* (1930), *Anything Goes* (1934), *Red, Hot and Blue* (1936) and *DuBarry*; and her recorded legacy has preserved the memory of one of the last major stars who did not need amplification. On the other hand, the stage charisma of William Gaxton, a successful leading man in *A Connecticut Yankee* (1927) and *Fifty Million Frenchmen* (1929) before teaming with Moore in the 1930s, is not evident from the few films he made between 1943 and 1945. Other factors must be considered, including the musical scores, of course, but it is probably not a coincidence that the four most popular musical comedy successes of the 1930s featured Gaxton, Lahr, Merman or Moore, alone or more often in combination: *Flying High* (Lahr), *Of Thee I Sing* (Gaxton and Moore), *Anything Goes* (Gaxton, Merman, and Moore) and *DuBarry* (Lahr and Merman). Some stars today can still launch or maintain a new show or a revival. The 1920s and 1930s contained a firmament of stars that could start (and stop) a show.

Although the stars of these shows deserve praise (the other unequivocal high point, the songs, will be discussed shortly), it must be said that musicals during this period were and remain accused of lacking strong books, especially by the standards set by the Rodgers and Hammerstein model. Surprisingly, unless the memory of earlier shows with still weaker books lingered, critics, even when they noted the failings of musical comedy books, did not seem too disturbed about it. Audiences, who were not unaware of well-made contemporary plays, did not mind either. For the most part the stories remained plausible, coherent and well crafted, presented a welcome series of opportunities to feature songs, dances and stars, and purposely contrasted with the integrated plot narratives found in contemporary American plays.

Because their books seemed so dependent on improvising comedy teams, even today such bona fide musical comedies as Flournoy Miller and Aubrey Lyles's *Shuffle Along* (1921) and the Marx Brothers' *The Cocoanuts* (1925) are commonly mistaken for a third type of musical, the revue. Like musical comedies and operettas a genre that gained its initial identity and prominence in the 1890s, revues feature intentionally loose and autonomous skits that exploit the idiosyncratic talents of star comedians, production numbers with beautiful girls, and, most memorably from a later perspective, songs – qualities that were by no means strangers to musical comedy. Revues may be organised around a unifying theme such as travel (*At Home Abroad*) or newspaper headlines (*As Thousands Cheer*), or they may reflect more generally the stylistic imprint of a producer such as Florenz Ziegfeld or George White. As the 1920s began, revues were the most popular form of musical theatre. In fact, before 1924 revues were the exclusive venue of Berlin (*Ziegfeld Follies* and *Music Box Revues*), Gershwin (*George White's Scandals*) and Porter (*Hitchy-Koo, Greenwich Village Follies*), while Rodgers, who spent these years writing amateur shows, made his hit debut in *The Garrick Gaieties*, a Theatre Guild revue from 1925 that introduced 'Manhattan'. By mid-decade, operettas and musical comedies vied for hegemony, with the former claiming seven of the decade's ten most popular shows (see chapter 3). In the 1930s musical comedy would eclipse both operetta and revues in quantity and popularity and could boast nine of the fifteen most popular shows (although the two longest-running shows of the decade, *Hellzapoppin'* and *Pins and Needles*, were revues).

Music and words

For most readers of this volume the central legacy of musical theatre of all types during this period remains the songs. Contemporary critics and audiences may have been willing to overlook the fact that musical comedy books lacked the qualities expected of the best plays, but a musical comedy score in the 1920s or 1930s without at least one notable song was unacceptable. Every successful show and the majority of those otherwise forgotten, offered one or more songs that continued with a life of its own. The Broadway and film songs of Berlin, Gershwin, Kern, Porter and Rodgers, among others, are still with us, frequently sung and increasingly revered. Even when heard in instrumental versions in shopping malls, elevators and lounges, they still retain a close association with their original verbal messages.

Several sociological and musical characteristics link the major songwriters, who shared lyricists, librettists, producers and stars, and knew, respected, learned from and sometimes, as in the unlikely friendship of Berlin and Porter, genuinely enjoyed each other's company. All were born between 1885 (Kern) and 1902 (Rodgers), nearly all in one of the New York City boroughs. Most were the sons of recent Jewish immigrants from Central and Eastern Europe or from Russia. Only Berlin, who arrived from Temun, Russia when he was five years old, was not born in America. The geographical and ethnic exception was Porter, a Protestant who grew up in Peru, Indiana, but who by the 1920s was self-consciously trying to emulate what he perceived to be Jewish melodic and harmonic characteristics.[6] Economic status ranged from poor (Berlin) to affluent or relatively affluent (Kern, Porter, Rodgers). Before establishing their careers, Kern, Porter and Rodgers received at least some formal musical education in theory and composition. At the age of eighteen Kern studied piano, counterpoint, harmony and composition at the New York College of Music. One year after graduating from Yale University Porter enrolled for a year in Harvard's music department and several years later continued his studies in composition, counterpoint, harmony and orchestration with Vincent d'Indy at the Schola Cantorum in Paris. At the age of twenty-one Rodgers studied harmony with the noted theorist Percy Goetschius at the Institute of Musical Art (renamed the Juilliard School of Music in 1946). Gershwin studied the piano, performing professionally as a song plugger from the age of fifteen and later as a rehearsal pianist and professional performer of his own music, and for the rest of his life absorbed what he needed from a sporadic procession of theorists and composers, including Edward Kilenyi, Joseph Schillinger and Arnold Schoenberg. Berlin alone was self-taught and barely capable of notating or playing his own songs. The songwriters in this short list quickly absorbed early ragtime and blues as well as operetta models and eventually incorporated

1920s jazz and 1930s swing styles into their musical language, harmonically conservative by modernist standards but often strikingly original.

The majority of their songs fitted a standard framework, widely known as 32-bar song form. In most cases the main part of the song, the chorus, was prefaced by a verse, a sometimes independent, sometimes thematically linked introductory section stylistically somewhere between speech and song, a bridge between spoken dialogue and a fully developed melody. Although a famous song such as Gershwin's 'The Man I Love' began its life as a verse, most verses lack the tunefulness or even the rhythmic regularity of the chorus, the portion that gives most songs their primary identity. On rare occasions, most famously in Kern and Harbach's 'Smoke Gets In Your Eyes' and 'Yesterdays', both from *Roberta*, verses are absent altogether. Popular and jazz artists and revivals that take up the song frequently removed verses also (or like Fred Astaire, sang them *after* introducing his recordings with the more familiar chorus), but most songs included verses when they made their musical comedy stage debuts. The 32 bars of each chorus were most frequently divided into four phrases of 8 bars each, with an A A B A scheme ('My Heart Stood Still' from *A Connecticut Yankee* is an example) making up the vast majority of songs. Numerous songs favoured the format A B A C (e.g. 'Embraceable You' from *Girl Crazy*). A related but distinctly different song form that had begun to wane by 1925 offers a more parallel eight-bar periodisation of the thirty-two bars with a complete break in the middle: A B // A B (as in 'Thou Swell' from *A Connecticut Yankee*) or A B // A C (as in 'My Romance' from *Jumbo*).[7] For the most part, the songwriters featured in this chapter shared Rodgers's view that he 'never felt restricted but rather enjoyed the challenge of coming up with something fresh within the prescribed regulations'.[8]

Early in their careers the major songwriters developed idiosyncratic musical characteristics. Gershwin often favoured pentatonic melodies ('I Got Rhythm'), blue notes ('I'll Build a Stairway to Paradise' and 'Somebody Loves Me' in *George White's Scandals*, and throughout *Porgy and Bess*), and a predilection for repeated notes, for example the release or B section of 'I Got Rhythm' (an A A B A song) and the 'no, no, they can't' portion of 'They Can't Take That Away'. Characteristically, as in the last-named song, Gershwin changes the harmony on each repeated note. Other harmonic features in Gershwin songs are the delayed resolution of the central key ('Slap That Bass') and the use of harmony for expressive textual purposes (the harmonically imaginative chord that fits the phrase 'just imagine someone' in 'Nice Work If You Can Get It'). These latter characteristics become increasingly prevalent in Gershwin's film songs, more than half of which also display at least one section that is either longer (or in one case shorter) than eight measures. Although they are almost invariably disregarded by the thousands of jazz musicians who play the 'I Got Rhythm' chord progressions (known as the 'rhythm changes'), two additional bars originally belonged to the final A section of this song.

Porter exhibits a strong predilection throughout his career for the juxtaposition of major and minor modes ('Night and Day'), release sections that closely parallel the main A sections ('Let's Do It' and 'Night and Day'), and exotic beguine and other Latin rhythms ('Begin the Beguine'). Rodgers's nearly ubiquitous trademark is the simple scale, either ascending or descending, both with Hart and later with Hammerstein, out of which he manages to develop a staggering melodic variety (from 'Mountain Greenery' to 'Do-Re-Mi'). 'My Heart Stood Still', yet another variation of this technique, consists of an ascending series of three-note descending scales that carefully avoid the climactic note until the word 'thrill' in the final A section. Among other prominent Rodgers trademarks are the intentionally surprising notes at the ends of phrases[9] and a long and impressive series of memorable waltzes from 'Falling in Love with Love' to 'Do I Hear a Waltz?'

Naturally, the subject matter of the vast majority of musical comedy songs is romantic love. Within this convention the lyricists Berlin, Ira Gershwin, Hammerstein, Hart and Porter manage to convey an impressive variety of individual responses and attitudes. Although their lyrical versatility and range defy comfortable generalisations, some characteristics did emerge during the course of their careers. Hart's lyrics tend to ponder the bittersweetness of unrequited love ('Glad to Be Unhappy') or even love as a sickness ('It's Got to Be Love' and its sequel 'This Can't Be Love'). Porter focuses more on the direct approach ('Let's Do It'). Philip Furia notes that Ira Gershwin 'situated most of his songs at the moment of falling in love'.[10] John Clum explores a possible gay subtext in Hart's lyrics and the more transparent references to homosexuality in Porter's.[11]

From the Rodgers and Hammerstein era onwards, lyrics typically came first, but in the 1920s and 1930s it was nearly always the music, unless, as with Berlin and Porter, the composer and lyricist resided in the same person. It may be constructive to compare the compositional methods of some of the leading songwriters. Early in his career Berlin summarised his life-long working methods in the following succinct terms: 'I get an idea, either a title or a phrase or a melody, and hum it out to something definite.'[12] In a 1936 interview Porter described a related working procedure: 'First I think of an idea for a song and then I fit it to a title. Then I go to work on a melody, spotting the title at certain moments in the melody. Then I write the lyric – the end first – that way it has a strong finish.'[13] In the same interview Porter also disclosed that he tried to pick rhymes for which he could assemble a long list with the same ending. Kern, the Gershwins and Rodgers and Hart almost invariably began with the music, often after a title had been determined. A rare if not unprecedented exception to Kern's music-first rule is the song 'The Last Time I Saw Paris', the Academy Award-winning song that the composer set at Hammerstein's request for the film *Lady Be Good* (1941). No extant documentation reveals that Rodgers ever set a Hart lyric for a full chorus.[14] But just as Berlin and Porter frequently begin their compositional process with a title, so did the Gershwins and Rodgers and Hart. When Rodgers composed 'My Heart Stood Still', for example, he was setting a title that formed the central starting point for Hart's future lyrics.[15] In this very real sense the words, or at least arguably the most important words, did indeed come first. What is remarkable, to continue with this famous song, is Hart's unusual sensitivity to Rodgers's music. The line 'my heart stood still' may have been a given, but Hart knew to pick a climactic word ('thrill') that corresponded perfectly to Rodgers's climactic melodic note (attached with a harmonic surprise, the IV chord).[16] In an interview that appeared in 1925 Hart offered a valuable insight about his working methods.[17] Hart's normal starting point was 'the most distinctive melodic phrase' of a Rodgers tune. The example he used was the musical phrase set to the word 'adorable' in the opening line, 'Here in my arms, it's adorable', from the song 'Here In My Arms' (*Dearest Enemy* (1925)).[18] This pivotal musical phrase also inspired a series of prominent multi-syllabic rhymes ('adorable/deplorable' and 'kissable/permissible' in the first stanza and 'affable/laughable' in the second). Many Gershwin songs began with an untitled (and unfinished) melodic fragment. In the case of 'Fascinating Rhythm', for example, something in the song eventually yielded a title and a rhyme scheme, i.e. a set of lyrics to match the fascinating musical rhythms.[19]

According to Stephen Banfield's theory of melopoetics, by the end of the songwriting process, and usually at the beginning, the music and words form a symbiotic, if not always inseparable, union.[20] This principle remains applicable, even in the songs of Rodgers and Hart with their striking opposition of soaring music and languishing and acerbic words. This is, of course, part of the secret of many great songs, whether by Schubert or by Berlin, but for the Broadway songwriters the creative process almost invariably serves both the union and the purposeful contrasts. This generality holds even when new lyrics are created for a song, either unused (a so-called trunk song) or recycled from a failed or otherwise abandoned show. Since the song is the staple of the show in the 1920s and 30s, it is probably unfair to deride a song for stopping the show, its avowed purpose. Like Mozart's arias, songs were often conceived to show off the strengths and minimise the vocal limitations of particular stars. Even if most of the books lack the integration of the Rodgers and Hammerstein era, they usually manage to place their characters in believable, if silly, dramatic situations, and they express the feelings and intellect of their characters. Nearly all the songs of Kern, the Gershwins, Rodgers and Hart, and Porter were conceived or revised for specific characters in specific situations, and contrary to the standard perception, do not characteristically arise meaninglessly out of nowhere.

Legacies: stage revivals, film adaptations, and reconstructed recordings

Soon after *Oklahoma!* (1943) cast albums became common and then a required byproduct for nearly every show. Song selections and in many cases relatively complete vocal scores became available for most shows, and by the 1950s aficionados could usually purchase scripts as well. Many shows from the Rodgers and Hammerstein era have been recreated – sometimes slavishly – in film versions, occasionally with the original stars (Rex Harrison in *My Fair Lady*, Robert Preston in *The Music Man*). More recently, some shows have been filmed in staged versions (Sondheim's *Sweeney Todd*, *Sunday in the Park With George*, *Into the Woods* and *Passion*). It is also the norm rather than the exception that post-Rodgers and Hammerstein shows appear in reasonably faithful staged revivals. Thanks to these developments the idea of an American musical as an integral unit, still a novel notion in the 1940s, is now an established standard by which musical theatre audiences, critics and even scholars embrace or dismiss a particular show. Although the primary concern of modern practitioners, like their predecessors, is the reaction of opening night audiences, after *Oklahoma!* those responsible for creating musicals realised that their products had a potentially longer shelf life than in previous decades.

In contrast to the well-preserved monuments of the post-Rodgers and Hammerstein era, the legacies of American musicals of all types from the 1920s and 30s pose difficult, occasionally insurmountable problems. Shows that lasted only three months could earn a profit; only sometimes were their lives extended by a national tour, a London production or (more rarely) a film adaptation. Complete, even representative recordings of a show from this earlier era are therefore rare, although the situation improves if one considers London cast recordings of Broadway exports.[21] Saleable songs were published individually in sheet music format, but scripts and complete scores appeared only sporadically.[22] Revivals and film versions as a rule altered either the stories, the scores or both, occasionally beyond recognition. In many cases no one now alive can remember what the shows looked like, how they worked, the indefinable dimension of star appeal, what words were spoken, how they were sung, or why audiences could not stay away. Despite our lack of familiarity with most of this repertory, in any form, American musical comedies of the 1920s and 30s have nonetheless left their mark through three frequently distorted yet valuable legacies, namely revivals, films and reconstructions, and one indestructible remnant – the songs.

For a variety of reasons, few of even the most popular musical comedies before *Oklahoma!* have made successful comebacks, at least in their original form. Consider the fate of the four musical comedies of the 1920s to receive over 500 performances, *Sally* (1920), *Shuffle Along* (1921), *Sunny* (1925) and *Good News!* (1927). The decade's first hit show, *Sally* (book by Bolton, lyrics by Clifford Grey, among others), enjoyed successful runs in London and Sydney and inspired the making of two films, both with the huge star who played the original Sally, Marilyn Miller. Perhaps the most lasting memory of the show is Judy Garland's performance of 'Look for the Silver Lining' (lyric by DeSylva), playing Miller in the hemidemisemi-biographical film about Kern's life, *Till the Clouds Roll By* (MGM, 1946). The 1948 revival, in which nearly half of the score was recycled from other Kern shows, closed after 36 performances. *Shuffle Along* (lyrics by Noble Sissle and music by Eubie Blake) which introduced 'I'm Just Wild About Harry', Harry Truman's campaign song of 1948, and interpolated 'How Ya' Gonna Keep 'em Down on the Farm' (music by Walter Donaldson), was a runaway hit of 1921. It is also credited as the launching pad of the Harlem Renaissance and the careers of several distinguished African Americans from Florence Mills in the replacement cast to Josephine Baker, Paul Robeson, and Adelaide Hall in the chorus, and inspired a long list of imitators for more than a decade.[23] Three attempts to revive the show with new material, *Shuffle Along: Keep Shufflin'* (1928), *Shuffle Along of 1933* (1932), and *Shuffle Along* (1952), however, all quickly closed. Kern's second 1920s hit, *Sunny*, also with Miller, fared slightly better than *Sally*. Although it too vanished after its tour, *Sunny* at least left a fine representative period recording of eight songs from the London cast, including two songs not heard in New York. It also marked the beginning of a collaboration with Hammerstein that would lead to *Show Boat* two years later. Again, its most lingering memory is a song, 'Who', featured in the *Sunny* sequence from *Till the Clouds Roll By*, sung and to some extent danced by Garland, then pregnant with Liza Minnelli.[24]

The fourth hit musical comedy of the 1920s, *Good News!* (lyrics by DeSylva and Brown, music by Henderson), alone managed to have a future on the wicked stage, albeit radically transformed. Thus the 1974 revival altered the setting, plot and book, raided other DeSylva, Brown and Henderson shows for formerly popular songs that a fresh audience might enjoy to join 'The Best Things In Life Are Free' and the 'The Varsity Drag', yet still closed after sixteen performances. In the 1990s Wayne Bryan and Mark Madama wrote another new libretto, which according to the notes that accompany the recording 'streamlines the romantic complications into a unified, fast-moving farce, whose characters have believable backgrounds and motivations', i.e. a musical that follows the Rodgers and Hammerstein model.[25]

The new *Good News!* exemplifies the *modus operandi* of revivals for the past fifty years. Even when the integrity of the earlier scores are largely preserved, as in the revival of *No, No, Nanette* in 1971 that successfully resuscitated hoofers from an earlier era and lasted for two years, and the impressive 1983 Broadway restoration of George Balanchine's choreography and Hans Spialek's orchestrations in *On Your Toes*, the books are invariably revised or rewritten in response to real and imagined modern dramatic expectations and sensitivities.[26] As with *Good News!* the most familiar practice is to invade other scores by the composer at hand and find a way in a new book to include as many familiar songs by that composer as possible. Among the most successful embodiments of this approach are *My One and Only* from 1983, a reworking of Gershwin's *Funny Face*, the 1962 off-Broadway and 1987 Broadway revivals of Porter's *Anything Goes*[27] and in 1992, *Crazy for You*, a major overhaul of Gershwin's *Girl Crazy* that ran for an astonishing 1,622 performances.

Good News! provides a useful starting point to introduce another lasting legacy of 1920s and 30s musical comedies: films. The second film incarnation of *Good News!* (MGM, 1947), which starred June Allyson and Peter Lawford and Mel Tormé, illustrates a familiar pattern. On this occasion the studio commissioned a new book by Betty Comden and Adolph Green, retained six songs from the 1927 score (about half), some with new lyrics, and added two songs by other composers. Film adaptations of other shows present a range of fates, none of which include fidelity to the staged originals. Even though the original creators were more likely to still be around to protest, however ineffectually, the general practice in film adaptation closely paralleled the distortions of stage revivals. Retentions usually (but not always) retained the basic story line, typically half or fewer of the songs, and occasionally only one (e.g., 'Night and Day' in *The Gay Divorce*, *Divorcée* on film, or 'Strike Up the Band' in the 1940 musical film of that title). Sometimes the original composer and lyricist added one or more new songs expressly for the film; in other cases new composers were brought in for this purpose. The creative control that Broadway composers had begun to exert in the 1920s was largely absent when it came to film adaptations. Original film musicals fared somewhat better.

A few examples will illustrate representative adaptive possibilities. *The Cocoanuts* (Broadway, 1925; Paramount, 1929), the first in a long and popular series of films with the Marx Brothers and Margaret Dumont, was perhaps the only significant contemporary film setting of a 1920s musical comedy.

Most of the original songs from the 1925 score were dropped, and the film added a new love ballad, 'When My Dreams Come True'. Surprisingly, *The Cocoanuts* film preserves extensive portions of Kaufman's published script (including Groucho's puns and other silly business) and presents a serious challenge to those who want to believe that the zaniness was mainly improvised.[28] The plot of Youmans's *Hit the Deck* (1927) was freely adapted in the Fred Astaire and Ginger Rogers film, *Follow the Fleet* (RKO, 1936). Additionally, the film offered an entirely new score, not by Youmans, but by Berlin, a fine film perhaps, but not quite the *Hit the Deck* Broadway audiences came to see in 1927. Two decades later a second film, now called *Hit the Deck* (MGM, 1955), dutifully used seven of Youmans's ten songs (including 'Hallelujah' and 'Sometimes I'm Happy'), but still managed to completely disregard the original book by Herbert Fields. Although the filming of *Funny Face* (Broadway, 1927; MGM, 1957) was delayed by thirty years, it managed to offer one of its original stage stars, Astaire. The film *Funny Face* also used a new screenplay, retained five songs, including 'How Long Has This Been Going On', cut from the original score, reintroduced a familiar Gershwin tune originally from *Oh! Kay!* ('Clap Yo' Hands'), and added three new songs by Leon Gershe and Roger Edens. With *Rosalie* (Broadway, 1928; MGM, 1937) the original double story (Lindbergh flight/Queen of Romania visit) was preserved, but the composite Gershwin/Romberg score was replaced by an all-new one by Porter.

Freewheeling adaptation practices would continue with musicals that first appeared in the 1930s. From the trio of Gaxton, Moore and Merman, only Merman remained in the first filming of *Anything Goes* two years later (Broadway 1934; Paramount, 1936). The film used Merman's songs, the title song, 'You're the Top', 'I Get A Kick Out of You', and 'Blow, Gabriel Blow', but only two songs of those originally sung by others, 'All Through the Night' and 'They'll Always Be a Lady Fair'. For the 1956 remake, starring Bing Crosby in the role introduced by Gaxton, now teamed with Mitzi Gaynor and Donald O'Connor, the story was more drastically altered. The film version of *Babes in Arms* (Broadway, 1937; MGM, 1939), starring Judy Garland and Mickey Rooney, preserved the basic story and spirit of Rodgers and Hart's Broadway show, but omitted the significant political and racial component and retained only two songs, the title song and 'Where or When', from a score that is widely regarded as one of the richest of any decade.[29] *The Boys from Syracuse* (Broadway 1938; Universal, 1940) with comedians Martha Raye and Joe Penner retained the basic story and four songs and added two new ones by Rodgers and Hart. When *Jumbo* (Broadway 1935; MGM 1962) was finally filmed, the story was considerably rewritten but nonetheless recognisable, half the original score and the original Jimmy Durante was preserved (along with his 'Elephant? What elephant?' routine);

the film also pilfered two vintage Rodgers and Hart songs from other shows, 'Why Can't I?' from *Spring is Here* (1929) and 'This Can't Be Love' from *The Boys from Syracuse* (1938).

Roberta (Broadway 1933; RKO 1935) stands out as perhaps the finest contemporary film of a staged musical comedy.[30] It also demonstrates how it is possible to retain a storyline while at the same time adapting new roles for new stars, especially if the stars are Astaire (as Huck Haines, now dancing in the formerly non-dancing role played on stage by newcomer Bob Hope) and Rogers (as Countess Tanka Schwarenka, impersonating the stage Countess Lyda Roberti's Polish-Hungarian accent). The original score, which included 'Yesterdays', 'Smoke Gets in Your Eyes', 'Let's Begin', 'I'll Be Hard to Handle', 'Something Had to Happen', 'The Touch of Your Hand', and 'You're Devastating', was already one of the most memorable of the 1930s. The film dropped the three last-named titles as song numbers, but retained the melodies of the last two to underscore the fashion-show sequence. On stage, 'Yesterdays' was sung by Aunt Minnie (Fay Templeton); in the film 'Yesterdays' joins 'Smoke Gets in Your Eyes' as Stephanie's (Irene Dunne's) second major song, leaving non-singing Helen Westley (Parthy in Universal's 1936 *Show Boat* classic) songless, a net gain. The combination of European elegance represented by Dunne and the addition of two new swing dance numbers for Astaire and Rogers, 'I Won't Dance' (reworked by Dorothy Fields and Jimmy McHugh from Kern's recent London flop with Hammerstein, *Three Sisters*) and 'Lovely to Look At' (composed expressly for the film by Kern and Fields), captures the best of both worlds and the best of what musical comedy of the 1930s has to offer modern audiences, even if viewers are asked to swallow the outrageous notion of an exiled Russian princess living in Paris in 1935, the 'Gee, that's swell' persona of the non-singing Randolph Scott and the unsightly fashions.

The third prominent modern legacy of the musical is the series of re-constructed recordings, sometimes referred to as 'restorations'. Among the chief instigators of this practice are the conductor John McGlinn (*Sitting Pretty, Show Boat, Anything Goes*), and Tommy Krasker, the archivist and administrator for the Ira and Leonore Gershwin Trusts. Taking advantage of such invaluable rediscoveries as the Warner Brothers materials in Secaucus Warehouse in 1982 and Tams Witmark Music Library in 1987, McGlinn and Krasker have been able to resurrect the original orchestrations by Hans Spialek and Robert Russell Bennett and salvaged even whole scripts and songs previously considered lost. Casts have been carefully chosen to paral-lel the original vocal types as closely as possible, and performing styles and tempos are carefully observed, when known. The end result may give present and future students of the 1920s and 30s their most reliable opportunities to hear relatively complete versions of these scores as New York audiences

Plate 5 Gertrude Lawrence with the doll that George Gershwin gave her to hold
while singing 'Someone to Watch Over Me' in *Oh, Kay!*

first heard them, along with musical numbers discarded on tryout tours and
during the early stages of their Broadway runs.

Those who wish to explore this literature should be advised, however,
that the restorations sometimes recreate versions that no first-night, or any
night, audiences may have heard or seen. In most cases scholars such as
McGlinn and Krasker are motivated by a desire to preserve an imagined
pristine pre-Broadway integrity. For example, the song 'Buddy Beware' was
cut from the first production of *Anything Goes* at the request of Merman in
favour of a reprise of 'I Get a Kick Out of You'. The McGlinn reconstruction
restores it.[31] With *Fifty Million Frenchmen* Krasker's restoration revised
Herbert Fields's script in order to recycle several songs dropped during the
pre-Broadway tryout ('I Worship You', 'Please Don't Make Me Be Good',

'The Queen of Terre Haute', and 'The Tale of the Oyster'). Another song dropped before Broadway, 'Down with Everybody But Us', however, is absent from the album. Early during the Broadway run 'Let's Step Out' replaced 'The Boy Friend Back Home'; both are included in the restored recording, albeit in different acts.[32]

Restorations commonly favour the initial vision of those that created the songs and tend to dismiss the practical concerns that led to pragmatic decisions by directors and producers and anyone under time constraints. To take one example among many, Krasker's restoration of *Oh, Kay!* returns to the way the show looked before its excessive length forced some cutting.[33] At the Philadelphia premiere the first three songs audiences heard were 'The Moon Is on the Sea', 'Don't Ask' and 'Someone to Watch Over Me', the last written for Gertrude Lawrence, the show's star and namesake. A fourth song, 'When Our Ship Comes Sailing In', originally placed between 'Moon' and 'Don't Ask', had been dropped during the rehearsals. At least in part as a solution to the excessive length, 'The Moon Is on the Sea' was dropped (along with 'Ain't It Romantic?' and the Finaletto to Act II, scene 1 from later in the show). 'A Woman's Touch' was relocated to start the show followed by 'Don't Ask', and 'Someone to Watch Over Me' became the first song of Act II. The shift of Lawrence's hit song created some dramatic problems that have not gone unnoticed. In a national televised broadcast Leonard Bernstein pointed out the silliness that results from the line 'Haven't found him yet' after Kay has already made it clear in the first act that she has in fact found the man whose initial she would like to add to her monogram. Bernstein interprets this incongruity as a sign that neither Broadway songwriters nor their audiences cared about dramatic credibility and nuance: 'As they said in the mad, gay Twenties, what's the diff?'[34] Bernstein's assessment is accurate in that the song 'doesn't *quite* fit the situation in which it was sung', and Ira Gershwin either did not notice or chose not to adjust his lyrics to the new situation. As originally conceived, however, the song did fit dramatically. Thus Krasker restored the appropriateness of a lyric, which depicts Kay looking for a man she had not only met but also saved from drowning the previous summer. Since one intention in a restored recording is to present as much of the original score as possible (and length is no longer an issue on a compact disc), listeners might welcome a return to the more substantial pre-Broadway concept. But what is being restored does not necessarily correspond to the solution agreed to by the original creators of the show (e.g. the inclusion of 'When Our Ship Comes Sailing In', a song dropped before the tryouts).[35]

The shortened *Oh, Kay!* became, after *Lady, Be Good!*, Gershwin's second biggest hit of the 1920s. On the other hand, Gershwin's penultimate musical comedy, *Pardon My English* (1933), never recovered from numerous cast changes and endlessly revised scripts and songs. At 46 performances, it failed in its own time, and it remains little known today beyond the songs 'Isn't It a Pity?' and 'My Cousin in Milwaukee'. It also poses extremely difficult reconstruction problems. The only extant Fields/Ryskind script is a draft that dates from 15 November 1932, two weeks prior to its Philadelphia tryout, making a Broadway version unsalvageable beyond a reconstruction of song order. After reviewing the earlier script and what is known about the changes in Philadelphia, Boston and Brooklyn over the next few months, Krasker's decision to use the Philadelphia song-lineup as the starting point was arguably more felicitous than the decision to restore the rehearsal and tryout versions of *Oh, Kay!*[36] Even if Krasker's restoration does not represent a version that any audience heard in 1932 or 1933, it does successfully rescue most of the extant music from an exceptionally fine Gershwin score. That's something to sing about.

Despite their liabilities and the perhaps inevitable fact that they reveal as much about a later time as they do about the 1920s and 30s, revivals, films, and reconstructions offer indispensable as well as more than occasionally entertaining glimpses into this unknown territory, a territory which extends far beyond *Show Boat* and *Porgy and Bess*. With the right casting and sense of period style, producers and directors might be surprised at the revivability of an undoctored *No, No, Nanette* or *Lady, Be Good!*, and *Oh, Kay!* in the 1920s, or *Anything Goes, On Your Toes, Babes in Arms, The Boys from Syracuse, Johnny Johnson, Knickerbocker Holiday*, and *The Cradle Will Rock* in the 1930s. Like most of the forgotten comic operas of the past 250 years, musical comedies, belonging perhaps more to their time than serious operas, music dramas, operettas or the integrated musical plays that began in earnest on Broadway in the 1940s, appear more susceptible to the ravages of time than more obliquely topical genres. This is as true today as it was in 1920. The shows of the 1920s and 30s may have ended but their melodies and words linger on. And to match these catchy tunes and clever lyrics, these musical comedies – however ephemeral and difficult to recapture – offer unsung dramatic treasures.

PART II

Maturations and formulations: 1940 to 1970

6 'We said we wouldn't look back': British musical theatre, 1935–1960

JOHN SNELSON

Between the early Edwardian musical comedies of the Gaiety Theatre and the recent mega-musicals of Andrew Lloyd Webber is a largely forgotten era in the history of the British musical of some twenty-five years. Between 1935 and 1960, 127 new British musicals were presented in the West End, but only a handful have survived into today's active repertory. *Me and My Girl* (1937; music by Noel Gay) was neglected for decades until it received a major London revival in 1984 and successfully transferred to Broadway. *The Boy Friend* (1953–54; Sandy Wilson), itself a tribute to an earlier style of show, has achieved an international prominence while *Salad Days* (1954; Julian Slade) has found popularity predominantly in Britain. Some individual songs from shows of this period are still favourites in the light music repertory – particularly those by Ivor Novello and Noël Coward – but almost always the songs have been divorced from any knowledge of the original shows. Based on this scant evidence, any view of British musical theatre in the mid-twentieth century is likely to be strange.

So what happened to all of the other shows? Why did most of them never receive more than one original professional production? Were they really so bad as to be better forgotten or did other factors lead to their neglect? This chapter will look at the major works of the period and provide some answers as to why this part of the British musical theatre has been and continues to be largely ignored.[1]

1935–1939

In 1935 there were seven new British musicals in the West End, including the 'sporting farce' of *Twenty to One* (music by Billy Mayerl), *Love Laughs – !*, (music by Noel Gay) and *Please Teacher!* (music by Jack Waller and Joseph Tunbridge). However, the show that was to have the most lasting effect on the West End and made 1935 a significant year for British musical theatre was *Glamorous Night*, the first of a series of musicals by Ivor Novello

Plate 6 Programme cover from original production of *Twenty to One* (12 November 1935, Coliseum). Photo from private programme collection of John Snelson.

(1893–1951). Novello dominated British musical theatre of the 1930s and 1940s with an extraordinary series of popular stage works that had huge national appeal, and yet almost never travelled beyond Britain. At the time of his sudden death in 1951 he was one of the most loved figures of British theatre and a household name. Half a century later he is largely forgotten.

Born David Ivor Davies, Ivor Novello formed his professional name from his own middle name and that of his mother, Clara Novello Davies; he changed his name formally to Ivor Novello by deed poll in 1927. Novello first came to public prominence with his music for the song 'Keep the Home Fires Burning', which fast became an anthem of World War I. In 1916 he was co-composer with Jerome Kern on *Theodore & Co*; in contemporary British terms Novello was the big name and Kern the newcomer. Novello wrote a series of musical shows and revues in the rest of that decade, but his contributions to such works in the 1920s were increasingly subject to his diversions into silent film as a romantic actor. After becoming the country's foremost matinée idol on film he began to develop a similar presence in the theatre, one which took over from film in the early 1930s. When the Theatre Royal, Drury Lane needed something spectacular to revive its fortunes in 1935, Novello's combination of musical, theatrical and performing skills made him the ideal choice for a big new work.

The resulting show, *Glamorous Night*, was a strange concoction of operetta, musical comedy and ballet, with a plot that combined old and new in the romance of a Ruritanian princess and a television inventor. But it was most notable for its scale. Everything about it was indulgent: lines of royal guards, a horse-drawn carriage and a gypsy wedding made the show a spectacular. Most strikingly, through the hydraulics of the huge Drury Lane stage, the sinking of a passenger liner was simulated, and stills from the show reveal how like film was the whole approach. And this is where Novello innovated: he brought the visual, geographical and temporal potential of film to the stage. He followed *Glamorous Night* with *Careless Rapture* (1936), *Crest of the Wave* (1937) and *The Dancing Years* (1939), which reinforced the image of a 'Novello' show as overtly emotive in music, romantically idealised in plot and rich in visual impact.

Today, the reputation of Novello stands in sharp contrast to his contemporary Noël Coward (1899–1973). In many ways their careers are similar. Both occupied the roles of playwright, film and stage actor, composer and (though to a limited extent with Novello) lyricist. They were both icons of their time, with Coward as the urbane sophisticate and Novello as the male romantic ideal. Yet any discussion of British musical theatre keeps returning to Novello as a pivotal figure, while Coward is largely incidental, in opposition to their more general theatrical reputations. Novello's eight shows were produced consistently between 1935 and 1951, with a common identifiable quality that allows his name to be used as an adjective for that style. Coward's musical theatre output in the same period constantly changed direction, through *Operette* (1938), *Pacific 1860* (1946), *Ace of Clubs* (1950) and *After the Ball* (1954), but continually failed to regain the public appeal of his first 'operette' *Bitter Sweet* (1929). While individual songs, often comic, from Coward's shows have found a life in cabaret, the lack of a common identity through his diverse stage works has left no sense of a distinct Coward musical theatre style. Coward now has an international profile whereas Novello is barely remembered nationally, although professional revivals of the musicals of both men are almost completely unknown. It is only the British music industry's annual Ivor Novello Awards that now gives his name any public prominence.

Today, however, the most widely known British musical of the 1930s, through a modern reworking, is not by either Novello or Coward. *Me and My Girl* (1937) became an immediate success through both its accessible, tuneful score and a storyline designed to showcase the performer Lupino Lane. The central character of Bill Snibson, a working-class cockney, was developed for the musical *Twenty to One* (1935), with music by Billy Mayerl (1902–59), who is now best remembered for his syncopated piano style and accompanying piano schools.[2] *Me and My Girl* was written to capitalise on the success of the Snibson character as performed by Lane, and with Gay's score became a success with hit songs. Of its numbers, 'Leaning on a Lamp-post' is characteristic of Gay's ability to write simple, instantly appealing melodies while the success of the cockney march 'The Lambeth Walk', complete with dance steps, gave the name to the film of the show (1939) and achieved remarkable fame. The show ran for 1,646 performances at the Victoria Palace, successfully toured and had West End revivals in 1941, 1945 and 1949. It was a much less sophisticated style of show than that of the Novello romances, relying on a farcical plot, slapstick humour, specialty dances, even audience vocal participation in 'The Lambeth Walk', all of which reveal links with the peculiarly British form of the pantomime, whose influence on the British understanding of the musical has generally been neglected.

Novello's best remembered and most performed show is *The Dancing Years*, which opened at the Theatre Royal, Drury Lane in March 1939. In the plot the composer Rudi Kleber (played, as usual, by Novello himself) is in love with the opera singer Maria Ziegler (Mary Ellis), but their affair is thwarted through misunderstandings. It was also a political musical, despite the operetta naivety of much of the on-stage world, as Novello made his central character an Austrian Jew in order to bring in overt criticism of the Nazi regime. While much of this theme was included in the production, the management tried to remove it on the grounds that it was inappropriate for a musical. It proved to be all too appropriate for the show and its time. As Coward had used the comparison of different ages and their ideals of love in *Bitter Sweet*, so Novello used a similar chronological contrast with the romantic Austria of operetta and the real effects of German political aspirations of the 1930s.

The music of the show is some of Novello's finest, and includes a number of stylistic references that root the work in European operetta while incorporating the later American developments of the 1920s. Viennese operetta is referenced in the waltzes (the song 'Waltz of My Heart' remains one of his most frequently performed and best-known songs) and through many deliberate allusions to Lehár's *Die lustige Witwe* (The Merry Widow), which, in its original London production, had been a formative influence on Novello. In *The Dancing Years*, for example, the opening section of the concerted number 'Lorelei' is based on an inversion of the melody and an exact repetition of the rhythm of the opening chorus of the first act of Lehár's classic operetta. The solos 'My Heart Belongs to You', 'I Can Give You the Starlight' and 'My Dearest Dear' are expansive 4/4 melodies that show the later influence of Romberg, while the pastiche 'Primrose', in the style of an Edwardian musical comedy number, is an acknowledgement of Novello's youth and the musical theatre with which he grew up. The shifting time periods of the plot, the range of musical influences and the references to contemporary European politics provided a broad base for audience appeal. Yet a cursory glance at listings of long-running shows does not indicate fully the popularity of *The Dancing Years*. Special circumstances conspired to make

Novello's most long-lived show the least successful if viewed only from the evidence of such raw statistics. Its initial London production ran for only 187 performances, closing on 1 September 1939.

Wartime

As soon as war was declared in September 1939 all the West End theatres shut down in anticipation of immediate bombing and more pressing priorities. Within a few weeks they opened again. In fact, throughout the war, the theatre benefited from something of a revival of fortunes. There was a high demand for live entertainment to raise morale and the number of professional actors consequently swelled numbers considerably, so much so that, after war's end, British Actors' Equity felt obliged to discuss methods of regulating entry into the profession in order to counter this influx of inadequately trained performers. Not surprisingly there were very few new works in the first years of the war, and the revivals included many operetta-style works. These included such comfortingly familiar favourites as *The Desert Song*, *Chu Chin Chow* (which began its initial record-breaking run during the First World War), *Maid of the Mountains*, *Rose-Marie*, *Show Boat* and *The Merry Widow*. Musical comedy revivals included *Twenty to One* and *Me and My Girl*. In 1943, however, two West End successes were the new shows of *Old Chelsea*, with music by the singer Richard Tauber, and *The Lisbon Story*, with music by Harry Parr Davies (1914–55), more familiar at that time as Gracie Fields's regular accompanist. The latter show involved British spies, the French resistance and had its heroine killed on stage at the end. It was tuneful, indulgently dramatic, and just sufficiently removed in location and events to tread a fine line between reflecting wartime concerns and providing a diversion from them. Novello had one of his few near-misses in 1943 with *Arc de Triomphe*, a biographical musical based on the life of Mary Garden, but reworked as the story of an imaginary French singer, Marie Forêt. For other West End composers it would have been considered a fair run, but 222 performances for Novello was well below his usual expectations. Yet an omnipresent feature of musical theatre around the whole country and in the West End during the war was his earlier show *The Dancing Years*. It had been deprived of the Theatre Royal, Drury Lane at the start of the war when the theatre was taken over as the headquarters of ENSA (Entertainments National Service Association). There was no other sufficiently large theatre available in the West End to which it could move. After a year's delay, it was launched as a national tour in September 1940, finally returning to the Adelphi in the West End in March of 1942 and playing there until July 1944. It was revived again in 1947, filmed in 1950 and entered the amateur dramatic repertory, where it still receives the occasional airing. A television version was broadcast in 1981, which was a rare honour indeed for a British musical. Its presence in the musical theatre world was consequently much greater than the length of its short initial run in London would indicate.

In April 1945, just before peace was declared in Europe, Novello launched his next show at the Hippodrome. Drury Lane was still occupied by ENSA and the association of Novello with that theatre was broken in practice if not in the mind of the public. *Perchance to Dream* followed an affair through reincarnations of the lovers over three eras: Regency (1818), Victorian (1843) and contemporary ('193–?'). Novello was able to revel in period costumes, and romantic figures such as the masked highwayman, familiar to audiences through the style of films from the Gainsborough Studio and from the novels of Georgette Heyer or Daphne du Maurier. The show was further decorated with a 'singing ballet' called 'The Triumphs of Spring', while the music included the waltzes 'Love is My Reason' and 'Highwayman Love', and a hugely popular pastiche of a Victorian parlour ballad, 'We'll Gather Lilacs'.

It was Noël Coward who relaunched Drury Lane after the war, perhaps remembering his great success in that theatre at the start of the 1930s with *Cavalcade*. The resulting work, *Pacific 1860*, which opened on 19 December 1946, is remembered as something of a disaster, set against a background of an unready and unheated theatre in the middle of a fearsome winter aggravated by fuel shortages, and dominated by the miscasting of Mary Martin in the leading role of Elena Salvador. (Serious miscasting also blighted Coward's 1954 show, *After the Ball*, in which his nostalgic remembrance of Mary Ellis's singing proved as out-of-date as the show itself.) As Coward represented an important strand of British theatrical continuity across the divide of World War II, the faltering of such a high-profile work as *Pacific 1860* in London's leading theatre for musicals made it a symbol of perceived British musical theatre decline. In retrospect the judgements of the time on *Pacific 1860* seem harsh. There is some wonderfully luxurious music in the score which, although not seeming as much of a whole as *Bitter Sweet*, still showed Coward to be inventive, and the work is no less indulgent or old-fashioned than the first American show that had opened in London after the war in March 1946, *Song of Norway*.

1947 and the 'American invasion'

The war changed the content and perception of West End musical theatre. A wartime combination of revivals of shows from up to thirty-five years previously with an absence of newer Broadway shows had held British musical theatre in a time-warp of its own. London saw few new American musicals between 1939 and 1946, and contemporary Broadway was thus principally represented by Cole Porter (*Let's Face It* and *DuBarry was a Lady*, both 1942, and *Panama Hattie*, 1943). The first new American shows to be produced after the end of the war were the contrasting demotic comedy of *Follow the Girls* (1945), led by British comedian Arthur Askey, and *Song of Norway* (1946), whose subject matter, musical style, geographical setting, operetta influences and British casting made it seem anything but an American show. Consequently the impact of the first distinctively American show after war – Rodgers and Hammerstein's *Oklahoma!* in 1947, some four years after Broadway – was significantly heightened. The British public, worn down by years of war and deprivation, principally responded to the escapist image of vigorous youth, but at the same time incorporated other qualities of *Oklahoma!* to form the notion of a 'post-*Oklahoma!*' musical, a phrase much used at the time but never explicitly defined. Opening shortly after *Oklahoma!* was Irving Berlin's *Annie Get Your Gun*, with Dolores Gray in the role created on Broadway by Ethel Merman. Again it was rapturously received as the new type of American show and, as with *Oklahoma!*, the energy and style of performance were emphasised in reviews. In terms of construction and staging these two American shows were far apart: Berlin's show was an old-fashioned star vehicle using front cloths for scene changes and a ball in Act II that is reminiscent of a British pantomime walk-down finale; Rodgers and Hammerstein's work was more evenly balanced and tightly structured. Crucially in the West End, *Oklahoma!* began with an almost exclusively American cast with the perceived authentic spirit of youthful America. As the long run progressed, the casting gradually shifted to British performers but with no detriment to the show. *Annie Get Your Gun* only had two American performers from the start, Dolores Gray as Annie Oakley and Bill Johnson as Frank Butler. So, the performing energy may have been American in spirit but was very much British in origin.

Such distinctions matter. The arrival of *Oklahoma!* and *Annie Get Your Gun* created a sense of an 'American invasion' and the term is increasingly applied in the late 1940s as indicative of successful, integrated, modern musicals from America driving out of the West End the old-fashioned and feeble British shows. In fact, it was not until 1953 that the production of new British musicals collapsed, principally because of the increasing lack of confidence of West End producers who preferred proven Broadway shows to the financial risks of unknown British ones. The idea that 'British = old' and 'American = new' was given a further spur into being by the long presence in the West End of a British work that had opened just a few weeks before *Annie Get Your Gun*. *Bless the Bride*, with book and lyrics by A. P. Herbert and music by Vivian Ellis (1904–96), was hugely successful and challenged the notion of an 'American invasion'; equally and paradoxically it probably also helped to form the concept.

In one sense, *Bless the Bride* seems to encourage the notion of an 'American invasion' and reinforces the idea that British musicals in the mid-1940s were old-fashioned. It tells the story of a young English girl, Lucy, in the Victorian England of 1870–71, during the lead up to and outbreak of the Franco-Prussian war. She falls in love with a dashing Frenchman, Pierre, and elopes with him on the morning of her intended marriage to a stereotypical upper-class Englishman, the Honourable Thomas Trout. At the outbreak of the war Pierre joins the French army and Lucy returns to England, distraught. In the last act Pierre, previously thought lost in action, returns and they are reunited. The show capitalised on the period costumes and imagery of its Victorian setting, while Vivian Ellis's music adopts a Gilbert and Sullivan idiom, considerably more 'old-fashioned' than his work for shows before the war, but appropriate to the setting. The show dealt with the consequences of war, but through a sufficiently distant time to dilute the pain of the all-too-recent events, yet contemporary relevance was expressed through, for example, the maiden swept away by the foreign stranger (for which could be read GI), a song to Lucy from her nanny on the eve of her wedding that has more in common with the words of a mother to her son leaving for war, suspicion of foreigners, and the eventual return from the dead of a loved one lost in action. Its concerns were specifically (but not exclusively) British, and A. P. Herbert made much of the ambiguous relationship between England and France in witty asides and exaggerated posturing in the script.

Vivian Ellis supported the themes of Herbert's libretto through music that built up its own patterns of national identity. The English are portrayed in four-square rhythms and four-part harmony, suggesting a communal and socially rigid character, while the French are given freer melismatic lines in dance rhythms suggesting individuality and freedom. Two examples illustrate the point. The opening of the first act presents a croquet game on the lawn, set to a relaxed 6/8 pastorale, but the following introduction of a foreign game 'tennis' (with licentious implications for the prudish British) is set to the equally foreign dance form of the polka. Later, when Pierre seduces Lucy in the shrubbery it is to another continental dance form, that of the waltz in the song 'I Was Never Kissed Before', again with sexually charged overtones, and contrasts strongly with the preceding constraint in Lucy's observations on her own engagement to Thomas Trout. With Trout she acts out of duty and the music is formal and restrained; with Pierre she is driven by emotion and her vocal line becomes increasingly free as the waltz number progresses under the encouragement of Pierre. Such contrasts throughout the work play subtly on British self-image and confidence in the face of Europe and the world. On the surface the show appears to be extremely dated yet it had strong contemporary undercurrents for a British

Plates 7–10 Programme covers from (7) the 1945 revival at the Victoria Palace of *Me and My Girl* (original premiere 16 December 1937, Victoria Palace; the design is the same as the original cover and Lupino Lane starred in both productions) and original productions of (8) *Bless the Bride* (26 April 1947, Adelphi Theatre), (9) *Gay's the Word* (16 February 1951, Saville Theatre) and (10) *Expresso Bongo* (23 April 1958, Saville Theatre).

audience. If the West End taste had changed towards American shows then *Bless the Bride* should have failed quickly. Instead, it was hugely popular; but the production was taken off after more than two years while still playing to capacity houses because the theatre impresario C. B. Cochran wanted to try something new with the same creative team of Herbert, Ellis and Toye. The subsequent work, *Tough at the Top*, was not the success for which Cochran had hoped.

The contrast of the plot, musical style and period design of *Bless the Bride* with those of *Annie Get Your Gun* and *Oklahoma!* was striking and reinforced the notion of 'English = old' and 'American = new'. Yet the appeal of the American works in the West End was escapist, while that of the British ones was a subtle reflection of matters still very close to the public psyche. *Bless the Bride* would have had different resonances on Broadway and was never transferred; the concerns of the show are those on an axis between Britain and Europe not Britain and the USA. To juxtapose *Oklahoma!* and *Annie Get Your Gun* with *Bless the Bride* is thus to compare shows that were through subtext not intended to be on the same continent. Yet the received reputation of *Bless the Bride* from some sixty years on is that of a 'Victorian' show failing to reach the length of run of the American import through its dated style and content. A recent London fringe revival was re-written and re-structured by an American director to make the work more accessible. In fact, it removed precisely those elements which gave the work its initial appeal and dramatic motivation. The context of the show is both its strength as a theatrical work and its weakness in entering a contemporary active repertory.

The biggest indication that the West End and Broadway markets were not the same and that there was a peculiarly British tradition of musical theatre received its best expression immediately post-war in *King's Rhapsody* (1949), the last of Novello's musical romances. It included everything that was against the spirit of the 'American invasion' yet was a great success. Set in the Ruritanian country of 'Krasnia', it concerned princes, kings, marriages, mistresses and abdications. The music was lush, with 'Someday My Heart Will Awake' in the best Novello waltz-song tradition, and the set pieces included a dramatic coronation scene as the finale of the show. Importantly, it concerned one dominating feature of the British social structure, a focal point at the time of war and an institution that provided a sense of national unity: royalty. Central to *King's Rhapsody* is the prince with the foreign mistress who gives up his throne rather than lose her, and the abdication of Edward VIII was a recent memory in the late 1940s. In addition, reference to living people was restricted under the Lord Chamberlain's censorship of the stage at the time, while the portrayal of royalty of the past couple of centuries was forbidden. Consequently, the use of the royal settings of European operetta had become one of the ways in which the British could see expressed on stage issues relating to royalty, and anything that presented the emotions and personal lives of these revered and distant figures was thus tantalising.[3] This aspect of the show's appeal is peculiarly British and it is hardly surprising from this perspective that one of the great West End successes of the immediate post-war years was never considered a candidate for Broadway.

King's Rhapsody maintained its popularity throughout its two-and-a-half-year run, with Novello playing the central character of Prince Nikki up until his sudden death from a heart attack just hours after his performance on Monday, 5 March 1951. Obviously the presence of Novello in the cast was a huge draw, but it ran for a further seven months after Novello's death with his role played by another West End legend, Jack Buchanan. At the time of the show's eventual closure, box office receipts confirm that a steady public interest had been maintained at near capacity despite this substitution in the central role. The show could have run in the West End for much longer, but went on tour from October 1951 until June 1952, still to great acclaim. A film was made in 1955 with Errol Flynn, past his best, in the Novello role. The music was altered so that no number was heard in full and the dubious talents of Anna Neagle did little for the role of the mistress. To compare this with the remarkably faithful and painstaking adaptation to screen of *Oklahoma!*, released in the same year, is to appreciate how much the British repertory has suffered through an ongoing inaccessiblity due to a lack of good – or indeed any – significant screen adaptations until those of *Oliver!* and *Half a Sixpence*. While key works of the American repertory are available today at the local video store there is no similar access to British works of the same period.

In the 1940s and 1950s America represented to the British the escapist, the optimistic, the future, all in strong contrast to the daily bleak reality of the after-effects of the war. Not surprisingly British writers of musicals addressed their home audience through the home concerns of the day, particularly those of post-war recovery and sometimes the perceived lack of it. This introversion accounts not only for the impenetrability of some shows at the time to foreign visitors, but also explains their increasing irrelevance to more modern generations. Such domestic concerns, although present as subtext (*Bless the Bride*, for example), were also presented explicitly. In 1949 Cicely Courtneidge starred in the musical play *Her Excellency* as a woman ambassador to a South American country, whose main purpose was to secure a meat supply contract for Britain. In many respects the plot foreshadows that of *Call Me Madam*, but whereas a British audience could understand many of the topical references to American financial imperialism towards Europe in Howard Lindsay and Russell Crouse's American book the British topical references in Archie Menzies and Harold Purcell's book defeated American understanding.

The subplot of *Her Excellency* involves the selling of British furniture to Latin America as part of the British export drive, while the main plot revolves around the British ambassador beating the American ambassador in securing the beef supply contract. Some of the jokes are still funny but, as much of the script was concerned with topical reference, the show cannot be understood outside of the context of food rationing, which had been introduced soon after the start of the war and was only completely discontinued in 1954.[4] The particular circumstances of 1947–48 inspired the context of the show as the meat ration hit its lowest level since the start of wartime rationing. The direct supply of beef to Britain from Argentina and not via the canning factories of the USA (as a part of Lend-Lease) was thus a theme of strong practical and symbolic value to a British audience in 1949. The language of the show also invokes symbols of England, with the song 'Sunday Morning in England' evoking a national image that played on both the symbols of a strong and proud past and those of a tired and run-down present. A crisis of confidence in the country comes through in many British shows of the period as they seek to address the long-term effects of World War II, particularly in the patriotic bolstering of national spirit. For example, *Tough at the Top* portrays a European princess enamoured of all things English (especially an attractive boxer) and who sings that 'England Is a Lovely Place'; in 1954 Harry Parr Davies's setting and Christopher Hassall's lyrics emote 'I Leave My Heart in an English Garden' (*Dear Miss Phoebe*, 1954). While these expressions of patriotism were hardly new – Ivor Novello's 'Rose of England' from *Crest of the Wave* is perhaps the best example of all – the grim aftermath of the war required an additional dose of patriotism.

Such nationalistic sentiment does not chime well with a modern audience, set against the tainting of patriotism with the racist and bigoted overtones of recent decades and the increasingly ambiguous position of the United Kingdom in relation to mainland Europe. Again, the contemporary strength of these works has proved a latter-day handicap. Generally the judgement of West End musicals after World War II has been viewed from a Broadway-led agenda which has denied these British shows their own home character, yet it is precisely this character that explains why British shows such as *Bless the Bride*, *Her Excellency* and *King's Rhapsody* could be successful despite being apparently so out of step with the prevailing notion of a modern 'post-*Oklahoma!*' musical.

The 1950s

Any retrospective look at the West End musical in the first half of the 1950s makes for uncomfortable reading from a British perspective. Contrasted with the American imports of *Carousel*, *Kiss Me, Kate*, *South Pacific*, *Call Me Madam*, *Guys and Dolls*, *The King and I* and *Pal Joey*, *Wonderful Town* and *Kismet* are indigenous shows such as *Ace of Clubs* (Coward), *Golden City* (John Toré), *Dear Miss Phoebe* (Harry Parr Davies), *Gay's the Word* (Novello), *Zip Goes a Million* (George Posford), *Wild Thyme* (Donald Swann), *The Water Gipsies* (Vivian Ellis) and *A Girl Called Jo* (John Pritchett).

Nothing of this British repertory has survived, while the American imports are mostly 'classics'.

There was an awareness at the time of a difference in style between British and American musicals and two British shows in particular adapted American models in response. In *Golden City* (1950) John Toré wrote a work that was essentially a copy of *Oklahoma!*, adapted to suit the different cultural resonances of a London audience. In the place of the Oklahoman frontier was that of South Africa; instead of farmers and cowboys there were the opposing groups of farmers and miners; the rustic dance of 'The Farmer and the Cowman' became the communal barbecue of 'Braavleis'. The music also used the features of contemporary American shows: 'It's Love, My Darling, It's Love' is a clear copy of the ideas and style of *Oklahoma!*'s 'People Will Say We're in Love', *Annie Get Your Gun*'s 'The Girl That I Marry' was transmuted into 'The Prettiest Girl in the Town', while the 'Oklahoma!' chorus itself became 'It's a Great Occasion', complete with high sustained chords for the women's voices, and the chanting of 'trekkin', ridin'' to match the now familiar rhythmic 'Ok-la ho-ma' of that title song's arrangement. In *Gay's the Word* (1951) Novello changed direction by writing for Cicely Courtneidge rather than himself (he was still performing in *King's Rhapsody*), and this provided an opportunity to adopt a different style, one through which he made the perceived contrasts between British and American shows the substance of the show itself. His ultimate conclusion as presented in *Gay's the Word* was that a confident style of presentation and energy in performance were lacking in British musical theatre at the time, a state further aggravated by a lack of respect for the individuality of British theatrical history. These were far more significant concerns than any notion of changing content. By creating for Courtneidge the character of Gay Daventry, a middle-aged musical comedy star, he was able to juxtapose images of bad old shows and good new shows as part of the dramatic construction. He also surprised his audiences through music which adopted a more popular American idiom, so much so that distinct models can be found for most of the numbers: the show's theme song 'Vitality' is clearly related to 'Another Op'nin', Another Show', the romantic ballad 'If Only He'd Looked My Way' shares crucial similarities of melody and harmony with 'Some Enchanted Evening', while the Novello waltz 'A Matter of Minutes' is not the expected broad sweeping melody but adopts a fast, short-phrased and repetitive structure indebted to Richard Rodgers. As with the theme of rationing in *Her Excellency*, the subject matter of *Gay's the Word* was not suited to export. While a battle between indigenous British musicals and imported American ones became a topic of some heat in the West End, it was an irrelevance for Broadway at that time. In addition to the show's strictly contemporary theme, its reliance on the skills of one unique comic performer and the current ambiguity of the title have contributed to the difficulties for any attempt at revival.

In 1953, however, the effects of an 'American invasion' were felt most strongly, with only two new British shows, one a disaster called *Happy as a King*, led by the much-loved comedian Fred Emney, and a musical pageant *The Glorious Days* which capitalised on the fervour of coronation year by having Anna Neagle play Nell Gwynn and Queen Victoria (both young and old). The Lord Chamberlain was sympathetic towards a slight relaxation of the conventions governing the presentation of royal personages on stage in the year that Elizabeth II became queen, and justified Neagle's portrayals in this show on the grounds that the drama took place in the imagination of a girl who had been knocked out during an air raid, and so was an imagined not actual portrayal of the Queen![5] The American productions that opened in the same year were *Paint Your Wagon, Guys and Dolls, The King and I* and *Wish You Were Here*, although most of their leading performers were British, in contrast to the position of some five years before. Only *Guys and Dolls* relied on leading American performers, with Isobel Bigley, Sam Levene and Stubby Kaye recreating their Broadway roles.

The effect of censorship on British writers is shown indirectly by comparison through the response of the Lord Chamberlain's office to the production of the American show *Wish You Were Here* and in a lesser way to *Call Me Madam*. The reader for the Lord Chamberlain completely missed the point of the social setting of the former work by Harold Rome, Arthur Kobler and Joshua Logan, equating it with the British family holiday camp of Butlins rather than an exclusive setting for priapic American youth. The only change required by the Lord Chamberlain prior to production was the replacement of a reference to the Duke of Windsor with an alternative. The need to remove his name was simply because of its existence. There was nothing in its context that was in any way offensive; it was, if anything, complimentary to the Duke by including him in a list of famous and influential world figures. Four months after the show opened a single complaint from a member of the public over its supposed decadent nature prompted a visit from a representative of the Lord Chamberlain's office, whose report makes for humorous reading today as each piece of dubious or suggestive movement is described in excessive detail.[6] The presentation of the show was subsequently toned down by order. In *Call Me Madam* a reference to Princess Margaret Rose had to be removed (simply because it existed) while the representation in the show of the real American congressman Dean Acheson was allowed on the grounds that it had not been objected to in America. In Britain the representation of real people was often prohibited, especially where offence could be taken by foreign powers, and such restrictions provided a challenge to the development of satire. By effectively banning the presentation of a real monarchy, political figures and any sense of sex (as opposed to idealised romance) the British musicals were inevitably behind the times when compared with the American ones whose censorship in London was more limited through a lack of understanding (as with *Wish You Were Here*) or a bending of rules.[7] American writers for the musical stage were more free to represent contemporary life than British counter-parts who existed in a long-established culture of compliance in which rules of censorship were subconsciously learned or actively considered at an early stage of writing. The play, rather than the musical, was generally the battle ground for contentious matters. It was only after the challenges to the Lord Chamberlain through straight theatre in the second half of the 1950s that the British musical began to escape this self-censorship, and with *Expresso Bongo* (discussed below) jumped forward decades in a single show.

What was perceived as a strike back at the American repertory began in 1954 with *The Boy Friend* (Sandy Wilson, b. 1924) and *Salad Days* (music by Julian Slade, b.1930; book and lyrics by Slade and Dorothy Reynolds). Both musicals were conceived as small-scale works for the specific companies of the Players' Theatre and the Bristol Old Vic respectively. In their different ways they present a particular sense of archetypal Britishness. In the case of *The Boy Friend*, although primarily a tribute to musical comedies of the 1920s, finishing schools, debutantes, aristocrats in disguise all played to notions of class, particularly upper-class, behaviour. *Salad Days* drew on the rarefied idyll of a Cambridge college, the select world of undergraduates, and family connections that extended to Whitehall. Both shows are also sexless, although sexuality through the codified language of a gay subculture casts a subtle shade. While *Wish You Were Here* was overtly displaying a cast of mostly sexually rampant semi-clad youths, the British response was to summarise romantic relations with a chaste kiss or two. One of the most well-known songs in *Salad Days* declares that 'We Said We Wouldn't Look Back', yet it is gently ironic in that the reminder not to be nostalgic prompts in the lyrics exactly that which it aspires to eschew. This duality of view, the present as interpreted through the past, is a common strand in British musicals, and *Salad Days* and *The Boy Friend* did look back in both musical and dramatic ways. *Salad Days* was conceived as an entertaining, ephemeral diversion, at the heart of which is a nostalgic innocence conjuring up an affectionate cartoon of certain English stereotypes. Whereas the passion of *West Side Story* invokes death, the 'romance' of *Salad Days* remains chaste. The lyrics of *Salad Days* are equally one-dimensional while its music is inoffensive, with diatonic (often pentatonic) melodies, simple harmony and the most straightforward of verse–refrain structures.

The Boy Friend was revised and extended from an original one-act ver-sion and eventually entered a mainstream West End theatre at Wyndhams in January 1954, running there for a month over five years; *Salad Days* went into the Vaudeville in August of 1954 and stayed there until 1960. Consequently, for the second half of the 1950s, the most enduring image of the British musical was of something with the parochial virtues of the village hall in *Salad Days* or the over-refined, nostalgic atmosphere of a fictitious and glamorised 1920s in *The Boy Friend*. For an American audience on Broadway in the mid-1950s – or, for that matter, all through the USA by virtue of extensive touring – *The Boy Friend* represented the only contact with contemporary British musical theatre, so reinforced the perception of a dated and retrospective British style. Nearly five years after *Salad Days* had opened at the Vaudeville theatre Jerome Robbins sat in foggy Manchester for the out-of-town tryouts of the first British production of *West Side Story*. An interviewer told him the plot of London's longest-running musical and quoted a few of its lyrics. After a short silence Robbins's response was a stunned 'You're kidding!'. How could you explain to one of the creators of such a socially aware show as *West Side Story* that its main London British rival, seen by some five million people by then, concerned a magic piano that made people dance? Yet *The Boy Friend* and *Salad Days* are about all that remains active of the British musical theatre repertory of the 1950s. Their continuing popularity is partly accounted for by their dramatic lightness, adaptability for performance and inoffensive natures, making them safe for school productions and amateurs. Both have received very occasional professional revivals, but only *The Boy Friend* has achieved an international dimension to its fame.

That *The Boy Friend* has been taken to be a leading example of the British musical in the 1950s is, however, in one sense particularly apt. The music of the show is derivative, using – albeit most skilfully – older styles. This approach is a constant one in British musical theatre. Novello consciously borrowed from a range of sources including classical music, Viennese operetta and certain characteristics of Richard Rodgers. Vivian Ellis's later works adopted period styles appropriate to their dramatic settings, while Coward relied strongly on Victorian parlour music and music-hall styles throughout his works. There was no specific sound that characterised the West End. The search for that distinctive voice brought about the chameleon-like shifts of Coward and the last change of direction (or return to his musical youth in one sense) for Novello.

Despite the impression given by the longest-running British musicals, the second half of the 1950s was a lively one for British theatre as a whole. John Osborne's play *Look Back in Anger* (1956) has become a symbol for the beginning of a move towards greater realism in theatre, although subject to some of the same over-stressed importance that *Oklahoma!* has received. The inoffensive styles of Slade and Wilson in their first big successes contrasted with the increasingly serious intent of other contemporary theatre works, especially those of the more politically driven theatre as characterised by Joan Littlewood's theatre company at Stratford East whose demotic show of 1959 (note that *Salad Days* ran until 1960), *Fings Ain't Wot They Used T'Be*, contrasted East End working class complete with resident prostitute with *Salad Days*'s middle-class 'niceness'. Yet for all the supposed realism of *Fings Ain't Wot They Used T'Be*, it shared with the Slade and Wilson shows a common naivety towards characters (as with the camp interior designer) and a certain predictability in the music. *Fings* extended the reputation of the up-and-coming songwriter Lionel Bart (1930–99) and only shortly preceded his international success *Oliver!* in 1960. Julian Slade followed up *Salad Days* with another escapist work, *Free as Air* (1957), but the conditions that had made inconsequential escapism a surprise hit in 1954 were sufficient only to sustain an existing reputation, not to support a new one. Wilson's attempt to adapt the novellas of Ronald Firbank as *Valmouth* (1959) became a cult success, although the baroque excesses of Firbank's characters proved too strange for a wider audience.

A further contemporary antidote to any British nostalgia was provided in *Grab Me a Gondola* (1956, with music by James Gilbert), whose central character was based on the British 'sex-bomb' Diana Dors. More significantly, David Heneker and Monty Norman's *Expresso Bongo* (1958) laid into the world of the pop singer and teenage heart-throb, bringing contemporary pop styles into the theatre along with the first electric guitar in a West End pit orchestra. (Amplified acoustic guitars had been in use at least since 1950.) *Expresso Bongo* is remarkable for the cynicism of its characterisations, which include the pelvis-thrusting singer Bongo Herbert, 'Me' who is a crooked agent ripping off Bongo's strictly limited talent and a predatory older actress keen to boost her own flagging career through some fame by association. One number proclaims that 'There's nothing wrong with British youth today' while comprehensively listing all the problems created in the world (most notably the atom bomb) caused by their own parents. It was compared to *Pal Joey* in the unpleasant range of its characters and hailed as the show in which the British musical grew up. The film version (1959) had Cliff Richard in the role of the pop idol, but the plot and style were so diluted as to undermine the thrust of the whole show, again depriving the future of a suitable advocate for an innovative show. The Lord Chamberlain's office worked overtime to tease out every innuendo it could from the book and lyrics, but ultimately failed to dilute the central message. The sexual puns in *Pal Joey* had not been censored for the West End in 1954 (although the 'Den of Iniquity' scene was cut when Princess Margaret visited a performance), but four years later *Expresso Bongo* had to fight over many lines. An air of deference to the Lord Chamberlain was fast being replaced by a cheeky rebellion, such that the alternative suggested by the authors to the censored line 'Go and stuff herself' was 'Go and screw herself'. They ended up with 'Get lost', which was not exactly at the hard edge of realism.

Expresso Bongo opened in the West End in the same year as *My Fair Lady*. It did not run as long and it has hardly been seen since, but its gritty cynicism, contemporary setting and pop score gained it many fans. It was voted Best British Musical of the Year in a *Variety* annual survey of shows on the London stage, with a ballot result far ahead of *My Fair Lady*, and was referred to in general as 'the other musical' to distinguish it from Lerner and Loewe's work. A London view of the musical in 1958 reverses the usual historical assumption in that the new American success was a costume and period work whereas the new British success was contemporary in its characters, setting, plot, language and music.

Conclusion

World War II interrupted the development of British musical theatre and led to a post-war dichotomy between the need to take up again and develop the interrupted past as an assertion of continuity and the need to embrace change in a world that could not be the same again. In musical theatre the British writers understandably tended to address the former need, while the imported American shows addressed for a British audience the latter. The focus of America was on America, the focus of Britain was on Britain. Not surprisingly the traffic in shows across the Atlantic was almost exclusively one-way as the British works had a social and political dimension alongside a general national mood that was not interesting or even comprehensible to a Broadway audience. Furthermore, the different aspirations of home-grown and imported West End shows were judged by the same criteria although fulfilling different functions, and the consequence of this approach towards their contemporary and subsequent interpretation and comparison has been seen in a reinforcement of an American-led musical theatre canon in Britain. In 1956 Vivian Ellis was moved to head an article for *Plays and Players* 'Give Us a Chance', which was 'an eloquent plea for the British composer, who is generally denied all the opportunities open to his American rival'.[8] In addition, the repertory has remained inaccessible owing to a lack of quality films of British stage shows and to a more limited representation on record than American ones; subsequent transfers from 78 to LP or more recently to CD have been negligible. This lack of exposure has prevented the development of an easy familiarity with some of the best works, and the resulting lack of opportunity to learn the canon has in turn reinforced its obscurity.

The heritage of the period still persists, partly through a distinctive British characteristic in musicals of retrospection. Constant reference to the past is found through plots, but also often through the remnants of musical hall and revue styles. The famous comic songs of Coward are from a music-hall tradition from the start of the century and subject to very little stylistic change throughout his life; David Heneker drew on music-hall sing-along styles in 'Flash-Bang-Wallop' (*Half a Sixpence*) as did Lionel Bart in 'Oom Pah Pah' (*Oliver!*) and the title song of *Fings Ain't Wot They Used T'Be*, itself indicative to some of a British state of mind. Coward's tendency towards allusion and clever lyrics often comes to the fore in British musicals, most directly in the works of Sandy Wilson who has followed this epigrammatic approach in lyrics at least. The style of Novello has been continued by Andrew Lloyd Webber, whose works exhibit the same predilections, with the large scale and the visual as strong components. Musically they have much in common in adaptable musical styles that reference classical elements and a tendency to go for the 'big tune' – 'Waltz of My Heart', 'Rose of England', 'Someday My Heart Will Awake' for Novello and 'Memory' or 'Music of the Night' for Lloyd Webber.

Knowledge of the past is important to the understanding of both the content and the appeal of the British musical mid-century, and the reassertion of its individuality as distinct from Broadway is a revealing consequence of this. Although 'we said wouldn't look back', in the case of this particular repertory, maybe we should.

7 The coming of the musical play: Rodgers and Hammerstein

ANN SEARS

Broadway was an exciting place to be in the 1920s, as many new voices were heard in American musical theatre. One important voice was that of jazz; other new voices included the composers George Gershwin, Vincent Youmans, Arthur Schwartz, Ray Henderson and, of course, the team of Richard Rodgers and Lorenz Hart. Rodgers (1902–79) and Hart (1895–1943) began their twenty-five-year collaboration during college productions at Columbia University. Their professional productions began with *Poor Little Ritz Girl* in 1920, and they attracted considerable critical and popular attention with their hit song 'Manhattan' in *The Garrick Gaieties* in 1925. By the end of the 1920s, several more of their shows had appeared on Broadway: *Dearest Enemy* (1925); *The Girl Friend*, a second *The Garrick Gaieties*, *Peggy-Ann* and *Betsy* (1926); *A Connecticut Yankee* (1927); *She's My Baby*, *Present Arms* and the disastrous failure *Chee-Chee* (1928); and *Heads Up!* (1929). By the end of the decade Rodgers and Hart counted among the most popular songwriters in America, but after the start of the Depression and with the arrival of sound in motion pictures, they turned to the promising opportunities of writing film scores in Hollywood.

Hollywood proved to be financially rewarding, and Rodgers and Hart created some of their most enduring songs for films produced in the early to mid-1930s, such as 'Isn't It Romantic', 'You Are Too Beautiful', and 'Easy to Remember'. However, the waiting game of writing a few songs for a film over which they had little artistic control was not for this energetic pair. They returned to Broadway in 1935 with *Jumbo*, an extravaganza staged by Billy Rose. The 233 performances of *Jumbo* began a five-year series of hit shows for Rodgers and Hart, and at one point they had three shows running simultaneously.[1] Most of these shows from the late 1930s were very successful and later appeared in film versions, including, for example, *On Your Toes* (1936), *Babes in Arms* (1937), *The Boys from Syracuse* (1938) and *Pal Joey* (1940). When their masterpiece *Pal Joey* appeared, Rodgers and Hart were at the peak of their creative partnership. The play's seamy plot and characters provoked much criticism, but by the time of its revival in 1952, *Pal Joey* was acknowledged as the most important work produced by Rodgers and Hart. The most integrated of all their musicals, *Pal Joey* is probably the only one of their shows that can be easily revived today.

By the 1940s Hart's lifelong battle with alcoholism and related problems had made meeting theatre deadlines extremely stressful. When the Theatre Guild directors Theresa Helburn and Lawrence Langner approached Rodgers about transforming Lynn Riggs's play *Green Grow the Lilacs* into a musical, the situation came to a head. Hart did not believe the play could be adapted successfully, and he refused to work on the project, even though Rodgers confronted him with the possibility of finding another lyricist. Rodgers had already discreetly spoken to the man he thought might replace Hart – Oscar Hammerstein II.

Hammerstein (1895–1960) came from a family with theatrical traditions in its bones. His grandfather Oscar Hammerstein I founded the Manhattan Opera Company in 1906, giving the American premieres of several important operas and featuring many famous singers. In 1910 he sold his interests in the Manhattan to the Metropolitan Opera.[2] Oscar I's sons William and Arthur were also successful producers and theatre managers. Although William's son Oscar II had promised his father that he would never become involved in show business, like Rodgers and Hart, he was drawn to amateur productions while at Columbia University; during law school at Columbia, he began working for his Uncle Arthur. Eventually he became a writer, collaborating with his mentor Otto Harbach on works by Vincent Youmans (*Wildflower*, 1923), Rudolf Friml (*Rose-Marie*, 1924), Sigmund Romberg (*The Desert Song*, 1926, and *The New Moon*, 1928), and most importantly, Jerome Kern (*Sunny*, 1925). In 1927, Kern and Hammerstein wrote *Show Boat*, a groundbreaking show often considered to be the 'prototype for the "musical play" – the singularly American type of operetta which was popularized by Hammerstein and Richard Rodgers'.[3] Hammerstein's great success with *Show Boat* was followed by two other successful shows with Kern, *Sweet Adeline* (1929) and *Music in the Air* (1932). Like many others, Hammerstein was drawn to Hollywood during the 1930s, contributing screenplay or lyrics to ten films.

However, for most of the 1930s Hammerstein's career was an odd patchwork of frustration and gratification. His stage works during the early 1930s had very short runs. *The Gang's All Here* (with Louis E. Gensler) opened to very mixed reviews and closed after only 23 performances. *East Wind* (with Romberg) also closed after 23 performances, and *Free for All* (with Richard A. Whiting) after a dismal 15. Two productions enjoyed respectable runs (*Ball at the Savoy*, London, 1933, 148 performances; and *May Wine*, with Romberg, 1935, 213 performances), and the 1936 film version of

Show Boat, for which Hammerstein wrote the screenplay and some new songs, was an instant critical and popular success; but several later stage shows were disappointments (including *Very Warm for May* with Kern, 1939, 59 performances). The early 1940s were likewise uneven. Although Hammerstein had written some of his most memorable lyrics in the years following *Show Boat* ('I've Told Every Little Star' from *Music in the Air*; 'When I Grow Too Old to Dream' from *The Night Is Young*; or 'All the Things You Are' from *Very Warm for May*), it seemed to most of the musical theatre world, and perhaps to Hammerstein himself, that his best work was behind him.

Having no specific commitments to either Hollywood or Broadway, Hammerstein turned to a project he had first contemplated in 1934 after hearing a concert performance of Bizet's opera *Carmen* at the Hollywood Bowl. He had tried to interest MGM in a film version of an opera, but they never followed through on the idea. Nonetheless, in 1942, listening to a recording of *Carmen* and with his career at a watershed point, Hammerstein began the transformation of Bizet's nineteenth-century Spanish gypsies into African Americans from the American South during World War II. By July 1942, he had completed the entire libretto of *Carmen Jones*. Condensing the original four-act libretto into two acts and moving the location from a cigarette factory in Seville, Spain, to a parachute factory near a southern town, Hammerstein set his new lyrics to the original music of the opera. He eliminated the recitatives from the opera, restoring Bizet's original balance of spoken dialogue and arias, and as closely as possible kept to the original order of the music.

Opening only a few months after *Oklahoma!*, *Carmen Jones* (502 performances) further signalled the return of the Oscar Hammerstein who had written works such as *The Desert Song*, *Show Boat* and *The New Moon*. The lyrics captured both the opera's tempestuous love story and the unique character of African-American culture. Critics noted how well Hammerstein had matched his words to Bizet's music and story. *Variety* stated that 'Hammerstein is now at the peak of his career'.[4] With such accolades pouring in and two successful Broadway runs launched, Hammerstein's career was reborn. Thus, both Rodgers and Hammerstein brought many years of theatrical experience to their new collaboration, each was intent on having the plot, music and lyrics closely knit together to form a coherent whole, and each was strongly influenced by the operetta tradition. As collaborators, Rodgers and Hammerstein reversed the writing process Rodgers had used with Hart. Rodgers usually wrote music first to which Hart then set lyrics. Now, however, after lengthy discussions about the play, the characters, and the function and placement of the songs, Hammerstein would carefully craft his lyrics, then turn them over to Rodgers, who in turn composed the music. Hammerstein had learned from the unhurried, concentrated writing of *Carmen Jones* that he did his best work when he took plenty of time to polish it. Having accommodated Hart for many years, Rodgers found the reliable, meticulous Hammerstein a comfortable partner.

The result of their initial efforts together was *Oklahoma!*, which exploded on Broadway in 1943 with unprecedented critical and popular acclaim that would have been unimaginable in previous decades. Even Hammerstein was surprised, having written to his son William that while 'here is the nearest approach to *Show Boat* that the theatre has attained' and 'it is comparable in quality', he didn't think that 'it has as sound a story or that it will be as great a success'.[5] Although the opening night performance in New York was not sold out, by the next day long lines waited at the box office. *Oklahoma!* ran for 2,243 performances on Broadway and toured for fifty-one weeks. A national company toured for ten years through over 150 cities, and the international companies included a USO unit in the Pacific that entertained American troops. The London production at the Drury Lane Theatre was the longest run in the history of that theatre. The show won a special Pulitzer Prize for Drama in 1944. The film version was made in 1955, winning two Oscars: Best Scoring of a Musical Film and Best Sound Recording.[6]

As he wrote the book and lyrics for *Oklahoma!*, Hammerstein aimed to keep the character of the original play, even quoting Lynn Riggs's opening paragraph:

> It is a radiant summer morning several years ago, the kind of morning which, enveloping the shapes of earth – men, cattle in a meadow, blades of the young corn, streams – makes them seem to exist now for the first time, their images giving off a golden emanation that is partly true and partly a trick of the imagination, focusing to keep alive a loveliness that may pass away.[7]

In the stage play, the story takes place in the Indian Territory of Oklahoma around 1900. Laurey, a young, innocent girl, lives on a farm with her widowed Aunt Eller. She falls in love with Curly, a cowboy. They are shy with each other, and to provoke Curly, Laurey agrees to attend a box social with Aunt Eller's farmhand, Jeeter Fry, whom she fears. At the social, Jeeter and Laurey argue, and Jeeter leaves. Soon after Laurey and Curly are married. During the shivaree on their wedding night, Jeeter appears and dies after falling on his own knife while fighting with Curly. Aunt Eller convinces the authorities to let Curly spend one night with Laurey before he is sent to jail.[8] Traditional folk songs were sung throughout the play.

Hammerstein used much of the original play and kept Riggs's arrangement of two acts, each with three scenes. However, he changed the second act considerably, compressing it and writing a new ending in which Jud (formerly Jeeter) Fry's death from his own knife while fighting with Curly is declared self-defence. Laurey and Curly can leave on their honeymoon. Additionally, Hammerstein created a secondary, comic love triangle by re-defining Ado Annie and inventing her suitors, neither of whom is in Riggs's play. The shy, quiet Ado Annie of the original becomes a brash, irrepressible girl who cannot resist men. The cowboy Will Parker and the Persian ped-dler Ali Hakim both attempt to woo her. Hammerstein expands the tra-ditional pairs of lovers, observed so frequently in opera, to pairs of love triangles.

As Rodgers and Hammerstein translated the play to a musical setting, they indeed took the musical in a new direction. While Broadway composers of the day might typically have placed an ensemble number early in the show, preferably with a bevy of beautiful girls singing and dancing, *Oklahoma!* opens with Aunt Eller alone on stage churning butter. The leading man, Curly, begins singing 'Oh, What a Beautiful Mornin'' off-stage and without accompaniment. The western setting dictated costumes that were rather homespun compared to the glittering revues and witty comedies of previous eras. No one believed that Rodgers and Hammerstein could sell a death in the second act, not even the accidental death of so disagreeable a character as Jud Fry. Rodgers and Hammerstein themselves joked about why the show could flop: 'the chorus girls didn't appear until the curtain had been up for forty minutes; the first act had no plot except a girl deciding which young man to go to a dance with; there were virtually no important new numbers in the second act; and so on'.[9] There were further examples of a new approach: the combination of both ballet and vernacular American dance used as a narrative element; long musical scenes and thoughtful use of song reprises; a plot about ordinary people and their ordinary, yet deeply dramatic lives; and the unusual way the romantic couple interact and fall in love. It all worked together to form a show that, like *Show Boat*, became a milestone, so that later historians writing about important moments in twentieth-century musical theatre would begin to identify eras according to their relationship to *Oklahoma!*, for example 'Act I: Before Rodgers and Hammerstein' and 'Act II: The Broadway Musical After *Oklahoma!*'[10]

Hammerstein's decision to follow the play's original arrangement of three scenes that developed character followed by three scenes more centred around the plot enabled him to create characters of such depth that the audience empathised with them at once. By the end of Act I Aunt Eller is established as a wise woman and earth mother. Laurey has revealed both her love for Curly and her fear of Jud Fry. Ado Annie is ripe for Will Parker's ultimatum about marriage, and the peddler Ali Hakim is bound to be caught by some enterprising young woman. Jud Fry is obviously the villain, but touchingly so, because we know from 'Lonely Room' and 'Pore Jud Is Daid' just how miserable he is. All the action of Act II follows from the emotions and events set up in Act I: Laurey and Ado Annie making choices about their love relationships, the resolution of conflicts between their men, the sad end of the villain, and the community moving towards statehood.

The flow of the dramatic action is helped along by the way Rodgers and Hammerstein use song reprises. For example, the two renditions of 'The Surrey with the Fringe on Top' in scene I are the first steps in the relationship between Laurey and Curly. As Curly begins to describe the beautiful surrey in which he will take Laurey to the dance that night, he is really telling her how much he wants to spend a romantic evening with her. Following the song, he discovers that she has agreed to attend the dance with Jud Fry. She realises that the wonderful surrey is not just Curly's imagination; rather, he has really rented it to drive her to the dance. The reprise of 'The Surrey with the Fringe on Top' is Curly's opportunity to tell her what she has missed, and it prompts her to reconsider her feelings for him. The last song in Act I, scene I, 'People Will Say We're in Love', functions similarly; in the rendition that ends Act I, scene I, an interaction is begun that must be completed later. After the anxiety set up by 'The Surrey with the Fringe on Top', 'People Will Say We're in Love' lets us see the first blossoming of serious romantic love between Laurey and Curly. Not until Act II, scene II do we hear the reprise of 'People Will Say We're in Love' and know that Laurey and Curly have sorted out their differences and agreed to marry, releasing the tension held from Act I, scene I. The resulting organic unfolding of the plot gives *Oklahoma!* a dramatic unity and momentum that had hardly been present in American musical theatre before 1943, and thus announces the arrival of the 'musical play'.

Although the self-effacing Hammerstein claimed that his lyrics were a result of a predilection for 'a more primitive type of lyric',[11] in fact, his fresh, romantic approach to poetry matched the tone of *Oklahoma!*'s story and frontier location perfectly. The repetition of lines in 'Oh, What a Beautiful Mornin'' captured the hushed, suspended serenity of morning in the country before the world was permeated by traffic noise. Country life was also echoed in the patterns of 'The Surrey with the Fringe on Top', where the first two lines are composed of a series of one-syllable words followed by two-syllable words at the end of the line, reminiscent of the true-to-life sounds of clip-clopping horses' hooves and the chicken yard, still familiar to many people in the 1940s. The patterns of his judicious use of western dialect add to the depth of characterisation. Special characters and tender moments are delineated by leaving off the dialect, for example, in Laurey's songs and in Curly's songs about his relationship with Laurey. When Curly sings with or about other characters, such as about Jud Fry in 'Pore Jud Is Daid', the dialect reappears. Hammerstein also disproved critics who thought he could only write sweet, sentimental, inspirational lyrics. Precisely matching his lyrics to Jud Fry's interior landscape he created a dark, introspective picture of *Oklahoma!*'s most sinister character, who describes his bleak world in the song 'Lonely Room'.

The music Rodgers wrote for *Oklahoma!* matched and amplified the brilliant characterisations of Hammerstein's lyrics. Curly's repeated opening lines ('There's a bright golden haze on the meadow' and 'Oh, what a beautiful mornin', Oh, what a beautiful day') are paralleled by repeated musical phrases. The repeated notes on 'looks like it's climbin' clear up to the sky' along with the other repetitions reinforce the environment of the Oklahoma territory: wide-open spaces, long days and repetitive tasks, and the deliberate unfolding of a daily life marked by occasional festivities. The hesitant steps Laurey and Curly take towards each other are mirrored in their songs, 'The Surrey with the Fringe on Top' and the 'almost love song' (also a 'list song'), 'People Will Say We're in Love'. Compelling characterisations and music are also given to the minor characters. For example, Will Parker's 'Kansas City' simultaneously introduces Will Parker and the context of the show to the audience. Ado Annie is given some of the most interesting characterisation in the show through her song 'I Cain't Say No', which leaves the audience with a crystal-clear understanding of what motivates her. 'Lonely Room' particularly shows Rodgers's ability to describe character through music. The dissonant intervals of a second that murmur through much of the accompaniment to the song also begin and end the vocal part, mirroring the pain within his psyche and his dysfunctional relationship with the world around him.

The dances in *Oklahoma!* were choreographed by Agnes de Mille, fresh from her triumphs of choreographing and dancing in Copland's ballet *Rodeo* with the Ballet Russe de Monte Carlo in 1942. The choice of de Mille seemed natural in view of the western theme and set of *Rodeo*. Her mixture of vernacular American dance and ballet turned out to be just right for *Oklahoma!*, continuing the character illustration and plot propulsion already inherent in the book, lyrics, and music. Will Parker's dance following 'Kansas City' uses a new social dance, the two-step, tap dancing with references to ragtime, and occasional square dance steps. It sums up the potpourri of popular culture at that time, neatly paralleling the dialect in which Will both speaks and sings. For the 'Dream Ballet' at the end of the first act, de Mille used ballet, flavoured with turn-of-the-century costumes, to reveal Laurey's psychological state and her fear of Jud Fry. While all kinds of dance had been incorporated in the shows of earlier eras, the profound connection of the 'Dream Ballet' to the plot of *Oklahoma!* revolutionised the use of dance in musical theatre. As her fellow choreographer Jerome Robbins said about the use of ballet to tell a story, 'Agnes made it stick'.[12]

There were many obvious innovations in *Oklahoma!* – the importance of the story; songs growing seamlessly out of the plot and characters; the complexity of the strong women characters; the use of lengthy musical scenes; the striking simplicity of the opening; the 'almost love song'; the narrative use of multiple dance styles; and the forthright approach to moral and social issues. Nearly all these elements had appeared to some extent in the work of Rodgers and Hart, who had always considered the integration of story and music a crucial factor in a successful show. For example, Rodgers and Hart had incorporated dance significantly in their shows, showcasing George Balanchine's ballets. As Hammerstein had in 'People Will Say We're in Love', Lorenz Hart often approached love song lyrics obliquely, sometimes even speaking of love more as a disease than an emotional state ('This can't be love because I feel so well'). Some aspects of the Rodgers and Hammerstein collaboration had been important in Hammerstein's earlier work as well. Hammerstein had tried the western theme in *Rainbow* (1928), and moved towards longer musical scenes in *Show Boat* with Kern. However, with Rodgers and Hammerstein these ideas coalesced, and their innovations would become the recipe for a series of Rodgers and Hammerstein hits. Part of *Oklahoma!*'s immediate success, along with the freshness and coherence of the production itself, was its appearance at the mid-point of World War II, a crucial time in the nation's history. In the context of a devastating world war, the outcome of which appeared far from certain, *Oklahoma!*'s story transmitted a powerful message about the American spirit to its audiences. After Hitler's advance through Europe, the shock of Pearl Harbor, and two brutal years of war, *Oklahoma!*'s celebration of the indomitable pioneer spirit was just what Americans needed to hear. The book, lyrics, costumes and music (especially 'Oklahoma', the 'song about the land' that closes the show) reflected currents in American art, music, and popular culture that looked at American life past and present through a haze of romanticism and nostalgia.

Shortly after *Oklahoma!* was launched, Hammerstein wrote the screenplay and lyrics for Twentieth Century-Fox's remake of *State Fair,* returning to the nostalgia of rural America. Rodgers and Hammerstein wrote two of their most memorable songs for the film, 'It's a Grand Night for Singing' and 'It Might as Well Be Spring', which won the Academy Award for Best Song that year. These songs and the title song continued the Rodgers and Hammerstein strategy of using songs to move the plot and explicate character. As the film opens, the title song 'State Fair' functions as an exposition of the story, carrying the action as the song is handed from one character to another, with each giving his or her description of the chief delights of attending the fair. 'It's a Grand Night for Singing' also moves the plot along as the characters hand this song back and forth while they move through the fair. The soliloquy 'It Might as Well Be Spring' provides the most personal, intimate observation of any character in this film, as we see a young girl learning about love between men and women. The making of *State Fair* was a better experience than most of either Rodgers's or Hammerstein's early Hollywood work, and it may have influenced them later to consider film adaptations of their stage productions.

Knowing that it would be difficult to surpass or even equal the triumph of *Oklahoma!*, Rodgers and Hammerstein carefully weighed possibilities for a new show. When the Theatre Guild suggested adapting Ferenc Molnár's play *Liliom*, they refused. After all, 'common knowledge' said that Molnár had refused even Puccini permission for an opera setting.[13] Furthermore, they thought that the Hungarian setting and the bitterness of the second act presented insoluble difficulties. The first challenge was met by having Molnár see *Oklahoma!* for himself, after which he happily gave permission for a musical setting. The other obstacle was overcome by moving the play to the coast of Maine in 1873, turning the leading lady into a wife rather than a mistress, and finding a more acceptable approach to the ending. Inspired by the carnival theme of *Liliom*, they called the new show *Carousel*.

The musical version begins without the customary overture; rather Rodgers settled on a 'Prologue (The Carousel Waltz)' that is an integral part of Act I. As the waltz plays (its orchestration reminiscent of genuine carnival music), a pantomime unfolds in which the two most important characters are introduced. The body of the play explores the relationship between Billy and Julie, who fall in love, marry and are expecting a child, and the moral choices they make. Julie's friend Carrie marries Mr Snow, providing a stable family story against which Billy and Julie's tragedy is counterposed. Having been fired from the carnival by Mrs Mullin, Billy is unable to support his family. He and his friend Jigger contemplate a robbery, during which Billy is killed. The celestial Starkeeper allows him to return to earth for one day, during which he tells Julie he loved her and encourages his daughter Louise to believe in herself, because she is not alone.

Many ingredients from the smash hit *Oklahoma!* reappeared in *Carousel*, including the use of long musical scenes and reprises. Dance was still an important element, with ensemble numbers for the whole cast and a ballet introducing Billy and Julie's troubled child, Louise. The 'almost love song' ('If I Loved You') appeared in an even more integrated way, emerging seamlessly from the dialogue. Moral choices were more realistically addressed, as conflicted leading man Billy Bigelow struggled with issues such as work and responsibility, domestic abuse, and whether to turn to a life of crime. Julie and Carrie joined Aunt Eller, Laurey and Ado Annie in the Rodgers and Hammerstein pantheon of strong, individualistic women characters. Rodgers and Hammerstein also added an element that would appear in all their subsequent shows: important child characters and issues concerning children.

Musically, the Rodgers and Hammerstein approach became even more organic. Many critics have noticed that 'The Carousel Waltz' of the 'Prologue' provides much of the musical material for the songs in the show.[14] Borrowing from melodrama, *Carousel*'s characters frequently speak over music, a technique that Hammerstein previously used in *Rose-Marie*, *Show Boat* and *The New Moon*. The greater complexity of all the characters, whose stories often involve conflict and resolution within themselves, is reflected in their music, particularly in Billy Bigelow's 'Soliloquy', an episodic song that moves far away from the traditional AABA form of the typical Broadway song and through several keys, and the reprise of 'If I Loved You' in Act II, in which Billy Bigelow finally allows himself to admit his love for Julie.

Like *Oklahoma!*, *Carousel* was produced by the Theatre Guild and supervised by Theresa Helburn and Lawrence Langner. The superb integration of all the show's elements was carefully overseen by a production team almost transplanted from *Oklahoma!*, headed by director Rouben Mamoulian. Agnes de Mille again choreographed the dances, and Miles White designed the costumes. Although some critics found the second act too slow and the ending peculiar, the opening reviews were generally enthusiastic. A few reviewers liked *Carousel* even more than *Oklahoma!* Anticipating Richard Rodgers's own opinion, Robert Garland wrote that 'when somebody writes a better musical play than "Carousel", written by Richard Rodgers and Oscar Hammerstein, Richard Rodgers and Oscar Hammerstein will have to write it'. Later Rodgers admitted that *Carousel* was his favourite of all his musicals, saying: 'Oscar never wrote more meaningful or more moving lyrics, and to me, my score is more satisfying than any I've ever written. But it's not just the songs: it's the whole play. Beautifully written, tender without being mawkish, it affects me deeply every time I see it performed.'[15] Certainly Rodgers and Hammerstein reached a more profound level of integration and dramatic sensitivity in *Carousel*.

Following *Carousel*, Rodgers and Hammerstein began a pattern of producing other work in between writing and producing their own. In 1946 they produced *Annie Get Your Gun* with a score by Irving Berlin, which went on to have successful runs in New York and London, and throughout Europe. By 1946 Hammerstein had running simultaneously on Broadway a string of hits that included *Oklahoma!*, *Carousel*, *The Desert Song* (with *Carmen Jones* to follow), *Show Boat* and two shows that he and Rodgers co-produced, *I Remember Mama* and *Annie Get Your Gun*. Rodgers and Hammerstein had become two of the most influential men in American musical theatre, and with theatre receipts and royalties flowing in steadily, two of the most affluent.

Their next show, *Allegro* (1947), is perhaps Rodgers and Hammerstein's most experimental work, but its 315-performance run could not compare to their first two outings. Based on the life story of a doctor from birth to the age of thirty-five, the show illustrates stages of his life through a 'Greek chorus', various lighting effects, lantern slides and rear-screen projections, short scenes, dances and songs. The idealistic doctor, Joe Taylor, marries a hometown girl, becomes corrupted by money and power, and loses his healing connection to his patients. Eventually his friend Charlie and Emily, a nurse who loves Joe, help him face his life and leave his unfaithful wife. They return to their hometown and their ideals of medicine. There is much speculation about the so-called 'failure' of *Allegro*. It was the first show Rodgers and Hammerstein created from scratch, whereas their previous two successful productions were based on strong literary sources. Agnes de Mille, who directed, found the play uneven. She thought the first act so beautiful that she cried when she first read it, but she felt that the second act, which Hammerstein wrote under time pressure, did not match the first act, either in quality of lyrics or in continuity of story. *Allegro* marked de Mille's directorial debut, and she struggled to direct, choreograph and manage the complicated, multi-level sets plus a large cast of forty-one principals and almost a hundred dancers and chorus singers. After a frantic rehearsal period and many revisions, *Allegro* opened to mixed reviews. Its forty-week run and thirty-one-week tour might have been a success had the production not been so expensive. However, the artistic failure distressed Rodgers and Hammerstein more than the financial loss. While some praised the show as 'unconventional' and 'a musical play without any of the conventions of form', Hammerstein knew that he had not written the story he really wanted to convey.[16] The commentary of the 'Greek chorus' seemed too moralistic, and it sapped the vitality of the characters and the action. The attempt to make characters less important while emphasising the other elements of the show – dancers, the chorus, the abstract set, the lighting effects – was lost on most people. Some people thought that Rodgers and Hammerstein's styles did not match well enough in the innovative *Allegro*, which may have been the first concept musical, and that Rodgers's music was too conventional for the book and lyrics Hammerstein had written.[17] In any case, the failure of *Allegro* was a misfortune for the world of musical theatre, because Rodgers and Hammerstein never again ventured into so radical a project. The rest of their collaboration was devoted to 'refining the dramatic musical play until they took their particular brand of it as far as it could go'.[18] However, Hammerstein retained an affection for *Allegro*, and was rewriting the musical for television when he died.

Returning to the successful approach that had produced *Oklahoma!* and *Carousel* required finding the right literary property to adapt. When Joshua

Logan suggested James Michener's *Tales of the South Pacific*, both Rodgers and Hammerstein were enthusiastic. A series of short stories about World War II in the South Pacific, the book included many characters and episodes. Hammerstein settled on 'Fo Dolla', the story Logan had first mentioned, and combined it with 'Our Heroine'. The resulting play revolved around two couples: Liat, a young Tonkinese girl, and Lt Joe Cable, an American from an aristocratic Philadelphia family; and Nellie Forbush, a young nurse from Arkansas, and Emile de Becque, a middle-aged French planter. Each couple faces the obstacle of racial prejudice. Lt Cable cannot imagine taking Liat back to America, and Nellie hesitates to marry de Becque after learning of his children born to his late native wife. Cable tells Liat he cannot marry her and leaves on a reconnaissance mission, during which he is killed. De Becque returns from the same mission to discover that Nellie has transcended her learned racism and awaits him with the children. Since having two serious romantic couples was unusual, two important, high-energy characters provided comedy: Bloody Mary, a native trader and Liat's mother, and Luther Billis, an entrepreneurial enlisted man.

Early in the writing of *South Pacific*, Rodgers and Hammerstein engaged Ezio Pinza, a bass with the Metropolitan Opera, and Mary Martin, whom they had wanted but could not get for *Oklahoma!* Having two major stars in the show created tremendous publicity, and the show's entire tryout week in New Haven was sold out. The Boston tryout was also well received, leading one critic to call the show 'South Terrific, and then some!' With such enthusiastic advance press, the New York opening on 7 April 1949 was equally triumphant.[19] *South Pacific* went on to run for 1,925 performances in New York, winning nine Donaldson awards, eight Tonys, and the coveted Pulitzer Prize for Drama. Many of its songs became familiar to the general public. The original cast album sold over one million copies, and in 1957 a film version appeared, directed by Joshua Logan.

Rodgers and Hammerstein's stamp was on every aspect of the production. They created another pair of strong female characters: nurse Nellie Forbush, who proves her spirit by overcoming her prejudices, and the irascible, incorrigible Bloody Mary. The spotlight on child characters begun in *Carousel* continued with Emile de Becque's two children. Furthermore, the children open and close the show with their song 'Dites-moi', illustrating their pivotal importance in the plot. The old device of a show-within-a-show appeared as a variety show for the troops in *South Pacific*. The show contained several stellar examples of Rodgers and Hammerstein's extraordinary ability to suggest a locale or a setting, from the exotic flavour of the beautiful, mysterious island described in 'Bali Ha'i' to the rowdy, slightly shady world of 'Bloody Mary' and the soldiers' world of 'There Is Nothin' Like a Dame' and 'Honey Bun'.

The refinements of their evolving formula were apparent in the dramatic use of two romantic couples, and the character-tailored music that fitted the vocal and acting talents of the two stars so well. A new level of dramatic maturity was noticeable in the social commentary of 'You've Got to Be Carefully Taught'. *South Pacific* also ventured into more adult territory with the sexual relationship between Liat and Lt Cable, engineered by Bloody Mary with the hope that Cable will marry her daughter.

Their next show would be an adaptation of Margaret Landon's 1943 *Anna and the King of Siam*, about British widow Anna Leonowens and her stint in the 1860s as tutor to the children of King Mongkut of Siam. The show featured the brilliant actress Gertrude Lawrence, who was not a particularly accomplished or reliable singer, but who had a wonderfully magnetic stage presence. Again the Rodgers and Hammerstein formula would be extended and refined; and again the expansion of the recipe would create a hit show. *The King and I* enjoyed a 1,246-performance Broadway run, toured for eighteen months and ran for 926 performances in London. After capturing three Tonys and five Donaldson awards as a stage production, the 1956 film version won six Academy Awards.

The charm of the show was obvious from the beginning, often in a way predictable from their previous three big shows. The fascination of the exotic time and place was gloriously emphasised by opulent sets and costumes designed after authentic models. Rodgers incorporated enough pentatonic melodies and Thai percussion motifs to imply a genuinely Oriental environment. Three significant songs featured adorable children of various ages: 'Getting to Know You', 'I Whistle a Happy Tune' and the 'March of the Siamese Children'. Jerome Robbins's imaginative ballet, 'The Small House of Uncle Thomas', retold the story of Harriet Beecher Stowe's controversial novel *Uncle Tom's Cabin*, pinpointing several important social issues, such as slavery and gender inequality. Dance and the 'almost love song' combined in 'Shall We Dance?'. Strong women characters abounded in this show: Anna, Lady Thiang and Tuptim.

The real story of *The King and I* was the relationship between Mrs Anna and the King. Bit by bit through the show, the audience observes the gradual understanding established between these two strong-willed characters, reaching towards each other across an enormous cultural abyss. Despite their political and philosophical differences, they grow to love and depend on each other. Their love is never overtly expressed, though coming close in 'Shall We Dance', when they talk about relationships and connect physically in the polka. As they gaze at each other breathlessly after dancing, the audience knows that the love between them hovers on the brink of speech. The tension is broken, not by spoken words of affection, but by the announcement that Tuptim has been found by the police. Any further progression of their feelings is prevented by the King's death, and the 'almost love song' becomes part of a compelling 'almost love story'.

With a fourth huge hit show behind them, Rodgers and Hammerstein had established a nearly infallible relationship with the theatre-going public. Consequently their next two shows managed respectable runs (*Me and Juliet*, 1953, 358 performances; *Pipe Dream*, 1955, 246 performances), but were far from their finest critical successes or best financial windfalls. As with *Allegro*, *Me and Juliet* was an original story by Hammerstein, in this case springing from Rodgers's desire to do a show about life in the theatre. Despite George Abbott's experienced direction, Irene Sharaff's costumes, and Jo Meilziner's ingenious set, the public did not respond to the story. *Pipe Dream* fared still less well, even with **a** story by John Steinbeck and glamorous opera star Helen Traubel in the cast. Unfortunately, Steinbeck's story and characters were closer to the world of Rodgers and Hart's *Pal Joey* than to the usual Rodgers and Hammerstein recipe. The failure of the production to recreate the earthy atmosphere of Steinbeck's novel and Helen Traubel's unsuitability in the role of whorehouse madam led to the shortest run of a Rodgers and Hammerstein show.

Despite the disappointments of *Me and Juliet* and *Pipe Dream*, Rodgers and Hammerstein forged ahead into new enterprises in the early 1950s. Rodgers wrote the music for a thirteen-hour television documentary series, *Victory at Sea* (1952), which covered important naval battles of World War II. Still popular today, the documentary is available in video format. The film version of *Oklahoma!* released in 1953 was the first film version of one of their shows, and they gave it careful attention, producing it themselves. A close reworking of the stage numbers, except for the omission of 'It's a Scandal! It's an Outrage!' and 'Lonely Room', the film repaid the time and money that went into it, winning two Academy Awards and becoming a screen favourite. They also wrote a well-received version of *Cinderella* (1957) for television that featured a young Julie Andrews, and assisted with producing film versions of *Carousel* (1956) and *South Pacific* (1958). Their new show *Flower Drum Song* began a 600-performance run in March of 1958. Both films and *Flower Drum Song* won Gold Records for their respective cast recordings and soundtracks, and *South Pacific* won an Oscar for Best Sound Recording.

As the 1950s closed, Rodgers and Hammerstein began a new show based on the story of the von Trapp family and their escape from Nazism. Early in the show's preparations, Hammerstein became ill and was diagnosed with stomach cancer. Nonetheless, they were able to write one of their most memorable works. Perhaps the best-known of all their shows because of the immense popularity of the film version, *The Sound of Music* was the epitome of the Rodgers and Hammerstein musical play. The components

Plate 11   Shirley Jones as Maria with the children in the 1977 production of *The Sound of Music* at the Starlight Theater, Kansas City, Missouri

that had guaranteed the success of the first big shows appeared in force in *The Sound of Music*: tightly integrated book, lyrics, and music with significant dramatic use of song reprises; an atypical love story; important child characters; strong women (a whole abbey of them, along with Maria von Trapp!); narrative use of dance, for example the 'Ländler' during which Captain von Trapp and Maria fall in love; the trademark 'almost love song'; and a brilliant depiction of the story's environment through poetic, musical and design elements. Hammerstein wrote some of his simplest, most heartfelt lyrics.

With memories of World War II and the Nazis' rise to power still vivid and reinforced by the spread of communism in Europe, and well-publicised stories about attempted escapes from communist countries in the American press, audiences took the singing von Trapp family to their hearts and made the show a hit. The artistic acclaim for the show meant even more to Rodgers and Hammerstein. Though some critics found it 'sticky with sweetness and light', many others considered it 'the full ripening of these two extraordinary talents'. Six Tonys, a Gold Record and a Grammy for the cast album, a *Variety* Critic Poll Award for Best Score, and a National Catholic Theatre Conference

Award were indisputable evidence of the show's immediate success. A two-year American tour and a 2,385-performance London run were followed by the film version (1965) which carried away five Academy Awards, a Golden Globe, a Gold Record for the cast album and various other awards. Although Hammerstein did not live to know of the remarkable popularity of this show and its film version, in many ways it was a most appropriate capstone to his career and in particular his collaboration with Richard Rodgers. Often decried as overly sentimental, Hammerstein's story and lyrics encoded his own values and principles that he thought audiences found important and believable. Over the years, his continued insistence on writing what he found authentic led to his development as a writer of great maturity, and combined with Richard Rodgers's musical and theatrical genius, produced a series of musical plays that revolutionised post-1943 American musical theatre.

Facing the certainty of his imminent death, Hammerstein encouraged Rodgers to find new projects and continue working with other lyricists. A second television documentary, *Winston Churchill – The Valiant Years* (1960), garnered Rodgers a second Emmy, and his television version of *Androcles and the Lion* (1967, book by Peter Stone, music and lyrics by Rodgers) was generously reviewed. Several new shows had impressive runs: *No Strings* (1962, 580 performances, book by Samuel Taylor, music and lyrics by Rodgers); *Do I Hear a Waltz?* (1965, 220 performances, book by Arthur Laurents, lyrics by Stephen Sondheim); and *Two by Two* (1970, 343 performances, play by Peter Stone, lyrics by Martin Charnin). While he proved his ability to write his own lyrics when necessary, Rodgers continued working with various writers. However, he never found a third collaborator who matched his own innate gifts so well as Hart or Hammerstein. Compared with most of his earlier work, his final two shows (*Rex*, 1976, 49 performances, and *I Remember Mama*, 1979, 108 performances) were failures.

Rodgers and Hammerstein's legacy rests on an astonishing body of work, first with other partners, and secondly on their collaborations, particularly their five best shows: *Oklahoma!*, *Carousel*, *South Pacific*, *The King and I* and *The Sound of Music*. All these shows had lengthy if not record-breaking Broadway runs, received significant Broadway show awards, and were issued in film versions. A long list of songs from their shows have become standard popular songs, heard around the world in a dizzying array of arrangements and contexts. Much of popular and even critical perception of their work is based primarily on knowledge of the film versions of their shows, sometimes softened and sweetened for accessibility. However, viewing stage versions, hearing original recordings or reading the plays makes clear the fundamental integrity and power of the shows, and their best work retains its significance at the dawn of a new century.

The vitality of the musical play that Rodgers and Hammerstein developed remains undiminished. Performances of their works in both amateur and professional theatres are ongoing, and the shows continue to find new venues. *Oklahoma!*, *The King and I* and *South Pacific* all enjoyed important London revivals in the late 1990s and early 2000s. A television version of *South Pacific* starring Glenn Close appeared in spring 2001; and *The Sing-along Sound of Music* has become the latest Rodgers and Hammerstein rage. We cannot know what Rodgers and Hammerstein might have thought about seeing long lines of movie-goers in their favourite characters' costumes from *The Sound of Music*, but the movie-goers' opinion is quite obvious: the Rodgers and Hammerstein phenomenon is alive and well! Various opinions have been offered as to the reason for Rodgers and Hammerstein's enduring popularity. Irving Berlin said that 'of all the Broadway lyricists, Hammerstein was the only one who was a poet'.[20] Oscar's own words about what he wanted to write may be the best description of his and Rodgers's work and its evergreen presence on the stage: 'The good and the simple and the true are alone eternal.'[21]

8 The successors of Rodgers and Hammerstein from the 1940s to the 1960s

THOMAS L. RIIS AND ANN SEARS
WITH WILLIAM A. EVERETT

Musical comedies that are recognisably American in tone or theme predate the opening of *Oklahoma!* by many years. At the turn of the century, critics applauded the shows of George M. Cohan for the original, furiously quick-paced action and vernacular dialogue that were his trademarks. Other non-operatic popular plays of the era with appealing music began to feature more kinetic staging, homespun and believable (if often silly) characters, and an air of optimism and headstrong abandon. The singing and dancing actors of Cohan's type, masters and mistresses of the Triple Threat,[1] bespoke a special brand of native entertainment as early as 1902. Fresh, clean, full of slangy humour and catchy songs, with plots loose enough to allow virtually any kind of specialty act to be inserted, truly American musical comedies like *The Belle of New York* (1897), *Little Johnny Jones* (1904, which featured the hit number 'Yankee Doodle Boy'), or *In Dahomey* (1903, the first major African-American musical comedy to put ragtime songs on Broadway) established a type that became the standard through the 1920s.

Nevertheless, in the mid-twentieth century *Oklahoma!*, not merely a hit but an indisputable blockbuster of remarkable coherence, presented a new thematic direction and dramatic formula that marked yet another turning point for musical theatre and would be widely emulated. *Oklahoma!*'s popularity signalled a turn away from the contemporary and topical subjects preferred during the Depression Era in favour of a more sentimental style and subject. Historical subjects, especially nostalgic or patriotic American ones, could and would be portrayed on stage in a manner that avoided farce or parody. The legacy of *Oklahoma!* and successive hits by Rodgers and Hammerstein was multifaceted, but one of its most important elements was the book, or the story. Before *Oklahoma!*, the term 'book show' meant little more than the bare outlines of a plot with a serviceable script about a more or less chronological set of events. Afterwards, it implied a story that was well made, capable of serious dramatic goals, and liable to stimulate the audience with genuine emotions other than laughter.

The Rodgers and Hammerstein approach advocated earnestness and honesty of expression, and it was hardly ever gruesome or visibly violent. Rarely was it sexually explicit, and of course, no overt nudity was permitted. It minimised slapstick antics and pun-saturated wit. Song lyrics and dialogues were romantic and thoughtful; they built story lines and, most crucially, they developed characters. Even dancing could be integrated into the movement of the play, becoming more than merely a diverting interlude. For example, Laurey's 'Dream Ballet' at the end of *Oklahoma!*'s first act permitted the exploration of deep feelings far more effectively than dialogue could ever do. Rodgers's musical language was conventional, but occasionally it included modern sounds to achieve pointed dramatic effect. His musical subtleties were not lost on his successors. Hammerstein's serious lyrics were often about something other than the ubiquitous subject of young love and romance, although certainly love songs are to be found in good supply. The critical element was primarily Rodgers and Hammerstein's integration of words, music, dance and story. This valued coherence had been a long-sought goal of operettas and even some Broadway productions in earlier decades, but it was achieved infrequently during the doldrums of the 1930s. Despite some remarkable works, such as George Gershwin's uniquely appealing folk opera *Porgy and Bess* (1935) and Rodgers and Hart's innovative dance show *On Your Toes* (1936), the 1930s favoured the revue format, in part because of its relatively modest production costs. However, after *Oklahoma!* the integrated show came into fashion again with a vengeance. This integration became one of the most prized aspects of the modern musical.

Oklahoma! also indicated to Broadway producers that certain formulas could be avoided without losing the audience. A full chorus of leggy women did not have to raise the first curtain. Mixed choruses could dance and even sing in parts – before this a style usually reserved for shows with serious operatic pretensions. Indeed, the use of an intelligent plot with a string of beautiful songs opened the door to many other sophisticated innovations, which could be slipped in without offending taste or inducing boredom. More flexibility in the creation of scenarios and even occasional violence resulting in an on-stage killing could be included, if the deserving characters were saved or exonerated in the end (as in both *Oklahoma!* and *Carousel*), thus raising the possibility of a fully formed musical with a tragic ending such as *West Side Story*.

Finally, *Oklahoma!* also reinforced other equally well-understood Broadway conventions that could *not* be discarded without careful consideration. By looking backwards in a few respects, it cleared the space for future experiments while underlining the need to retain always some elements of familiarity and contact for the audience. Like countless melodramas before it, the show's action is dominated by the activities and songs of two couples (one serious and one comic), one ethnic comedian and one villain. The plot's progress from character exposition to complications whereby the lovers are alienated from one another and then reconciled is its most obvious cliché.

Oklahoma!'s seemingly endless run (2,212 performances over six years at the St James Theatre), the continuing productivity of Rodgers and Hammerstein through the late 1950s, and the team's involvement in the production end of the business with shows other than their own all guaranteed that their influence would be profound. But their first and most important contribution was the works themselves, solidly built on universally understood themes with a wide appeal to people of all social and economic classes in mid-twentieth-century America. These works greatly shaped Rodgers and Hammerstein's contemporaries and, more significantly, became models for the succeeding generations of musical theatre composers and lyricists.

The 1940s

Musical theatre in the 1940s faced enormous difficulties, but there was also a resurgence of creative energy. Despite the economic challenges of getting new productions on stage during the 1930s and the resulting exodus of Broadway's best composers to Hollywood's more financially rewarding film opportunities, Broadway began to recover from the Depression by the late 1930s and early 1940s. Along with the old-guard writers Irving Berlin, Richard Rodgers and Lorenz Hart, Cole Porter, Arthur Schwartz and Howard Dietz, and Harold Arlen, a new generation of composers and lyricists either appeared on Broadway for the first time or produced their first important shows, including such writers as Alan Jay Lerner and Frederick Loewe, Jule Styne, Robert Wright and George Forrest, and Frank Loesser. The extraordinary efforts of America to mobilise for the war effort and the concurrent welling up of patriotic feeling throughout the country may have provided some impetus for the material of Rodgers and Hammerstein's *Oklahoma!*, and the wartime atmosphere certainly created a climate in which a show about the American frontier spirit was welcomed and could remain a hit for years to come. While the social and technological changes spurred by the war created an open atmosphere for new ideas and experimentation, the acceptance of innovation in theatrical works was balanced by an appreciation of American life and history, both present and past. Revues, shows exploring the usual romantic relationships (for example, Wright and Forrest's *Song of Norway*, 1944, or Cole Porter's *Kiss Me, Kate*, 1948) and shows based on fantasy (Lerner and Loewe's *Brigadoon* and Harburg and Lane's *Finian's Rainbow*, both opening in 1947) appeared during the 1940s; and an astonishing number of shows centred around Americans' experiences at home and abroad and around American military life opened on Broadway in the 1940s and 1950s (Berlin's *This is the Army*, 1942, Bernstein's *On the Town*, 1944, Harold Rome's *Call Me Mister*, 1946). With an almost uncanny understanding of the public's state of mind, Rodgers and Hammerstein combined the nostalgia for early American rural life with dramatic innovation to produce *Oklahoma!*, the biggest hit and most influential show of the 1940s.

The initial impact of *Oklahoma!* was felt almost immediately with the E. Y. Harburg/Harold Arlen show *Bloomer Girl* in 1944, featuring the story of the Civil War crusader for comfortable women's clothing, Amelia ('Dolly') Bloomer. Set safely in the colourful past, with a dance choreographed by Agnes de Mille focusing on women's personal anguish as the men go off to war – a transparent reference to the ongoing world war – and introducing the subject of slavery into the plot, *Bloomer Girl* captured in song and story many elements from the Rodgers and Hammerstein prototype, even using its star dancer, Joan McCracken, and its comic singer, Celeste Holm, who had played Ado Annie. Although Herzig and Saidy's libretto was less seamless than Hammerstein's, Arlen's music is undeservedly neglected. A romantic duet, 'Right As the Rain', the character Jefferson Calhoun's song to his love, 'Evelina', and the black servant's plea for racial harmony, 'The Eagle and Me', make a good effect. The show has seldom been revived; although it emphasised the most important social issues of the Civil War period, the book came across as 'superficial and somewhat silly', and certainly not comparable to *Oklahoma!*'s 'artistic cohesiveness'.[2]

Arlen's second show, this time with lyricist Johnny Mercer, was *St Louis Woman* (1946), with an all-black cast featuring such well-known artists as the Nicholas Brothers, Harold and Fayard, Pearl Bailey, Rex Ingram and Juanita Hall. Although the score contained some beautiful songs, such as 'Come Rain or Come Shine' and 'I Had Myself a True Love', the weak libretto foretold a brief run. The writer, Countee Cullen, died before the show made it to New York. Not even the extensive revisions of the replacement director, Rouben Mamoulian, who had directed both the original productions of Gershwin's *Porgy and Bess* (1935) and Rodgers and Hammerstein's *Oklahoma!*, could sustain the show beyond 113 performances, but the original cast album made later in 1946 eventually led to the critical recognition the fine score deserves. *St Louis Woman* was in many ways a worthy successor to some striking stage works focusing on African-American life and culture during the 1930s and early 1940s, among them *The Green Pastures* (1930), *Porgy and Bess*, *Cabin in the Sky* (1940) and Oscar Hammerstein's *Carmen Jones* (1943). Both of Arlen's first two Broadway shows reflected his long-standing interest in African-American music and his understanding of the issues facing African Americans in the United States. Having written arrangements for Fletcher Henderson's band and music for Cotton Club Revues from 1930 to 1934, Arlen had thoroughly absorbed the melodic, harmonic and rhythmic elements of black music, particularly the blues form. His ability to synthesise blues, jazz and Tin Pan Alley styles in popular song form gave his music a strong individual stamp as well as an unmistakably American identity, but his score has been lost for posterity because of the poor book. *St Louis Woman* never returned to Broadway, but the music later appeared in an operatic version in Amsterdam (1959) and Paris.

If one way to define the Rodgers and Hammerstein formula was simply operetta plus Americana, *Up in Central Park* (1945) fitted the bill perfectly, with a book by the experienced brother and sister team Herbert and Dorothy Fields, and music by the veteran operetta composer Sigmund Romberg. Complete with an American hero in the form of a journalist battling the corrupt politician Boss Tweed and Tammany Hall, it is set well back from modern times in New York of the 1870s. Although critical opinion of this show suggests that it failed to live up to the highest standards of its creators, its relatively lengthy run of 504 performances (and later preservation on film in 1947 with Deanna Durbin and Dick Haymes) implies that the writers and composer were giving the public what it wanted. A sumptuous production by Mike Todd and choreography by the emerging Helen Tamiris, who would later go on to stage the dances for the revival of *Show Boat* in 1946 and the original production of *Annie Get Your Gun* (1948), also helped to guarantee its warm reception, but the show is little known today.

Irving Berlin's *Annie Get Your Gun* (1946) did not seek to imitate Rodgers and Hammerstein in its details, although the team produced the show. The third-longest-running musical of the 1940s, it demonstrated that even after *Oklahoma!* and *Carousel*, good songs well performed could still make for a Broadway smash hit. The liveliness of the historical title character played by the triumphant Ethel Merman helped as well. Herbert and Dorothy Fields's book, while not strictly adhering to the facts of sharpshooter Annie Oakley's life, at least avoided the hackneyed melodrama of days gone by, and if Berlin's melodies are easily extractable from the show, they are no less worthy for that. The perennial creator of American popular song produced a string of superb numbers for the show, such as 'Doin' What Comes Natur'lly', 'Anything You Can Do', and 'They Say It's Wonderful'. The classic 'There's No Business Like Show Business', which entices Annie to join Buffalo Bill's Wild West Show, simply brings down the curtain better than any other song ever written for Broadway. The show has played in many countries and its revival on Broadway in the late 1990s with Bernadette Peters – succeeded in the role by actors such as Cheryl Ladd, Reba McEntyre and Crystal Bernard – demonstrates its continuing popularity.

Miss Liberty, Robert Sherwood and Irving Berlin's show of 1949 (with director Moss Hart and choreographer Jerome Robbins), once again invoked a patriotic theme, this time about the search for a girl to pose as the model for the Statue of Liberty, and an old-fashioned setting from 1885. Because of advance sales, the show played for over 300 performances; however, the tuneless score and heavy-handed libretto with its shocking failure to provide a final love interest for the 'girl next door' character put off audiences from the outset. Even with its all-star production team, the only memorable number from the show is the final hymn-like setting of the popular poem inscribed on the statue's base, 'Give Me Your Tired, Your Poor'.

Jule Styne (1905–94) had received classical training, made a success of himself in Hollywood song-writing and was a practised vocal arranger. Long before he reached Broadway in 1947, Styne had collaborated successfully with good lyricists such as Frank Loesser and Sammy Cahn on scores for over fifty films. He mixed writing and producing all through his career, and at his peak (1959–67) wrote music for television and the live stage, as well as popular songs. Over the years it became apparent that he possessed a discerning eye for talented women and was adept at making vehicles for them. (Styne also boosted Ethel Merman, Barbra Streisand and Mary Martin, and he had even coached Shirley Temple and Alice Faye years before.) Carol Channing became a star after her first important Broadway role in Styne's *Gentlemen Prefer Blondes* (1949), where 'Diamonds are a Girl's Best Friend' became her anthem. Like many American musicals, the show enjoyed runs in London and Germany as well. It was revived as *Lorelei* in 1973, again with Channing as the star, a production that reached Broadway the following year. The importance of a star like her in the show is underscored by the short-lived revival at the Lyceum in 1995.

High Button Shoes (1947) was Styne's first foray onto Broadway after working in Hollywood. He was assisted by Sammy Cahn's lyric writing and considerable rewriting by the noted director George Abbott. The book is formulaic and all the specialties (separate acts featuring the talents of individual performers but not contributing to a plot) of the show collectively make up its main attraction. These included the fresh comedy of Phil Silvers, the duo dancing of Nanette Fabray and Jack McCauley in 'Papa, Won't You Dance with Me', and an elaborate chase scene/ballet, choreographed by Jerome Robbins. Styne and Cahn's score was well liked and the sum total of these parts spelled a hit even as Rodgers and Hammerstein were experimenting with one of their least successful vehicles, *Allegro*. (*Allegro* opened on the day after *High Button Shoes* but enjoyed fewer than half as many performances on Broadway – 315 versus 727.) Both shows avoided colourful features of American history or operetta. Further versions of *High Button Shoes* have included two for American television in 1956 and 1966 and several regional productions. Styne's Broadway career was only beginning, but it was taking off at a time when the standard expectations for both song lyrics and quality of book were reaching an extraordinarily high level. With the clever literary texts of Lorenz Hart or Ira Gershwin fresh in people's minds, along with the production savvy of the Rodgers and Hammerstein team, a young musical newcomer like Styne could only benefit from close observation of the shows around him.

In *Gentlemen Prefer Blondes* (1949) the true genius of Jule Styne began to emerge. Rarely has a musician been more perfectly attuned to a medium than Styne was to the Broadway stage. He understood the larger-than-life quality of live theatre, the flair required to put over a song, the graphic gestures needed to make comedy convincing and the visible tear to evoke sympathy. Speaking in purely musical terms, Styne melodically derives from Irving Berlin, who always demanded a radically simple match between tune and text. Styne's love of show-business razzle-dazzle and his ability to bring filmic intensity to the live stage mirrored the widespread passion of Broadway denizens in his time. Just as so many Hollywood musicals are really about the process of making a show, so Styne's Broadway creations reflect the obsessions connected with the experience of putting a story with music and dance on stage. Styne was also involved in producing musicals, and until the late 1950s occupied himself with directing the revival of Rodgers and Hart's *Pal Joey* (1952) and Jerry Bock's *Mr Wonderful* (1956), a vehicle designed to introduce Sammy Davis Jr to the musical theatre stage.

With *Brigadoon* (1947), their third show and first hit together, Alan Jay Lerner (1918–86) and Frederick Loewe (1901–88) easily established themselves as the heirs apparent to the Rodgers and Hammerstein tradition. Although Lerner and Loewe had written two earlier musicals, in *Brigadoon* they settled on a style which followed Rodgers and Hammerstein in its combination of a well-written book with elements of operetta, for example, an exotic location, operetta-influenced music which demanded well-trained voices, and the incorporation of ballet. Loewe further reflected Rodgers's influence in writing idiomatically for the voice and effectively capturing the flavour of the faraway locale in music. Like Rodgers and Hammerstein, they had a series of hit shows produced during a partnership over a decade long (*Paint Your Wagon*, 1951; *My Fair Lady*, 1956; *Camelot*, 1960; and the film *Gigi*, 1958). Also like Rodgers and Hammerstein, Lerner and Loewe wrote in a 'words first, music second' fashion. After extensive discussions about the book, character development and placement of songs, Lerner sketched lyrics that Loewe then set to music. Revisions were done in a collaborative fashion, often working together. *Brigadoon* ran for 581 performances, a successful show in comparison to other shows on Broadway that year, even though it was not quite an '*Oklahoma!*' Set in the misty Scottish Highlands, the story concerns two American tourists who happen on a town that only awakens every one hundred years. It begins rather simply, again recalling *Oklahoma!* As the plot unfolds, three love stories must work themselves out, and the visitors must decide whether to remain in the enchanted village or return to New York. Lerner's eloquent lyrics and Loewe's music were complemented by the brilliant choreography of Agnes de Mille. The reviews exceeded Lerner and Loewe's wildest hopes: Brooks Atkinson of the *New York Times* praised their work as a 'major achievement on the musical stage', noting that 'it is impossible to say where the music and dancing leave off and the story begins in this beautifully orchestrated Scottish idyll'.[3] With such acclaim, Lerner and Loewe were well launched on their Broadway careers, and if they did not quite overturn Rodgers and Hammerstein's domination of American musical theatre, they did loom large over most of their contemporaries during the late 1940s and 1950s. As authors of three shows that have had frequent revivals, Lerner and Loewe remain one of Broadway's most important creative teams.

Burton Lane and E. Y. 'Yip' Harburg's *Finian's Rainbow* (1947) opened shortly before *Brigadoon*. It was the third of Burton Lane's stage musicals written in the 1940s, interspersed among his highly successful assignments for the Hollywood films that were the primary focus of his career from 1933 to 1954. Academy Award nominations for best song 'How About You' from *Babes on Broadway* (1941) and 'Too Late Now' from *Royal Wedding* (1951, starring Fred Astaire) indicated Lane's standing in film music, but musical theatre was his real interest, and he returned to New York in 1955 to concentrate on Broadway productions. Like *Brigadoon*, *Finian's Rainbow* was based on a fantasy story and featured a lush score. Its 725-performance run outlasted *Brigadoon*, but in any case both shows proved that when well done, fantastic and imaginative settings were viable topics for Broadway. *Finian's Rainbow*'s bittersweet ending did not detract, and the gems in the score carried the show, for example, 'How Are Things in Glocca Morra', 'Look to the Rainbow' and 'Old Devil Moon'. The show has been revived several times, including at the City Center in 1955, 1960 and 1967. The 1960 production was moved to the 46th Street Theater, but it folded after twelve performances.

Cole Porter's *Kiss Me, Kate* (1948) is considered by many to be the masterwork of his output. Similar to Kern's and Gershwin's experience, Porter's career began in 1915 writing songs for interpolation into musicals. His first success with a complete score came with *Fifty Million Frenchmen* (1929), followed by *Gay Divorce* (1932, starring Fred Astaire), and *Anything Goes* (1934) and *Panama Hattie* (1940) with Ethel Merman. By the 1940s he had a firmly established reputation. The seven shows Porter wrote in the 1940s encountered mixed success, but *Kiss Me, Kate* opened to rave reviews and ran for 1,070 performances. Based on Shakespeare's *The Taming of the Shrew*, with a brilliant book by Samuel and Bella Spewack, the story of *Kiss Me, Kate* cleverly paralleled the lives of Shakespeare's characters Petruchio and Katharina with the lives of a pair of divorced actors who play their parts in the show-within-the-show. As the Shakespeare play proceeds with the feuding divorced couple reciting Shakespeare's lines, the actors make up, just as do Petruchio and Kate, and they are reunited in the end. A secondary actor/actress couple also work out their difficulties throughout the show. As usual, Porter wrote both his own lyrics and the music. Porter's sophisticated lyrics matched the ebullience of Shakespeare's play, and the elegance of the entire production assured that it became the fourth-longest-running musical of the 1940s, quite a record considering that Rodgers and Hammerstein's *Oklahoma!* swept all attendance records for the entire decade. Furthermore, Porter's show has remained popular, as is shown in the important recent productions in both New York and London in 2000 and 2001. It has also played in Australia, Germany, Austria and France, among other countries. *Kiss Me, Kate* was a departure from the musical comedies Porter wrote earlier in his career, proving that he too had learned important lessons from such shows as *Oklahoma!* and *Carousel*. The theatre historian Gerald Bordman notes that in *Kiss Me, Kate*, 'all the ideals that musical plays had been striving for were triumphantly realized'. He points to the 'remarkably lifelike, believable protagonists, with every character having a sensible and important bearing on the plot, with every song perfectly related to the action and more often than not advancing it', and lyrics and dialogue 'that remained literate and witty or touching throughout'.[4] Many songs from *Kiss Me, Kate* became popular, including 'Another Op'nin', Another Show', another actor's anthem, much in the spirit of Irving Berlin's 'There's No Business Like Show Business'; 'Wunderbar', a waltz that even Richard Rodgers might have been proud of and a brief echo of the operetta tradition; and 'So in Love', a slow but passionate ballad.

The 1950s

Irving Berlin's next show, *Call Me Madam* (1950), was a far cry from Rodgers and Hammerstein in its tone of parody, and its wit and music kept it running on Broadway for well over a year. Similar in attitude to political shows of the thirties, it managed to be both modern and old-fashioned. Its plot arose directly from President Harry Truman's decision at the time to appoint Washington hostess Perle Mesta as Ambassador to Luxembourg. In the musical, the socialite Sally Adams, played by the ever-popular Ethel Merman, is the new minister to the mythical country of Lichtenburg. Love interests and complications ensue. American gaucherie is played off against European sophistication, reminiscent of operetta situations a half-century before. Berlin's songs were hailed and a movie, also starring Merman, was made in 1953. The show has seen a few revivals, including one at the Victoria Palace in London in 1983.

Call Me Madam was directed by the legendary George Abbott (1887–1995), who was as essential as anyone in creating what is often described as the 'Rodgers and Hammerstein type' of musical. His first musical was Rodgers and Hart's circus show *Jumbo* (1935), with the score realised by Paul Whiteman's orchestra. Having a great deal of experience from the legitimate theatre and film arenas in the 1920s and 1930s, Abbott was highly regarded on Broadway by mid-century. He believed in well-constructed plots, attentive actors who gave clear and crisp line delivery, and well-planned stage movement, rather than improvised business. His method was formulaic but extremely effective and required a high degree of precision. While he demanded efficiency and eschewed excess, he was not afraid of innovation, especially when it came to twists in theme, plot or choreography. He made his mark permanently on the acting style of the genre. From the 1940s until nearly the end of his long life, Abbott wrote, produced and directed shows with many of the greatest composers and lyricists of American musical theatre, including Irving Berlin, Leonard Bernstein, Comden and Green, Jule Styne, Frank Loesser, Arthur Schwartz, Adler and Ross, Bob Merrill, Jerry Bock, and Stephen Sondheim. The title 'show doctor' is perhaps more appropriately applied to him than almost any other figure in recent Broadway history.

Frank Loesser (1910–69), like Jule Styne, had extensive experience in writing songs for motion pictures before arriving on Broadway, although almost all of that experience came with writing only lyrics. Doing both words and music for his wartime hit 'Praise the Lord and Pass the Ammunition' inspired him to expand his horizons, and he joined George Abbott, who wrote the book and directed, to rework the classic English farce *Charley's Aunt* into the musical *Where's Charley?* The first of Loesser's five complete Broadway scores, the show was a slow starter, but ultimately became a successful vehicle for dancer Ray Bolger, who returned to Broadway in 1951 for forty-eight performances and appeared in the 1952 film version.

Loesser's masterpiece, *Guys and Dolls* (1950), reflects a debt to Rodgers and Hammerstein in its recognition of the essentially collaborative nature of modern musical theatre. The team coordination brought about by Loesser, who wrote music and lyrics, and Abe Burrows, the book-writer who developed the script from Damon Runyon's tales of New York City's underworld, tells much about how to do it right. The producers, Cy Feuer and Ernest Martin, were inspired by the unusual love interest represented by Nellie and

Emile in *South Pacific*. In light of that show's success, the unlikely pairing of the earnestly evangelical Sarah Brown and the high-rolling sportsman Sky Masterson in Runyon's 'The Idyll of Miss Sarah Brown' seemed at least plausible in a popular musical context. However, Loesser and Burrows put their own stamp on *Guys and Dolls* only after realising that they needed to deviate from the serious emphasis of *South Pacific* and give the comic aspect of the story free play in both dialogue and situation. Since Loesser had already written the songs, Burrows was presented with the unique challenge of writing a comic script to surround fully composed music. Unburdened by previous experience in writing for Broadway, Burrows succeeded brilliantly. *Guys and Dolls* was a perfect blend of romantic fun and funny romance. Even better, the floating crap game and the Save-a-Soul Mission were both located in the heart of the city, close to Broadway itself, that most American of thoroughfares. George M. Cohan would have loved it, and audiences have continued to applaud the show, one of the most frequently revived from the period. It has done very well in English-speaking countries, but has proven less popular elsewhere.

Guys and Dolls together with Rodgers and Hammerstein's *Carousel*, *South Pacific* and *The King and I* represent especially well the new blend of moods possible within the well-written script of the time. Both romance and comedy not only coexisted in different characters and situations but could be expressed – along with a generally wider range of emotions – at times by the *same* character. The music placed characters in a new realm outside the spoken play and hence could express what was otherwise unsayable within the typical serious drama. The inarticulate, abusive Billy Bigelow could be a touching optimist as he soliloquises about his unborn child. The brutal and arbitrary King of Siam can express 'A Puzzlement' and vulnerability in song when confronting the equally formidable but tender-hearted Anna.

Loesser's other Broadway hits did not equal his triumph with *Guys and Dolls*, but they represent a continuing willingness to deviate from stock dramatic scenarios filled with besotted but otherwise uninteresting young lovers. In *The Most Happy Fella* (1956) in particular, the ageing winemaker Tony, betrothed to the ultimately unfaithful but realistically frustrated and passionate waitress Rosabella, is reminiscent again of the ages and per-sonal issues that divide *South Pacific*'s Nellie Forbush and Emile De Becque. *The Most Happy Fella* also represents a vote for musical integrity and se-riousness but without reverting to operetta in the old style or trying to appeal to an audience beyond a typical Broadway crowd. Loesser's *How to Succeed in Business Without Really Trying* (1961) as a parody of corpo-rate climbing and opportunism was about as far from a Rodgers and Hammerstein *theme* as could be imagined. Yet the quality of its book, only the fourth ever to win a Pulitzer Prize for drama – the previous winners had been *Of Thee I Sing* (1931), *South Pacific* (1949) and *Fiorello!* (1959) – indicated that the creative team, essentially the group that had confected *Guys and Dolls*, all subscribed to Lehman Engel's dictum that great musicals begin with great books, a principle Engel had derived from his observations of and participation in the shows of Rodgers and Hammerstein from the conductor's podium. *How to Succeed in Business* became a successful film, played well in other English-speaking countries, and reappeared in a successful Broadway production in the 1990s with Matthew Broderick as the star.

Lerner and Loewe's first Broadway offering of the decade was *Paint Your Wagon* (1951), a Gold Rush story inspired by Lerner's reading of Bret Harte's rough and ready frontier tales. The show was beset with problems from its very beginning: Loewe had to be coaxed to work on it; the production team argued over casting choices; and by Lerner's own admission, he struggled to create a coherent musical play that combined the realism of actual frontier life and robust entertainment. Despite the contributions of the experienced producer Cheryl Crawford and the choreographer Agnes de Mille, the popularity of several memorable songs (for example, 'I Talk to the Trees' and 'They Call the Wind Maria') and a run of 289 performances, the show lost money. Indicating Rodgers and Hammerstein's continued sway over Broadway, critics described Lerner's lyrics in contrast to Hammerstein's (they lacked his 'honest sentiment'); and they compared Loewe to Rodgers as well as Loesser (Loewe had written the 'most accomplished music Broadway had fallen heir to since *The King and I* and *Guys and Dolls*').[5] *Paint Your Wagon* and its ambivalent reviews in no way prepared either audiences or critics for Lerner and Loewe's next production, *My Fair Lady*, which became their biggest success, while *Paint Your Wagon* has fallen into relative obscurity.

My Fair Lady (1956) began as the brainchild of film producer Gabriel Pascal, who originally approached Rodgers and Hammerstein to write the musical adaptation of George Bernard Shaw's *Pygmalion*. Unable to solve the problems presented by Shaw's insistence that *Pygmalion* was not a love story, Hammerstein withdrew from the project.[6] Interested by the story, Lerner and Loewe began working on the book, and Pascal signed an agreement for production with the Theatre Guild. After a few months, Lerner and Loewe admitted defeat as had Rodgers and Hammerstein; Pascal was subsequently refused by Noël Coward, Cole Porter, Schwartz and Dietz, and Fred Saidy and E. Y. Harburg. After half-hearted efforts on a number of new show possibilities and writing the screenplay for the successful film of *Brigadoon* (1954), Lerner read in the newspaper that Pascal had died, leaving a complicated estate that included the rights to *Pygmalion*. Lerner and Loewe went to work, resolved to 'do Pygmalion simply by doing Pygmalion',[7] while their attorney sorted out the legalities. The musical was a very faithful adaptation, changing little of the play except the addition of three scenes, including the

Ascot Racetrack Scene and the ending: in the original play, Eliza walks out on Higgins but in a postlude Shaw suggests that she might have married young Freddie; in the musical, she returns to the irascible Higgins. Lerner retained as much of the dialogue as he could, blending his own dialogue and lyrics almost flawlessly with Shaw's own words. He and Loewe aimed to 'musicalise' the play with 'fresh expressions' of the conventions of 'the balance of the score, the proper distribution of solos, ensemble singing, and choreography', so the 'characters arrive at the emotional moment that demands the right kind of music to balance the score'.[8] Loewe's charming music, if redolent of the operetta of an earlier day, added to the lavish, stunning period costumes designed by Cecil Beaton. A superb cast, headed by Rex Harrison as Higgins, included a young, radiant Julie Andrews as Eliza and veteran character actor Stanley Holloway as Eliza's father. The night of the opening in New Haven, Connecticut, a blizzard struck, and nervous about his foray into musical theatre, Rex Harrison announced that he was not yet ready to appear in the role. Yet, after a few changes in New Haven and a second tryout period in Philadelphia, *My Fair Lady* opened in New York to unanimously glowing reviews, one of which said, 'Don't bother reading this review now. You'd better sit right down and send for those tickets to *My Fair Lady*. First things first.'[9] Acknowledging that the Shavian story was an atypical Broadway approach to romance, critics praised the thoughtful use of Shaw's original play, the brilliance of the lyrics, and Loewe's well-integrated score. Brooks Atkinson wrote in the *New York Times* that 'in taste, intelligence, skill and delight, *My Fair Lady* is the finest musical play in years'. *My Fair Lady* was undoubtedly the 'most influential musical of the Fifties'.[10] The cast album was a best seller, and the 1964 film starring Rex Harrison and Audrey Hepburn won Academy Awards for best picture, best actor and best director. Even with the memory of distinctive performances of the original cast, the show has remained a favourite in revivals in many countries, including anniversary productions on Broadway in 1976 and 1981, the latter again starring Rex Harrison. Like all the important Rodgers and Hammerstein shows, *My Fair Lady* succeeded partially because it was based on an original literary work of the highest quality. Lerner and Loewe's smash hit further harked back to Rodgers and Hammerstein's latest big show *The King and I* in its half-sung/half-spoken part for the hero, more overtones of romance between the leading couple than in the source material, and Loewe's operetta-flavoured music. Apparently, the Rodgers and Hammerstein formula still provided a framework for artistic and commercial success.

As Rodgers and Hammerstein continued their march across musical theatre history and the careers of Lerner and Loewe peaked, something of an era ended when Cole Porter returned to Broadway in the 1950s for his last two musicals, *Can-Can* (1953) and *Silk Stockings* (1955), his fifth and sixth musicals with French settings. *Can-Can* is set in Paris in 1893, telling two stories side by side. A young judge investigates the scandalous can-can danc-ing at a café, but falls in love with the café owner and then helps legalise the dance. One of the dancers is pursued by a sculptor and an art critic, who attacks the sculptor's work. Of course, all ends happily. Like many of Porter's scores, *Can-Can* was poorly received initially, but became a hit with five new standards, among them 'I Love Paris'. The show was helped along by the sizzling dancing of the young Gwen Verdon in her first major Broad-way role. It was revived at the City Center in 1962, but critics found the book dated in a 1982 production at the Minskoff, despite Abe Burrows's revision of his original text. *Silk Stockings* was inspired by the 1939 film *Ninotchka*, starring Greta Garbo. The story is about Ninotchka, a beauti-ful but icy Russian woman official seduced both by the luxuries of western culture and by a talent scout who wants a Soviet composer to write the score for a movie version of *War and Peace*. When the composer opts to stay in Paris, Ninotchka is sent to bring him home. Pursued to Russia by the talent scout, she returns with him to the West. Full of clever allusions to the ongoing Cold War, the lyrics are Porter's usual polished, topical, erudite work; and the score of *Silk Stockings* contained some of his favoured Latin-influenced, beguine-like melodies. The show has rarely been revived, and the story remains best known in the original film version.

Among the most conventional of successful musicals in the post-*Oklahoma!* decade was *Kismet*, which had its premiere on 3 December 1953 at the Ziegfeld Theatre and ran for nearly 600 performances. The secret of its success lay in the use of thoroughly romantic and exotic music by the Russian composer Alexander Borodin (1833–87) matched to a gaudy story of magic and adventure set in ancient Baghdad. Robert Wright and George Forrest added the lyrics for 'Stranger in Paradise' and 'Baubles, Bangles, and Beads' to Borodin's instrumental works ('Polovtsian Dances' from his opera *Prince Igor* and the second string quartet, respectively). Charles Lederer and Luther Davis rewrote the play based on the 1911 Oriental chestnut by Edward Knoblock. The make-believe operetta world that *Kismet* inhab-its is seldom absent from Broadway for long – one can see traces at least as far back as *The Black Crook* of 1866. But the show's appeal, during an otherwise unremarkable Broadway season, underscored the basic need for both musical and dramatic solidity within an idiom that audiences readily understood. The classical music was put together with the same building blocks that Rodgers and others used so well in their songs. *Kismet* remains among the shows from the period that have been revived, playing in New York in 1962, 1965 and 1976. The 1976 production appeared in London the following year.

The appropriateness of Borodin's music, with a vocabulary that serves the tonal world of much nineteenth-century classical music as well as Tin

Pan Alley, begs a further comment on Rodgers's stylistic legacy, which claims both a classical and a popular resonance. Rodgers was nothing if not flexible, and his ability to generate and maintain an overall sound was crucial to his success in so many shows with his principal collaborators, Hart and Hammerstein. In *South Pacific, The King and I* and *Flower Drum Song,* despite the harmony or instrumentation of a vaguely or superficially Asian nature, the main tunes come unmistakably from Rodgers's pen, using the song formulas that he uses in the other non-ethnic shows as well. The most talented musicians who created scores for shows between 1945 and 1970, such as Irving Berlin, Cole Porter, Kurt Weill, Leonard Bernstein, Harold Arlen, Frank Loesser, Jule Styne, Frederick Loewe and Charles Strouse, were similarly adaptable.

A host of neophytes led by the Broadway giant George Abbott created *The Pajama Game* in 1954. With a little bit of politics blended with the required romantic story, a healthy dose of comedy and several good songs, the vehicle ran efficiently for over 1,000 performances at the St James Theatre before hitting the road. Richard Adler and Jerry Ross wrote their first songs for a book show, including 'Hey, There, You With the Stars in Your Eyes', 'Hernando's Hideaway' and 'There Once Was a Man'. Co-director with Abbott was the young Jerome Robbins. The cast included the veterans John Raitt, Janis Paige, and Eddie Foy Jr, as well as the newcomer Shirley MacLaine. Hal Prince, Frederick Brisson, and Robert Griffith produced their first major show. The twenty-six-year-old choreographer Bob Fosse created his first big Broadway dance for 'Steam Heat', rich with the jazzy and angular gestures that would become his signature moves.

In 1955 virtually the same creative team followed up on *The Pajama Game* with the equally successful *Damn Yankees*, this time featuring the lithe and youthful Gwen Verdon (as Lola, the devil's assistant who typically gets what she wants). Ray Walston played the Tempter himself, the character called Mr Applegate, who transforms a middle-aged baseball fan into the youthful sports star Joe Hardy, played by Stephen Douglass, in exchange for his soul. Since devils and seductive temptresses had been appearing on stage since the Middle Ages, a certain sense of familiarity was inevitable, but the baseball-centred theme and Fosse's choreography added zip to the whole Faustian affair. Ross's death from leukaemia in 1955 (at the age of twenty-nine) ended what would undoubtedly have been a far more extended career on Broadway. Both of his musicals have been revived, including *The Pajama Game* in New York in 1973 and at the New York City Opera in 1989, and both often play in regional theatres.

Harold Arlen appeared on Broadway in his last musical theatre endeavours in the 1950s, beginning with *House of Flowers* (1954). Based on Truman Capote's short story about a bordello in Port-au-Prince, Haiti (which he himself had frequented), it tells the story of two competing houses of

pleasure. The House of Flowers run by Madame Fleur features employ-
ees with flower names; the rival house is run by Madame Tango. When
sailors bring a mumps epidemic and consequent financial ruin to the House
of Flowers, Madame Fleur contemplates selling her employee 'Violet', but
Violet prefers to marry her sweetheart. Despite a kidnapping plot, the sweethearts are married, but the House of Flowers survives when Madame Tango's
entire establishment sails away on a world cruise. The high points of the show
were the beautiful sets by Oliver Messel and Arlen's wonderfully atmospheric
score. The sets and score did not carry the show, however, and it ran for a
barely respectable 165 performances.

Arlen's 'Caribbean companion' to *House of Flowers* was *Jamaica* (1957).
Koli, a poor fisherman on an island off the coast of Jamaica, loves the ravish-
ing Savannah, who wants to live in New York. She is tempted by a city-slicker
pearl broker, but after Koli saves her little brother's life, she chooses to remain
with the simple fisherman. In a clear reference to *Oklahoma!*, she visits New
York in a 'dream ballet'. Lena Horne's appearance in the leading role and
in eleven of the twenty-one numbers of the show guaranteed the show a
remunerative run of 558 performances, but critics agreed that the score was
derivative at best.[11] *Saratoga* (1959), Arlen's final show of the 1950s, was
a period piece adapted from Edna Ferber's novel of the same name, and
closed after only ten weeks. Despite stage and revue successes and the many
popular songs from those efforts, and a thorough biography available, Arlen
remains most famous for his work in musical films, especially the ubiquitous *The Wizard of Oz* (1939). Although his musical style is innovative
and original, and the catalogue of his works extensive, Arlen's lack of name
recognition even now indicates that he has not yet found his rightful place in
American musical theatre history.[12] None of his Broadway shows remains
in the popular consciousness.

Bells Are Ringing (1956) marked the first full-blown musical of Betty
Comden and Adolph Green with Jule Styne. It also became their longest-
running collaborative effort, with over 900 performances at the Shubert
Theatre. (The team had made the composer's professional acquaintance
during their work together on *Peter Pan* and worked with him on eight
shows in all.) The story, a modern romance between a telephone switchboard
operator and a playwright, was intended as a vehicle for Comden and Green's
friend and earlier performing partner Judy Holliday. Two great songs, 'Just
in Time' and 'The Party's Over', along with spirited dancing, snappy list-
making lyrics, a New York setting and the personal charisma of Holliday
gave this show an old-fashioned, but well-made quality. The show is still
sometimes seen, for example in the 2001 Broadway revival starring Faith
Prince, but it is now overshadowed by a number of more famous musicals
from the decade. It has played in several foreign countries.

Styne's magnum opus was *Gypsy* (1959). Key to its success was the coming together of many phenomenal talents – lyricist Stephen Sondheim, choreographer Jerome Robbins, Arthur Laurents as author of the book (just two years after all three helped create the classic *West Side Story*), together with David Merrick and Leland Hayward to produce and Ethel Merman at her brassy, belting best. Merman insisted that someone more experienced than the young Sondheim create the music. Enter Jule Styne. It was immediately obvious from its opening that the show was a vehicle for the player of Mama Rose (rather than the title role, Gypsy Rose Lee), and in revival *Gypsy* has enjoyed success with good actresses, including Angela Lansbury and Tyne Daly in that part. However, *Gypsy* is one of those rare shows in Broadway history whose quality in the eyes of critics has changed for the better over time, chiefly because of the surprising durability of both Laurents's book, with its concentration on the inner turmoil of a middle-aged mother, and Styne's enhancing music. The prospects for future revivals are high, especially as burlesque, the genre in which Gypsy Rose Lee perfected her striptease entertainments, becomes more and more distant, a quaint rather than lurid bit of our theatrical past.

Meredith Willson's *The Music Man* (1957) – set in the genteel Midwest of 1912 – was a startling contrast to the other big hit show of the year, *West Side Story* (see pp. 177, 201–3 below). A charismatic con man plans to sell musical instruments to school children and then skip town, but is found out by, and enamoured of, the town librarian. Forced to stay in River City, Iowa, and teach the children, although he cannot read music himself, Hill leads the climactic parade. Though a dreadful din, it sounds wonderful to the loving parents and enthusiastic townspeople. Willson, who had grown up in Iowa, authentically captured the nostalgia and sentimental sweetness of a bygone era. Several appealing songs from the show became popular ('Seventy-six Trombones', 'Good-night, My Someone', and 'Till There Was You'), and the show ran for almost twice as long as the gritty, realistic *West Side Story*. It remains popular for revivals in summer stock and schools, and has played in many other countries as well.

Jerry Bock's *Fiorello!* (1959) was based on a ten-year period of the colourful New York politician Fiorello La Guardia's life before he became mayor of New York City. Covering such events as La Guardia's election to Congress before World War I, his joining the Air Force, his first race for mayor against the seemingly invincible James J. Walker, the death of his first wife, a financial scandal and preparations for the successful 1933 campaign, the show included various styles of music. *Fiorello!*'s Pulitzer Prize award inevitably invited comparison with George and Ira Gershwin's Pulitzer Prize-winning political satire, *Of Thee I Sing* (1931); however, *Fiorello!* did not quite measure up to the humour, wit and unity of the earlier musical. The Pulitzer

Prize notwithstanding, *Fiorello!* has hardly been seen since its original production. Bock would create his most important work a few years later with
Fiddler on the Roof.

The 1960s

Most Americans of the 1960s, certainly the vast majority of Broadway
habitués, intuitively understood the Rodgers and Hammerstein synthesis,
at least in its broadest strokes, and they took it for granted. In 1967 the
conductor and composer Lehman Engel hailed the arrival of the modern
musical, which he linked to *Pal Joey* and *Oklahoma!*, for representing models
of dramatic maturity, formal integrity and artistic excellence.[13] (He then
expanded on his thesis by discussing eleven shows in detail, including three
others by Rodgers and Hammerstein.) Any would-be achievers on Broadway
in this period had to begin with what Rodgers and Hammerstein had done.
As always, young newcomers could seek to introduce further innovations
of the proven formulas, but the basic template was clear.

Bye Bye Birdie (1960), with book by Michael Stewart, choreography
by Gower Champion, music by Charles Strouse and lyrics by Lee Adams,
was a hit in the year of Oscar Hammerstein's death, and perhaps symbolically represents a passing of the torch to a new generation. *Bye Bye Birdie*
is unquestionably a show of its era, an observation that could be taken as
either a compliment or a criticism. Its talky-teens-in-middle-America theme
guaranteed instant identification across the land. *Birdie* was the first full
Broadway show by its young creative team. Strouse wrote many excellent
tunes ('Put On a Happy Face', 'A Lot of Livin' to Do', 'Kids'), an uproarious
Shriners' Ballet, and a charming love ballad ('Baby, Talk to Me'). The show
ran for over 600 performances, and several of its stars – Dick Van Dyke,
Paul Lynde, Kay Medford, Michael Pollard, Chita Rivera – went on to more
exciting careers as a result of their exposure here. The parodic quality of *Bye
Bye Birdie*, however, while never flagging in sharpness and energy, imparted
a second-hand feeling to the show, whose intensity will likely increase over
time. The show's use of teenagers and its youthful spirit have made it a
favourite for high school productions, and in 1991 a major touring production starred Tommy Tune and Ann Reinking.

Because of its subject matter, the imminent departure of a rock star for
the military (a spoof on the early rock icon Elvis Presley), *Birdie* was widely
sold as a rock 'n' roll musical. In fact, the musical idiom is traditional
Broadway through and through. Conrad Birdie only appears as the image
of Elvis, not as the real thing. Attempted revivals have not been especially
successful, and the show has travelled poorly outside the United States.
In retrospect *Bye Bye Birdie* closely resembles the ubiquitous college-kid

musicals of the 1920s, blessed with charming melodies, a few clever lyrics, a dose of inventive dance and staging, with teens on the telephone in 'The Telephone Hour', and a harmless and relatively fast-moving plot. Strouse, of course, went on to write several more shows, but only *Applause* (1970) and *Annie* (1977) had the drawing power of *Bye Bye Birdie*. Like Frank Loesser, with whom he worked in the 1950s, Charles Strouse possesses prodigious musical gifts, showing a technical command of musical language that allows him to recreate nearly any period style or sound. Trained by several greats of the classical world, including Aaron Copland, Nadia Boulanger and David Diamond, he has written many songs for television and the movies, as well as live theatre, without always being recognised as an individual voice.

Strouse and Adams's only other major show of the 1960s was *Golden Boy* (1964), a remake of the Clifford Odets play of 1937, with one inspired twist sanctioned by the author, namely changing the name and race of the main character, a conflicted and doomed prize-fighter, from that of an Italian American to an African American. A considerable amount of the plot of the original script was deleted when the show was made into a musical. Strouse's songs were unexceptional, but with Sammy Davis Jr in the main role, the show ran for a year and a half at the Majestic Theatre. By creating a musical play focused on a substantial social issue, albeit with a certain amount of character complexity removed, Strouse and Adams once again invoked the spirit of Rodgers and Hammerstein. The jazzy score did not much resemble Rodgers in style, but Donald McKayle's choreography – especially in the final concluding boxing match – was widely hailed for its poetic appropriateness, a distant echo of Agnes de Mille in *Oklahoma!* and *Carousel*. *Golden Boy* has never been revived on Broadway, but a revised version played in Brooklyn, Florida and Connecticut in 1985 and 1991.

The Fantasticks also premiered in 1960, the year after *The Sound of Music* triumph. Probably no musical could be less like a Rodgers and Hammerstein show on the surface – with simple sets and a virtual annihilation of local colour – yet its perennial popularity can be linked to the values of Hammerstein in particular. The first act features an old-fashioned love story of thwarted meetings between two naifs and idealistic marriage triumphant. There is plenty of worldly-wise comedy provided by the fathers of the two lovers who at first obstruct, then engineer their children's romance. This obvious manipulation is carried off with great charm and sweet music. In the second act, reality sets in. Only in boring lives, filled with unrealised potential, do things ever proceed 'happily ever after'. The Candide-like moral, 'without a hurt the heart is hollow', confirms what we suspect all along, that new life and strength can only come out of pain and experience with the wider world. The mask of tragedy does not cover up a clearly optimistic tone that still manages to avoid strident preaching or rosy unreality.

The barebones sets and costumes for *The Fantasticks*, the most obviously unspectacular feature of the show, is precisely the thing that has maintained its appeal for off-Broadway audiences, not to mention innumerable high school, college and community productions.

The music is fully up to the standards of Rodgers and Hammerstein, and there is a kind of simplicity and universality about *The Fantasticks* that has aided its popularity in over tens of thousands of performances in thousands of productions in dozens of countries. The direct appeal of a romantic situation bound up with issues of families experiencing seasonal changes of the sort that occur everywhere is close to the centre of *The Fantasticks*'s incomparable success. Its humour wears well also. This kind of appeal can be found in many Rodgers and Hammerstein vehicles, most obviously in *Carousel* and *The Sound of Music*. Because of the restraint required in production of *The Fantasticks*, the warmly emotional text and tune of 'Try to Remember', for example, does not tumble into an embarrassing or cloying sentimentality. Harvey Schmidt's music matches Tom Jones's lyrics in much the same way that Rodgers was able efficiently and delicately to complement Hammerstein's poetry.

Lerner and Loewe's last collaboration, *Camelot*, opened late in 1960, almost as a last gasp of the Rodgers and Hammerstein type of musical play. Anxiously awaited by theatre-goers and critics alike, it was Lerner and Loewe's first show since *My Fair Lady*. Based on T. H. White's novel, *The Once and Future King*, *Camelot* told the story of the medieval King Arthur, his marriage to fair Guenevere, the creation of the idealistic Round Table, Guenevere's romance with Lancelot, and the villain Mordred's revelation of the illicit affair in order to provoke the destruction of Arthur's dream. With his Round Table in shambles and war raging in France, Arthur charges the young boy Tom to flee the battle, but always to remember and work to rebuild the ideals of Camelot. The king's final ringing soliloquy reminded many of the young, inspirational President Kennedy (elected in 1960) and his glamorous wife, Jacqueline. The public's willingness to associate a new Broadway show with a contemporary presidency reveals the extent to which America was attuned to New York's theatrical life in its heyday. Much of the group that assured *My Fair Lady*'s immense success joined Lerner and Loewe for *Camelot*, including Julie Andrews (leading actress), Moss Hart (director) and Oliver Smith (designer). Rex Harrison's leading-man counterpart in *Camelot* was the British actor Richard Burton, noted for dramatic roles. Opulent sets, elegant costuming and Lerner and Loewe's lyrics and music made a splendid vehicle, and several hit songs became very popular, especially 'If Ever I Would Leave You'. However, despite its 873-performance run, a successful touring company and at least three New York revivals, for most critics, *Camelot* was a disappointment after the delights of *My Fair*

Lady, which was the pinnacle of Lerner and Loewe's work together. It was ironic that both the Lerner and Loewe collaboration and the Rodgers and Hammerstein creative and business partnership ended the same year, one pair having essentially begun the move towards the integrated musical play and the second pair having helped close that chapter of American musical theatre history.

The last show to open on Broadway in 1960 (on December 26) was Garson Kanin's music industry satire about the selling of jukeboxes, *Do Re Mi*. Comden and Green provided the lyrics with Jule Styne's music, and the show enjoyed a good run of 400 performances, owing primarily to its clownish stars, Phil Silvers and Nancy Walker, and the beautiful tunes of Styne, especially 'Make Someone Happy'.

By the 1960s the time was ripe for new ideas. The final proof of the power of the status quo was the vehemence with which newcomers struggled to break from patterns that Rodgers and Hammerstein had relied on so often. One example of interesting innovation was Bob Merrill's *Carnival* (1961), based on a current film about Lili, an orphan who joins a carnival, falls in love with the magician Marco the Magnificent and ends up with the carnival's crippled, bitter puppeteer. Forgoing the use of any stage curtain and having performers entering and exiting through aisles, the director and choreographer Gower Champion staged some of the most exciting dances Broadway had seen in years. *Carnival* swept theatre awards that year and ran for 700 performances, and was revived by the City Center in 1968.

Apparently unstoppable, Richard Rodgers continued to work after the death of Oscar Hammerstein, writing both music and lyrics for *No Strings* (1962). He created a show about Barbara Woodruff, an African-American fashion model, and David Jordan, a Pulitzer Prize-winning author from Maine, who meet in Paris and fall in love. They travel to exotic locales together, but part when the writer decides to return to Maine in order to resume writing. Barbara declines to accompany him, aware of the prejudice they would meet. They part, their time together having been spent with 'no strings attached'. Rodgers's work was innovative: the orchestra sat backstage, musicians accompanied singers on-stage, principals moved scenery and props in view of the audience, and the orchestra contained no string instruments. Although Rodgers was admitted to be 'still a magician of the musical theater' and his score full of 'enchanted music', *No Strings* received very mixed reviews. Nonetheless, the show ran for 580 performances and enjoyed both successful tours and a London production in 1963. Rodgers continued his efforts with *Do I Hear a Waltz?* (1965), this time leaving the lyric writing to Stephen Sondheim. Since Sondheim had been a protégé of Oscar Hammerstein, many in the theatrical world had assumed that Rodgers and Sondheim might work together at some point. The bleak story concerns American spinster Leona Samish, who has an intense but hopeless affair with a married merchant in Venice. Sondheim's lyrics, described by Gerald Bordman as 'competent', the gloomy plot and a slow-moving production limited the run of *Do I Hear a Waltz?* to 220 performances, the shortest run of a Rodgers show during the entire decade.

Harvey Schmidt and Tom Jones's *110 in the Shade* (1963), based on the successful play by N. Richard Nash, *The Rainmaker* (1954), played for a creditable 330 performances on Broadway, but its songs never caught on once removed from the stage production. Despite a superficial resemblance to *Oklahoma!* in the show's western setting, use of a shady character (the rainmaker Starbuck) and focus on the romantic dreams of a young woman, the show sets its own tone. Starbuck, a far cry from *Oklahoma!*'s Jud, is saved from exposure by the miraculous arrival of rain, but heroine Lizzie Curry still resolves her wanderlust by opting for her dependable boy friend, Sheriff Fife, rather than the handsome stranger.

The ability of many of Rodgers and Hammerstein's songs to fly on their own was, of course, harder to imitate than their stage conventions. If it was difficult to write a new show that would succeed like *Oklahoma!* at a time when everyone alive knew the formula, it has always been challenging to write a great popular song that could stand on its own. *110 in the Shade* had no such song, and Schmidt and Jones's final collaboration of the sixties, *I Do! I Do!*, had only one. Produced by David Merrick and Gower Champion, and starring Robert Preston and Mary Martin, *I Do! I Do!* is a monothematic play tracing the fifty years of married life of the two characters. A work of taste, charm and sweet sentiment, it looked more towards the concept shows of the years to come. The show's intimacy and small staging demands have encouraged later productions in England, Australia and Germany.

Bob Merrill and Jule Styne's *Funny Girl* ran for 1,348 performances at the Winter Garden starting on 26 March 1964. The 'funny girl' referred to in the title was the vaudevillian, film and radio comedienne and torch singer Fanny Brice (1891–1951). The show illustrates some of the problems associated with using a historical figure in the relatively recent past as a focus, as opposed to merely a period setting. Life and art sometimes conflict, and audiences notice. Stanley Green reports several changes of production personnel and no less than forty rewrites of the final scene required before the show was deemed ready for an official premiere. On the other hand, *Funny Girl* benefited from the quite conscious parallels attempted with Styne's earlier woman-centred show, *Gypsy*. *Funny Girl* was also the show that made Barbra Streisand's stage career. The song 'People' became a runaway hit even before the opening. (Oscar Hammerstein's protégé Stephen Sondheim was first approached to write the story of Fanny Brice, but turned it down.) The show became a worthwhile film and it has remained in the popular consciousness, playing regularly in regional theatres in several English-speaking countries.

Jerry Bock's most spectacular show, *Fiddler on the Roof* (1964), was his greatest success and became the first Broadway musical to run for more than 3,000 performances.[14] The theatre historian Gerald Bordman has described the show as the 'last of the great masterworks of the era'.[15] Based on Sholom Aleichem's short stories, 'Tevye and His Daughters', it relates the experiences of a Jewish family in Russia around 1905 trying to survive poverty and religious persecution in a too quickly changing world. The story entwined issues of family relationships with romantic love interests to create a plot that appealed to a wide and diverse audience. The title and the fiddler who plays off and on throughout the show was inspired by the Russian artist Marc Chagall's painting 'The Green Violinist', in which a fiddler appears to be dancing on the roofs of a village.[16] Although the plot, lyrics and music are at times overwhelmingly sentimental and nostalgic, the realisation that the story mirrored genuine experiences of Jewish immigrants from the *shtetls* of the Ukraine gave the production unique credibility and power. Several songs from the show became standards almost overnight (such as 'Tradition', 'Matchmaker, Matchmaker', 'If I Were a Rich Man', and 'Sunrise, Sunset'). An impressive production team assembled the show: Hal Prince produced, Jerome Robbins directed and choreographed, and Zero Mostel, who played Tevye, displayed a phenomenal range of acting ability from the poignant to the comic. *Fiddler on the Roof* exhibits much of Rodgers and Hammerstein's recipe for success: a compelling, original literary source; a well-written libretto with intelligent theatrical pacing; beautifully written songs, many of which spring naturally from the action and contribute to character development; and sentiment which is natural and genuine enough to convince the audience this show is well worth seeing again. It is still produced in various types of venues throughout the world.

Jerry Herman's first Broadway show, *Milk and Honey* (1961), was set in Israel and told the story of American tourists and their desert romance. The show ends with the married but separated man aiming for a divorce in order to marry his new love. The song 'Shalom' became a hit, and Herman won a Tony award, but even better times were ahead for him when *Hello, Dolly!* opened in 1964, ran for 2,844 performances and won ten Tony awards. The title song, recorded by Louis Armstrong, was a staple on the song charts that year, greatly adding to the popularity of the show. The story had a long history, first appearing on the London stage in 1835, and eventually appearing as Thornton Wilder's play *The Matchmaker*. The plot centres around Dolly Levi, an 1890s New York matchmaker who sets her cap for her client Horace Vandergelder and entraps him for herself with some high jinks along the way, including a riotous evening at the Harmonia Gardens restaurant

Plate 12   Carol Channing in 1977 production of *Hello, Dolly!* at the Starlight Theater, Kansas City, Missouri

where she is welcomed by the staff ('Hello, Dolly!'). Neither innovative nor unusual in any way, it succeeded as a brilliant spectacle. Direction by the gifted Gower Champion and tasteful, turn-of-the-century-influenced sets provided a backdrop against which a long list of Broadway's most glamorous leading ladies played Dolly. Carol Channing made the role very much her own, and she was succeeded by the likes of Ginger Rogers, Martha Raye, Betty Grable, Pearl Bailey, Phyllis Diller and even the redoubtable Ethel Merman, who had turned down the invitation to create the role. Channing returned to the part several times during her career, and remains closely identified with both the character and the title song. It is no surprise that *Hello, Dolly!* remains exceedingly popular with the theatre-going public and has been produced in several languages. Herman scored another coup with *Mame* (1966), which received the Tony as best musical of the year and ran for 1,508 performances. The story of zany Auntie Mame and the adventures of her nephew as she raises him (amid the stock market crash, an attempt to break into musical theatre, subsequent marriage to a rich man who is killed while climbing the Alps, and then helping her nephew find the proper mate) gave Angela Lansbury the same kind of opportunity *Hello, Dolly!* had given Carol Channing, and she too became an important Broadway star through a Herman show. However, a revival of *Mame* with Lansbury in the summer of 1983 failed.

Several other significant shows opened in the mid-1960s. Mitch Leigh's only big hit, *Man of La Mancha* (1965), resembled Herman's two big shows of the 1960s in that it depended on the leading character for much of its energy. *Man of La Mancha* was a show-within-a-show production, where the novelist Cervantes is imprisoned for debts during the Spanish Inquisition and tells his fellow prisoners the story of Don Quixote, his faithful servant Sancho Panza and Aldonza, a servant girl whom Quixote sees as an idealistic 'Dulcinea' and for whom he is willing to fight any battle. By the end of the show, Aldonza/Dulcinea believes in Quixote's 'The Impossible Dream', too. The show is still produced often around the world and has been revived on Broadway.

Burton Lane and Alan Jay Lerner collaborated together to write *On a Clear Day You Can See Forever* (1965), from which the title song became a long-remembered favourite, but the libretto was loosely constructed and the fantasy theme involving extrasensory perception proved awkward. The title song is still well known, but the seldom-seen show is far better recognised from the 1970 film featuring Barbra Streisand.

A few other important collaborators also contributed their most important work to Broadway during the 1960s. Bricusse and Newley's *Stop the World – I Want to Get Off* (1962) and *The Roar of the Greasepaint – The Smell of the Crowd* (1965), and Sherman Edwards's *1776* (1969) enjoyed successful runs. The latter has proven most popular in regional and community theatres, especially around 1976, the year of the American Bicentennial, but its appeal outside the US has been limited. One of the most important new partnerships of the 1960s was formed by John Kander and Fred Ebb, whose first musical, *Flora, the Red Menace* (1965), provided Liza Minnelli with her first Broadway role. Their second show, *Cabaret* (1966), was set in the Kit Kat Klub of Berlin during the Nazis' rise to power. The love relationship between the American actress Sally Bowles and the aspiring young American writer Clifford Bradshaw, and Cliff's doomed friendship with the German Ernst Ludwig, who befriends Cliff and smuggles to help the Nazi cause, unfold amid conflicts related to anti-Semitism, social justice, personal freedom and abortion. The ironic, Brecht–Weill-influenced score, the clever unifying use of the Master of Ceremonies character, brilliantly played by Joel Grey, and the bitter undercurrents of the story made *Cabaret* an unusually powerful theatrical piece. It remains an utterly convincing show, although revivals are hampered by the strong identification of Joel Grey's masterly delineation of decadence captured in the well-adapted film version. Liza Minnelli's Sally is undoubtedly her best work on film.

A considerable part of Rodgers and Hammerstein's constructive legacy extends to the choice and formation of books, although here the point is one of general procedure on the road to achieving a script rather than the use of specific themes or techniques. As Lehman Engel and others have observed, nearly all successful musicals written between *Pal Joey* and *A Chorus Line* originated in a previous form, whether dramatic, literary or filmic. The challenge of developing a completely 'original' libretto has been met occasionally in a concept musical, such as *Company* (see pp. 184–5 below), and even in an old-fashioned book show like *Bye Bye Birdie*. However, beginning with someone else's play, poem, short story or biography seems to be the surer road to success. Rodgers and Hammerstein's ill-fated *Allegro* of 1947 and the successful but flawed *Me and Juliet* in 1953, coming amidst so many other successes for the team, seem to prove the rule.

The achievements of the major Broadway artists working between 1943 and 1970 transformed virtually all elements that make up what is known today as the American musical. Rodgers and Hammerstein led the way in the deft construction of plots, the invention of brilliantly singable poetry, the provision of consistently attractive music and the devising of stylised choreography for an entire evening's entertainment. Besides calculating the balance of forces and combining all elements to evoke a deep emotional response from a large and diverse audience in individual shows, they also paved the way for an era. Most remarkably, they succeeded in navigating the zone in which one could create with artistic integrity without sacrificing accessibility and popular appeal.

Recordings and Revivals (by William A. Everett)

Musicals from the mid-twentieth century have enjoyed lives far beyond their original stage incarnations through sound recordings – both original cast and studio – film and television versions and amateur and professional stage productions.

Before the popularity and common availability of video cassettes in the 1980s and DVDs in the 1990s, people experienced the world of musical theatre outside physical theatres (e.g., in their homes) primarily through sound recordings. The commercial viability of the 33rpm LP record in the late 1940s provided a new means for the distribution of musical theatre works. *South Pacific* (1949) was the first musical to have an original cast LP album. The commercial success of this venture led to the practice of releasing original cast albums that continues to the present day.

In addition to original cast recordings, the seemingly timeless allure of these golden-age works inevitably led to a multitude of studio cast recordings. While it is impossible to chronicle all of these here, some particular trends in the 1980s and 1990s can be noted. Dame Kiri Te Kanawa made a series of so-called crossover recordings in the 1980s that included *West Side Story* (1985, with José Carreras, Tatiana Troyanos and Kurt Ollmann, conducted by the composer), *South Pacific* (1986, with José Carreras, Sarah

Vaughan and Mandy Patinkin) and *My Fair Lady* (1987, with Jeremy Irons, John Gielgud, Warren Mitchell and Jerry Hadley). In the 1990s, John McGlinn conducted recordings of *Annie Get Your Gun* (1991) with Kim Criswell and Thomas Hampson and *Brigadoon* (1992) with Brent Barrett, Rebecca Luker, Judy Kaye and John Mark Ainsley, following the model of his pivotal rendition of *Show Boat* (1988) with Frederica von Stade, Jerry Hadley and Teresa Stratas. One of the most star-studded features in this constellation was the 1992 recording of *The King and I* with Julie Andrews, Ben Kingsley, Lea Salonga, Peabo Bryson and Marilyn Horne, conducted by John Mauceri. Two recordings of Bernstein's *Wonderful Town* appeared in the late 1990s: the 'first complete recording' with Rebecca Luker and Karen Mason, conducted by John Owen Edwards (1998) and a recording linked to a performance on the BBC Proms with Kim Criswell and Audra McDonald, conducted by Simon Rattle (1999).

Performers from a wide variety of backgrounds and styles have recorded discs devoted to musical theatre repertory. Barbra Streisand's *The Broadway Album* (1985) and *Back to Broadway* (1993) contain renditions that are worlds away from Kiri Te Kanawa's *Kiri on Broadway* (1993) or Dawn Upshaw's *I Wish It So* (1994) and *Dawn Upshaw Sings Rodgers and Hart* (1996). Bryn Terfel's *Something Wonderful* (1996, songs of Rodgers and Hammerstein) and *If Ever I Would Leave You* (1998, songs with lyrics by Lerner) demonstrate the Welsh opera singer's fondness for the American musical theatre. The legendary Julie Andrews released albums of music by Richard Rodgers (1994) and songs with lyrics by Alan Jay Lerner (1996). Broadway singers who made their mark during the late 1990s also have recorded discs on which they combine songs from earlier in the century with ones by living composers. Audra McDonald's *How Glory Goes* (2000) and Kristin Chenoweth's *Let Yourself Go* (2001) exemplify this contemporary approach.

The film versions of mid-century musicals, like those of operettas (chapter 3), rock musicals (chapter 13) and megamusicals (chapter 14), are the means – along with recordings – through which most people know (or think they know) the shows discussed in Part II of this volume (pp. 101–66). Through video releases, countless children are captivated constantly and consistently by these endearing works; not surprisingly, many youngsters can recite entire segments from the films – if not the entire films – by heart. This phenomenon is undoubtedly creating a new generation of musical theatre fans.

Film versions can be quite close to the stage originals, with only minor modifications, as in the case of the Rodgers and Hammerstein and Lerner and Loewe adaptations. On the other hand, substantial differences are often made, as in *Guys and Dolls* (1955), *1776* (1972) and *A Chorus Line* (1985), to offer a few examples. The dramatic needs of the film medium and its star system frequently account for changes in plot and/or concept.

In the 1990s, new screen versions of some classic Broadway musicals appeared. This trend paralleled the filming of Andrew Lloyd Webber musicals such as *Evita* (1996) for the big screen and others for television broadcast and subsequent video release (see Chapter 14).

The animated version of *The King and I* (1999) was very different from the original. If the creators' efforts were to fashion a version of the tale in direct contrast to either the original stage play or the 1999 film *Anna and the King* with Jodie Foster and Yun-Fat Chow, they certainly succeeded. The story was radically altered. A villainous sorcerer who wants to usurp the throne is the antagonist, helped by a dim-witted assistant taken from classic animated stock. A mischievous pet monkey, chase and rescue scenes and martial arts sequences all detract substantially from the Rodgers and Hammerstein exemplar. Most disturbing for purists is the ending of the film, where the King and Anna perform 'Shall We Dance?' in a happily-ever-after moment.

Tim Robbins's *Cradle Will Rock* (1999) – without the definite article – was based on Marc Blitzstein's *The Cradle Will Rock* (1938). The film incorporated the 1938 left-wing musical as a 'show within a show' into a plot that (somewhat) chronicled the final days of the Federal Theatre Project.[17]

As significant as the big-screen embodiments of mid-century shows are the television adaptations that appeared during the 1990s and early 2000s, all of which were subsequently released on video and/or DVD. These versions indicate the continued viability of the original shows as well as the networks' belief that people will invite them directly into their homes. Television versions of musicals have existed since the electronic medium began, but the versions from the 1990s confirm a renewed interest in the genre. This is undoubtedly rooted in the same aesthetic and love for the classics that infuse the popularity of revivals on Broadway and in the West End. Important television versions to appear since the early 1990s include *Gypsy* (1993), *Cinderella* (1997), *Annie* (1999) and *South Pacific* (2001).

In the CBS television broadcast of *Gypsy* in 1993, Bette Midler recreated the Merman role, making it her own. The lavish worlds of vaudeville and burlesque are vividly recreated in the musical's small-screen treatment. The new interpretation of Rodgers and Hammerstein's *Cinderella* on ABC's *The Wonderful World of Disney* in 1997 was the third incarnation of the television musical. The first two, both on CBS, were aired in 1957 and 1965. Brandy (star of the television show *Moesha*) played the title role to Bernadette Peters's wickedly intoxicating stepmother. Peters's interpolation of Rodgers and Hart's 'Falling in Love with Love' (from *The Boys from Syracuse*) accompanies the stepmother and stepsisters' preparation for and journey to the ball. The inclusion of the number is a fitting tribute to Rodgers's collaborations with both of his legendary lyricists, Hart and Hammerstein. Other actors in the telefilm include Paolo Montalban (Prince), Whitney Houston (Fairy Godmother), Whoopi Goldberg (Queen) and Victor Garber (King). Both royal marriages and even Cinderella's own stepsisters were cast 'colour blind'. This was a radical departure from the attitudes towards race exhibited in *South Pacific* and *The King and I*, and even more from the blatantly racially tagged animated features that Disney produced earlier in the century. Singing styles are as much about individual performers (Brandy, Peters, Houston) as dramatic characterisation, and the lavish choreographed scenes and clever photographic images endorse the traditions of film musicals and Disney fantasy.

Like *Cinderella*, *Annie* first appeared on ABC's *The Wonderful World of Disney*. The 1999 telefilm's cast included Kathy Bates, Alan Cumming, Audra McDonald, Kristin Chenoweth and Victor Garber – some of the biggest names on Broadway. Alicia Morton played the title role in a fresh manner, singing naturally and purely without any overdone affectations. Disney's version, like its *Cinderella*, features a multi-ethnic cast and eliminates the character of Punjab, Warbucks's frightfully stereotyped Indian butler.[18]

Only a year and a half later, the 2001 television version of *South Pacific* emulated the cinematic craze for World War II subjects. First broadcast on 26 March, the version of the classic Rodgers and Hammerstein musical starred Glenn Close and Rade Sherbedgia as Nellie Forbush and Emile De Becque. Harry Connick Jr took second billing for his role as Lt Joseph Cable, the tragic young crooning hero. Connick rendered the impassioned 'You've Got to be Carefully Taught' in a brooding manner, in duple metre rather than the original triple metre. Visuals for the number showed multiracial military units working together – a sign that prejudice could and should be overcome.

Cinematic images akin to those in the blockbuster film *Pearl Harbor* (2001) and the acclaimed ABC (the same network that broadcast the 2001 film) television series *China Beach* (1988–91) appear throughout *South Pacific*. *China Beach* concerned nurses during the Vietnam War, and although the war was different, the popularity of the series certainly influenced the film's focus on women's contributions. Similarly, *Pearl Harbor* and Steven Spielberg's *Empire of the Sun* (1987) clearly inspired the massive airfield and aviation sequences.[19] Wartime tragedy appears on-screen in the sequence showing Cable's death from stepping on a landmine – an event only referred to in previous versions of the musical. The realistic approach of turn-of-the-twenty-first-century war films thus replaced the fundamental escapism and romance of the original stage musical.

Mid-century musicals continue to receive live performances in many venues, both amateur and professional. Countless high schools throughout the United States turn to this repertory for their annual musicals, and the shows are equally popular with dinner theatres (US equivalent of British cabaret) and amateur companies.

Revivals played such a fundamental part of Broadway offerings in the 1990s that in 1994, a new Tony Award category, 'Best Revival (Musical)', was established. Mid-century originals to receive the honour include *Carousel* (1994), *The King and I* (1996), *Annie Get Your Gun* (1999) and *Kiss Me, Kate* (2000). By-products of these highly remunerative Broadway revivals are the plethora of new cast recordings with artists such as Nathan Lane (*Guys and Dolls*), Bernadette Peters (*Annie Get Your Gun*) and Faith Prince (*Guys and Dolls, Bells Are Ringing*).

The shows that represent the mid-century maturation of American musical theatre continue to be performed, cherished and remounted. The memorable melodies, sympathetic plots and characters, and inherent accessibility of these musicals continue to entertain performers and audiences alike. Their extraordinary popularity and subsequent canonisation keep them alive as perennial offerings around the world.

9 Musical sophistication on Broadway: Kurt Weill and Leonard Bernstein

BRUCE D. MCCLUNG AND PAUL R. LAIRD

What a marvellous sight, looking out the window during the rehearsal and seeing the students sitting around listening, some even singing the 'Moritat' ['Mack the Knife'] already. I don't think I will ever hear the music played as beautifully as when Lenny did it. It was so magical and effortless.[1]   LOTTE LENYA

So recalled Kurt Weill's widow about the performance of *The Threepenny Opera* at Brandeis University's Festival of the Creative Arts on 14 June 1952. The concert featured Bertolt Brecht and Weill's 1928 work, *Die Dreigroschenoper*, in an English translation by Marc Blitzstein, who also served as narrator. Nearly five thousand people filled the new Adolph Ullman Amphitheatre, and Lenya stopped the concert cold with her rendition of 'Pirate Jenny' (see accompanying photograph). The following year, a fully staged *Threepenny Opera* opened at the Theater de Lys in Greenwich Village. It ran for 96 performances, but closed because of a previous booking at the theatre. Reopening the following season, *The Threepenny Opera* ran for 2,611 performances to become (for a time) the longest-running musical in American history.[2] Lenya won the Tony for best featured actress in a musical, and the production garnered a special Tony, highly unusual for an off-Broadway show.

The conductor for the 1952 concert performance of *The Threepenny Opera* had been Leonard Bernstein, then a Brandeis faculty member. The concert proved a turning point for both Weill's and Bernstein's careers. Weill, who died in 1950 at the age of fifty, had fled Germany in 1933 and emigrated to the United States two years later. The Brandeis concert ushered in the so-called 'Weill renaissance' and the rediscovery of his German works by American audiences. *The Threepenny Opera*'s 'Mack the Knife', in renditions by Louis Armstrong, Dick Hyman, Bobby Darin, Frank Sinatra and Ella Fitzgerald, successively climbed the hit parade to sell over ten million records. As for Bernstein, his first opera, *Trouble in Tahiti*, had premiered at Brandeis two days before the *Threepenny* concert. Although his conducting career was firmly established, the period following the *Threepenny* concert was devoted to the stage: *Wonderful Town* opened on Broadway in 1953, *Candide* in 1956 and *West Side Story* in 1957.

Plate 13 Lotte Lenya (wife of Kurt Weill) performing the song 'Pirate Jenny' with Leonard Bernstein conducting (at left) during concert production of *The Threepenny Opera* at Festival of the Creative Arts, Brandeis University, 1952

When asked about Weill's possible influence on Bernstein, Lenya responded,

> I think surely Leonard Bernstein knows every note of Kurt Weill. I'm sure he does. Oh, he knows more than *The Threepenny Opera*. And he is the one who took up after Weill's death. I think Leonard Bernstein is the closest to Kurt Weill.[3]

Indeed, both composed in cultivated forms, such as the symphony and chamber music, and in vernacular genres, such as film scoring and the musical. Today both are regarded as prototypical 'crossover' composers who exploited the respective technologies of radio and television to reach broader audiences. Both drew musically on their Jewish heritage in such large-scale works as Weill's Biblical epic, *The Eternal Road* (1937), and Bernstein's Third Symphony ('Kaddish'), in vocal settings of the liturgy (the 'Kiddush' for Weill, the 'Hashkiveinu' and 'Yidgal' for Bernstein) and in settings of Hebrew folk songs. Although they arrived on Broadway from different avenues (for Weill via experimental drama, for Bernstein via modern dance), both brought a new level of musical and dramatic sophistication to the genre.

When Weill arrived in New York in 1935, economics were squeezing Broadway: the Depression had diminished investors' capital for new shows, the film industry had lured away the most talented writing teams, top ticket prices had been driven down from $6.60 to $4.40, and Hollywood 'talkies' and radio were giving live entertainment a run for its money. The only two musicals to run for more than 500 performances during the 1930s were topical or escapist revues: *Pins and Needles* (1937) and *Hellzapoppin'* (1938). Despite the grim outlook for the book musical, the first show Weill saw on Broadway was probably a rehearsal of *Porgy and Bess* (1935).[4] This exposure to one of Broadway's most unusual and lofty offerings of the thirties exerted a profound influence on Weill.

The Group Theatre, the noted company associated with Harold Clurman, recruited Weill for what became his first American stage work. Known for its leftist leanings, the Group brought Weill together with playwright Paul Green for a play with music entitled *Johnny Johnson* (1936). The story follows the adventures and psychological downfall of Johnny, an ordinary soldier who opposes the war he finds himself fighting. An example of how Weill creates intra-textual allusions in a score full of parody and musical quotations is 'Johnny's Song', which closes the show and attempts to encapsulate its pacifist message. Green recalled Weill telling him, 'If we can send the audience out humming a melody . . . it will be like a leitmotif.'[5] Weill included the melody of 'Johnny's Song' at critical junctures in the drama, foreshadowing its full statement at the denouement. One tabloid reporter described 'Johnny's Song' as 'the one song that is haunting everybody, that is hummed, sung and whistled on streets, in subways, in bathtubs and on terraces from one end of this comely island to the other'.[6] Nevertheless, *Johnny Johnson* failed to find an audience for its satire and closed after sixty-eight performances.

Weill's next collaborator was Maxwell Anderson, winner of the 1936–37 Critics' Circle Award for *High Tor*. As Weill had done in Germany, he was involving leading dramatists in musical theatre:

> One of the first decisions I made was to get the leading dramatists of my time interested in the problems of the musical theatre. The list of my collaborators reads like a good selection of contemporary playwrights of different countries: George Kaiser and Bert Brecht in Germany, Jacques Deval in France, Franz Werfel, Paul Green, Maxwell Anderson, Moss Hart . . . in America.[7]

Together Weill and Anderson fashioned a musical version of Washington Irving's *The History of New York by Diedrich Knickerbocker*. Although now primarily remembered for 'September Song', *Knickerbocker Holiday* (1938) gently lampooned Roosevelt's New Deal while telling a traditional love story. Weill's score is closest to operetta, with twenty-eight musical numbers invoking models from Gilbert and Sullivan to Sigmund Romberg. Weill bucked many of Broadway's conventions, chief among them not entrusting his

scores to professional orchestrators. (This was remarkable, but not unprecedented: Victor Herbert had orchestrated his operettas.) Weill described the
gruelling schedule of orchestrating his own shows:

> You sleep about two hours a night for the four weeks that it takes, but it's
> fun. Not until the rehearsals get under way can you start your
> orchestrating... since until you know who the singers are going to be you
> can't tell what key to put each number in.[8]

In his *New York Times* review, Brooks Atkinson described *Knickerbocker
Holiday* as 'vigorous composing for the modern theatre, superior to Broad-
way songwriting without settling in the academic groove'.[9] *Knickerbocker
Holiday* played for 168 performances, but failed to recoup its investment.

Lady in the Dark (1941) provided Weill with his proverbial big break.
The musical play, which dramatised a woman undergoing psychoanalysis,
brought together the playwright Moss Hart (author of a string of comedies
with George S. Kaufman), the lyricist Ira Gershwin and Weill. Sam Harris's
production was strictly first class. Gertrude Lawrence signed for the title role
at a minimum of $2,000 per week against 15 per cent of the box office. To
enable nearly instantaneous scene changes, Harry Horner placed *Lady* on
four hand-operated turntables. With a cast of fifty-four, a twenty-member
orchestra, and a stage crew of forty-one, the mega-musical's budget grew
to an astronomical $127,715. *Lady* played for two seasons on Broadway
and toured ten cities with a Broadway reengagement for a jackpot of 777
performances. The crush for seats established the practice of advance sales
on Broadway, while Paramount Pictures' $285,000 bid broke the previously
held record paid for film rights.

Lady in the Dark's commercial success, however, did not overshadow its
revolutionary form. Music was restricted to three through-composed dream
sequences which articulate the heroine's subconscious. Music was also at the
centre of the plot: the key to the 'lady's' neurosis was the recollection of a
childhood song ('My Ship') of which a fragment recurs in her nightmares.
Weill expanded the leitmotivic technique of *Johnny Johnson* not only to
create a web of allusions, but also to provide a musical analogue for the
drama. The first two phrases of 'My Ship' are tonally ambiguous, arpeggiat-
ing a complex of notes whose constituents are D minor and F major triads.
Weill worked out this musical riddle over the course of the drama: the 'incorrect' minor submediant giving way to the 'correct' major tonic to parallel
the heroine's psychoanalytical treatment.[10] Atkinson in a *Times* article for
Lady's second season deemed Weill 'the best writer of theatre music in the
country'.[11]

Weill's next offering was as close as he ever came to a regulation musical
comedy, and, perhaps not coincidentally, it enjoyed the longest continuous

Broadway run of his American shows (567 performances before heading out on tour). His collaborators included the lyricist Ogden Nash and the Marx Brothers' scriptwriter S. J. Perelman. Based on F. Anstey's 1885 novella *The Tinted Venus* (a remake of the Pygmalion/Galatea myth), *One Touch of Venus* (1943) told the story of a barber, Rodney Hatch, who slips his fiancée's ring on a statue of Venus. The goddess comes miraculously to life, and, much to Rodney's panic, sets out to win him away from his sweetheart. *One Touch of Venus* starred Mary Martin, who popularised 'That's Him' and 'Speak Low'. Agnes de Mille's two ballets capitalised on her previous success with *Oklahoma!* (see chapters 7 and 11). *One Touch of Venus* provided escapist fare during the war, made Mary Martin a star and saw 'Speak Low' climb to the top of the charts.

In 1944 Weill and Ira Gershwin reunited for a musical version of Edwin Justus Mayer's 1924 play, *The Firebrand*, about Benvenuto Cellini. Weill's intentions, preserved in a letter to Gershwin, were to turn it into a 'smart, intelligent, intimate romantic-satirical operetta for the international market'.[12] At the Boston tryout, George S. Kaufman attempted his renowned play doctoring, but to no avail. *The Firebrand of Florence* (1945), despite an astronomical budget of $225,000, closed on Broadway after a mere forty-three performances and represents Weill's only fully-fledged American flop. Lenya may have been miscast as the Duchess and the production may have been leaden, but in any case European operetta's brief renaissance on Broadway was nearly over.[13] *Song of Norway* (1944), presented earlier that season, had captured the best vocalists and audience. Despite its shortcomings, *The Firebrand of Florence* was the lengthiest of Weill's scores for the American theatre to date, sprawling to some 650 pages of orchestral score. The opening scene of Cellini's near execution and pardon was remarkable on Broadway: twenty minutes of continuous music incorporating recitative, aria, choruses and dances.

Street Scene (1947) fulfilled two of Weill's dreams. The first, evidently sparked by *Porgy and Bess*, was to write an American opera. The second was to create 'a special brand of musical theatre which would completely integrate drama and music, spoken word, song and movement'.[14] Elmer Rice's Pulitzer Prize-winning play of 1929 contained all the necessary ingredients, as Weill explained:

> It was a simple story of everyday life in a big city, a story of love and passion and greed and death. I saw great musical possibilities in its theatrical device – life in a tenement house between one evening and the next afternoon. And it seemed like a great challenge to me to find the inherent poetry in these people and to blend my music with the stark realism of the play.[15]

Weill and Rice collaborated on adapting the play, and the poet Langston Hughes was the lyricist. Rather than unify the score through a single idiom, Weill chose as an analogue for the melting pot a disparity of musical styles: 'I discovered that the play lent itself to a great variety of music, much as the streets of New York themselves embrace the music of many lands and many people'.[16]

Street Scene's diverse score reveals something about each of the characters: the central story of betrayal and murder in the Murrant family is told through the heightened musical language of late nineteenth-century Italian opera. Other inhabitants of the brownstone sing in their respective idioms: a blues-inspired number for the black janitor, a jitterbug for the nightclub hoppers, a children's game-song for the young people, etc. 'Opera was a way people lost money' on Broadway, quipped Oscar Hammerstein II. Consequently, *Street Scene* was billed as a 'dramatic musical'. Lest anyone be fooled, the two dramatic leads were cast from the Metropolitan Opera and a thirty-five-piece orchestra filled the pit. Olin Downes, the *Times*'s music critic, called it 'the most important step towards significantly American opera' to date.[17] Although *Street Scene* had an impressive opening, it was not able to hold its own against that season's *Finian's Rainbow* and *Brigadoon*. It closed after 148 performances – a disappointing run for a 'dramatic musical', but an impressive record for 'An American Opera', as it was subtitled when the piano-vocal score was published.

Never one to repeat himself, Weill's next show was worlds away from opera. He conceived with Alan Jay Lerner what was to become the proto-typical 'concept musical'. Subtitled 'A Vaudeville', *Love Life* (1948) carried an explanatory note in its playbill regarding its unusual form:

> *Love Life* is presented in two parts, each consisting of a series of acts. The sketches, which start in 1791 and come up to the present day, are presented in the physical style of the various periods. The four main characters, Susan and Sam Cooper, and their children, Johnny and Elizabeth, who present the story, do not change in appearance as time moves on. The vaudeville acts which come between each sketch are presented before a vaudeville drop and are styled and costumed in a set vaudeville pattern.

The book scenes record economic effects on the Coopers' marriage: from the transition of an agrarian to industrial economy, through the halcyon days of the 1920s to the post-War period. Intervening vaudeville acts comment on the book scenes and keep the audience from getting too emotionally involved with the Coopers.

Love Life, with its book scenes of the Coopers' marriage in six periods (from 1791 to the 'today' of 1948), adumbrates the concept musical through its series of vignettes. The vaudeville acts prefigure the use of the Kit Kat Klub numbers of *Cabaret* and the comment songs in *Company*. The overriding concept of the economic effect on the institution of marriage was reflected in all the disciplines of the production. Lerner, credited with book and lyrics, recalled, 'What made writing *Love Life* so much fun was discarding a lot of old rules and making up your own as you went along. We knew what we wanted to say. The problem was finding a way to tell our story.'[18] *Love Life* paved the way for such later concept musicals as *Cabaret* (1966), *Company* (1970), *A Chorus Line* (1975), *Chicago* (1985) and *Assassins* (1991). Weill's score ran to 738 pages – a full two hours of music. *Love Life*, starring Nanette Fabray and Ray Middleton, chalked up a respectable 252 performances.

Weill's last musical for Broadway was an adaptation of Alan Paton's anti-apartheid novel, *Cry the Beloved Country*. Weill and Maxwell Anderson planned a 'musical tragedy' (an inversion of 'musical comedy') with the chorus as the central musical element. On top of this layer, they fashioned a handful of songs for individual characters. Weill scored the work for twelve instrumentalists which gives it a transparent, chamber texture. After *Lost in the Stars* (1949) opened, Olin Downes wrote a letter to Weill complaining about the use of numbers in American popular song form (AABA) in a work with such operatic power. Weill defended his use of the form:

> Personally, I don't feel that this represents a compromise because it seems to me that the American popular song, growing out the American folk-music, is the basis of an American musical theatre (just as the Italian song was the basis of Italian opera), and that in this early stage of development, and considering the audiences we are writing for, it is quite legitimate to use the form of the popular song and gradually fill it with new musical content.[19]

Lost in the Stars, despite a strong opening, struggled to find an audience. The stress exacerbated Weill's hypertension, hastening a heart attack. Anderson and he had begun work on a new musical (*Huckleberry Finn*), but Weill did not live to see it completed. In eulogising Kurt Weill, composers, critics and collaborators attempted to sum up his contributions to the American musical theatre. Virgil Thomson wrote in the *New York Herald Tribune*, 'every new work was a new model, a new shape, a new solution of dramatic problems'.[20] The *New York Times* obituary quoted Brooks Atkinson's 1941 review, 'He is not a song writer but a composer of organic music that can bind the separate elements of a production and turn the underlying motive into a song.'[21] Maxwell Anderson in *Theatre Arts* magazine wrote, 'We have had no other rounded and complete composer, able to help on the book and lyrics, consummate as arranger and orchestrator, bubbling with original and unhackneyed melodies.'[22] Nine days after *Lost in the Stars* closed (after a run of 281 performances), ten thousand people attended a Kurt

Weill Memorial Concert at Lewisohn Stadium. Olin Downes, in previewing the concert, concluded, 'He has written for the stage with a technic and imagination and heart which make him one of the central figures in the development of an American form of opera.'[23]

Leonard Bernstein's stage career overlapped with that of Weill by only six years, and the only musical he wrote before Weill died was *On the Town* (1944). Despite its success, Bernstein did not return to Broadway for almost a decade. Except for his three musicals in the 1950s – *Wonderful Town* (1953), *Candide* (1956) and *West Side Story* (1957) – Bernstein was an irregular presence on Broadway, in part because of his many other activities, but his importance comes in the prominence of these four shows. From the time of his appointment as assistant conductor of the New York Philharmonic in 1943, Bernstein was seldom far from a podium, making his compositional activity sporadic. His interest in the stage began as a teenager when he put on versions of Gilbert and Sullivan shows and Bizet's *Carmen* with friends. While still at Harvard he directed Marc Blitzstein's *The Cradle Will Rock* (1937), taking the composer's famous role as pianist and narrator. Blitzstein attended the production and was most impressed, launching their long-term friendship.

Bernstein's entrance into the Broadway musical came through modern dance. Jerome Robbins, a young dancer with the American Ballet Theatre, sought a composer to score a wartime ballet concerning three sailors on leave in New York City. He found Bernstein, who took to the idea and the vernacular dance music that Robbins wanted in the score. The ballet *Fancy Free* (1944) is a delightful romp through many twentieth-century styles, including blues and big band jazz. It became a hit, and the ballet's set designer, Oliver Smith, and his business partner Paul Feigay saw the makings of a good Broadway musical. They convinced Robbins and Bernstein, who insisted that his friends Betty Comden and Adolph Green write the book and lyrics. The addition of the veteran director George Abbott helped secure funding, including some from MGM in return for the film rights. All agreed that the show should reflect Broadway's recent trends towards the integration of plot, music and dance, exemplified the previous season by *Oklahoma!*. Abbott asserted creative control and moulded the play, songs and dances through many cuts and changes. After a Boston tryout, the show opened at New York's Adelphi Theater on 28 December 1944. The cast included only two noted personalities: Sono Osato, a featured dancer in *One Touch of Venus*, and the comedienne Nancy Walker. Comden and Green played roles in addition to their writing duties. *On the Town* surged forward breathlessly in locales all over New York City, propelled by Abbott's excellent sense of pacing, Robbins's energetic dances and Bernstein's eclectic score. The show included six dance sequences – often accompanied by the complex music associated with modern dance – and songs that more or less fitted in the Broadway mould. *On the Town*'s dances each helped advance the plot. Their importance has been recognised by Denny Martin Flinn: 'In one startling night . . . and 436 subsequent performances, *On the Town* created and established the greatest of all American contributions to the stage arts: American theatre dance.'[24]

Bernstein composed the music for the dance numbers himself, a job often assigned to a dance arranger, but unlike Weill, he did not do all of his own orchestrations and received assistance from Hershy Kay, Don Walker, Elliott Jacoby, Bruce Coughlin and Ted Royal.[25] Three of the dances are heard in Bernstein's symphonic work *Three Dance Episodes from 'On the Town'*: 'The Great Lover Displays Himself', a lively swing movement from the dream ballet in Act II; 'Lonely Town: Pas de Deux', an arrangement reminiscent of Copland (following the ballad's performance in Act I); and 'Times Square: 1944', a jaunty exploration of 'New York, New York' that serves as the finale of Act I. *On the Town*'s songs demonstrate Bernstein's witty manipulation of American vernacular music. 'I Feel Like I'm Not Out of Bed Yet' includes prominent use of blues notes, and 'New York, New York' includes a surprisingly dissonant fanfare, jazz rhythms, and canonic imitation. The raucous 'Come Up to My Place' is a dialogue with Chip and Hildy, singing, respectively, with boogie-woogie and blues references. 'Carried Away' is a quasi-operatic duet in an unexpected minor key. The ballad 'Lonely Town' is perhaps the most typical Broadway song in the show, with a bluesy melody and an AABA form. 'Carnegie Hall Pavane (Do-Do-Re-Do)' begins stiffly classical, but becomes a parody of the Andrews Sisters.

Bernstein's next score on Broadway was incidental music and songs for J. M. Barrie's *Peter Pan*, followed in 1952 by his one-act opera *Trouble in Tahiti*, which ran for a time on Broadway in 1955. *Wonderful Town*, somewhat in the mould of *On the Town*, provided Bernstein, Comden and Green with another hit. The musical was based upon stories by Ruth McKenney about two sisters who move from Ohio to New York, further popularised by Joseph Fields and Jerome Chodorov in their play *My Sister Eileen* (1940). They had adapted the play as a musical and the producers Robert Fryer and George Abbott held an option on Rosalind Russell to star in the show. The first team hired to write the score failed to do so, and Abbott asked Bernstein, Comden and Green to join the project before losing the option on Russell. They completed the score in just five weeks in late 1952.

Wonderful Town was essentially a musical comedy with songs strategically placed in the plot. The show included important dance numbers choreographed by Donald Saddler (with unattributed assistance from Jerome Robbins[26]), such as Russell's hilarious 'Conga!' with Brazilian sailors and the 'Ballet at the Village Vortex', but the songs carried the evening. Comden and Green's evocations of 1930s culture, such as the questions that Ruth asks the Brazilian sailors in 'Conga!', help set the time and place, and Bernstein captured the era through music. 'Christopher Street' opens the show with a tour of Greenwich Village, spiced with delightful blues references and rich tempo and mood changes. 'One Hundred Easy Ways' balances musical interest and clever lyrics while working around Russell's limited singing ability. 'Swing!' evokes music of the thirties and 'Wrong Note Rag' brings rhythmic and harmonic complexity to the service of comedy, one of Bernstein's greatest compositional gifts. *Wonderful Town* ran for 559 performances, with Carol Channing replacing Rosalind Russell near the end of the run. The *Times*'s Olin Downes was among those who found the show a major step forward:

> This is an opera made of dance, prattle and song... We are coming to
> believe that when American opera created by a composer of the stature
> of the Wagners and Verdis of yore does materialize, it will owe much more
> to the robust spirit and the raciness of accent of our popular theater than
> to the efforts of our emulators... of the tonal art of Bartok, Hindemith,
> and Stravinsky.[27]

Bernstein's next Broadway projects came in collaboration with the dramatist Lillian Hellman, starting with incidental music for Hellman's *The Lark* (1955), a translation of Jean Anouilh's French play on Joan of Arc. In *Candide* (1956) Hellman and Bernstein set out to demonstrate in the McCarthy era that the United States was not 'the best of all possible worlds'. The long search for a lyricist included early work with James Agee, Dorothy Parker and John LaTouche before they found Richard Wilbur.[28] Unfortunately, the collaborators never agreed what *Candide* was: Hellman wrote heavy-handed satire, and Bernstein and Wilbur produced an operetta. The show's director was the famous Tyrone Guthrie. Much has been written about the difficulty of the collaboration and concept. Guthrie emerges as a believable source when he calls *Candide* 'wildly pretentious'. He notes Hellman's disadvantage because they had to cast singers rather than actors and writes that his own direction 'skipped along with the effortless grace of a freight train heavy-laden on a steep gradient'.[29] Despite a sumptuous production and some positive notes from Brooks Atkinson and other critics, *Candide* never found an audience and closed after seventy-five performances.

But *Candide*, of course, did not die in the 1950s. Bernstein's score is a charming romp through many European dance forms and genres with several unforgettable numbers, inspiring several revivals, including Hal Prince's so-called 'Chelsea' version of 1973, where Hellman's book was replaced by that of Hugh Wheeler, and new versions in the 1980s. Bernstein fashioned the score basically without his usual jazz and blues influences. He mined other musical traditions and produced a Broadway score of rare sophistication and range. Among the gems in *Candide* are the rollicking Overture, the gavotte 'Life is Happiness Indeed', Candide's laments, the witty 'Auto-da-fé', the laughing-song 'Glitter and Be Gay', the tango 'I Am Easily Assimilated', the schottische 'Bon Voyage', and the inspiring, Copland-like finale, 'Make Our Garden Grow'.

Where *Candide* failed in the collaborative process, *West Side Story* (1957) succeeded because its four main creators – director and choreographer Jerome Robbins, writer Arthur Laurents, Bernstein and lyricist Stephen Sondheim – worked together to make the dancing, script, music and lyrics an artistic whole. The show's integration and use of dance is considered in chapter 11; here we explore Bernstein's unification of the score through recurring musical styles and intervals. Bernstein employs various musical styles in *West Side Story* to describe different groups in the story. Complex rhythms and mixed metres capture the violence of the gangs, heard in the 'Prologue', 'Jet Song', 'Cool' and 'The Rumble'. Latin rhythms evoke the background of the Puerto Rican gang, the Sharks. Bernstein included Latin dances in 'The Dance at the Gym' and 'America' and used hemiola in the accompaniment of 'Something's Coming', a *tresillo* $(3 + 3 + 2)$ bass line for 'Maria', and a beguine accompaniment for 'Tonight'. More traditional Broadway fare such as lyrical ballads and waltzes appear in songs involving the lovers Tony and Maria. Ballads include 'Maria', 'Tonight', and 'Somewhere'. 'One Hand, One Heart' is a slow waltz, but 'I Feel Pretty' is faster and perhaps infused with the spirit of the Aragonese *jota*. *West Side Story*'s various styles come together dramatically in 'A Boy Like That/I Have a Love', where Anita's unpredictable, violent song is vanquished by Maria's sweet statement of devotion to Tony.

A number of commentators have noted Bernstein's use of two intervals – the tritone and minor seventh – to unify the score.[30] The opening motive of *West Side Story*, an ascending perfect fourth followed by an ascending tritone, announces the latter interval's importance. The tritone is the first interval heard in the melodies of 'Maria' and 'Cool', and occurs early in 'Something's Coming'. It figures prominently in the accompaniment of a number of other songs. The 'Dance at the Gym' includes a number of obvious tritones, especially when Tony first sees Maria, and then the melody of the song 'Maria', with its tritone, sounds in the 'Maria Cha Cha'. The minor seventh is less important in the score, but its strong association with the song 'Somewhere' allows for several satisfying moments of dramatic unity.

About the time *West Side Story* opened, Bernstein assumed co-directorship of the New York Philharmonic with Dimitri Mitropoulos. The orchestra soon named Bernstein music director. During Bernstein's sabbatical in

1964–65 he tried to adapt Thornton Wilder's *The Skin of Our Teeth* as a musical with Robbins, Comden and Green, but the effort failed.[31] In 1968 another project with Robbins that came to nothing was an adaptation of Bertolt Brecht's play *The Exception and the Rule*.[32] *Mass* (1971), written for the opening of the Kennedy Center in Washington DC, included elements from Broadway, but is an entirely different sort of work.

Bernstein's last musical was *1600 Pennsylvania Avenue* (1976), with book and lyrics by Alan Jay Lerner. Lerner and Bernstein wrote a strident plea for racial tolerance, including both white and black occupants of the White House: presidents and first ladies, slaves and servants. As was the case with *Love Life* by Weill and Lerner (1948), the show skipped through history and followed one or more themes, drawing parallels between different times. *1600 Pennsylvania Avenue*, however, suffered from a cumbersome book and many urged Bernstein and Lerner to revise it or cancel the project. The show opened on Broadway on 4 May 1976 and closed after seven performances. Bernstein's score fared better in reviews than the book, but its reception was at best mixed, and Bernstein refused to allow an original cast album. In subsequent years some have praised Bernstein's use of nineteenth-century musical styles and such songs as 'Duet for One' and 'Take Care of this House'. Bernstein's estate issued a concert version in 1997 called *A White House Cantata*. It was first performed at London's Barbican Centre on 8 July 1997 and has been recorded.[33]

Weill and Bernstein shared similar approaches to the Broadway musical, both making fresh use of vernacular musical styles and bringing a musical sophistication unusual for Broadway. As Lotte Lenya suggested, it was Bernstein who continued Weill's trajectory as a composer of dramatic music on Broadway in the 1950s. In an age when many were content to follow the lead established by the success of Rodgers and Hammerstein, Weill, Bernstein and their collaborators continued to challenge Broadway's prevailing norms and produce some of the more artistically influential musicals of the 1940s and 1950s.

PART III

Evolutions and integrations: after 1970

10 Stephen Sondheim and the musical of the outsider

JIM LOVENSHEIMER

In a *New York Times Magazine* interview with Frank Rich, Stephen Sondheim (b. 1930) told an anecdote as revealing as it was charming. Reminiscing about the New Haven opening of *Carousel* in 1945, when he was fifteen, the composer/lyricist recalled the emotional impact of the first act's closing moments. 'I remember how everyone goes off to the clambake at the end of Act One and Jigger just follows, and he was the only one walking on stage as the curtain came down. I was sobbing.'[1] In the next paragraph, however, Sondheim displays a more characteristic caginess when considering why *Carousel* is his second favourite score. (*Porgy and Bess* is his favourite.) After suggesting that he might be drawn to *Carousel* 'because it's about a loner [the protagonist Billy Bigelow] who's misunderstood', Sondheim dismisses the thought, calling it 'psychobabble'.[2] Later in the interview, he returns to this somewhat defensive argument, noting that, after all, 'the outsider is basic to a lot of dramatic literature. This country's about conformity. And so nonconformity is a fairly common theme.'[3]

Nonconforming outsiders are indeed inherent in much dramatic literature. American musicals, however, have generally avoided them, and certainly their presence as protagonists in musicals before *Carousel* is rare. Even their existence as important supporting characters is unusual. Notable exceptions exist, of course. They include the mulatto Julie in *Show Boat* (1927), the discovery of whose racial heritage results in her dismissal from the showboat company and her subsequent tragedy, and Jud Fry in *Oklahoma!* (1943), whose angry isolation is voiced in the disturbing number 'Lonely Room'. With the possible exceptions of *Pal Joey* (1940) and the opera-derived *Carmen Jones* (1943), however, musicals before *Carousel* were not about these outsiders. Instead, these were secondary characters whose conflict with society usually resulted in society's triumph. Interestingly, each of these rather atypical works, with the exception of *Pal Joey*, had book and lyrics by Oscar Hammerstein II, Sondheim's mentor and close personal friend. Only after *Carousel*, which also was written by Hammerstein, do we find the outsider increasingly cast as the principal figure in a musical, particularly a musical by Stephen Sondheim. Perhaps, as Sondheim acknowledges, this is because the nonconformity of the outsider is 'obviously something I feel, belonging to a number of minorities'.[4] (Sondheim is Jewish and gay.) Or perhaps, as he quipped earlier in the interview, such observations really are psychobabble. Either way, Sondheim's body of work for the musical theatre thus far suggests that his early emotional reaction to a work about a disenfranchised member of society, a nonconformist, was an indication of the theme upon which he since has written many variations, each of them in a distinct and personal style. He seems always to have been attracted to characters whose actions place them outside the boundaries of mainstream society. Neuroses are plentiful in these musicals, and they are found in characters whose complexities often recall the loner who troubled and moved the young Sondheim.

Sondheim's first Broadway shows were *West Side Story* (1957) and *Gypsy* (1959), for which he provided the lyrics to Leonard Bernstein's and Jule Styne's scores, respectively, and even they are concerned with outsiders and/or the disenfranchised. Already Sondheim's lyrics create sharply drawn characters who express, among other feelings, a frustration with, or even contempt for, mainstream society. *West Side Story*, for example, concerns several layers of social ostracism: a white gang (the Jets) aggressively treats a Puerto Rican gang (the Sharks) as outsiders from American society, and the Sharks deeply resent and violently challenge that status; both gangs are disenfranchised from society in general (in the clever lyrics of the number 'Gee, Officer Krupke!', the Jets chronicle their misfit status); and the lovers Tony and Maria are rejected by both gangs because of their relationship. Sondheim's lyrics for the show create an expressive vernacular that emphasises the strained social relationships between the two gangs. *Gypsy*'s Mama Rose thumbs her nose at 'respectable' bourgeois society: 'they can stay and rot', she sings, 'but not Rose'. Only at the end of the show, when Rose breaks down in the number 'Rose's Turn', does the audience see the toll that this disenfranchisement has taken. Furthermore, both early works also feature a motive common to several of the later works: the outsider's ability, or at least hope, to escape reality through dreams or dreamlike fantasy. *West Side Story* contains a dream ballet in which the two principal characters imagine a life in which none are outsiders; and *Gypsy* is full of Rose's leitmotif 'I had a dream', with which she confronts various crises. Many of Sondheim's subsequent outsiders also express themselves in or through dreams, or in dreamlike detachments from reality. In *Follies*, for instance, the neurotic and emotionally frazzled characters take turns performing acts in an imaginary and nightmarish vaudeville. Much of the action of *Company* (1970) occurs in a timeless and dreamlike suspension of reality in which Robert, an emotionally detached bachelor, comes to grips with what he really wants from life. In the second act of

Sunday in the Park with George (1984), the twentieth-century George is consoled and inspired by the dreamlike apparition of Dot, a character from another century (and another act), and in *Assassins* (1991), the characters fervently, if desperately, believe that 'Everybody's got the right to their dreams.'

A consideration of Sondheim's scores as representations of the outsider provides an entrée to discussing some of their general and specific stylistic traits. These traits create what Sondheim scholar Steven Swayne has called Sondheim's 'multiple musical voices', many of which are imitative or referential.[5] Specifically, argues Swayne, Sondheim exploits this 'range of musical voices in pursuit of his singular voice: the voice of character delineation'.[6] While Sondheim's principal purpose, therefore, is the clear depiction of individual characters, his means for achieving it are as diverse as the concepts for the shows in which those characters exist.

The introduction above of the word 'concepts' in turn demands mention of the term 'concept musical', for it is often applied to Sondheim's work in general and relates specifically to any discussion of his means of creating characters for a given show. Joanne Gordon sums up this term as follows:

> Concept, the word coined to describe the form of the Sondheim musical, suggests that all elements of the musical, thematic and presentational, are integrated to suggest a central idea or image . . . Prior to Sondheim, the musical was built around the plot . . . The book structure for Sondheim, on the other hand, means the idea. Music, lyric, dance, dialogue, design, and direction fuse to support a focal thought. A central conceit controls and shapes an entire production, for every aspect of the production is blended and subordinated to a single vision . . . Form and content cannot really be separated, for the one dictates and is dependent on the other.[7]

In other words, Gordon continues, Sondheim 'develops a new lyric, musical, and theatrical language for each work. Sondheim's music and lyrics grow out of the dramatic idea inherent in the show's concept and themselves become part of the drama.'[8]

Two compositional techniques especially facilitate Sondheim's ability to change musical languages without losing his own 'singular voice': the use of motives, or short, recognisable musical ideas that sometimes represent non-musical concepts or characters and that are often used as structural cells for lengthier musical statements and the use of pastiche, which is the presence of music and/or musical styles from various sources in a single work. While the first of these is observable as early as *Company* and, after *Sweeney Todd* (1979), becomes increasingly important, the second appears as a recognisable trait even earlier and is variously exploited by Sondheim in nearly all his works.

Company, then, serves as an early example of one way Sondheim uses motives to define the character of an outsider. Throughout *Company*, Sondheim uses a recurring motive, the 'Robert' or 'Bobby' motive, as a cell, or building block, for much of the score, as Stephen Banfield has demonstrated.[9] (The motive, first sung to the words 'Bobby, Bobby', consists of a descending minor third followed by a descending major second. The initial pitch of each interval is the same.) What Banfield does not mention, however, is the careful utilisation of this motive in relation to Robert and the other characters, and as a musical symbol of Robert's detachment from his married friends. It is heard almost immediately at the show's beginning, and a development of it introduces the opening title song. After this, the motive is used between scenes and before, or as part of, musical numbers involving Robert and his married friends, a group from whom he is an outsider despite the mutual affection between them.

The motive does not introduce songs that involve characters or their observations without Robert, however. This is evident in 'Little Things', a commentary by the acerbic Joanne on another couple's scene as well as on marriage in general, and 'Sorry Grateful', the men's reflective answer to Robert's question, 'Are you ever sorry you got married?' The motive neither introduces nor appears in songs that involve Robert on his own or without the couples, such as 'Someone is Waiting', or 'Barcelona', his emotionally removed duet with a flight attendant. Although these numbers do not quote the motive, they are frequently built on it, often by inverting it, as Banfield points out. Perhaps the most dramatic use of the motive is in the dance sequence 'Tick Tock', omitted from the revised version of the show. In this number, the audience hears taped dialogue of Robert and the flight attendant during sex. At a critical, post-coital moment, she says, 'I love you', and the motive is heard. It signifies what the couples all along have been wanting Robert to hear and experience; it represents their hopes fulfilled, as well as their presence in even his most intimate life. Robert, however, can only respond with 'I … I …', at which point the orchestra plays a dissonant fragment of the motive that signifies Robert's inability to express what everyone else wants him to express.

The central character's inability to respond reinforces his outsider status in the world of the married and emotionally committed. It is a telling moment, harking back to an earlier moment in the second act when, in the course of a production number, several couples perform a call-and-response tap dance break; when it is Robert's turn, there is a call but no response. Robert's motive, therefore, is expressive of the gulf between Robert and the couples, between Robert and thoughts of marriage, and between Robert and any kind of emotional commitment. On his own, Robert can only recall the motive by transforming it into something else. Woven into the show's

Plate 14   Production of *Company* in 2001 at the Missouri Repertory Theatre. Left to right: Cathy Barnett, Tia Speros, Cheryl Martin, Paul Niebanck, Lewis Cleale (as Robert, the 'other' who is unable to make a connection with his friends)

texture, the motive and its transformations, along with the accompanying lyrics, create a web that is present in some form throughout the show, and that defines Robert as a singular figure on the outside of a world of couples. This kind of motivic development is later greatly utilised by Sondheim, especially in *Sunday in the Park with George* and *Into the Woods* (1988).

Sondheim's use of pastiche appears even earlier, as noted above. In *Anyone Can Whistle* (1964), his second produced show as both composer and lyricist,[10] Sondheim made use of what he calls 'traditional musical comedy language to make points. All the numbers Angie [Angela Lansbury, one of the show's co-stars] sang in the show were pastiche – her opening number, for instance, was a Hugh Martin–Kay Thompson pastiche. The character always sang in musical comedy terms because she was a lady who dealt in attitudes instead of emotions.'[11] Interestingly, Sondheim has also said of this show that, 'Essentially the show is about, on one level, non-conformity and conformity in contemporary society.'[12] The show ran for only nine performances, but features a score that anticipates Sondheim's more mature work. Original and often memorable, it explores subjects like sanity, depression and twentieth-century fears with a decidedly musical theatre vocabulary.

As in *Anyone Can Whistle*, Sondheim uses the vocabulary of the musical theatre in *Follies* (1971). Because *Follies*, in the words of director/producer Harold Prince, 'deals with the loss of innocence in the United States, using the Ziegfeld Follies . . . as its metaphor',[13] musical pastiche is a natural choice for realising that metaphor. Here, however, he gives resonance to characters who, unhappy with the present, look back to a past best recalled by its music and by their memory of having sung it. (The characters are former showgirls and their husbands, and the title refers to their former employment as well as to their personal delusions.) As Joanne Gordon observes, 'The work is a voyage into the collective unconscious of America's theatrical imagination. Nostalgia is not merely the mood, it is the subject matter.'[14] To this end, Sondheim writes musical numbers that recall the past eras referred to in the script and for which the characters express nostalgia, as well as numbers that are 'book' songs sung by the characters in the unhappy present. Because the script calls for the representation of the characters in their past youthful days as well as their present middle age, Sondheim sometimes combines the two styles of writing and creates a surreal blend of past and present.

The pastiche numbers, however, are most effective in the last section of the show, a kind of musical revue–nervous breakdown in which each of the four principal characters expresses his or her individual neurosis. Sally, a former chorus girl who is now unhappily married to a travelling salesman and living a nondescript suburban life in the American southwest, expresses her long-standing love for Ben, a friend's husband whom she has quietly loved for years, in a Gershwin-like torch song. The rather mousy and decidedly unglamorous Sally stands alone in a circular spot, clad in a clinging silver gown evocative of Jean Harlow, and passionately sings 'Losing My Mind', one of Sondheim's most powerfully emotional love songs. Her husband Buddy, on the other hand, sings a patter song about loving one woman (Sally) but finding affection only in the arms of another. The upbeat and funny vaudeville quality of the song, a baggy pants routine, barely masks Buddy's desperate frustration with a lifetime of watching his wife love another man. Phyllis, Sally's former best friend and the wife of the man Sally loves, has a production number that speaks of her schizophrenia: 'The Story of Lucy and Jessie' depicts Phyllis as a young woman, warm and loving but fearful of life, and as a middle-aged woman, classy but emotionally dead. The irony is that each wants to be the other. This number recalls both Cole Porter and Kurt Weill, especially 'The Saga of Jenny' from *Lady in the Dark*.

The final number in this follies of the mind is for Ben, Phyllis's husband and the man loved by Sally. This is a top hat and tails number that also recalls Gershwin or, perhaps, the syncopated dance tunes of Irving Berlin. As Ben swaggers to the song, cane in hand and backed by the ensemble, he quite literally falls apart, forgetting his lyrics and losing control until the nightmare takes over and the revue literally explodes in a cacophony of musical fragments and shadowy images. Sondheim's choice of material to parody in this final section of the show is what makes the numbers so effectively devastating, and it is his most powerful and successful use of pastiche up to that point. His portraits of the neurotic and troubled characters are almost painful to watch, and they are created with great sympathy for the individuals who yearn for a time that was not nearly as happy, or tuneful, as they like to remember.

The complex web of relationships that forms *A Little Night Music* (1973) is one of outsiders. In this cast of misfit outsiders, it is Henrik who exemplifies this state more than any other character in the musical. He goes from being a misfit at the seminary to being a misfit at home to being a misfit at Mme Armfeldt's estate. Desirée Armfeldt, an ageing actress, seeks consolation amongst her fellow malcontents. Her dramatic soliloquy 'Send in the Clowns' is one of Sondheim's best-known songs. The number is preceded by an underscored speech for Desirée's former lover Fredrik, in which he tells of what *is* and what he wishes *was*:

> FREDRIK: When my eyes are open and I look at you, I see a woman that I have loved for a long time, who entranced me all over again when I came to her rooms . . . who gives me such genuine pleasure that, in spite of myself, I came here for the sheer delight of being with her again. The woman who could rescue me? Of course.
> (*Pause*)
> But when my eyes are not open – which is most of the time – all I see is a girl in a pink dress teasing a canary, running through a sunlit garden to hug me at the gate, as if I'd come home from Timbuktu instead of the Municipal Courthouse three blocks away . . .

Fredrik, like all the characters in the musical, is an outsider. He comes to Desirée desiring the companionship he so woefully misses with his new, young wife. He is outside of the bliss he sought in his marriage to Anne, and wants to find solace with Desirée.

One of the most original creations for the musical theatre, *Sweeney Todd, The Demon Barber of Fleet Street* (1979) is filled with outsiders. Sweeney Todd, the half-mad barber bent on revenge; Mrs Lovett, the pie shop owner with a business problem (not being able to find meat for her meat pies); the menacing Judge Turpin; the ever-in-love Anthony; his beloved Johanna (Todd's daughter); the assistant Tobias; and the Beggar Woman: these colourful characters are all dispossessed persons, outsiders in nineteenth-century London. Sweeney Todd, alias Benjamin Barker, comes to London to murder Judge Turpin, and when the intended victim escapes Todd's blade, Todd swears to kill all who visit his barber's chair until he cuts Turpin's throat.

In 'Epiphany' Todd's inner need for revenge is awakened to some of the angriest and most disturbing music ever written for the musical theatre. In the subsequent duet 'A Little Priest', Todd and Mrs Lovett devise a plan to solve both of their problems – Todd getting rid of his murdered bodies and Mrs Lovett finding a source of meat for her pies. The cannibalistic fantasy with its grotesque lyrics that describe how members of various professions would taste appears as a light-hearted waltz. The counterpoint between the lyrics and the music accentuates the macabre nature of the duet.

The idea of using the waltz idiom – associated with escapism – to accompany dark and menacing lyrics was of course nothing new. Sondheim himself had used it throughout *A Little Night Music*, but in *Sweeney Todd* the style took on an even more demonic character. This would become manifest in two numbers in *Assassins*, as we shall see: the opening sequence, where 'Hail to the Chief' is transformed into a waltz, and 'Gun Song', where the carefree waltz is the musical identifier in a number that celebrates the weapon of assassination.

In the fairy-tale-based *Into the Woods* (1987), Sondheim once again has non-traditional characters as the central figures in his musical. Little Red Riding Hood, Cinderella, Jack (of beanstalk fame), Rapunzel and even Snow White appear in this musical about outsiders, all of whom have their own personal issues, working together to solve bigger problems. Encased in a larger tale of a baker and his barren wife who is under the spell of a witch, the stories of the familiar fairy tales are enhanced through their dramatic and musical treatment. Rapunzel's Prince and his brother, Cinderella's Prince, sing the waltz duet 'Agony' and the instructive ballads 'No One is Alone' and 'Children Will Listen' have enjoyed lives of their own outside of theatrical contexts. 'No One is Alone' is a benevolent anthem to outsiders – people are never completely disconnected from others in their thoughts and actions.

Important to Sondheim's work is the way in which stories are told. The audience members themselves in some ways become outsiders as they observe the various non-narrative structures. *Company* and *Follies* are 'concept musicals', as described above. *Merrily We Roll Along* (1981) is told backwards in time: the reasons behind an ended relationship are unravelled, making the dramatic action and its audience outsiders in the normal progression of time.

Narration in a non-traditional sense pervades *Sweeney Todd*, *Into the Woods* and *Assassins*. In *Sweeney Todd*, it is the chorus who intone the recurring 'The Ballad of Sweeney Todd'. The other two shows both have a narrator who relates the tale, the character being dubbed 'The Balladeer' in *Assassins*. In both instances the narrator is killed – in *Into the Woods* he is sacrificed to the giantess and in *Assassins* he is enveloped by the assassins in 'Another National Anthem'. The narrators cannot and do not survive in the midst of outsiders. The elimination of the narrator enhances the power of the outsiders. In *Into the Woods* the narrator's death propels the surviving characters to join together to overcome adversity, while in *Assassins* it allows the climactic scene to take place: the convergence of the assassins in the Texas Book Depository on 22 November 1963 as Lee Harvey Oswald contemplates the assassination of President John F. Kennedy.

And it is this latter work, *Assassins*, where Sondheim is at his best portraying the neurotic outsider. Nowhere in Sondheim's work is this character type created with more explicit sympathy, humour or irony. *Assassins* is a troubling work that perplexed and even angered some critics and still has the power to disturb American audiences.[15] In this piece, all the characters are would-be or successful assassins of American presidents. They are also unhappy loners and, from society's perspective, losers. In *Assassins*, furthermore, Sondheim and the playwright John Weidman suggest that, with the exception of John Wilkes Booth, none of these singular figures acts out of any specific political motivation. Instead, their acts are explosive expressions of their hopeless and powerless positions in a system that seems, to them, to have been designed for the well-being of someone else. Individually and as a group, these men and women feel cheated and deprived of a happiness they view as their right. They express these feelings in one of Sondheim's most accomplished scores. How he gives voice to these outsiders, and how his technique for doing this is unique in this work, is fascinating.

Weidman and Sondheim, who had earlier collaborated on *Pacific Overtures* (1976), created *Assassins* after the model of a vaudeville-like revue, a choice that contributed in several ways to the successful presentation of the disenfranchised titular characters. It encouraged Sondheim to exploit pastiche in new and sophisticated ways. Previously, as noted above, the composer/lyricist used familiar and traditional musical theatre song styles to underscore aspects of situations and characters. In *Assassins*, however, the reach of Sondheim's stylistic net is much wider. The sources for his pastiche include pre-existent and often familiar pieces of music from the mid-nineteenth century to the 1980s. He also parodies familiar popular song styles from nineteenth-century parlour songs to 1980s pop love songs, as well as popular dance styles such as cakewalks, Sousa marches and hoe-downs. Non-musical sources include historical poems, lyrics, interviews and quotations. In addition, historical characters are interwoven throughout various eras to create relationships that would have been chronologically impossible. Such an extended use of historical materials, musical and textual, is unprecedented in Sondheim's work. He exploits these sources to probe the troubled psyches of deeply disturbed, and disturbing, outsiders.

By taking the familiar vocabulary of American music and using it to give voice to the disenfranchised and the desperate, moreover, Sondheim uses pastiche to particularly ironic effect. Comfortable and sometimes comforting styles of American popular music are used to depict an underside of American society, a depiction that in turn causes discomfort. Sondheim recasts or defamiliarises the comfortable styles by using them for characters who make us squirm but whose disenfranchisement, we begin to see by the show's end, is just as American as the 'comfortable' musical space it inhabits. When Sondheim uses popular song styles in ways that subvert the connotations they have carried for a century or more, he is taking a drastic stylistic step, one that cannot but disturb and unsettle American audiences. Sondheim thus creates a network of textual references to give individual numbers, and even the entire score, meanings they might otherwise lack. The whole work is a carefully spun web of various references that maintains cohesion in part through the manipulation of these references and the viewer's assumed knowledge of them. This combination of references, demonstrated below, is adroit and powerful.

The vaudeville model for *Assassins* allows each character to have his or her appropriate turn, or specialty number, each following the other in no particular order and each in a different musical style. Giuseppe Zangara sings his Sousa-inspired number strapped in an electric chair, looking as if he might at any moment make a Houdini-like escape; Charles Guiteau sings and dances a jaunty cakewalk up and down the hangman's scaffold; and Samuel Byck dictates monologues into his tape recorder as if performing stand-up comedy. This combination of seemingly unrelated styles and personalities is, of course, characteristic of American vaudeville, which was derived from, and often satirised, established genres of entertainment. The unrelated styles also allow the distinctness of each character from the others, as well as from society in general. The individual messages from the fringe are similar, but they are spoken with different musical vocabularies.

The choice of the vaudeville model no doubt also suggested the non-linear structure for *Assassins*. Like *Follies* and, especially, *Company*, the show moves smoothly but non-chronologically through time. Sometimes its dejected historical characters meet in locations non-specific to any one time period: a saloon in downtown New York City, for instance, that looks the same today as it did in 1900. Other times, however, the setting is almost painfully specific: the penultimate scene takes place in the Texas School Book Depository in Dallas, just before the assassination of President Kennedy. Sondheim also creates extended musical scenes through collections of numbers related by dramatic content and musical styles. 'How I Saved Roosevelt' is a collection of closely related but meaningfully contrasted dances. 'Gun Song' is a collection of waltzes, each of which deals with a different aspect of handguns and features a character from a different era. These waltzes are stylistically diverse, but they are connected by a refrain and preceded, as

well as followed, by a sombre ballad, also a waltz. 'The Ballad of Guiteau'
mixes hymn, parlour song, and cakewalk. Stephen Banfield has called these
sequences 'suites'.[16]

The focus of one of these 'suites' ('How I Saved Roosevelt') is Giuseppe
Zangara, an Italian immigrant who, in February of 1933, attempted to kill
president-elect Franklin Delano Roosevelt in Miami. He failed, but he managed to wound several others, including the mayor of Chicago, Tony Cermak,
who subsequently died from his wounds. After Cermak's death, Zangara's
life sentence was changed to death by execution in the electric chair. Zangara's
only political agenda was his simple if fervent anti-capitalism: he was neither
an Anarchist, for instance, nor a Socialist nor even a Communist. He bore
no grudge towards any individual figure, including Roosevelt.

While 'How I Saved Roosevelt' creates a vivid portrait of Zangara, however, it also contrasts him with a group of patriotic Bystanders, as Sondheim
calls them, all of whom claimed to have thwarted the assassination attempt.
These individuals each received and enjoyed much attention in the press
and became momentary celebrities for their claims of having saved FDR.
The contrast of Zangara's passionate anti-capitalism with the all-American
absorption with self-promotion and celebrity in the press creates the bipo-
lar perspective of the musical scene. When we add to this the fact that,
before Roosevelt's appearance, a band gave a concert at Bayfront Park's new
bandshell,[17] we have the makings of a musical number, and it is from here
that Sondheim works his magic.

Through an onstage radio, we hear the activities at Bayfront Park: a
performance of Sousa's march 'El Capitan'; an announcer's description of
the festive scene, and then of the unsuccessful assassination. The announcer
summarises the ensuing events, ending with, 'We take you now to a group
of eyewitnesses who will tell us what they saw.' The lights come up on five
Bystanders and, as the band resumes 'El Capitan', they begin singing.

Sondheim's choice of 'El Capitan' is interesting. One of Sousa's best-
known marches, it, too, is a pastiche of unrelated musical numbers from
Sousa's most successful operetta, also titled *El Capitan*. This lighthearted
work is also concerned with political insurrection and turmoil. After opening
his number with a direct quote of the march's four-bar introduction in 6/8
time, and thus emphasising the diegetic aspect of the march being played
in Bayfront Park, Sondheim builds a melody related to Sousa's, albeit more
of a recognisable reminiscence than a direct quote. In the third strain of
the march, Sondheim changes the character through a shift to sustained
quartal harmony (i.e. harmony based on fourths). This serves as Zangara's
introduction into the number, and the lights come up on him confined
in the electric chair. In the middle of this section, after the minor mode
unambiguously appears, Zangara's music is transformed into a tarantella.

Whereas the character of the Sousa march indicates the patriotic American middle class and its capitalist system, the tarantella is, in this context, distinctly 'other' and foreign. Its heritage as a folk dance reflects Zangara's poor Italian background and provides a clear contrast to the Sousa march's more bourgeois origins. Since both are in 6/8 time, transition from one to the other is relatively simple.

After Zangara's interlude, the strains of 'El Capitan' return, and the Bystanders begin again. After they sing the same musical material as in the opening section of the number, Sondheim takes another surprise turn and introduces 'The Washington Post', another Sousa march that operates on more than one level. The first, of course, is that the 'The Washington Post' represents the establishment press to whom the Bystanders are so eagerly and self-importantly telling their stories. The other level is that of yet another dance style. After its composition in 1899, 'The Washington Post' was chosen by a group of dance instructors as suitable for a new and fashionable dance called the two-step, which in many places is still referred to as 'The Washington Post'. This dance, then, implies another contrast in social class.

When the music yet again returns to 'El Capitan', a Bystander refers to Zangara as 'Some left wing foreigner'. Zangara, however, refutes the term 'left wing' with a chilling section best described as a miniature mad scene. Here the orchestra plays dissonant snippets of the march melodies in counterpoint to Zangara's increasingly higher, and increasingly intense, vocal line. After asserting 'Zangara no foreign tool, / Zangara American! / American nothing!' Zangara begins asking about the photographers. He sings, 'And why there no photographers? / For Zangara no photographers! / Only capitalists get photographers!' Odd though it is, this ranting is based on fact: in its report of Zangara's execution in March of 1933, *Newsweek* reported that Zangara said, 'No camera man here? No one here to take picture? Lousy capitalists! No pictures! Capitalists! All capitalists! Lousy bunch! Crooks'.[18]

What Sondheim does with this outburst is particularly ingenious. Zangara's diatribe about photographers equates him with the Bystanders, who are smitten with the press and excited by their importance to it. To point out this new, if fleeting, relationship between Zangara and the Bystanders, Sondheim again quotes the second strain of 'El Capitan' and has Zangara sing a countermelody while the Bystanders sing the original melody. Zangara's identifying tarantella, then, transforms into an integral section of the march. After Zangara asks, 'And why there no photographers? / ... / Only capitalists get photographers', he comments 'No right! / No fair / Nowhere!' as the Bystanders sing, 'I'm on the front page – is that bizarre? / And all of those pictures, like a star!' The implication is that, for at least this one moment in his life, Zangara envies the capitalist middle class more than perhaps he ever dreamed possible, even as he distinguishes himself from them. Because of Zangara's presence on stage with the Bystanders, the original lyrics for this phrase in Sousa's operetta are almost eerie: 'Gaze on his misanthropic stare. / Notice his penetrating glare.' As both Zangara and the Bystanders reach the end of the number, Zangara sings, 'Pull switch!' and a hum of electricity accompanies the number's final cadence.

Sondheim again references and/or quotes other texts, musical and non-musical, in his portrayal of Charles Guiteau in 'The Ballad of Guiteau'. On the surface an affable lunatic who shot James Garfield to preserve the country and promote the sales of his book, the singular Guiteau is given a pathetic and angry underside. This is done in part through recalling writings by the character as well as subsequent folksongs about him. (Indeed, the body of extant folksongs in general about political assassination in fact suggests that *Assassins* is the latest in a long line of works in popular genres about this aspect of the American character.)

On the day of his execution, Charles Guiteau wrote a poem that begins, 'I am going to the Lordy; / I am so glad. / I am going to the Lordy / I am so glad. / I am going to the Lordy, / Glory Hallelujah! Glory Hallelujah! / I am going to the Lordy.'[19] This poem intrigued Sondheim, who first encountered it in the short play by Charles Gilbert that inspired *Assassins*, and he opens Guiteau's number with its first lines. They are sung hymn-like and unaccompanied, and Sondheim continues to use the line 'I am going to the Lordy' as a recurring refrain between the number's sections. The contrast of Guiteau's fervent yet hymn-like poem with the musical styles that follow it suggests Guiteau's mental imbalance, a trait the audience has already seen. He is glib, frequently charming and completely insane.

Sondheim first contrasts Guiteau's mad hymn with a parlour song in 3/4 time sung by the narrating Balladeer. The opening lines also recall the opening exhortation of the folksong mentioned above, which is, 'Come all ye Christian people, wherever you may be, / Likewise pay attention to these few lines from me.'[20] Sondheim distils this to 'Come all ye Christians, and learn from a sinner.'

Musically, Sondheim constructs a useful structure for all this textual reference. As noted above, the opening is an unaccompanied hymn sung by, and with lyrics by, Guiteau himself. Because the lights come up to reveal him at the foot of a scaffold, his reference to 'going to the Lordy' is amusing. The music, however, is a straightforward and almost austere hymn, sixteen bars of increasingly wider intervals. The initial hymn section segues into the Balladeer's triple-time parlour song, mentioned above. The parlour song leads into a sixteen-bar cakewalk refrain for Guiteau, by the end of which he has danced himself one step closer to the hangman's waiting noose. The upbeat character and tempo of the dance are reflected in Sondheim's optimistic lyrics for Guiteau. Each refrain begins 'Look on the bright side' and continues with appropriately optimistic homilies that, along with the cheerfulness of the cakewalk, provide ironic contrast to the ominous scaffold on which they are delivered. The first two statements of the refrain are upbeat, but the third is slower, more resolute and accompanied by strong chords played on the beat, and ends abruptly after only four bars. At this point, Sondheim returns to the hymn. Now, however, it is played as a resolute and forceful dance: a *danse macabre*. At the end of the forceful hymn section, the Balladeer begins his refrain, this time in the previous fast tempo, and he and Guiteau sing an extended ending. As the refrain, and the number, are finally allowed to conclude, Guiteau is blindfolded and, as the lights blackout and the final chord is played, the Hangman pulls the lever that releases the trap door under Guiteau.

The implications of the cakewalk, of course, are fascinating. The dance was originally a dance of outsiders, created by plantation slaves as a means of ridiculing their white owners. It was theatrical from its conception, with its prancing, high steps, its forward and backward bowing and its practice of dressing up in costume to impersonate others. Later, when the cakewalk was included in minstrelsy, it included acknowledgement of the audience. The cakewalk was eventually accepted by all of society and it became quite popular with American and European dancers, white as well as black. Guiteau's self-consciously theatrical performance of the number recalls the cakewalk of minstrelsy and its winks and bows to the audience, and the absurdity of its urgent cheerfulness, under the circumstances of its performance, suggests Guiteau's insanity. The changing reception of the cakewalk, furthermore, suggests Guiteau's desperate desire for the respectability he thought fame and success would bring. Interestingly, the nature of the cakewalk, in its origins and later as a popular dance, was competitive. The slave who best impersonated the masters was rewarded with a prize – a cake – and later dancers also competed for prizes and acclaim. In *Assassins*, the disenfranchised seek a prize withheld by society, and their increasingly angry demand for that prize culminates in the powerful musical number 'Another National Anthem'. Guiteau's cakewalk simply and subtly drives home the idea that he, like each of the characters, is waiting for a prize, but not necessarily the noose and trap door.

The skill demonstrated in the creation of these two musical numbers suggests why Stephen Sondheim is among the most accomplished and influential composer-lyricists of the American musical theatre. His mastery of the styles that inform the score for *Assassins* is nothing less than stunning, and each musical number displays a virtuosity similar to that found in 'How I Saved Roosevelt' and 'The Ballad of Guiteau'. Even the musical interludes refer to music other than that in *Assassins* and at one point are self-referential: Samuel Byck's first monologue, a humorous if unsettling message to Leonard Bernstein dictated into a tape recorder, ends with Byck singing Sondheim's lyrics to 'America' from *West Side Story*. Sondheim then parodies Bernstein's music for 'America' to close the scene. First quoting the number and then paraphrasing it, Sondheim uses his own work as a historical source. The moment is as chilling and ironic as it is amusing. Later, before the scene in the Texas School Book Depository, Sondheim uses actual recorded music – The Blue Ridge Boys singing 'Heartache Serenade' – to give the scene an especially eerie sense of reality that is made surreal when John Wilkes Booth appears before Lee Harvey Oswald.

Drawing on the body of American popular culture to give voice to the characters as well as to make critical commentary about them, Sondheim leaves the audience with the act of assassination as a collective cultural memory that uncomfortably lingers. The bitter observations of 'Gun Song', for instance, have the capability to haunt the viewer long after the final curtain. The communal desperation of 'Another National Anthem' fades into the quieter desperation of Lee Harvey Oswald, whose violent act, still vivid in the minds of many in the audience, is the climax of the show. There is no song for Oswald because his feelings have already been anticipated and expressed: he is the culmination of all the assassins and all the songs that have gone before him. Of course, he too is the victim of assassination, an act that provokes the final chorus of 'Everybody's got the right to be happy'.

This one score, perhaps the most indigenously 'American' of all Sondheim's output given its sources, displays a master at a high point of his career. *Assassins* is representative of Sondheim's work in its use of pastiche, its experiment with form and its representation of outsiders looking at a society that, for whatever various reasons, excludes them.

In all his work, Sondheim's musical languages are varied yet identifiably his own; perhaps they are more like different accents of the same language than altogether different languages. His harmonic vocabulary is vast and he alters it somewhat with each project; but the end result is always recognisably his own.[21] His musical treatment, as well as the vocabulary of the lyrics in his own scores (Sondheim has criticised some of his earlier lyrics as inappropriate),[22] display an unerring sense of character as well as theatricality, and no false note or word appears in any of his mature work. Returning to his scores again and again, the listener is continually informed, surprised and entertained by them. In *Assassins*, Sondheim's musical pastiche is a tool for revealing aspects of the American national psyche, including the American proclivity for assassinating elected leaders. The initial and nervous critical reception of *Assassins* in the United States perhaps suggests that Sondheim reveals too much too clearly. Each of his works operates in similar, although outwardly different, ways.

The sensitivity that caused the fifteen-year-old Stephen Sondheim to cry at the first act curtain of *Carousel* is still present in his maturity. *Sweeney Todd, Into the Woods, Assassins* and *Passion* are each as heartbreaking as they are disturbing and amusing. In *Assassins*, Sondheim's outsiders find a national anthem for all the 'others' as well as for themselves in a musical score of inordinate richness. In musical after musical, Sondheim offers a moving reminder about those people who 'can't get in to the ball park', and he offers this reminder in a most American way: through the voice of America's own songs.

11 Choreographers, directors and the fully integrated musical

PAUL R. LAIRD

Can one recapture the excitement that *A Chorus Line* brought to Broadway? The Broadway musical seemed moribund in the first half of the 1970s. The big hits of the previous decade, such as *Hello, Dolly!* and *Man of La Mancha*, had closed and the era of the great musical plays that followed the Rodgers and Hammerstein model was over. Stephen Sondheim and Hal Prince combined for major artistic successes between 1970 and 1973 with *Company*, *A Little Night Music* and *Follies*, but the appeal of these shows was limited, as can be seen by the length of their runs and mixed commercial success. The rock musical had become a Broadway reality with *Hair*, *Two Gentlemen of Verona* and other shows, but rock was a new musical language that many in the traditional Broadway audience had not yet accepted. Creators of the musical theatre searched for a new mould that might combine new musical styles and contemporary thinking with tradition, building upon the genre's proud history. *A Chorus Line* did all of this as a veritable celebration of Broadway dance and dancers, bringing new life to the genre and taking it into the colossal hit era of 6,000-performance runs.

Those who saw *A Chorus Line* during its original run will not easily forget it. The plot was minimal and somewhat artificial, but the characters were engrossing. We recognised types of people that we knew and with each part of their stories were further consumed. The singing and dancing had a special immediacy because, within the world that the director Michael Bennett magically created, we knew that these characters would express themselves through music and movement.

The creators of *A Chorus Line* built upon decades of Broadway history when dance was integrated into the musical as a crucial part of character development and dramatic impact. It had taken years in the musical comedy to integrate plot and any aspect of the music, but by the time of *Show Boat* (1927) and *Of Thee I Sing* (1931), song placement had become more careful in some shows and plots sometimes advanced during songs. Although this trend could hardly be described as linear, by the time Rodgers and Hammerstein wrote *Carousel* (1945), songs were often an important part of the plot and extended musical sequences were more common.

The integration of dance with a show's plot was a slower process. Victor Herbert, a Broadway pioneer in several areas, wrote some of the first dance musicals, such as *The Lady of the Slipper* (1912).[1] In such shows, Herbert used dance for its spectacular effect with entire scenes based on dances, surpassing the usual limited use of dance for variety. The famous team Vernon and Irene Castle were hired to show the latest ballroom steps, but were dismissed in Philadelphia because part of their dance seemed too suggestive. During the 1920s dances would follow a song, and various stage personalities offered dance specialties that had nothing to do with the plot. For example, according to Hugh Fordin, the *Sunny* star Marilyn Miller interrupted Oscar Hammerstein II as he described the plot, wondering when she would do her specialty tap number.[2] There were a number of fine dancers on Broadway in the 1920s, including Fred and Adele Astaire, Ann Pennington and Marilyn Miller, who helped introduce dance as a way of describing their characters, but for the most part dance remained part of the musical's quest for variety. Most shows included dances added solely for entertainment; *A Connecticut Yankee* and *Show Boat* were two exceptions. Dances designed by such leading choreographers as a Busby Berkeley were fairly predictable and resulted only in the credit line 'dances by'.[3]

As Hollywood musicals appeared and confirmed the public's interest in watching stars dance (perhaps a metaphor for what could not be shown), Broadway followed suit. Ethan Mordden describes the continued development of the character dance in 'Clifton Webb's unassuming soft shoe or Tamara Geva's ballet glide' and the continued popularity of the kick line.[4] (The latter, of course, never died; *A Chorus Line* exploited the appeal of the long, shapely female leg and a line's drilled precision.) By the second half of the 1930s, however, more ambitious dances appeared in shows, first and most famously in *On Your Toes* (1936), with a score by Rodgers and Hart and direction by George Abbott. George Balanchine, the famed Russian choreographer, worked on the show and was the first honoured with the credit line 'choreography by'. His major contribution was the ballet 'Slaughter on Tenth Avenue', danced by Ray Bolger, Tamara Geva and George Church. Abbott remembered the segment as 'one of the best numbers I've ever seen in the theatre, both musically and choreographically'.[5] The show also included a ballet in the first act, 'Princesse Zenobia'. The dances were part of a story about a vaudeville hoofer trying to make it in ballet. The dances were praised at the time, but, as Marian Monta Smith has noted, they were seen as an exception and the production had little immediate influence.[6] Balanchine's role on Broadway is really no more than a historical curiosity because his other shows (*Keep Off the Grass*, 1940; *The Lady Comes Across*, 1942; *What's Up*, 1943; *Courtin' Time*, 1951) are mostly forgotten.[7]

It is significant that George Abbott, a major influence on the continuing integration of the musical and on two important choreographers who later became directors, directed *On Your Toes*. As extensive use of dance became part of the musical, the director became the force who assembled the show's elements into a creative whole. By the 1960s, several of the most important directors were choreographers. Two of these, Jerome Robbins and Bob Fosse, worked with Abbott and learned to direct the book from him. The line continues with Hal Prince, who, although not a choreographer, also explored the musical's greater integration. He began his Broadway career working for Abbott in the early 1950s and learned direction from both Abbott and Robbins.

The greater integration of dance, specifically ballet, into the musical required the willing cooperation of Broadway creators and understanding talent from the ballet world, a combination that came together in *Oklahoma!* Rodgers, Hammerstein, and the producers Theresa Helburn and Lawrence Langner of the Theatre Guild sought to make ballet part of the show's plot apparatus and hired Agnes de Mille as choreographer. She had handled western themes with her 1942 ballet *Rodeo*, with music by Aaron Copland. De Mille's work in *Oklahoma!* is legendary, from her insistence on real dancers and separate rehearsals to her battles with the director, Rouben Mamoulian.[8] Such dances as 'Laurey Makes Up Her Mind' at the end of the first act changed Broadway history. De Mille's dancers served as substitutes for the principal actors during the ballet and made convincing on stage the notion of Laurie dreaming her way to a choice between Curley and Jud. De Mille's use of counterpoint in her ballets, with characters doing different movements at the same time, added to the visual appeal.[9]

Broadway creators are nothing if not imitative, and several immediately capitalised on the new idea of taking the highbrow art of ballet into the middlebrow world of the Broadway musical. De Mille played a major role throughout the 1940s. She next worked on *One Touch of Venus* (1943), with music by Kurt Weill and lyrics by Ogden Nash, who co-authored the book with S. J. Perelman. A show about Venus coming to life invited fanciful ballets. De Mille contributed 'Forty Minutes for Lunch' in the first act, where Venus meets New York workers in Rockefeller Center, and 'Venus in Ozone Heights' as the second act's dream ballet, where Venus discovers suburbia. De Mille went on to *Bloomer Girl* (1944), with music by Harold Arlen and lyrics by E. Y. Harburg, where she contributed a ballet based on an 'Uncle Tom' show and a Civil War ballet in which female dancers expressed the feelings of those watching husbands and sons go off to war.

De Mille returned to work with Rodgers and Hammerstein as choreographer for *Carousel*, where her dances again played a major role in plot development. The opening ballet-pantomime introduces the scene and mood, and in the second-act dance, Billy Bigelow's daughter expresses her frustration. De Mille next choreographed *Brigadoon*, Lerner and Loewe's break-through hit, including atmospheric Scottish dances and the chase ballet in the second act. De Mille became the first choreographer-director in Rodgers and Hammerstein's *Allegro* (1947), where she tried to unify a rambling plot, a singing Greek chorus and many musical numbers calling for motion. She included a fantasy ballet where, in a manner reminiscent of *Our Town*, characters both living and dead appear. The show would have challenged any director, but de Mille demonstrated comfort with all types of stage motion.

Agnes de Mille's peers, who helped dance become a more important part of the Broadway musical, included, among others, Jack Cole, Michael Kidd and Jerome Robbins. Cole helped establish the Broadway vernacular dance tradition with his imaginative use of steps from ethnic and ballroom dances and acrobatics, often set to big band music.[10] He also added ballets to shows, such as his slow-motion softball game in *Allah Be Praised* (1944). Michael Kidd choreographed *Finian's Rainbow* (1947), *Guys and Dolls* (1950) and *Can-Can* (1953), showing an admirable range, but he never had much success as a director. Jerome Robbins, one of Broadway's most important choreographers, was the first dancer to become a truly successful director.

Jerome Robbins straddled ballet and Broadway for much of his career, but worked little on Broadway from the mid-1960s to the 1980s. His first major ballet was the popular *Fancy Free* in 1944, created with the composer Leonard Bernstein. They brought the ballet's energy, references to vernacular music and dance, and a plot concerning three sailors on leave in wartime New York to Broadway in *On the Town*, which also involved the lyricists Betty Comden and Adolph Green and the director George Abbott. Much about the show was memorable (see chapter 9), especially its frenetic energy and constant motion. In her autobiography *Distant Dances*, Sono Osato, a ballet dancer who played Ivy Turnstiles, describes her work with Abbott and Robbins:[11] Abbott directed the book scenes, but Robbins had a free hand with the dances. The two major ballets were 'Miss Turnstiles' and 'Gabey in the Playground of the Rich', the latter a dream ballet near the end of the show. Both helped propel the story. Osato danced the latter ballet with a dancer substituting for the actor who played Gabey. Abbott allowed Robbins to show how dance could be incorporated in varied situations, leading finally to shows such as *West Side Story*.

Robbins continued to work on Broadway as well as in ballet and modern dance. In 1945 he contributed the ballet 'Interplay', with music by Morton Gould, to the vaudeville *Concert Varieties*.[12] In December of that year, *Billion*

Dollar Baby opened, starring the dancer Joan McCracken with dances by Robbins. Far more famous is Robbins's work with George Abbott during the 1947–48 season, including *High Button Shoes* (1947) and *Look, Ma, I'm Dancin'* (1948). Abbott directed and wrote *High Button Shoes*, a fast-paced farce built around Phil Silvers. The score was Jule Styne's first for Broadway. He considered himself a songwriter, but Robbins convinced him to score the 'Mack Sennett Ballet', where leads were chased by Keystone Kops and a bear. All finally land in a pile topped by a flag-waving policeman. The number was repeated in the retrospective *Jerome Robbins' Broadway* (1989). *Look, Ma I'm Dancin'* was a vehicle for Nancy Walker conceived by Robbins. Walker played a brewery heiress who becomes a patron for a ballet company and finally dances with it, a hilarious possibility given her clowning skills. Robbins's 'Sleepwalker's Ballet' was one of the highlights in a show that ran for only six months because of Walker's ill health. Robbins also worked with Abbott on *Call Me Madam*, a vehicle for Ethel Merman with a score by Irving Berlin, but the show is remembered more for its star and score than for its dancing. Abbott reports that Robbins started rehearsals early to create his dances, but the major number was removed before opening night. Abbott reveals his faith in spoken materials, predictable for one of the genre's best book directors: 'Time and time again the ambitious dance effort will fail, whereas something conceived for practical purposes and on the spur of the moment will be a success. This is equally true of songs.'[13] Abbott's type of show, the fast-paced comedy, however, was in decline as dance became more an integral part of the musical.

In 1951 *The King and I* opened, a much-loved show by Rodgers and Hammerstein that included Robbins's lengthy ballet 'The Small House of Uncle Thomas', which offers interesting commentary on the plot's theme of East meeting West. The dance also appeared in *Jerome Robbins' Broadway*.

In 1954 Abbott gave Robbins billing as co-director for *The Pajama Game* (considered below), partly because of his success at working with such dancers as the star Carol Haney. The show's choreographer was Bob Fosse, and other important newcomers to Abbott's team were the producers Hal Prince and Robert Griffith, who later produced *West Side Story*.

Robbins earned his first full credit as a Broadway director in *Bells Are Ringing*, a show with little important dancing, music by Jule Styne, lyrics by Comden and Green and a delightful star in Judy Holliday. It ran for two years. At this point Robbins was ready to spread his wings by taking on both direction and choreography. He realised this ambition the following year with *West Side Story*.

West Side Story (1957) marks the full integration of dance into the Broadway musical and the arrival of the choreographer-director. Plans for a modern version of *Romeo and Juliet* involving Robbins, Bernstein and

Arthur Laurents had started as early as 1949.[14] Their original thought was that the lovers should be Catholic and Jewish and the story should occur around the time of Easter and Passover, but they were unable to work together with any consistency and the project was shelved. Bernstein and Laurents ran into each other in Beverly Hills in August 1955 and decided to move the story to New York's West Side and pit gangs of Puerto Ricans against the white 'Americans'.[15]

As director and choreographer, Robbins was responsible ultimately for the full integration of each element into a dramatic whole. He believed in method acting, dividing the cast into the two gangs and forbidding them to socialise on the set. His intensity in rehearsal was legendary. Carol Lawrence, who played Maria, remembers working with Robbins:

> You have to understand that Jerry Robbins was the motivating force in all of this. He was the eternal perfectionist. The fact that one can never attain perfection did not deter him for a second. That was what he wanted and if he ended up killing you in the interim, well that was okay too![16]

West Side Story was cast from a pool of dancers. Even the romantic leads, Carol Lawrence and Larry Kert, had extensive dance training. In effect, Robbins choreographed every movement in the show. Dance provided motion in the action sequences (such as in the 'Prologue' and 'The Rumble'), served as an expressive device both for inarticulate characters ('Dance at the Gym' and 'Cool') and in numbers designed to release tension (such as in 'I Feel Pretty' and 'Gee, Officer Krupke!').[17] How dependent the show was on dance became clear when the company arrived at the Washington theatre for its out-of-town try-out and discovered that the stage was significantly smaller than at the Winter Garden in New York, for which it was choreographed. Carol Lawrence remembers that Robbins had to rework the ballets and 'there was so much dance, almost nothing but dance in the show'.[18]

Bernstein wrote the dance numbers as well as the songs. Robbins was a close collaborator, often suggesting changes and at times making them himself. Bernstein showed fine command of Latin dances and various types of jazz, producing a score that still sounds contemporary. Especially effective moments include the mambo in the 'Dance at the Gym' and the rich references to cool jazz in the song 'Cool'. Bernstein uses melodies from the songs in dance sequences to great dramatic effect, such as the tune 'Maria' in the 'Maria Cha-Cha' of the 'Dance at the Gym' sequence, heard there before Tony sings the song for the first time. The song 'Somewhere' also appears in dance passages, tying the dream sequence between Tony and Maria to the show's plot.[19]

West Side Story was Bernstein's last important Broadway show, but Robbins continued to work there consistently into the mid-1960s. Two of his

West Side Story collaborators – Arthur Laurents and Stephen Sondheim – joined the composer Jule Styne on *Gypsy* in 1959. Choreography was far less important here than in some of his previous shows, but Robbins again showed his deft staging touch, beautifully evoking the vaudeville and burlesque while allowing room for one of Ethel Merman's greatest roles. His next show was *Fiddler on the Roof* (1964), another triumph of mood and atmosphere in a book musical. Along with the set designer Boris Aronson and the costume designer Patricia Zipprodt, Robbins convincingly recreated the Jewish *shtetl* of Anatevka. Robbins designed some of his most imaginative dances, using both Jewish and Russian elements to add to the show's true-to-life quality. Two memorable sequences included a joint dance by Jewish and Russian characters in the inn and the bottle dance at the wedding. The show marked Robbins's last work on Broadway before the anthology *Jerome Robbins' Broadway* of 1989.

The next great choreographer-director in the line of Agnes de Mille and Jerome Robbins was Bob Fosse (1926–87), a dancer from Chicago who began his career in vaudeville and burlesque.[20] As noted above, George Abbott was important to Fosse's career development, hiring him as choreographer in *The Pajama Game* (1954). Unlike Robbins, Fosse came to Broadway through the world of ballroom and ethnic dances, showing the influence of Jack Cole's jazz-dancing techniques. Fosse's dances for *The Pajama Game*, especially in 'Hernando's Hideaway', kept up the frenetic pace popularised by Abbott and Robbins. For the star Carol Haney, with whom Fosse had worked in Hollywood, he created 'Steam Heat', which she danced with Peter Gennaro and Buzz Miller. The show bubbled over with major dance numbers, including 'Once a Year Day', '7$\frac{1}{2}$ Cents', and 'I'll Never Be Jealous Again'. Fosse also worked with Abbott in *Damn Yankees* (1955), which included a number of dances based upon typical baseball moves and 'Who's Got the Pain?', conceived for Gwen Verdon, Fosse's third wife and frequent collaborator. Fosse also worked on the film versions of *The Pajama Game* (1957) and *Damn Yankees* (1958). In 1956 Fosse assisted Robbins with the choreography for the Broadway show *Bells Are Ringing*, including the number 'Mu Cha Cha'. Fosse's last show with Abbott was *New Girl in Town* (1957): their break-up was caused by Abbott's moral objections to Fosse's dream ballet in a bordello. Fosse often cultivated the suggestive in his dance routines, perhaps an influence from his days in burlesque. Christine Colby Jacques, a dancer who worked with Fosse on *Dancin'*, notes that Fosse often ironically parodied suggestive movements:

> the 'American Women' section in *Dancin'* (1978), presented three women
> with long-stemmed roses in their mouths. With hips thrust forward, hands
> on hips and elbows squeezed together in back, they took three long,

Plate 15 Ann Reinking, P. J. Mann, and Christine Colby Jacques in 'Stout-Hearted Men', a dance number from Bob Fosse's *Dancin'* in 1979

exaggerated steps across the stage. Their feet came together, and looking over their shoulders out toward the audience, each woman swayed her hips side to side ever so slightly in an up, even tempo. The impact was a clear, yet comical comment on the pouting and sensual manner women sometimes use to manipulate men. So much of Fosse's choreography reflects a tongue-in-cheek look at ourselves, whether it's sensual movement or gestural movement... Fosse directed us to think of ourselves as little girls with sway backs and protruding little bellies, sucking our thumbs.[21]

Fosse became Broadway's third important choreographer-director in the late 1950s, starting with *Redhead* (1959), a vehicle for Gwen Verdon, including the dances 'Pick-Pocket Tango' and 'The Uncle Sam Rag'. Fosse shared director's credit with Abe Burrows in *How to Succeed in Business Without Really Trying* (1961), where Fosse did the 'musical staging'.

Fosse's next show was *Little Me* (1962), starring Sid Caesar. Among Fosse's dances was the effective 'Rich Kid's Rag'. His next major work was for Gwen Verdon in *Sweet Charity* (1966), which Fosse conceived, directed and choreographed. Fosse's dances included 'I'm a Brass Band' for Gwen Verdon (with the male chorus performing his trademark posture of locked ankles and a backward lean), 'Big Spender' for the hostesses at the Fandango Club, and 'The Rich Man's Frug', a satire of recent dance fads in discothèques. Fosse struggled through the film version of *Sweet Charity*, but resurrected his career by directing the highly successful film adaptation of *Cabaret* (1972), winning the Oscar for best direction. He also directed and choreographed the film *All That Jazz* (1979), which many considered Fosse's autobiography and which included brilliant dancing segments.

Fosse's last three Broadway shows included some of his most popular work. *Pippin* (1972) had a weak plot, enlivened by Fosse with characters based upon *commedia dell'arte* clowns and several large-scale song and dance numbers, and assisted greatly by the energy and gregarious personality of Ben Vereen. *Chicago* (1975) was yet another show starring Gwen Verdon, joined by Chita Rivera. They played murderesses who form a nightclub act. Fosse's staging was lean and effective with dance an integral part, led by Verdon and Rivera, who allowed Fosse to parody their fading youth in brief costumes and suggestive poses. The show is a series of vaudeville acts, each advancing the plot, with a band on stage. Fosse's choreography made frequent use of the soft-shoe and Charleston, emphasising the 1920s setting. *Dancin'* (1978) was Fosse's answer to *A Chorus Line*: another show about dancing conceived in a workshop situation. Using music by many composers dating back to Bach, *Dancin'* includes no plot and little singing. Critics offered mixed reactions but the audience did not, propelling *Dancin'* to a run of 1,774 performances. The show was a monument to Fosse the entertainer and his eleventh Broadway hit in a row. His final Broadway show was the unsuccessful *Big Deal* (1986). A retrospective of Fosse's work, *Fosse*, ran on Broadway and in the West End and toured in the late 1990s and early 2000s. It was conceived by Richard Maltby Jr, Ann Reinking and Chet Walker with the assistance of Gwen Verdon. Reinking has had a successful career as a choreographer, for example following Fosse's work in the hit revival of *Chicago* which ran for years on Broadway (starting in 1996) and in the West End (starting in 1997).

Another of Broadway's important choreographer-directors was Gower Champion, who started as a Broadway dancer in the 1940s. He went to work in Hollywood, and then returned to Broadway as choreographer-director of *Bye Bye Birdie* (1960), a fairly simple show whose major dance was the wild 'Shriners' Ballet'. His next show was *Carnival* (1961), where Champion brought the audience into the action by dispensing with the curtain and using aisles for entrances and exits. The memorable choreography included the 'Grand Imperial Cirque de Paris'. Champion's biggest hit was *Hello, Dolly!* (1964). Although more famous for the hit title song and Carol Channing's inimitable presence, the show benefited enormously from Champion's staging, which included extensive business from the dancers. He made Channing the centrepiece whenever possible and crafted one of the greatest entrances in theatre history with the hilarious 'Waiter's Gavotte' before Dolly Levi descends the stairs at the Harmonia Gardens. The extensive use of choreography was also found in 'It Takes a Woman' and 'Before the Parade Passes By'. Champion's career continued for another fifteen years with both hits and flops, including *I Do! I Do!* (1966), *The Act* (1977) and *42nd Street* (1980). The latter was an unabashed return to the days of tap-dancing chorus complete with story and music from old movies. Champion died the day the show opened.

Although not a choreographer-director, Hal Prince has played a major role in the development of the musical since the 1950s.[22] Like Robbins, he learned his craft from George Abbott. He played a role in several of Abbott's shows during the 1950s and emerged from the older man's shadow when he produced *West Side Story* with Robert Griffith in 1957. Following Griffith's death in 1961, Prince produced such shows as *She Loves Me* (1963) and *Fiddler on the Roof* (1964). He made his directing debut with *Cabaret* (1966), a book show that he treated like a concept musical, with an inspired staging that commented on the story through the cabaret entertainment. Its run of 1,166 performances did much to establish Prince as one of the most sought-after new directors. In 1970 he began his artistically successful collaboration in concept musicals with Stephen Sondheim in *Company* (1970), *Follies* (1971) and *A Little Night Music* (1973), three shows without conventional plots where staging played a huge role. Prince took staging nearly to the extreme limits in *Follies*, helping to create the spectacular effect of a theatre crumbling, but at the same time losing $685,000 during the one-and-a-half-year run. More recently, Prince has worked on some of Broadway's biggest successes with scores by Andrew Lloyd Webber, but his artistic vision had the most influence in the 1960s and 1970s, when he played a major role in the continuing integration of music, dance and drama in the musical. Like Robbins, he wielded great power in a production and helped make the director one of Broadway's most important figures.

The next important choreographer-director was Michael Bennett, creator of *A Chorus Line*. From a young age he showed great interest in dance and made his professional debut while still in his teens in a stock production of *West Side Story*. He later toured Europe in the show and became intimately familiar with his idol Robbins's work. Bennett became a Broadway gypsy in the early 1960s but worked in no memorable shows. He choreographed stock productions and achieved his first Broadway credit in *A Joyful Noise* (1966), which ran for twelve performances.[23] Critics praised Bennett's work, as they did his dances for *Henry, Sweet Henry* (1967), also a flop. Bennett finally worked on a hit in *Promises, Promises* (1968), directed by Robert Moore. The final version of the show included only one major dance number, but, as Ken Mandelbaum reports, 'Bennett was able to make an enormous contribution to the show by weaving scene into scene, staging marvelous "crossovers", with secretaries spinning through revolving doors in stylized movements reminiscent of... "go-go" steps.'[24] *Promises, Promises* was the first show where Donna McKechnie was Bennett's principal female dancer. She eventually became for Bennett what Gwen Verdon was to Bob Fosse. Bennett and McKechnie were also married for a time.

Bennett's next show as choreographer was *Coco* (1969), a vehicle for Katherine Hepburn directed by Michael Benthall. With both star and director working on their first musical, Bennett's role was very large. He choreographed dances around a largely stationary, charismatic star, and worked on book scenes; Mandelbaum called *Coco* Bennett's 'unofficial directorial debut'.[25] He gained valuable experience in the concept musical *Company* (1970), working with Hal Prince. Bennett had considerable influence on the show's staging, especially in the musical numbers, such as 'You Could Drive A Person Crazy', 'Side By Side By Side', 'What We Would Do Without You', and 'Tick Tock', Donna McKechnie's memorable solo dance. Bennett wanted to direct, but worked with Prince on *Follies* (1971), this time billed as co-director. Reviewers recognised his important contribution to the show's staging, especially in numbers like 'Who's That Woman?' Walter Kerr wrote in the *Sunday Times*: 'Michael Bennett's dazzling dance memories and perpetually musical staging are as seamlessly woven into [Sondheim's musical] personality as they are into Prince's immensely creative general direction.'[26]

Bennett had become highly regarded for his imaginative staging ideas and was ready to direct on his own. Before *A Chorus Line* he directed two non-musical plays and *Seesaw* (1973), a troubled musical that he took over in Detroit and brought to Broadway for a respectable ten-month run. Bennett received full artistic control over the show and brought in his usual assistant choreographer Bob Avian along with the dancers and choreographers Tommy Tune, Baayork Lee, Thommie Walsh and others, several of whom later worked in *A Chorus Line*. *Seesaw* had a successful national tour and made Bennett a major player in the Broadway community.

A Chorus Line started with Bennett's inspiration to do a show about dancers, a group he did not feel received its due on Broadway.[27] Along with Tony Stevens and Michon Peacock, with whom Bennett had worked in *Seesaw*, he arranged a meeting to discuss with eighteen colleagues on 18 January 1974. It was an extraordinary evening on which many felt moved to tell their life stories.[28] Bennett recorded the stories, as well as the conversations at the second such session on 8 February. After initial work with the tapes by Stevens, Peacock and the dancer-writer Nicholas Dante (whose story became the character Paul in the show), Bennett bought the rights of the raw material for *A Chorus Line*.

Bennett, Avian and Dante held more interviews and chose an audition format where dancers were encouraged to tell their stories. Early in the process Bennett decided to cast the show before even writing it and sold the workshop idea to Joseph Papp of the New York Shakespeare Festival. Papp agreed to pay Bennett and the dancers each $100 per week and let them work in his Newman Theater. Workshops had been used in plays for years, but *A Chorus Line* was the first musical produced through this method.

Bennett assembled his creative team. The co-writers were Bennett and Dante. Marvin Hamlisch became the composer and Edward Kleban the lyricist, both writing songs in the workshop. The first workshop, beginning in August 1974, lasted five weeks of fourteen-hour days, and after auditions included several of Bennett's favourite dancers. At the end of the workshop, however, they had only staged a few numbers. A second workshop began in late December, for which Bennett brought in writer James Kirkwood to help Dante with the script. The second workshop yielded a workable show. Kirkwood recalled the process:

> The material – book, music, lyrics, and staging concepts – changed
> daily . . . the show became structured and focused. The key to this was the
> invention of the character of Zach. In the first workshop, there had been an
> amorphous God-like figure billed only as 'Voice.' There was now an actual
> director character leading the audition, one who would soon be given a
> past involving one or more of the characters.[29]

Along with the character Zach came Cassie, his ex-lover, a small plot around which the remainder of the show could form. The workshop was highly collaborative, ensuring the seamlessness of the final product. It is impossible to sort out who was responsible for each contribution. For example, Bennett often asked another dancer, such as Avian, McKechnie or Baayork Lee, to design steps that he could edit.

Formal rehearsals began in March 1975 with the first preview on 16 April 1975. The buzz around Broadway was that the show was a sure hit, and tickets at the tiny Newman Theater (299 seats) were scarce. The public remained infatuated with the show through the official off-Broadway opening on 21 May 1975 and the move to the Shubert Theatre for its Broadway opening on 19 October 1975. *A Chorus Line* ran for fifteen years, paving the way for the megamusicals of the 1980s and 1990s, but without the huge stage effects that mark many of those shows.

Bennett brought to *A Chorus Line* rich Broadway experience as a dancer, choreographer and director, and the vision to forge an unconventional show. Placing the story in the context of an audition gave the audience the feeling of peeking backstage, even though the device was essentially unrealistic. Of course no Broadway director would have cared about the life stories of auditioning dancers, but these real-life vignettes did help to give the show a sense of truth.

Although some of his signature numbers in other shows involved elaborate costumes and sets, Bennett realised that *A Chorus Line* would work best with a nearly bare stage and rehearsal clothes as costumes. He satisfied the audience's craving for Broadway glitz in the closing number, 'One', performed by the entire cast in full costume, but that seemed appropriate because the chorus had been chosen and it was time for the show to open.

The show's intensity came from its rapid pace and lack of intermission. In earlier shows Bennett had used 'cinematic' techniques of directing, fading from one scene to another through action on stage, as in the dancing secretaries between scenes in *Promises, Promises*. Such pacing had begun with George Abbott in the 1930s. Prince and Bennett used the technique in *Follies*, and in *A Chorus Line* one finds its full realisation. The curtain never does go down during the show. Bennett had found success with montage scenes before, and designed his masterpiece in the long 'Hello Twelve, Hello Thirteen, Hello Love' (Martin Gottfried notes that it is one-fifth of the length of the script[30]), where the characters explore the pains of adolescence. Much of the show's action seems to occur in real time, a huge tribute to Bennett's direction.

Another major factor in the show's success is its saturation with dance and the various levels at which the audience perceives the dancing. One expects dancers to dance at an audition, so the audience accepts it as the show's basic language, and revels in watching those auditioning learn the steps, some succeeding and others cursing their efforts. Dance enters the characters' stories as they are told, such as the delightful tap dance 'I Can Do That', in which Mike tells of his early and natural talent. Finally, dance allows characters to express deeper feelings, especially Cassie in 'The Music and the Mirror', McKechnie's memorable solo number in which she shows that Cassie has the talent to be a solo dancer, even if that career has not worked out. Soon thereafter, the audience learns the difference between solo and chorus dancing, as Zach berates her for not dancing in unison with the others.[31]

Sometimes lost in the excitement about the show is the music, but this is partly because of the convincing way that songs and dance music are integrated with the rest of the show. In an essentially plotless musical a song cannot advance the narrative, but it can fit in with the dramatic concept of the moment, and all songs do. Most help tell a character's story, the only real exceptions being 'What I Did For Love' and 'One'. Many have criticised 'What I Did For Love' as Marvin Hamlisch's crass attempt at a hit song. The lyricist, Edward Kleban, hated it and wanted something different,[32] but the song is meaningful. After telling the most dramatic story of any of the characters, Paul falls and re-injures a knee. His career might be over. Zach asks the dancers what they will do when they can no longer dance. Diana's answer is this song, which, in the musical language of a 1970s pop anthem, answers the question by stating that one works for love of the art.

Like most Broadway scores, Hamlisch's effort in *A Chorus Line* is eclectic, including a number of styles from twentieth-century popular music. 'I Can Do That', a tap number, has the character of 1930s jazz with melodic blues touches and much use of jazz rhythms. 'One', in the style of a 1930s soft-shoe, is a production number from the show the dancers are auditioning for, and excerpts from it sound throughout the score. 'At the Ballet' alternates between a rock beat and a waltz with effective musical representation of speech rhythms in the rock section. The montage 'Hello Twelve, Hello Thirteen, Hello Love' is especially eclectic, befitting its length and complexity, with many characters interjecting segments of their stories. 'Nothing', part of the montage, combines an easy rock feel and the sound of a traditional Broadway ballad. The end of the montage borrows much from the sound of gospel music. 'The Music and the Mirror' provides another short tour of 1970s commercial music, moving mostly between jazz and funk.

It could be said that Hamlisch's score is firmly rooted in the 1970s (as is obvious from the instrumentation on the original cast recording), but most Broadway scores are products of their time. *A Chorus Line* probably carries the deepest meaning for Americans who grew up in the two or three decades following World War II. Bennett made a show about himself and other people willing to make sacrifices to work in their chosen fields. Few who saw *A Chorus Line* were professional dancers, but almost everyone understands what it means to want something as badly as those dancers wanted a job. Despite his other shows, the most successful of which was *Dreamgirls* from 1981 (another masterpiece of integration of drama, music and dance), Bennett spent much of the remainder of his life overseeing *A Chorus Line*. He assembled touring companies and ensured that each company maintained the requisite energy and quality.

Tommy Tune has been another important Broadway choreographer/director. Born in Wichita Falls, Texas in 1939, Tune danced in a touring version of *Irma La Douce* in the early 1960s. He choreographed the touring version of *Canterbury Tales* in 1969 and appeared in films. His first major

Broadway credit was the number 'It's Not Where You Start (It's Where You Finish)' in *Seesaw*, which Michael Bennett allowed Tune to choreograph. After five years without Broadway work, Tune began a string of hits as choreographer-director of *The Best Little Whorehouse in Texas* (1978), which ran for 1,584 performances. Tune's next success was sharing the choreography credit with Thommie Walsh in the New York version of the British show *A Day in Hollywood, A Night in the Ukraine* (1980). In 1982 he directed *Nine*, an adaptation of Federico Fellini's film *8½*. Walsh again shared the choreography credit and Tune's innovative staging won a Tony. Tune won the Tony for best actor and shared the award for best choreography with Walsh for *My One and Only* (1983), a substantial reworking of *Funny Face* (1927). Tune then won Tonys for both choreography and direction in *Grand Hotel* (1989) and *The Will Rogers Follies* (1991). In both of these shows, Tune demonstrated his talent for mining the history of American entertainment for ideas and styles and then adding his own special energy and panache.

Choreographers and directors continue to strive to make the songs and dances of a Broadway score an integral part of the plot rather than a distraction from it. An example of a successful recent effort was *Ragtime* (1998), directed by Frank Galati with choreography by Graciela Daniele. The road from Victor Herbert's *The Lady of the Slipper* to *Ragtime* is long and winding, but most stops along the way were attempts to improve the artistic integration of the Broadway musical: a seminal trend in the genre's history.

12 Distant cousin or fraternal twin? Analytical approaches to the film musical

GRAHAM WOOD

After the demonstration of a synchronized soundtrack, studio head R.F. discusses the new technology with his colleagues.
R.F.: Well?
MAN #1: It's just a toy!
WOMAN #1: It's a scream!
WOMAN #2: It's vulgar!
MAN #2: R.F., do you think they'll ever really use it?
R.F.: I doubt it. The Warner brothers are making a whole talking picture with this gadget – *The Jazz Singer*. They'll lose their shirts! What do you think of it Dexter?
DEXTER: It'll never amount to a thing.
COSMO: Yeah, that's what they said about the horseless carriage.

SINGIN' IN THE RAIN

Prologue

While I was channel surfing one evening at a friend's house, the familiar faces of Peter Finch and Michael York caused me to pause briefly. The spectacular scenery and epic sheen suggested a big-budget 1970s adventure movie. After only a couple of minutes of casual viewing, however, I gasped audibly and recoiled in horror as Michael York burst into song. For this was no ordinary film but was the 1973 remake of Frank Capra's classic *Lost Horizon* (1937) with the addition of songs by Burt Bacharach and Hal David. More troubling than the comic earnestness of the singing was the fact that I – an unabashed fan of both stage and screen musicals – would have been shocked at all by the mere occurrence of someone breaking into song at the top of a hidden mountain land. For surely therein lies the essence of the most popular (mis)conception of the movie musical – the spontaneous bursting forth of the human spirit in song and (almost as frequently) dance in unlikely or fantastical locations and for reasons which, if apparent at all, are mostly paper-thin at best. What is it about that moment where song takes over from speech that when treated with skill and finesse can seem like the most natural thing in the world, yet when carelessly done is jarring and comic in the extreme? Indeed, such is the ubiquity of this musical cliché that comedians ranging from the Monty Python team to Mel Brooks and, more recently on TV, the makers of *The Simpsons* and *South Park*, have made an art of parodying this essential element of movie musicals.[1] We could only find these comic renditions amusing if we accepted, at least in part, the artificiality of someone breaking into song in the ultimate medium of documentary realism: film.

Even at this early stage in our inquiry, questions arise. Can film musicals be studied as a unique medium? Or should they be considered part of a larger repertory including musicals for the stage? Stage and screen musicals are indisputably and intimately connected in terms of their history, content and style and must be considered as such if a full picture of either genre is to emerge. Certainly, one advantage movie musicals have over stage shows is the benefit of a relatively permanent record that can be infinitely repeated and studied. Stage musicals, in contrast, truly exist only in live performance. Yet the similarities and differences between screen and stage do require us to consider the specific qualities that make film musicals special, and the music in film musicals distinct from the *live* music in the theatre.

Introduction

Three discrete areas of investigation immediately present themselves as a means of examining the movie musical: (1) technology, (2) genre and (3) style. Although there is a good deal of overlap between these areas, they can serve as a useful matrix for preliminary analysis, and will be considered in turn in the sections that follow.

Under technology the principal areas of focus are advances in sound and colour, the mobility of the camera, and the way in which such changes affect the way musicals look and sound. Questions of genre explore the difference between stage transfers (those based on a pre-existing stage show) and original movie musicals (those with no stage musical precedents), different versions of a show, and the sources of the music. Also important is the sub-genre of biopics, movies about the life and work of actual show-business personalities. Issues of style subdivide into three areas: musical, visual and dance. Musical style includes the notion of *diegesis* – that is, the extent to which music featured on the soundtrack could plausibly emanate from a source within the visual frame or the narrative as a performance, a rehearsal, or some other likely musical activity. Visual style focuses on contrasts of realism, abstraction and fantasy, the comparison of spectacles that are either stage-influenced or movie-specific, and recurring iconographical symbols. Dance style considers an array of dance types – ballet, jazz, tap and ballroom – and the number of people involved in performance.

One notion in particular permeates all aspects of the movie musical: *self-reflexivity*. This term refers to those aspects of a musical that quote or allude to their own history – the history of musical theatre, the entertainment industry or the process of making musicals. This might occur through plot (movies about putting on a show or making a movie), songs (including those filmed as performances or rehearsals, those with lyrics that refer to singing or other aspects of performance and/or those that quote elements of an existing song or earlier musical style) or star personae who have a prior relationship with the genre or the entertainment industry. *Singin' in the Rain* (1952) is the archetypal self-reflexive musical. The movie concerns the making of early movie musicals, shows songs in rehearsal and performance, has songs about performance and the entertainment industry ('Singin' in the Rain' and 'Make 'Em Laugh') and features an established star with a prior history in stage and screen musicals (Gene Kelly).

It goes without saying that the creative teams involved in musical production – studios, producers, directors, songwriters, actors, singers and dancers – were central in the realisation of these visions, in formulating the combination of sights and sounds that filled the screens. Many team members had experience with stage musicals and transferred aspects of their craft to the film medium.

Technology

Once sound could be coordinated and then synchronised with film, the creative possibilities of the film musical genre expanded exponentially. The early successful examples of Warner Brothers' *The Jazz Singer* (1927) and Disney's animated *Steamboat Willie* (1928) demonstrated to audiences and, more importantly, to other film studios what was possible when sight and sound were combined with precision.

The next technological advance in sound concerned the way in which musical numbers were recorded. Early musicals required huge sound stages where music, singing and choreography were recorded simultaneously. The noisy camera needed to be encased in a soundproof booth, severely restricting its flexibility. Later, the sound for musical numbers was recorded separately then played back during the filming with singers lip-synching. This freed the camera from its relative immobility and soon, as Fehr and Vogel describe, 'cameras began moving more sure-footedly than ever and blending wide- and mid-angle shots with pans or dollying into close-ups at will. Film editors sped up the pace of musical films while adding variety to the visual menu.'[2] These changes challenged both silent-movie actors, who had to learn to use their voices and a new way of acting, and technicians, who had to rapidly master new equipment. But the great gains, artistic and financial, were soon clear.

Concurrent with advances in sound was the development of colour film. In order to compete with the live spectacle of Broadway, the major studios

began to use a two-strip Technicolor process, at first just in select musical sequences, but later in entire movies. Technical problems prompted continued
experimentation until a three-colour process was developed in the 1930s,
and from the end of the decade entire musicals in colour would become
increasingly common. Unfortunately, film using the two-colour process
was highly susceptible to damage and fading and many movies degraded
irreversibly, some only a few years after being made.

Genre

The first task for any genre-based study of musical films is to distinguish
them from those that are 'non-musical'. Many movies have theme songs,
more have musical numbers, but not all of them qualify as true musicals. It
is not so much a question of the quantity of music or the number of songs,
but rather one of approach. Gerald Mast states it most succinctly: 'A play
or film is a musical if its primary entertainment value and investment lie in
the musical numbers themselves.'[3]

Once separated from the body of 'non-musical' films, movie musicals
may then be viewed along a spectrum. At one end are movies originally conceived for the screen with no stage precedents – see the discussion on p. 217
below. At the other end are the stage-to-screen transfers that recreate, to
varying degrees, elements of a prior stage production – such as *My Fair Lady*
(1956/1964), *West Side Story* (1957/1961), *The Sound of Music* (1959/1965)
and *Cabaret* (1966/1972).[4]

The movie version of *My Fair Lady* is one of the more faithful of these
transfers in that scene by scene and song by song it closely follows the sequence of the original stage production. Not only that, but it also presents an
actor who originated one of the title roles (Rex Harrison as Henry Higgins)
and recreates the lavish costumes and high production values of the stage
version. As Mast has noted, the movie version of *My Fair Lady* 'is not an original musical conception for cinema but a theatrical conception brilliantly
inflected by cinema values . . . a permanent record of an ephemeral event'.[5]

A similar comparison of the stage and screen versions of *West Side Story*
reveals some small but telling changes. The songs 'Cool' and 'Gee, Officer
Krupke!' have switched places, the sequence of the 'Balcony Scene' and
'America' has been reversed (male Sharks have also been added to 'America')
and the ballet sequence in the stage version has been entirely removed. Ex-
changing 'Officer Krupke' with 'Cool' has specific dramatic ramifications
for the movie version. First, a different singer is needed to sing 'Cool' since in
the film Riff is now dead. Also, no other song has quite the vaudevillian humour of 'Officer Krupke' and its original placement in the latter half of Act II

in the stage version brings much needed comic relief to the Shakespearean tragedy that has engulfed these young people. With 'Krupke' placed in the first half of the movie, there is nothing to alleviate the steady tragic slide from that point on to Maria's final outburst. In the stage show, 'Cool' is a hip attempt to quell youthful anger and frustration, whereas in the movie it comes across as a harrowing effort to suppress the panic and shock engendered by the two unexpected deaths that occur during the rumble. According to Block, this exchange of songs for the two different versions represents the difference between the 'theatrical truth' and the 'literal truth',[6] or, in other words, it illustrates the difference between what is dramatically convincing in a live theatrical genre and what is equally convincing in the film medium.

Similarly, the movie version of *The Sound of Music* is widely regarded as one of the more successful Rodgers and Hammerstein transfers to the screen, despite changes in the plot and the score. The director, Robert Wise, takes full advantage of the stunning Austrian scenery, allowing Maria and the von Trapp children to leap from one glorious location to another, often in the middle of songs. Wise thus maximises the possibilities that film offers and, through creative editing and camerawork, creates a world far larger than any Broadway stage. (From this point of view, the opening of *West Side Story* is also promising in purely cinematic terms because the Sharks and Jets dance through the back streets of New York. Thereafter, however, the movie becomes closely bound to its backlot set.)

Bob Fosse's 1972 film version of *Cabaret* also departs from its stage version in terms of plot and character, and, in contrast to *The Sound of Music*, all but one of the songs are performed indoors on the stage of the Kit Kat Klub. Particularly successful is *Cabaret*'s combination of camerawork, design and lighting and the way in which the stunning performances by Liza Minnelli and Joel Grey are cunningly interwoven into the off-stage narrative. This produces a penetrating psychological drama driven as much by visual effects and choreography as by plot and character. What Fosse's adaptation reveals is that a pure scene-by-scene comparison of stage and screen versions, while necessary and valuable for understanding the effect of the differences between them, may not be an appropriate means by which to evaluate the success of either version. It may, in fact, inhibit discussion of something that is so *cinematic* in execution.

The inevitably close relationship of stage and screen musical genres has often precluded a serious consideration of movie transfers on their own terms as opposed to the extent to which they reproduce or deviate from the stage production. Busby Berkeley's *Babes in Arms* (1939) is one example from many such transfers that carry the name and a couple of songs from the original, but scarcely anything else. The movie version bears little resemblance to the 1937 Rodgers and Hart stage show except for the use of

'Where or When', the title song 'Babes in Arms', an instrumental reference to 'The Lady is a Tramp', and some tangential plot elements. Yet viewed on its own terms it captures the triumph of youthful persistence and energy in the face of adversity and elders' disapproval that is the central theme of the original, even though its manifestation is different. Energetic performances from Mickey Rooney and Judy Garland as they attempt to put on their own show propel a narrative that is greatly enhanced by Berkeley's thoroughly cinematic direction. An early montage sequence cleverly intercuts snippets of performances, off-stage scenes, New Year's Eve balloons and newspaper headlines ('Talkies Arrive', 'Vaudeville Doomed') to indicate that Mickey's character is growing up just as his parents' profession is being eclipsed. Also visually striking is the 'Babes in Arms' sequence that masterfully juxtaposes images of adult revolution – angry marching through streets and backyards carrying flaming torches – with such symbols of childhood as see-saws, chutes, swings and skipping in circles. As a musical corollary, the robust march-like chorus is intercut with snatches of nursery tunes. Together these visual and musical symbols reinforce the central theme of the original stage show, though in a uniquely cinematic way.

At the other end of the spectrum are movies originally conceived for the screen with plots based on short stories, novels, fairy tales and so forth, or on newly invented narratives, but specifically *not* on stage musicals. Examples span the whole history of the genre from *The Jazz Singer* to *Moulin Rouge* (2001). Some of the more outstanding examples include: *42nd Street* (1933), *Top Hat* (1935), *Snow White* (1938), *The Wizard of Oz* (1939), *Meet Me in St Louis* (1944), *Easter Parade* (1948), *An American in Paris* (1951), *Singin' in the Rain*, *Beauty and the Beast* (1991), *The Lion King* (1994) and *Dancer in the Dark* (2000). And while the influence of theatrical conventions, styles, plots and performers is frequently felt, what distinguishes these works is the way in which they employ the medium of film.

With these generic categories now in place, the study of movie musicals should then take into account the origins of the score. Is it a newly composed set of songs written specifically for a film by a single songwriting team, or a combination of old and new songs by a variety of composers and lyricists? The five songs for *42nd Street*, for example, were all written specifically for the movie by Al Dubin and Harry Warren. The score for *Easter Parade* contains sixteen songs all by Irving Berlin, some newly composed, some interpolated from prior contexts. All eight of the songs for *An American in Paris* are by George and Ira Gershwin, but were assembled for the movie long after George's death. More recently, the score for *Moulin Rouge*, although set in late nineteenth-century Paris, consists of a freewheeling array of pop songs from the 1950s to the 1990s including numbers associated with pop culture icons Marilyn Monroe, Madonna, The Beatles, David Bowie, Elton John and Sting.

Adaptations from stage to screen might contain songs from the original stage production, new songs or a combination of the two. This seemingly arbitrary phenomenon must be understood in the context of the working methods of the studio system. Once studios realised the economic rewards to be gained from movie musicals, production increased rapidly, causing a sudden need for songs. The larger studios bought up New York publishing houses as a way of feeding their new children. Having made such an investment, the studios were subsequently reluctant to pay royalties for the use of songs they did not own. Instead, they either had staff writers in their employ compose new songs to be added to an existing score, or interpolated one or more of the many songs whose copyright they already owned. This often resulted in scores with over half a dozen different songwriters, as is the case in the movie version of *Babes in Arms*. The musical and narrative effects of such composite scores have yet to be fully explored. For example, can older songs be used to evoke an earlier time period in a specific narrative framework? These and similar questions about the narrative function of songs remain to be answered.

An important subgroup of film musicals comprises biopics – movies about show-business personalities. Singers and songwriters are the typical subjects of biopics, but bandleaders, impresarios, dancers and choreographers are also occasionally featured. The biopic provides ample occasion for musical numbers as the careers of stars unfold, and also incorporates features of the backstage or 'show' musical. *Till the Clouds Roll By* (1946), the screen homage to Jerome Kern, contains a series of delightfully staged numbers including a substantial chunk of *Show Boat*. Interestingly, the two renditions of 'Ol' Man River' that occur in the movie are diametrically opposed in their settings. Caleb Peterson as Joe sings in the staged *Show Boat* excerpt while Frank Sinatra appears in a fantasy cloudscape dressed in a white tuxedo, symbolically representing Kern's spiritual and musical ascent to the pantheon of great songwriters. These contrasting representations clearly illustrate how popular singers have always mined musical theatre repertory as a source for their songs. *The Jolson Story* (1947) and its highly successful sequel, *Jolson Sings Again* (1949), chart the life of the charismatic performer who kicked off the genre with *The Jazz Singer*. The second movie allows for some interesting moments of self-reflexivity when Larry Parks, playing Jolson, encounters Larry Parks playing himself playing Jolson as the sequel documents the making of the earlier movie. The real Jolson even appears uncredited in a long-shot sequence on his famous theatrical runway that extended into the middle of the audience.

Another charismatic performer, Elvis Presley, made a series of movies beginning with *Love Me Tender* (1956) that took him to various modern fairy-tale locations and allowed him to play characters not far removed from his stage persona. The Beatles also provided new twists to the biopic in their first two pop movies, *A Hard Day's Night* (1964) and *Help!* (1965). Here they playfully mixed their original songs with pseudo-autobiographical exploits that grew increasingly fantastic until live action became too restrictive and they delved into the world of animation for their next movie – the psychedelic *Yellow Submarine* (1968). This combination of documentary style with performances in plausible and implausible locations may well be the source for the visually adventurous music videos pioneered by Michael Jackson and Madonna in the 1980s as well as more recent band biopics such as *Spice World* (1997), featuring the real but 'manufactured' girl group The Spice Girls. Other spins on this ever-flexible subgroup include *Stop Making Sense* (1984), essentially a filmed rock concert featuring David Byrne and the Talking Heads, and the cult spoof rock documentary *This is Spinal Tap* (1984).

Biopics and other musicals provide opportunities for a particular manifestation of self-reflexivity: the foregrounding of the technology of the industry. Here, images of cameras, projectors, microphones and recording studios fill the frame, to which are frequently added audiences that observe both stage and screen performances and rehearsals. *Singin' in the Rain* has many such scenes, but there are countless other musicals that employ this device as a way of letting us in on a secret only to hide it from us at another level – we are, after all, still watching a movie.

The opening sequence of the movie version of *Evita* (1996) is a recent example of how deftly these self-reflexive relationships can be juggled. Over the opening black screen the names of the creators and stars of our movie appear along with sound effects and Spanish conversation. Abruptly, the screen is filled with black and white images – a shock since we surely expected colour. Next follows a shot of the internal audience viewing what we now realise to be the movie within our movie. For a brief moment, both external and internal audiences watch the same movie unaware of the other's presence, but when we see them, the illusion is over. The next shot, however, shows us both the movie screen and the projector – the source of the on-screen illusion and also the source of *our* movie. Such masterly blurring of the boundaries between on- and off-screen audiences also mirrors the blurring between the lives and personae of the two charismatic female subjects of the movie: Evita and Madonna. The stage production of *Evita* (1978) also opens inside a movie theatre, but cannot refer to itself visually in quite the same way as the movie version.

Any analysis of musical theatre and film should take into account the central importance of race and culture both in the creative process and in the final product. This area is not without its difficulties since modern audiences will continue to find the ethnic stereotyping in many musicals distasteful, particularly the practice of 'blacking up' by both white and black actors in the earlier musicals from *The Jazz Singer* to *Holiday Inn* (1942). Yet provocative connections between Yiddish theatre, minstrelsy, blacking up, Tin Pan Alley and the music of the Broadway theatre have already been noted in the literature. Surely, therefore, a consideration of the influence and impact of both Jewish and African-American culture should be an important part of the analytical and critical enterprise of musical film studies.[7]

Issues of gender and sexuality also surface regularly in this genre – directly and indirectly. For example, cross-dressing occurs in *Victor/Victoria* (1982) and *Yentl* (1983). Also, a camp sensibility in visual and performance styles permeates the genre to such an extent that an expression of interest in musicals can be virtually synonymous with coming out as gay (at least in American culture).[8] The reception of Judy Garland as an icon for gay men has already been convincingly explored.[9] Gerald Mast has also posited a close connection between Jewish culture and gay culture as two marginalised groups that were drawn to the entertainment industry because it was a safe professional haven where they could express themselves with less fear of discrimination.[10] Our willingness to address and deal sensitively with these issues must surely be one of the priorities of future research on musical film specifically and musical theatre in general.

Visual style

The silver screen contains a fundamental dualism between realism and fantasy: realism because movies and TV report the news, war, natural disasters, sport and events that have actually occurred; fantasy because that same medium, through acting, *mise-en-scène*, creative camerawork, editing and special effects, can create entire new worlds that do not exist anywhere but on that same screen. This tension is not nearly so pronounced in the stage musical because theatre audiences have learned, over centuries, to suspend their disbelief in the illusion of reality that they observe. For movie audiences, although they can be transported to much more complete and detailed worlds of fantasy than stage audiences, the memories of wreckage from the latest plane crash or blood-soaked bodies from a terrorist shooting are not far away. For film musicals this has always presented the central problem of how to effect a smooth and convincing transition from speech into song. This dualism affects visual style in a number of ways, most obviously in the contrast between 'realism' and 'fantasy', such as Dorothy's black and white Kansas versus the Technicolor Oz. But there is also a tension of visual style created by the contrast of realism and abstraction. The camerawork of Busby Berkeley is one example.

Berkeley was the dance director for three Warner Brothers productions in 1933: *42nd Street*, *Gold Diggers of 1933* and *Footlight Parade*. His now infamous and much-quoted style in these and later movies is characterised by a much more imaginative use of the camera than had ever been observed in musicals. Having choreographed the large-scale production numbers, Berkeley's camera then becomes a roving eye that reduces the multiple body parts of chorines into geometric shapes seen from all possible angles. In a sense, he caught the mood of the times by suggesting the dehumanising of his dancers as cogs in a larger visual machine while making them the voyeuristic subject of a visual spectacle – but a spectacle governed by a distinctly filmic sensibility. As Fehr and Vogl have noted, Berkeley 'elevated the movements of a chorus line to the highest imaginative level. In fact, no other artist of the period was more responsible for establishing the format of the 1930s big-budget production numbers than he... [Berkeley also] refused to accept the movie set as a West Coast proscenium. The camera was free to roam at will.'[11]

Animated musicals demonstrate the spectrum of visual styles from illusory to realistic particularly well and it may be that the role of the Disney studio has been underestimated in the history and generic development of the film musical. The opening sequence of *Dumbo* (1941), for example, shows a sky full of parachuting baby animals that bears a striking resemblance to World War II newsreel footage. Disturbing, too, are the harrowing scenes of the circus train journey through the rain that conjure up even more disquieting war-related images. Yet against this realistic background, Disney creates a striking visual contrast. When Dumbo accidentally drinks some beer, the three-dimensional depth, natural tones and realistic detail of the visual frame (talking animals and birds notwithstanding) is replaced by a flat, black background, against which surreal, garish colours play amidst logistically improbable animal mutations and abstract transformations. The pink elephant sequence is rendered all the more fantastic because its style of animation is so completely counter to the surrounding elements of the movie. The combination of highly abstract and stylised visuals and sinister minor-key music strengthens the impact of the sequence, which becomes, in effect, the show's big production number. Macabre and menacing, yet plausible because of Dumbo's alcohol-enhanced state, the sequence is also crucial to the narrative because for the first time Dumbo is able to visualise the impossible and actually fly himself – the next morning he wakes up high in a tree with a hangover as a little piece of fantasy spills over into the real world.

Dumbo's drunken vision is related to the dream sequences that occur in many stage musicals such as *Betsy* (1926) and *Babes in Arms* (1937). Dream sequences or dream ballets, as they sometimes were, transferred to some of the screen adaptations such as *Oklahoma!* (1955) and also appear in original movie musicals such as *The Wizard of Oz*, *Yolanda and the Thief* (1945), *The Pirate* (1948) and *An American in Paris*. Most often these sequences play out the psychological dilemmas of the main characters in fantastical worlds that are related to but far removed from their everyday experience.[12]

A more recent animated example of how contrasting visual styles combined with contrasting musical styles can enhance the narrative is Disney's *The Lion King*. Here Disney recreates the world of the African savannah by combining nature-documentary-style visuals and 'African-sounding' pop songs by Elton John and Tim Rice. Hans Zimmer's orchestrations effectively provide the required ethnic ambience that the songs themselves lack. Set against this overall visual style of panoramic long shots and leaping gazelles is the occasional use of non-realistic, stylised animation with savannah beasts doing things that you'd never see them do on televised nature programmes. In 'I Just Can't Wait to Be King', Simba launches into an early Michael Jackson-style number that simultaneously abandons visual realism for hyper-real colours, flat backgrounds and abstract patterns formed by a conveniently situated chorus of usefully marked animals. The style of Busby Berkeley immediately springs to mind (as it does in the 'Be Our Guest' production number from *Beauty and the Beast*), except that here it is the noble animal rather than Berkeley's chorus girl that is visually dismembered. The good humour of the animal play hides any apparent exploitation and once again the musical refers to its own past. Yet, as in *Dumbo*, this musical number is crucial to the narrative because Simba is giddy with the anticipation of regal power and the freedom from regulations that he thinks it will provide. The number thus becomes a space where the possibility of a positive future can be imagined. In contrast to *Dumbo*, the sinister element in *The Lion King* is reversed. Dumbo's dream is far more frightening than reality, whereas the party atmosphere of Simba's production number is quite unlike the harsh reality of actually being king – an awesome responsibility that is placed on his young shoulders after the accidental death of his father. The terrifying realism of the wildebeest stampede and destruction of the pride lands that follows sheds a darkness over Simba's world that is entirely absent both visually and musically from his earlier song.

Another visual device that can add to the impact of musical numbers is the use of symbols. Powerful images of steam trains occur in such movies as *The Harvey Girls* (1946), *Oklahoma!* and *Evita*. Train iconography is a vital part of the American visual landscape, as many nineteenth- and twentieth-century paintings, prints, murals and Western movies show. And aside from being a vital means of transportation for an expanding frontier, the iron horse brought along with its dirt and noise the ideas and social codes that would ultimately lead to the civilising of the continent. The song 'On the

Atchison, Topeka and the Santa Fe', from *The Harvey Girls*, celebrates the railroad line that will allow the Girls to bring a feminine brand of civilisation to the West, while 'Kansas City' and 'Buenos Aires', from *Oklahoma!* and *Evita* respectively, demonstrate the potent fascination that the modern city has for rural communities. Also, these last two songs take advantage of the film medium by changing their location from the stage versions specifically in order to incorporate close-ups of real engines that powerfully reinforce the sense of urban modernity. Similarly, 'The Trolley Song' in *Meet Me in St Louis* is heading for the 1903 St Louis World's Fairground – a symbol of progress and the inescapable internationalism of the twentieth century. The family in this lavishly detailed period piece does not need to move to New York; modernity will reach them soon enough. Once again, movie musical characters are being thrust into the future through song. What these and my earlier observations illustrate is how the visual style and setting of musical numbers can affect the overall narrative framework of the movie.

Musical style

No study of this rich cultural product would be complete without a treatment of the music and its relationship to surrounding elements.

Song

The basic component of the musical, the song, can be understood as a very flexible template, whose lyrics may provide narrative thrust, insight into a character's psyche or reflection on a external object. From the 1920s to the 1950s most of the popular songs used in movies exhibit a plan that consists of three discrete sections: an instrumental introduction, a verse and a chorus. Built into the pattern is the potential for repetition of the verse and the chorus. This overall plan continued to be used in later decades, but the increasing use of rock and other popular styles led to a greater variety of song patterns in musicals from the 1960s onwards.

The verse and chorus have either a single text or multiple texts that require musical repetition. Single-texted choruses may also be repeated many times. In general, the chorus carries the most musical and dramatic weight because it contains the most important musical and textual material and because of the frequency with which that material is repeated. The most common plan for choruses is four eight-bar phrases that form a 32-bar pattern. Sometimes these eight-bar phrases can break down into two- and four-bar units. Thematically, choruses are most likely to fall into one of two distinct patterns that describe the eight-bar phrases: A B A C and A A B A. The first pattern is the more symmetrical and has a strong half cadence at the mid-point leading to the repeat of the A section. The second pattern has a strong half cadence at the three-quarter point leading to the final repetition of A, giving more musical weight to the latter half of the pattern. Extensions and variations add nuance to certain phrases, but these two basic patterns form the backbone of the song repertory used in movie musicals. Rather than being abstract or arbitrary patterns, however, each has a quite different emotional effect. The A B A C pattern tends to feel more balanced and suggests restraint and elegance, whereas the A A B A pattern drives more forcefully towards its final goal and, as a result, is often more passionate and direct in content and delivery. When combined with specific musical styles, time signatures and orchestrations, the choice of pattern can greatly enhance the meaning of the words and the specific dramatic context of the song itself.[13]

Diegesis

Even before the advent of the synchronised soundtrack, the movie-going experience had always been associated with the continuous playing of accompanying background music on piano, organ or even orchestra: these movies were thus never really 'silent'. After the advent of talkies and the fixing of sound to visual images, both musical and non-musical films persisted in their use of background music, or underscoring. Film scholars refer to this special category of sound as non-diegetic music, that is, music that does not clearly emanate from a performance or other sound-generating source within the visual frame. But because movie musicals frequently contain so much diegetic music – actual performances, rehearsals, recording sessions and the like – they have been able to take this technological advance and turn it to aesthetic ends. For what this phenomenon allows is a more subtle transition from non-diegetic underscoring to actual diegetic performance. Since both musical and non-musical film use orchestral underscoring, the onset of a section of orchestral background music might be perceived as underscoring for a new scene, or the non-diegetic introduction to a song. It could also be music from a diegetic orchestra playing just off-screen – something that may not be apparent until a subsequent visual edit cuts to a shot of the musicians and/or singers in a night club or dance hall. Transitions into environments associated with live performance or rehearsal are much easier for an audience to accept than a less obviously musical environment because we would expect music to be present even if we do not at first see the source. Thus a diegetic performance can be used to accomplish transitions from one scene to another and to smooth over visual edits. Sensitivity to this blurring of diegetic and non-diegetic music can greatly enhance the viewing experience as well as furnishing a greater understanding of musical syntax in this genre.

Transitions

The makers of movie musicals have devoted a considerable amount of attention to the problem of how to effect the transition from speech into song, often with ingenious results. For example, Fred Astaire's apparently spontaneous rendition of 'No Strings' in *Top Hat* is, in fact, very carefully prepared. Playing unobtrusively underneath Fred's banter prior to the song is non-diegetic orchestral underscoring. As the conversation turns towards marriage, the dialogue introduces the topic of the song. Since Fred's delivery of his lines is so lyrical and his singing voice so effortlessly conversational, it seems as if he has started to sing the song before we realise it. Simultaneously the underscoring becomes Fred's orchestral accompaniment. By omitting the verse and leaping directly into the chorus of the song, Fred is able to project an air of spontaneity and immediacy. Later in the same movie, when Fred and Ginger are sheltering from the rain in a bandstand, a clap of thunder cleverly sets in motion a timpani roll that allows Fred to begin the verse of 'Isn't It a Lovely Day'. Again the preceding dialogue is directly related to the first sung words of the song and its overall theme. Visual clues – a few music lyres in the background and the bandstand itself – also provide a setting ripe for music making.

One of the more unusual approaches to solving the transition problem was the use of rhyming dialogue. Seen most effectively in two movies with scores by Richard Rodgers and Lorenz Hart, *Love Me Tonight* (1932) and *Hallelujah, I'm a Bum!* (1933), a middle zone between speech and song is created through extended passages of rhymed, rhythmical and patterned dialogue, frequently with underscoring. Sometimes these passages lead into a full-blown song, at other times they conclude with a brief antecedent–consequent phrase in arioso style that functions like a Shakespearean rhyming couplet signalling the close of an act. Although rhyming dialogue was not widely used in subsequent movies, as a unique solution it deserves further scrutiny.

Transitions out of songs also present a challenge to the movie director. Common strategies at the end of songs include a shot of the audience applauding, a view of the performer(s) from the wings of the theatre (for diegetic performances), fading to black or cutting directly to a new scene (for non-diegetic performances). Sometimes more humorous and inventive endings are fashioned. The opening number of *Gold Diggers of 1933*, for example, appears to be an electrifying live stage performance of 'We're in the Money'. It is not until the performance is interrupted that we realise this was merely a rehearsal – albeit an astonishingly well-polished one. A variant on this approach is an apparent stage performance that turns out to be a take for a movie. When someone off-screen shouts 'cut' at the end of the song, the illusion is broken.

Recent Disney styles

The Disney Studio has dominated the production of feature-length animated musicals since *Snow White* (1938). Even when live action musicals
grew scarcer from the 1970s onward, Disney continued to produce musicals on a more regular basis than anyone else. Finding renewed momentum
with *The Little Mermaid* (1989), Disney has produced a string of modern classics that have earned numerous best song Oscars, utilise the latest
computer-generated animation techniques to enhance visual splendour and
are in many ways worthy successors to the classic musicals of the 1940s and
1950s.

Disney has also continued to experiment with musical style. *The Little
Mermaid* and *Beauty and the Beast*, for example, both employ Broadway-
style scores by Howard Ashman and Alan Menken where full-blown songs
arise as a means of providing a narrative climax. In contrast, the score
for *Pocahontas* (1995) by Menken and Stephen Schwartz contains several
passages of singing that do not form complete or discrete songs in themselves but seem closer to the more continuous fluid style of Alain Boublil
and Claude-Michel Schoenberg's musicalised French epic *Les Misérables*.
Here, speech-like singing and smaller lyrical units are woven around more
traditional musical numbers. Different again is *The Lion King* with songs
by the pop mega-star Elton John and the Broadway veteran Tim Rice. The
rock orientation of the score combined with Hans Zimmer's stylish and
slick orchestrations made the CD soundtrack of *The Lion King* considerably
more marketable than earlier scores. Overall, *The Lion King* returns to the
earlier format of distinctly separate numbers. This successful formula is
repeated in *Tarzan* (1999), with another rock mega-star, Phil Collins, writing
and performing songs that are greatly enhanced through exhilarating visual
effects. As the above examples show, the unique contribution of the animated
Disney musicals must be included in future studies of the genre.[14]

Song migration

An interesting phenomenon occurring in this repertory is songs that appear
in more than one movie. Songwriters for stage shows have often canni-
balised their own songs for re-use in later productions and the tradition of
interpolating other people's songs into a show is well established. In movies,
however, these practices are applied with considerably greater freedom. This
is partly due to the lesser degree of control that songwriters had over the
musical aspects of movies produced in a studio system. In any case, examining the different contexts of each version can be revealing. Irving Berlin's
'Blue Skies' appeared in no less than four movies after its initial stage appearance in Rodgers and Hart's *Betsy* (1926).[15] Belle Baker, the star of *Betsy*,
was concerned about not having a show-stopping number and asked Berlin

to oblige. 'Blue Skies' did stop the show – much to the consternation of the show's creators. Al Jolson's version of the song in *The Jazz Singer* (1927) is a diegetic parlour room performance to his mother in charismatic style and optimistic mood – not a cloud in sight here. 'Blue Skies' next appears in *Alexander's Ragtime Band* (1938), again as a diegetic performance – this time in a nightclub and sung by Ethel Merman. Here the mood is quite different: the tempo is slower and the performance is tinged with melancholy. The nightclub audience joins in with a spontaneous accompanying choral refrain. Bing Crosby's non-diegetic outdoor performance in *Blue Skies* (1946) is also fairly slow, but his unique crooning voice projects reassurance and optimism. Mother Nature even obliges by quelling the rainstorm before the end of the song. A fourth filmed version of 'Blue Skies' occurs in *White Christmas* (1954) and again features Crosby, this time dancing with Danny Kaye. The context is a live stage performance with an unseen but presumably diegetic orchestra. This upbeat dance number in vaudevillian style has the duo sporting straw boaters and canes and is more in the charismatic tradition of Jolson than the other versions. By tracing the progress of a song as it appears in various shows, the dramatic context for each version can be compared and contrasted, as can the orchestrations, tempos, performers and musical style. This is essentially the same song, but meaning in each case is located in the combination of a variety of factors.

Singing and lyrics

The use of microphones in the making of movie musicals allowed for the possibility of a more intimate singing style. No longer did performers have to sing as if they were projecting to the back row of a theatre or filling a large auditorium with their voice. As Miles Krueger has noted, Paul Robeson chose to sing quietly with the microphone only two feet away when recording 'Ol' Man River' for the 1936 movie version of *Show Boat*.[16] The singing style of different performers also translates differently onto the screen. Compare, for example, the singing styles of Fred Astaire and Al Jolson. Jolson's personality fills the screen and his huge voice is barely contained by the soundtrack. Astaire's style, on the other hand, is more intimate and refined. Also, since vocal projection over a great distance is less crucial here, Astaire can focus on the clear diction and suave, elegant phrasing that is his forte. Technology can also affect the lyrics of songs. Before the regular use of amplified sound in theatres, lyricists developed the technique of placing long vowel sounds at the ends of lines to aid with projection ('day/free/high/show/you' etc.). But the intimacy of the recording studio allowed more complex lyrics to be fashioned that could, for example, end lines with short vowels and clipped consonants that would have been lost in a theatre environment.[17]

Dance style

A wide variety of dance styles are present in this genre, ranging from high to low, elite to popular. They may be performed by a solo dancer, a couple, or a large ensemble in a 'production number'. Contrasting styles are sometimes played off against one another – usually with the more popular styles winning out. Gene Kelly, Fred Astaire, Eleanor Powell and Ann Miller are the best of the solo dancers. Fred Astaire and Ginger Rogers set the benchmark for the special chemistry that can be generated from the couple dance in Cole Porter's 'Night and Day' from *Gay Divorcée* (1934), a remake of the 1932 stage show *Gay Divorce*. This number established new standards of direction, design, choreography, camerawork and editing, not just for the team's subsequent dances, but for many other couples as well. In a similar way, the production numbers of Busby Berkeley greatly influenced subsequent large-scale ensemble dances.

Concluding example

Clearly, the elements I have isolated above do not operate alone in the projection of a narrative and should, ideally, be considered in conjunction with one another. A final example attempts to bring together some of the approaches suggested above.

The example, 'Slap That Bass' from the *Shall We Dance?* (1937), was, like all the songs in the movie, written especially for the film by George and Ira Gershwin. It was the last of the RKO studio series to feature Fred Astaire and Ginger Rogers as dancing partners. The movie was as much a meditation on the difficulty of maintaining any kind of relationship under close public scrutiny as it was a polemic on the cultural struggle between Europe and America and the challenge of forging a viable dance style out of two seemingly opposed traditions. The song is staged in the engine room of a luxury ocean liner on which Fred (Pete Peters) and Ginger (Linda Keene) are travelling. Ginger/Linda has just seen through Fred/Pete's pretence of being the Russian ballet dancer Petrov, and he now seeks to shake off all European influences and immerse himself thoroughly in American popular music in order to achieve his dream of dancing jazz/tap instead of ballet.

The song's opening shot shows three black workers who move and hum in time to the ship's engines – a scene suggesting both urban modernity and outdoor work songs. The polished black engine room floor and pristine white machinery become the 'stage'. When one of the workers begins to sing the verse, other workers form a chorus, a diegetic engine-room band, and an audience of which Fred/Pete is at first a member. The verse begins in the minor mode, but swings around symbolically to the major at the words:

> Happiness is not a riddle
> When I'm listening to that big bass fiddle.

At this point Fred/Pete leaps up, apparently spontaneously, and takes the lead by singing the chorus. Now the workers are *his* accompaniment and audience. The opening of the chorus returns to the minor mode again but ultimately achieves a stable major by the final phrase, symbolising the transformative powers of (listening to) popular music. The lyrics of the chorus use the short, clipped words at the ends of phrases that are possible with a microphone ('bass/tonic/rhythm'). The only long vowel, 'flow', is placed on the longest and highest note in the whole chorus, giving musical and lyrical emphasis to the anticipation of the Elysian rewards promised in the line 'And the milk and honey'll flow!' The Gershwins even use a melodic, rhythmic and textual fragment ('all got rhythm') that recalls one of their earlier songs, 'I Got Rhythm' from the stage show *Girl Crazy* (1930). Through its allusion to the last line of the quoted song – 'Who could ask for anything more?' – this brief moment of self-reflexivity suggests that the man who performs with spontaneity and rhythm is truly free and requires nothing else in life. As the song concludes, Fred/Pete, still searching for that freedom, casts off his jacket (that European influence?) and begins to dance in the hoofing style of Bill Robinson – an influence that Fred had already acknowledged on screen during 'Bojangles of Harlem' in *Swing Time* (1936). The on-screen audience is now out of view – we the off-screen viewer have become the audience. Next, Fred/Pete symbolically flouts convention by ignoring the stairs to the next level and instead leaps and climbs up to the balcony. In the ensuing section, the regular pulse of engine-room machinery is Fred/Pete's only accompaniment. And as he moves in tandem with huge pistons his body becomes a symbol of urban modernity as well as metaphor for the long hours of disciplined practice required for dance at this level. As Fred/Pete searches for a new style he accidentally executes an old ballet move which he instantly rejects because he is looking for a way to transform old-style tap into something even more modern. He wants to forge a new style for himself that is definitely *not* ballet. Music returns in the final section of the dance and Fred/Pete spins across the balcony to a new space: 'Yes, that's it! I've found it!' his ecstatic apotheosis seems to say. At the end of the number, the camera pulls back to show Fred/Pete high above the workers who began the song. Although visually separated from the workmen, he acknowledges them both as his audience and as the source of his inspiration as he returns to his own level/world forged anew.

Summary

Seemingly infinite access to seventy-five years of movie musicals through video, DVD and cable/satellite TV, along with the high movie-like production values of music videos and the impressively slick and continuously inventive medium of TV commercials, has tended to lessen the craving for the large-scale visual spectacle with music and song of which the movie musical was once the sole provider. Yet the apparent decline of a tradition (is the movie musical dead or just reinventing itself?) may be precisely the point at which it is time to stand back and reflect. Perhaps we are now distant enough from the corpus to bring serious analytical consideration to these powerful cultural artefacts. As other disciplines have already shown (films studies, cultural studies, American studies), the study of movie musicals can yield rich rewards. Perhaps the recent growth of scholarly interest in musical theatre will encourage the continued exploration of this magical screen counterpart.

13 From *Hair* to *Rent*: is 'rock' a four-letter word on Broadway?

SCOTT WARFIELD

Among the etymological legacies of the 1960s is the once ubiquitous family of musical categories distinguished by the word 'rock' somewhere within a compound name. Today one seldom hears such terms as 'jazz rock' or 'symphonic rock', but on Broadway the term 'rock musical' has retained currency, either as a show's formal subtitle or as an appellation casually used by critics and others to describe a particular work. Yet despite widespread use of the term over the past three decades, no scholarly or even semi-formal definition of the 'rock musical' has ever appeared in print. Instead, the 'rock musical' has remained an extremely pliable category, capable of embracing a wide range of characteristics.

Despite the lack of rigour with which the term has been used through the years, a number of common features identify 'rock musicals'. Virtually anyone who has written on the history of the musical has remarked – positively or negatively – on the first appearances of rock-influenced music on Broadway in the mid-1960s.[1] *Hair*, subtitled 'An American Tribal Love-Rock Musical', has been universally accepted as the first example of the genre. Almost immediately after that landmark show, other works appeared with similar subtitles, but there were also shows with rock scores that were never identified as such by their producers. In fact the latter case soon predominated, and consequently, many New York critics began to employ the term 'rock musical' to identify any stage work with even the slightest hint of popular styles.[2] Even twenty-five years after *Hair*, the closest thing to a definition of the 'rock musical' was John Rockwell's brief discussion in his article on 'Rock Opera' in *The New Grove Dictionary of Opera*. For Rockwell, both the 'rock opera' and the 'rock musical' were simply variants of their parent genres 'in which the musical idiom is rock and roll'. Following the lead of New York newspaper critics, however, Rockwell identified two Broadway shows, *Godspell* and *The Wiz*, as 'rock musicals', even though neither was ever promoted as such. Similarly, Stanley Richards's *Great Rock Musicals* lumps together a disparate group of shows – *The Wiz*, *Two Gentlemen of*

Verona, Grease, Jesus Christ Superstar, Your Own Thing, Hair, Tommy and *Promenade* – as the leading examples of this genre.[3]

Despite the casual and often contradictory usages of the term, one can identify a number of New York productions generally associated with the 'rock musical' and from them identify a series of categories and traits that might define this genre. Avoiding temporarily the question of precisely what the music in a rock musical is like – while acknowledging that rock (at any point in its history) differs significantly from Broadway's traditional sound – four distinct categories of shows that use rock music emerge. First are those works – such as *Hair* and *Your Own Thing* – that were identified by their creators and producers as 'rock musicals' either by subtitles or in advertisements. A second category consists of works that began as concept albums – such as *Jesus Christ Superstar* – which were marketed and sold to fans of rock music before they were ever staged. The third and most arbitrary category consists of works – such as *Godspell* – that used rock styles, either in whole or in part, yet were never called 'rock musicals' by their creators. At the same time many shows that some critics label 'rock musicals' have music that is clearly not rock. Fourth are musicals – such as *Grease* – that emulate earlier styles of rock 'n' roll. This category then leads to shows that simply appropriate old songs for their nostalgic value, as in *Smokey Joe's Café*. These four types are not rigid, of course, as some shows straddle categories.

The first musical to include songs in a rock 'n' roll style was *Bye Bye Birdie* (1960). The product of Broadway newcomers Charles Strouse and Lee Adams, it revolved around the televised farewell of Conrad Birdie, a rock 'n' roll star who had been drafted into the army. The character and plot were shamelessly modelled on a conflation of Elvis Presley's own 1958 departure into the military, his staged farewell and his earlier television appearances. Although the show-within-a-show storyline included two tame rock 'n' roll numbers, *Bye Bye Birdie* owed its success to more conventional Broadway elements, including a light-hearted plot and a good variety of tunes in traditional musical comedy styles. The role of Birdie, as created by Dick Gautier in a lamé jumpsuit, was also just a caricature of Elvis, devoid of the physical and vocal sexuality that the model clearly had, and thus, despite its few rock 'n' roll elements, *Bye Bye Birdie* was not really a rock musical.

Even though *Bye Bye Birdie* proved that rock 'n' roll could be used in a musical, it was seven years before rock returned to Broadway. The reason for this gap was doubtless the declining economic conditions for New York theatres. Beginning with a strike in 1960 that raised labour costs significantly, Broadway experienced a series of disastrous seasons that reached its nadir in 1967 with the fewest new shows produced in Broadway's recorded history. In those strained financial times, essentially conservative producers grew even more so and refused to back anything but escapist fare aimed at middle-aged businessmen and theatre parties from the suburbs. Such dated material exacerbated the problem by alienating youthful customers, who felt that Broadway was disconnected from the fundamental changes then being wrought in American society.

Despite Broadway's inherent conservatism, the New York theatre community in the 1960s did include many devoted to revitalising the form and making it more relevant to modern life. One of the most innovative groups was Ellen Stewart's La Mama Experimental Theatre Club, the company that originated *Hair*.[4] Although myth would have it that *Hair* was a fluke creation by neophytes, James Rado and Gerome Ragni were both young veterans of the New York stage, and the classically trained Galt MacDermot was a successful composer of jazz and pop tunes. In 1965, Rado and Ragni found themselves drawn into the anti-war movement, which they studied in the youth culture of New York's Greenwich Village. Over the next two years they used La Mama's workshops to transform their observations into a rough script that was soon making the rounds of New York producers.

Joseph Papp agreed to mount a limited run of the music-less musical to demonstrate the social relevance of his new non-profit Public Theater. MacDermot came aboard to write songs, and in about two weeks he composed the first score of *Hair*. Gerald Freeman, the Public Theater's Artistic Director, reworked the material into a loose story that centred around the drafting of a young man named Claude and his indecision over whether to fight in Vietnam. That character stands in contrast to Berger, a high school dropout who leads a hippy commune. Instead of a logical narrative, *Hair* was more of a rambling diatribe against all authority figures and a glorification of drugs, free love, racial tolerance, respect for the individual and environmentalism. The most passionate moment came in the penultimate scene of Act II, a stylised set piece that railed against the futility of war. The story ends with Claude accepting his call into the military, followed by his death.

When *Hair* was premiered on 2 December 1967 as the Public Theater's inaugural production, it was set for an eight-week run, but Michael Butler, a wealthy liberal with anti-war sentiments, wanted the show seen by a wider audience and thus took over as producer. The Papp production then moved uptown to a discotheque called the Cheetah for 45 additional performances and from there to the Biltmore Theatre, where it opened on 29 April 1968 and ran for 1,742 performances. Before it moved to Broadway, however, important changes were made to accommodate the production to a larger theatre and to sharpen its anti-establishment message. MacDermot composed thirteen new songs and Tom O'Horgan, one of the driving forces in La Mama, came in to direct.

Using the techniques of avant-garde theatre, O'Horgan sought to involve the audience as much as possible in the action by eliminating the

Plate 16   The original production of *Hair* in 1968. Shelley Plimpton is on the mattress and the creators of the show, James Rado and Gerome Ragni, are in the group over her to the rear left. Jonathan Kramer is on all fours and in the foreground on the right is Hiram Keller

proscenium's fourth wall. The stage had no curtain, and cast members were continually moving into and throughout the audience. The band, enlarged from the five-piece rock group used in Papp's production by the addition of four horns, was placed on stage. To be heard above the amplified ensemble, singers used hand-held microphones that they simply passed from one performer to another. To maintain naturalness, cast members were encouraged to improvise, and everyone in the company was expected to be able to cover any role on short notice. To emphasise the lifestyle of the hippies, everyday language, including profanity, was used freely, and the first act ended with a now famous nude scene, which audience members sometimes joined. In short, there was to be no theatrical artificiality in O'Horgan's conception; rather, the show was to be more like a spontaneous 'happening'.

Hair's music was quite unlike anything that had ever appeared on Broadway. While MacDermot's songs were not cutting-edge rock, his arrangements were all in an unmistakable, amplified rock style, with prominent bass lines and strong backbeats. At the same time, nearly every song used the verse–chorus format long favoured on Broadway and eschewed the blues and other simple circular progressions from early rock 'n' roll. MacDermot also used the harmonic language of mid-1960s rock, which stood in stark contrast to the often complex and sophisticated harmonies that had been heard on Broadway for years. Remarkably, at least five songs from *Hair* – 'Aquarius', 'Hair', 'Easy to Be Hard', 'Good Morning Starshine', and 'Let the Sunshine In' – all became US Top Forty hits. Indeed, 'Aquarius' became a virtual anthem for the youth movement in the late 1960s. Yet although MacDermot captured the sound of mid-1960s rock, his music remained within the bounds of what most Broadway audiences would accept, which was a remarkable achievement given the wide gap between Broadway and rock at the time. The majority of *Hair*'s songs are quite tuneful and many have remained pop standards, even if the show itself has aged poorly.[5]

The extraordinary financial success of *Hair*, which had been produced for less than a third of the typical $500,000 cost of a musical in the mid-1960s, spawned the inevitable imitations. Within a season of *Hair*'s premiere, two new rock musicals were playing off-Broadway, and by the early 1970s more than a dozen shows with pop/rock scores had been produced on Broadway. Yet only one explicitly labelled 'rock musical' lasted a full season, while a few other shows with rock-tinged scores succeeded in varying degrees.

Your Own Thing, like *Hair*, was premiered off-Broadway and remained there for its entire 933-performance run. Its plot, loosely adapted from *Twelfth Night*, concerned a marooned rock band in search of a gig, and the confusion between Shakespeare's twins was reflected in gender-crossing hairstyles and clothing. Both the cast's psychedelic costumes and the dialogue's youthful slang date the production almost to the year. The show's title, in fact, was a catch phrase of the day for an individual's right to be free from the crush of society's ways. Again as in *Hair*, an on-stage rock band provided the music. Unlike *Hair*'s score, however, the music of *Your Own Thing* – in the unmistakable electric style of late-1960s rock – was utterly lacking in individuality, and when this second rock musical closed, it vanished without a trace. *Your Own Thing* reflected its era's preoccupation with the under-thirty generation, yet with its emphasis on young love – as opposed to the serious issues confronted in *Hair* – the show was closer to the old-fashioned boy–girl musicals of the 1930s and 1940s. Finally, *Your Own Thing* cost a mere $45,000 to produce. When the New York Critics' Circle named it Best Show of 1968, producers surely noticed the substantial returns possible from the minimal investments that a rock musical required.[6]

In the five seasons after *Hair*, several other shows with rock music (or marketed as such) were premiered on or off Broadway, with those labelled explicitly as 'rock musicals' enjoying the least success. *Salvation*, New York's third rock musical, began downtown in the spring of 1969 as a loosely structured rock concert with dialogue that parodied a revival meeting. When it moved uptown that autumn, critics hailed it as the 'son of *Hair*' and Broadway's 'second rock musical' (*Your Own Thing* had meanwhile remained off-Broadway).[7] *Salvation*'s relative success enabled its co-creators, Peter Link and C. C. Courtney, to create a fully-fledged musical two seasons later. *Earl of Ruston* – billed as a 'country rock musical' – told the story of their uncle Earl, the town 'crazy' of Ruston, Louisiana. Critics faulted the story for its lack of development, and the music – played by the obligatory on-stage rock band – was considered a 'disappointment' after *Salvation*. *Earl of Ruston* folded after less than a week in May 1971.[8] The next two rock musicals suffered similar fates. *Soon*, the story of a rock musician who sells out for commercial gain, lasted just three performances in January 1971, and *Hard Job Being God*, attempting to trade on *Godspell*'s success, closed after only six shows in May 1972. Both were panned for poor music and weak books.[9]

After *Hair*, Galt MacDermot wrote three more scores for Broadway. In 1971, Joseph Papp mounted *Two Gentlemen of Verona*, another update of Shakespeare, although less explicitly contemporary than *Your Own Thing*. Critics raved about the production, but only a few singled out MacDermot's music, which Clive Barnes described as a mix of 'rock, lyricism [and] Caribbean patter' and 'more subtly shaded and more variegated than his score for *Hair*'.[10] MacDermot's two attempts in the following season, *Dude* and *Via Galactica*, both suffered from expensive, troubled productions. The score for *Dude* was praised, but the music for *Via Galactica* was seen as yet another step downward for MacDermot, who never had another Broadway hit.[11]

Following all of these failures, the designation 'rock musical' fell into disuse just as rock and pop styles began to find a place in New York's theatres. *Oh! Calcutta!*, a long-running revue first produced in 1969 and remembered now only for its gratuitous nudity, had a small on-stage band playing an eclectic mix of contemporary sounds that included rock. *The Last Sweet Days of Isaac* was a 1970 off-Broadway success that had a four-piece band playing 'soft rock'.[12] Two other shows, one a quick failure and the other a major success, demonstrated the growing symbiosis between Broadway and the recording industry. *Georgy* (1970) was an adaptation of the 1966 motion picture *Georgy Girl* and its popular title song. George Fischoff's music for the Broadway show was described as 'mediocre, an easy-listening kind of rock crammed into a show-tune style, orchestrated with disinterest', and *Georgy* closed after only four nights.[13] Burt Bacharach's score for *Promises, Promises* was certainly not rock, but the show's title song did do well on the pop charts. The production's real innovation, however, was in the pit, where every member of the band, including four female backup singers, was miked. A sound engineer controlled the mix, which was sent out to the audience through loudspeakers on either side of the house. Audiences quickly came to expect theatrical performances to match the sound of commercial recordings.[14]

Interestingly, the only successful original rock musical that premiered in New York in the early 1970s was never explicitly promoted as one.[15] When it moved uptown in 1976, *Godspell* was roundly panned for its saccharine book, weak score, amateurish staging and lack of dance movement, but after 2,118 performances off-Broadway, the show was essentially critic-proof.[16] John-Michael Tebelak had first drafted this modernisation of the Gospel of St Matthew for his master's degree, and it was subsequently reworked at La Mama's. There the original music was discarded, and a newcomer, Stephen Schwartz, was brought in to compose a replacement score.

Tebelak had envisaged *Godspell* as something for teenagers, and the show's relentlessly upbeat tone and childlike innocence were perfect for its intended audience. The minimalist set vaguely resembled a bare schoolyard playground; the staging was just a series of sketches in which the small company acted out Biblical parables in imitations of television shows, comic strips and circus acts. The book made frequent references to current events, and the cast – costumed in brightly coloured rags and clown-like facial paint – often impersonated well-known performers of recent years. All of this also appealed to adults who might not have cared for the more realistic and scruffy hippies of *Hair*.

Schwartz's music provided a good match for the production's celebratory mood. Although the band was yet another four-piece rock ensemble, the addition of tambourines and acoustic instruments often gave the music the feel of folk-rock and even gospel. The repetitive lyrics, mirrored in the simple forms of the songs, helped to create the atmosphere of a revival meeting or a church service. 'Prepare Ye (The Way of the Lord)', for instance, is nothing but a repeated single phrase, while 'Day by Day' consists of only a few motivic fragments arranged into a standard song form. Many songs also begin slowly with quiet accompaniments, but quickly transform themselves into energetic gospel numbers through increases in tempo, the addition of drums and amplified instruments, and the use of improvisatory call-and-response patterns. The first act finale, 'Light of the World', dispenses with the sedate opening, and instead launches itself immediately into the sound of black soul music that builds continuously until the curtain. In contrast, the strong country beat of 'We Beseech Thee' evokes the feeling of a white revival meeting, while various other easy-listening styles and even a soft-shoe number, 'All for the Best', are also part of the show. Despite this stylistic eclecticism, the score holds together well in the youthful celebration of spirituality that permeates *Godspell*.

Only a few months after *Godspell* began its off-Broadway run, a second youth-oriented rock musical with a religious theme opened in New York and thereby highlighted two emerging theatrical trends. With over two million copies of its double album sold long before its stage production opened, *Jesus Christ Superstar* (music by Andrew Lloyd Webber, lyrics by Tim Rice) abandoned the usual Broadway marketing model, in which ticket sales were the primary source of revenue and recordings only souvenirs, and instead followed the practice of pop music, in which live performances promoted recordings. *Jesus Christ Superstar* also reflected the rise of progressive rock in the late 1960s. With a sonic palette that admitted any sound source up to a symphony orchestra and an expanded harmonic vocabulary that ranged from nineteenth-century Romanticism to Stravinsky, progressive rock was able to sustain interest for the album-length works that this new style promoted. The same applied to a Broadway show.[17]

The New York production was a note-for-note rendition of the album and included all the elements of progressive rock. The heart of the show's sound is a six-piece rock ensemble, frequently augmented by a small orchestra on the recording or by synthesisers and a few horns in the theatre. The musical style, although strongly influenced by rock, already reflects Andrew Lloyd Webber's trademark eclecticism. The overture is a microcosm of his technique. Beginning with a solo electric guitar, it proceeds like any Broadway overture through a series of excerpts from the show. There are frequent shifts from rock timbres to synthesised sounds, mixtures of rock and traditional instruments, and ultimately a symphonic finale. In the show itself, a hard rock tune like 'Judas' Death' follows the campy 'King Herod's Song', which is in the style of a vaudeville number, and a soft rock tune like 'Everything's Alright' leads into a scene that includes recitative mixed with rock. One innovative element for Broadway is the frequent use of irregular metres, such as 5/4 in 'Everything's Alright' or 7/8 in 'The Temple'. In setting every bit of text to music, Lloyd Webber also went far beyond the alternation of spoken and sung passages typical of most Broadway shows, and for its use of recitative *Jesus Christ Superstar* stands closer to a rock *opera*, as the recording was billed.

The early 1970s was a high-water mark for the rock musical. The successful runs of *Godspell* and *Jesus Christ Superstar* proved that *Hair* was no fluke and thus solidified rock's position on Broadway. Beginning in the 1970s, an ever-increasing number of shows had rock-influenced scores, yet very few of them – and no commercially successful shows for nearly two decades – were ever promoted as 'rock musicals'. Simultaneously, the use of the term 'rock musical' by critics declined but never quite disappeared. Usually the term was applied to a show with a small ensemble and, presumably, music that approximated a rock or pop sound. For instance, *The Lieutenant*, a now obscure work from 1974–75 that dealt with the Vietnam War's My Lai massacre and closed after only nine performances despite much critical acclaim, was always described as either a 'rock opera' or a 'rock musical' in theatre listings, reviews and its own advertisements. Nothing was ever mentioned about the sound of its music, however.[18]

From the 1970s onwards usage of the term 'rock musical' by critics became quite inconsistent. In 1975, *The Wiz* arrived on Broadway with a score that pulsed with the sounds of soul, gospel and other Black pop and rock styles, and it was followed six years later by another musical built on the Motown sound, *Dreamgirls*. Neither was ever widely identified as a 'rock musical', although a few reviews of *The Wiz* did describe its score as rock or rock-related.[19] Reviews of *Dreamgirls*, however, said almost nothing about its music, as critics chose instead to focus on the show's lavish costumes, big dance numbers and high-tech stagecraft.

Between those two productions were two 1978 shows that some critics and music theatre historians consider rock musicals, even if others hesitate to use that label. The occasional identification of *I'm Getting My Act Together and Taking It On the Road* as a rock musical may simply stem from its plot, which concerns a female singer preparing to tour with a rock band, and the fact that its soft-rock and pop score was played by a small ensemble. The other show, *Runaways*, was a story of adolescents forced to fend for themselves on the streets, and at least one reviewer compared it favourably with *Hair*, without calling it a rock musical. Its music included everything from disco and salsa to blues and country-and-western, and was performed by a six-piece ensemble that was based around a piano–guitar–drum trio.[20] Both shows, moreover, had originally been developed as limited-run off-Broadway productions by Joseph Papp.

Clearly more than just the sound of a show identified it as a rock musical. Small guitar-and-drum ensembles playing contemporary musical styles was a significant trait, and several failed rock musicals had nothing in common with *Hair* and *Jesus Christ Superstar* except for their small bands playing amplified music. At least part of a rock musical's identity seemed to derive from rock's status as an 'outsider' genre. Plots that dealt with issues important to young people in the 1970s – the Vietnam War (*Hair* and *The Lieutenant*), spiritual values (*Jesus Christ Superstar* and *Godspell*), self-identity (*The Last Sweet Days of Isaac* and *I'm Getting My Act Together*) and the problems of growing up (*Runaways*) – also marked a show as something beyond the usual Broadway fare. Such topics did not usually attract financing from established Broadway producers, and thus many rock musicals were born and nurtured in places like La Mama's and Papp's Public Theater. In contrast, *The Wiz* and *Dreamgirls* were both traditional, big-budget Broadway shows in slick productions.

The basic problem for rock musical composers was an old one, which Walter Kerr, the *New York Times*'s senior critic, summed up in a review of *Dude*:

Rock musicals, if they are to sustain themselves as genuine theatre pieces rather than arena concerts, are going to have to meet the obligations earlier musicals have accepted, always with difficulty, often with pain. Music *is* the ultimate making of any musical. But the music must have something to stand on, something other than its own beat to move it, something to demand one particular song rather than another at a particular moment, [and] hopefully something in the way of wit to keep it company.[21]

Thus, although a few shows may have succeeded on the novelty of contemporary sounds, the key to a winning production remained the integration of rock music with the book and the staging. Reviews of failed rock musicals in the 1970s suggest that there was often no compelling reason for the use of rock in a particular show and, moreover, that the music itself was frequently not very good. Admittedly, those productions usually also had serious problems with their books, staging and other elements, but it is almost impossible to find a failed rock musical in which critics praised the music and condemned the rest of the show.[22] In short, the fate of a rock musical hung chiefly on its music, which had to be both good – or at least inoffensive – and relevant in some way to the action on stage. Some Broadway producers, however, seemed to treat rock music as just another element that could be grafted onto a big-budget musical, and the results were sometimes spectacular failures.

Chess, a failure on Broadway in 1988, is a good example of a production that appropriated rock as its musical idiom for no urgent reason. Its plot concerns a championship chess match between an American and a Russian during the Cold War. The work, with lyrics by Tim Rice and music by Benny Andersson and Björn Ulvaeus (the male half of the Swedish pop vocal group Abba), was initially issued in 1984 as a concept album and then performed throughout Europe in a concert version that generated two hits on European pop charts. Two years later, a London production began a three-year run, but in New York, *Chess* was a $6.6 million disappointment.

Although the score included a variety of musical styles, rock numbers in Abba's trademark style – primarily power ballads and up-tempo songs with a strong dance beat – predominated. With no gradations in energy levels, the result, according to Frank Rich, was that 'for three hours, the characters on stage yell at one another to rock music'.[23] For instance, when the American, Freddie Trumper, first meets the reporters ('Press Conference') near the beginning of Act I, the accompaniment is a strong rock beat, synthesisers and snarling guitars, and his vocal line ascends regularly to its upper limits.[24] The purpose of this scene is merely to introduce Trumper and reveal his arrogance, but such an intense vocal display so early in the show leaves no room for later climaxes. Despite this sort of dramatic miscalculation, *Chess* contains some of the best pop/rock music ever used on the stage. 'One Night in Bangkok' – the curtain-raiser for Act II in London, and a production number in Act I on Broadway – is a first-rate disco tune, and 'I Know Him So Well' – the show's first European hit song – is a fine rock ballad.

Such keen interest on Broadway in older, familiar rock and pop styles can be traced back to at least 1972, when *Grease*, 'a new '50's rock 'n' roll musical', premiered. The story, set in 1959, was a nostalgic look back at 'greasers' and their girls, built around a simple teenage love story. After the turbulent 1960s, *Grease* was a gentle parody of almost idyllic times, with a series of faux fifties tunes that poked fun at the teenage angst of that era. The show's success, despite mediocre reviews, was extraordinary, and *Grease* played out the decade on Broadway. Once it was apparent that imitations of old rock 'n' roll could succeed on Broadway, the genuine article came into the theatre in Tom O'Horgan's 1974 off-Broadway staging of the Beatles' album as *Sgt Pepper's Lonely Hearts Club Band on the Road*, followed by *Beatlemania* (1977), a curious mixture of concert and theatre that ran for two years on Broadway. In 1982, Dick Clark tried to mount a broader retrospective, but *Rock and Roll! The First 5,000 Years* closed in only a week. In 1989, *Buddy: The Buddy Holly Story* opened in London and a year later came to Broadway. Marketed as a 'bio-musical' and using Holly's music, the first half of the show traced his rise, while the second act recreated his final concert. Another big success in the 1990s, *Smokey Joe's Café*, was an expensively produced revue of songs by Leiber and Stoller, perhaps the most famous rock 'n' roll songwriting team of the 1950s and 60s.

By the 1990s, rock – or at least a conservative form of it – was in widespread use on Broadway, making the rift between theatrical and popular music narrower than it had been at any time since just before the premiere of *Hair* in 1967.[25] It was again possible to hear songs in a Broadway theatre that were also regularly played on radio and easily available in stores, and major rock musicians were now courted by Broadway. In the mid-1990s, two veteran pop/rock songwriters of the first rank, Randy Newman and Paul Simon, each tried unsuccessfully to compose a Broadway musical. Newman's *Faust*, described as a 'rock 'n' roll travesty of Goethe's poem', died in 1996 after tryouts in San Diego and Chicago, but even before the first production was mounted, a CD was issued, with Newman joined by rock legends James Taylor, Don Henley, Linda Ronstadt and Bonnie Raitt.[26] Although eagerly anticipated on Broadway, Simon's *The Capeman* – described in one review as a 'pop-operatic retelling of a street gang murder in 1959' – struggled through its previews only to be savaged by the critics on opening night.[27] The *New York Times* called the show 'one solemn, hopelessly confused drone' and went on to comment on its twin problems of integrating pop sounds into a theatrical work and the frequent lack of stage movement. As with *Faust*, a CD, made by Simon and top session musicians, was issued before the stage premiere. Purely as a recording, *The Capeman* stands with Simon's best work, but his laid-back mix of 1950s doo-wop and Latin rhythms lacks even the occasional energetic number that might have suggested some striking stage movements.

In addition to those two well-financed failures, Broadway in the 1990s saw the frequent return of older pop and rock materials. In the autumn of 1999, a stage version of the 1977 motion picture *Saturday Night Fever* was premiered with music just slightly revised from the Bee Gees' film score. The following year, another relic from the 1970s, *The Rocky Horror Show*, which had played briefly and unsuccessfully on Broadway in 1975, returned to New York on the strength of its classic cult film version of nearly the same name. Yet another musical that found new life in revival is Willy Russell's *Blood Brothers*. When it first opened in London in 1983, it ran for only eight months, but successful regional productions eventually led to a 1988 London revival that is booked through the year 2002. A New York production opened to poor reviews in 1993, but lasted for 839 performances on the strength of its word-of-mouth.[28] *Blood Brothers* has been a quiet phenomenon with younger listeners, especially teenagers, who apparently identify with the story of twins separated at birth whose reunion years later has tragic consequences. The youthful vogue for this piece has doubtless been helped by recordings that feature such pop stars as Kiki Dee, David and Shaun Cassidy, and even the 1960s pop icon Petula Clark, despite critical opinion that Russell's music is simplistic and derivative.

Finally, the continuing popularity of Abba's music has led to one of the most unusual musicals in Broadway's history. The book of *Mamma Mia!* – a newly invented story about a young girl's impending marriage – was written specifically to showcase twenty-seven Abba hits from the 1970s and 80s. Less than a year after its 1999 London premiere, two productions were touring North America, one of which opened at the Winter Garden theatre (former home of *Cats*) in New York. The London production recouped its costs in less than seven months, and sell-out houses on the road, strong album sales and an advertising campaign that includes a state-of-the-art website suggest that the Broadway run will be long and lucrative.[29]

While it is doubtful that any of these shows – from *Grease* to *Mamma Mia!* – truly deserves the designation of 'rock musical', all of them have been described somewhere as such. This linguistic imprecision, moreover, confirms the desire of producers to exploit the popularity of rock, while simultaneously suppressing its rebellious spirit and most extreme sounds. Instead of the real thing, Broadway has offered up a diluted pop sound and even an air of nostalgia that appeals to typically older theatregoers but still draws some younger customers into theatres. In an environment where some form of watered-down pop-rock has become the *lingua franca* of Broadway, one might ask if a genuine rock musical in the spirit of *Hair* is still a possibility. The answer would seem to be a qualified 'yes', if one is willing to look beyond the major theatres just north of Times Square.[30] Off-Broadway, experimental theatres and even regional companies remain vital forces for reinventing the musical, and in the late 1990s, three new works from those non-traditional milieus played in New York to excellent reviews.

Jonathan Larson's *Rent* – winner of the 1996 Pulitzer Prize for Drama, that year's Tony Award and numerous other accolades – has been compared to *Hair* for its similarly stunning impact on a sclerotic theatrical world.[31] *Rent*'s genesis, likewise, mirrors the struggles of many early rock musicals, with a beginning in an off-Broadway theatre workshop and marginal financing. Larson's death at the age of thirty-five, due to an undiagnosed aortic aneurysm, on the eve of *Rent*'s first preview, moreover, gave the opening an air of almost gothic tragedy and generated an extraordinary amount of publicity for the show.[32] In fact, Larson's career had been on a slow but steadily upward trajectory well before *Rent*. Two awards in 1988–89 brought him to the notice of Stephen Sondheim, who then became a mentor, and a $45,000 Richard Rodgers Development Grant in 1994 paid for the first workshop performances of *Rent*.

In retelling Puccini's *La bohème*, Larson transplanted the story of four struggling young artists to his own New York neighbourhood, the East Village, where Rado and Ragni had also found their inspiration for *Hair*. Larson based his songs and scenes on people he knew, but sentimentalised nothing. Nearly all of the principal characters are HIV positive, several are current or former drug users, and a number are also gay. Mimi, Puccini's meek, tubercular seamstress, is transformed into a dancer at a sadomasochism club, and everywhere are homeless people and other dregs of society. All of these characters are unflinchingly real, a point underscored by their ordinary clothing and an industrial grey set.[33] Despite the potential for offending an audience who had to deal regularly with these sorts of people on the streets of New York, Larson made his characters sympathetic and even attractive by focusing on how they lived with their diseases and problems, rather than on their dying. To underline that point, Mimi does not die at the end of *Rent*, as she does in *La bohème*.

The vitality of *Rent*'s characters is emphasised by the pervasive rock feel of the entire score. During pre-production, Larson insisted that a rock beat was essential for his songs, but that the words must always remain audible. Consequently, the engineer/arranger, Steve Skinner, worked hard to balance the competing needs of the singers and the five-member band.[34] The show's rock sound begins with the electric bass and drum set, which is the driving force in up-tempo tunes like 'Rent' and 'Out Tonight', and even songs with more moderate tempos, such as 'I'll Cover You', project a solid rock feel because of the strong support of bass and drums. Prominent acoustic guitars give the ballads – 'Life Support', 'Without You', 'Your Eyes' and 'Will I?' – a soft rock feel, while the influence of gospel is evident in the celebratory tones of 'La Vie Boheme' and 'Seasons of Love'. Many bits of dialogue that might have been spoken are also accompanied by rock vamps. Remarkably, virtually all of the show's songs contribute to plot or character development with a realistic text that includes justifiable use of common vulgarities. Nevertheless, Larson's word play is often theatrically quite clever, as in the lists of 'La Vie Boheme', which obviously owe something to Sondheim's example. Larson's artistic achievement, which never resorts to artificial devices, is especially impressive when viewed against the backdrop of vacuous, big-budget entertainments dominating Broadway at the end of the century, and his use of rock music to portray these gritty characters is exactly right. It is impossible to imagine how a more conventional Broadway score could tell this story as well.

The two remaining shows could not be more different from *Rent* and also from one another, yet each exhibits a level of honesty about its subject matter seldom found on Broadway. Despite such frankness, *Hedwig and the Angry Inch* – the invented story of an East German transsexual who was the victim of a botched sex-change operation – played to audiences for two years after being premiered off-Broadway in 1998. The show was more a glam-rock concert than a traditional theatrical staging, and its hard rock music went far beyond the bounds of any previous rock musical, with several numbers that exhibit a punk sensibility. In contrast to the bizarre, adults-only world of *Hedwig*, *Inappropriate* dealt with the problems of teenagers in an equally direct and sometimes raw fashion. This show originated at the DeSisto School, a private boarding academy for troubled adolescents in Stockbridge, Massachusetts. Over the years their theatre programme fashioned scenes out of students' journals, which Michael DeSisto then set in musical styles ranging from rock to rap. The resulting show was performed by students from the school in a brief two-week run off-Broadway in 1999, and its success was such that a longer second run was mounted the following year. Although critics noted the production's unevenness, they also praised its honesty and noted how its expression of youthful anger, hurt and exuberance echoed the same elements in *Rent* and *Hair*.[35]

By the time the first wave of baby-boomers began approaching retirement at the end of the twentieth century, rock music had become the soundtrack of America. From television commercials selling automobiles to radio stations that programmed by the desired decade, rock was everywhere, including Broadway. While some ageing Americans might still think of rock as the music of youthful rebellion, by the late 1980s rock was a safe and respectable commodity. In its place, the hip-hop culture of black urban youths – chiefly in the form of 'gangsta rap' – had become the new sound of the disenfranchised. Similarly on Broadway, by the late 1980s middle-of-the-road rock was an unexceptional sound. No 'rap musical', however, has ever appeared in order to call attention to rock's new insider status, and thus the term 'rock musical' retains at least a tenuous connection with the rebellious traditions of early rock musicals. Still, it is almost impossible to think of a mega-hit from the 1980s like *Les Misérables* – described by some critics as 'the musical cum rock opera' and a 'pop opera' – as the same type of show as *Hair*.[36]

Nevertheless, at the beginning of the third millennium, there has been a modest renaissance of 'rock musicals' in the tradition of *Hair*. *Rent*, *Hedwig and the Angry Inch* and *Inappropriate* all present honest, youthful attitudes similar to those that fuelled the first rock musicals over thirty years ago, and while *Rent* quickly moved uptown, it was again off-Broadway that gave birth to these three shows. Beneath their vastly differing aural surfaces they speak for and to a generation that has not previously been heard on (or off) Broadway. Significantly, the generation that looks to *Rent* as its anthem are the children of the generation that embraced *Hair*. While it is too soon to say if the recent upsurge of the rock musical can or will be sustained, the odds nevertheless seem pretty good that the grandchildren of the *Hair* generation will surprise their parents with a musical of their own somewhere off-Broadway in about twenty-five years.

14 The megamusical and beyond: the creation, internationalisation and impact of a genre

PAUL PRECE AND WILLIAM A. EVERETT

Nowhere in the realm of the musical theatre is technology more evident than in the world of the megamusical. These 'larger than life' visual and aural spectacles dazzle audiences and are among the most popular musical theatre works at the beginning of the twenty-first century. *Les Misérables*, billed as 'the world's most popular musical' and *Cats*, heralded as 'now and forever', are but two shows where commercial slogans enlist, endorse and promote their mass appeal.

But what exactly are megamusicals? Terms such as 'through-composed popular operas' and 'poperas' have also been used to describe the phenomenon of sung-through musicals where set design, choreography and special effects are at least as important as the music. They are overtly romantic and sentimental in nature, meant to create strong emotional reactions from the audience. Stories merge aspects of human suffering and redemption with matters of social consciousness.

The concept of the megamusical constitutes a reinvigoration of nineteenth-century French grand opera. Whereas audiences in the late twentieth century were dazzled by stage effects such as the chandelier and underground lake in *The Phantom of the Opera*, the staircase in *Sunset Boulevard*, the barricade in *Les Misérables* and the helicopter in *Miss Saigon*, their nineteenth-century French counterparts saw the eruption of Vesuvius in Daniel-François-Esprit Auber's *La muette de Portici* (1828) and the St Bartholomew's Day Massacre in Giacomo Meyerbeer's *Les Huguenots* (1836).

If one central figure had to be identified as the driving creative force behind this late twentieth-century genre, it would almost certainly be the producer Cameron Mackintosh (b. 1946). His collaboration with Andrew Lloyd Webber on *Cats* in 1981 transformed the style of musical theatre. His success at creating musical theatrical experiences can be seen in many of the shows that virtually define the megamusical, including *Les Misérables*, *The Phantom of the Opera* and *Miss Saigon*. His revivals of such classics as *Oliver!*, *My Fair Lady* and *Carousel* won critical praise, and the 1997 Royal

Gala Performance, released on video as *Hey Mr Producer! The Musical World of Cameron Mackintosh*, was an all-star tribute to the producer. The video is self-described as 'a magical night of theatre that could only take place in your dreams... until now'. The pure theatricality of Mackintosh's vision – taking the aural and visual components and creating something greater than the mere sum of its parts and then marketing it with remarkable efficiency – defines so much of what makes the megamusical a critical part of today's musical theatre.

While it is Mackintosh's vision that defines the genre theatrically, parallels must be drawn between the Scottish producer and one of his nineteenth-century predecessors in Paris, Louis Véron, director of the Paris Opera and a major force in nineteenth-century French Grand Opera. By definition, works in this genre related some sort of socio-political message through a grandiose medium that combined music, drama, dance, lavish costume and set designs, and special effects. It comes as no surprise that the creators of *Les Misérables*, Claude-Michel Schoenberg and Alain Boublil, are French and that the original concept for 'the world's most popular musical' was in the French language. Frequently, French Grand Operas were set against war backgrounds; likewise, all four Schoenberg–Boublil musicals, *La Révolution française* (1973, Paris), *Les Misérables* (1980, Paris; 1985, London; 1987, New York), *Miss Saigon* (1989, London; 1991, New York) and *Martin Guerre* (1996, London; revised 1998, London; revised 1999, West Yorkshire Playhouse) have war settings. Sharing the desire for bringing about some sort of social change with their nineteenth-century predecessors, Schoenberg and Boublil include some sort of edifying message in their shows, whether it be the power of forgiveness in *Les Misérables*, the hideous personal consequences of war in *Miss Saigon* or the repercussions of deception in *Martin Guerre*.

Schoenberg–Boublil musicals have their musical basis in folk-like melodies that are given a lavish treatment, largely through orchestration. This Gallic concept permeates their three English-language shows. Pentatonicism is especially prominent, creating a sense of populist fervour in *Les Misérables*, orientalism (Vietnam) in *Miss Saigon* and medieval French folk music in *Martin Guerre*.

Mass choral numbers, generally accompanied by inventive choreography suggesting a specific time and place, are central to the musical and dramatic structure of each show. Social injustice in the nineteenth century dominates 'At the End of the Day', 'Do You Hear the People Sing?', 'One Day More' and similar numbers in *Les Misérables*, while in *Miss Saigon*, 'The Heat Is On in Saigon' depicts Americans in Vietnam and 'The American Dream' incarnates the plight of Vietnamese wanting to emigrate to America. 'Working on the Land' celebrates the sense of community in *Martin Guerre* and 'Welcome

Plate 17   The original London cast of *Les Misérables*, Palace Theatre, 1985

Home' acclaims the supposed return of Martin Guerre to his native village. The driving rhythms throughout the last score accentuate both the folk element and the drama of the libretto.

Because of the Gallic musical theatre tradition of audience edification, each of the shows also contains at least one song of social injustice. 'Do You Hear the People Sing?' and 'One Day More' in *Les Misérables* offer a hope for a future free from oppression of any sort. In *Miss Saigon*, the anthem 'Bui Doi', accompanied by emotional photographic images, educates the audience on the plight of children fathered by American soldiers in Vietnam. *Martin Guerre*'s 'The Impostors' is an anthem of self-reflection, the characters begging themselves and the audience to look inward and see if they are truly as forthright as they themselves claim to be.

In *Les Misérables*, Victor Hugo's immense novel receives a three-and-a-half-hour musical treatment, long for a musical, but brief considering the vast amount of source material. The human condition, the focus of the novel, is also that of the musical. Jean Valjean represents the inherent good in every person while Javert symbolises its antithesis. A single act of mercy on the part of a bishop causes Valjean to radically alter his ways, and the sacrificial deaths of Fantine, Cosette and the students for the cause of justice, personal or social, are among the most poignant moments in the show.

Recurring melodies enhance developments in the dramatic plot. Valjean and Javert share much of the same music, thus demonstrating that they represent two sides of the same human condition. For example Valjean's

'Who am I?' is reprised in 'Javert's Suicide'. The finale includes reprises of several musical numbers, some with new texts, and ends with a 'finale ultimo' rendition of the show's central anthem, 'Do You Hear the People Sing?'

Les Misérables epitomises the pan-national production of megamusicals. The show began life as an 'arena version' at the Palais des Sports in Paris on 18 September 1980. Cameron Mackintosh heard the recording of the production and subsequently took on the task of overseeing the show's metamorphosis. The English-language result, a collaboration between Mackintosh and the Royal Shakespeare Company and first performed at the Barbican Theatre in London on 8 October 1985, was an immense success. It transferred to the Palace Theatre in the West End on 4 December 1985, and since that time has continued to draw packed houses. The New York production opened on 12 March 1987. Colm Wilkinson dazzled audiences as Jean Valjean in both London and New York, as did Frances Ruffelle as Eponine. Patti LuPone, Alun Armstrong and Michael Ball were featured in the London production, while Terrence Mann, Judy Kuhn and David Bryant appeared in New York.

Translations into many languages quickly followed. Within two years of the show's London success came performances in Hungary and Iceland in the vernacular languages of those countries. Subsequent productions opened in Norway, Austria, Poland, Sweden, the Netherlands, France, Germany, the Czech Republic, Spain, Israel, Japan, Denmark and Finland, each in the vernacular. Furthermore, recordings of the show have appeared in English, Hungarian, German, Swedish, Dutch, French, Czech, Danish, Hebrew, Japanese and Spanish. The historic tenth-anniversary concert that took place in the Royal Albert Hall on 8 October 1995 included a surprise grand encore that proved the international appeal of the musical. Seventeen actors who had played Jean Valjean in various national productions processed into the hall to sing the anthem 'Do You Hear the People Sing?', each in his native tongue. Central issues associated with the megamusical – theatricality, social responsibility and international popularity – were evident in this celebratory encore.

The international popularity of the megamusical and its specific association with France was further manifested at the opening ceremonies for the Olympic Games in Sydney on 15 September 2000. When the French team entered the stadium, it was to the strains of 'Do You Hear the People Sing?' This musical choice was telling on many levels, for it simultaneously endorsed the worldwide reputation of the song, its universal audience appeal and its inherent Frenchness.

Following the success of *Les Misérables* came *Miss Saigon* and *Martin Guerre*. *Miss Saigon*, set in the final years of the Vietnam War, shares its plot with Puccini's opera *Madame Butterfly*. Lea Salonga and Jonathan

Pryce astounded audiences and critics in both London and New York. *Martin Guerre*, yet to play in New York at the time of writing (2002) is set in sixteenth-century France against the backdrop of Protestant–Catholic religious conflicts. Its fundamentally folk-based musical style also includes sentimental ballads and dazzling dance numbers. The show has experienced numerous revisions during its existence; a 1999 cast recording made in conjunction with the West Yorkshire Playhouse documents the show's continuing evolution.

While Schoenberg–Boublil musicals address broad social issues, those of Lord Andrew Lloyd Webber (b. 1948) focus on personal healing or catharsis. But there is much more to Lloyd Webber's approach to the musical theatre than this one central theme – commercialisation, pop icons and pure theatricality also loom large in his work.

When *The Beautiful Game* (2000, London), Lloyd Webber's twelfth work, opened in September 2000, it joined its West End sisters *Cats* (1981, London; 1982, New York), *Starlight Express* (1984, London; 1987, New York), *The Phantom of the Opera* (1986, London; 1988, New York) and *Whistle Down the Wind* (1998, London). Five Lloyd Webber musicals were thus playing simultaneously in London. The popularity and longevity of Lloyd Webber's canon is staggering.

The numbers speak for themselves as far as the success of Lloyd Webber's shows is concerned. The original production of *Cats* has the distinction of being the longest-running musical both in the West End and on Broadway. The New York production, which opened on 7 October 1982 and closed on 10 September 2000, played for 7,485 performances and was seen by over ten million people. When the announcement was made in 2002 that the London production was going to close, it resulted in increased ticket sales and additional performances beyond the announced closing date. In December 1999, it was reported that *Phantom* alone had taken in more money than any other production on stage and screen (£1.88 billion/ approximately $2.8 billion), surpassing huge money-making films such as *Star Wars* and *Titanic*. Twenty-seven productions of Lloyd Webber's work were playing around the world in July 2000.[1]

Films and video versions provide another venue for dissemination, including the theatrical films of *Jesus Christ Superstar* (1973) and *Evita* (1996) and the home video versions of *Cats* (1998), *Joseph and the Amazing Technicolor Dreamcoat* (1999) and *Jesus Christ Superstar* (2000). A film version of *The Phantom of the Opera* is in production at the time of writing (2002). Andrew Lloyd Webber – composer, businessman and visionary – is doing something right.

Norma Desmond, the Phantom, Jesus, Joseph, Evita, Grizabella and the dancing chorus of *Cats*, and Rusty and the skating Starlight trains are all

Lloyd Webber prototypes that have been elevated to pop icon status, placing them firmly in the twentieth-century lexicon of musical theatre characters. As postmodern hero-protagonists they all search for immortality, deliverance and redemption from some real, imagined or self-imposed darkness. They are true 'superstars', to use the Warholian term, created and lifted to this status by Lloyd Webber's 'music of the night' and 'technicolor' imagination. His musical vision is as theatrical as it is operatic and his imaginative approach is rejuvenating and resuscitating, if not revisionist. Credited with having composed some 350 songs, Lloyd Webber, in the words of his biographer Michael Walsh, is 'a musical pack rat, salting away useful tunes in the knowledge that someday they will come in handy'.[2] He is as acutely aware of the visual possibilities of representation and the utility and potential of stage technology. Furthermore, he is cognisant of the 'really useful' need for select collaboration with creative lyricists, designers and stage directors.

Founded by Lloyd Webber in 1977, The Really Useful Group Ltd is the organisation that administers the rights to all of the composer's works from *Cats* onward. The Group has offices in London, New York, Los Angeles, Hong Kong, Singapore, Sydney, Basel and Frankfurt. In addition to involvement in management, production, recording and music publishing, the Group also owns several London theatres, including the Palace Theatre (home to *Jesus Christ Superstar* and, since 1985, to *Les Misérables*), the New London Theatre (home to *Cats*), the Adelphi Theatre (where *Sunset Boulevard* played), the Palladium, the Cambridge (home to *The Beautiful Game*), the Theatre Royal Drury Lane (where *Miss Saigon* enjoyed its tremendous run) and the Apollo Victoria (home to *Starlight Express*). The Group also controls The Really Useful Store, where Really Useful Merchandise is sold. The branded products carrying logos of Lloyd Webber shows comprise everything from T-shirts to thermo-reactive mugs. Production, promotion and product manufacturing and marketing are therefore all under the auspices of the same umbrella organisation.

Lloyd Webber, a baby boomer, began composing at the age of seventeen. From an early age he had an interest in music, stagecraft and architecture and was fascinated by the musical stage and its treasures. As befits a true child of the fifties, the evident influence of Elvis, rock 'n' roll and the Beatles intermingle with his knowledge of Prokofiev, Puccini and the classical repertory instilled largely by his father, William S. Lloyd Webber, a church organist and professor of composition at the Royal College of Music and eventually director of the London College of Music. But it was with the American musical theatre and its composers that his infatuation grew. He cites Richard Rodgers as a primary influence and reveals candidly, 'Musical theatre is the only thing that's ever made me tick.'[3]

From his early 'through-written' or 'through-composed' techno-music spectacles to his later more traditional adaptations, Lloyd Webber establishes dramatic and musical primacy and admits, 'I'm quite incapable of writing the words, but I lay out what I believe the libretto ought to be. That is one of my strongest assets.'[4] His self-confessed first rule is 'It's not the subject, it's the treatment.'[5] His librettos are cinematic, fantastic, dreamlike, sweeping, lush and conceptually rich in possibility. Whether developed from a film (*Sunset Boulevard*), a work of fiction (*The Phantom of the Opera, Aspects of Love, Whistle Down the Wind*), a collection of poems (*Cats*), a Biblical or historical figure (*Jesus Christ Superstar, Joseph, Evita*) or simply an imaginative idea (*Starlight Express*), Lloyd Webber's (re)sources are magnified musically and theatrically.

As mentioned above, it is the search for some sort of redemption that connects all of Lloyd Webber's lead characters. Perhaps this is the influence of his father's involvement with Anglican church music and theology. Lloyd Webber's shows fall into three categories based upon subject matter: (1) immortality musicals; (2) competition musicals; and (3) intimate musicals. (See Table 14.1.) The immortality musicals fall into two categories, those based on Biblical or historical figures and those focusing on singular personalities who are in search of immortality. In the Biblical musicals, *Joseph and the Amazing Technicolor Dreamcoat* and *Jesus Christ Superstar*, the title characters are imprisoned or destroyed by a group (Joseph's brothers in *Joseph*; Judas, Pontius Pilate and soldiers in *Superstar*). At the same time, a

Table 14.1 *Categories of musicals by Lord Andrew Lloyd Webber*

I Immortality musicals

A RELIGIOUS/HISTORICAL
Joseph and the Amazing Technicolor Dreamcoat (1968–72, book and lyrics by Tim Rice)
Jesus Christ Superstar (1971, lyrics by Tim Rice)
Evita (1978, lyrics and book by Tim Rice)

B PERSONALITY
The Phantom of the Opera (1986, lyrics by Charles Hart, book by Richard Stilgoe, based on the novel by
   Gaston Leroux)
Sunset Boulevard (1993, lyrics and book by Don Black and Christopher Hampton, based on the Billy
   Wilder film)

II Competition musicals

Cats (1981, lyrics by T. S. Eliot, book based on Eliot's *Old Possum's Book of Practical Cats*)
Starlight Express (1984, lyrics by Richard Stilgoe, story by Andrew Lloyd Webber)

III Intimate musicals

Song and Dance (1982, lyrics by Don Black and Richard Maltby Jr)
Aspects of Love (1989, lyrics and book by Charles Hart and Don Black, after the novel by David Garnett)
Whistle Down the Wind (1998, lyrics by Jim Steinman, book by Patricia Knop, Gale Edwards, and Andrew
   Lloyd Webber, after the original novel by Mary Hayley Bell and the Richard Attenborough film)
The Beautiful Game (2000, lyrics and book by Ben Elton)

character exists in each show who looks to the protagonist for redemption (Pharaoh in *Joseph*, Mary Magdalene in *Superstar*).

Both *Joseph* and *Superstar* incorporate a variety of pop-rock styles, including Elvis-style and calypso numbers in *Joseph* and various rock styles in *Superstar*. *Joseph* began life as a 'pop cantata' for the choir of St Paul's Junior School at Colet Court, Hammersmith. It was first performed on 1 March 1968 in a concert at the Old Assembly Hall and lasted a mere fifteen minutes. It finally found life as a full-length production in 1973, after the success of *Superstar*. Further productions appeared, and the 1999 video/DVD release starring Donny Osmond, Richard Attenborough, Maria Friedman and Joan Collins made the show more accessible than ever. By contrast, *Superstar* began life as a double album. Concert tours of the rock opera followed, and a stage version ultimately emerged. The 1973 film version starred Ted Neeley and Carl Anderson. Both shows, therefore, had origins that were atypical for canonical works in the musical theatre.

Lloyd Webber's technicolor rendition of the Old Testament story of Jacob's favourite son, *Joseph and the Amazing Technicolor Dreamcoat*, is a sung-through loosely linked series of novelty numbers. The show is circular in nature, reflected in a line from the finale, 'let us return to the beginning ... any dream will do'. This concept of the dream reappears in *Sunset Boulevard* when Norma and her associates ponder 'new ways to dream'. *Joseph* concludes with the knowledge that a lesson has been taught and learned. It is youthful, energetic, fast-paced, lively and childlike, and its music is sweet and easily accessible, with 'Close Every Door' being the show's most haunting original tune.

Whereas *Joseph* is buoyant and light-hearted, positive and uplifting, *Jesus Christ Superstar* is brooding and imbued with a dark sense of foreboding. The last week of Jesus' life, his betrayal and Passion as seen through the eyes of Pontius Pilate, constitute the scenario. There are glorious moments of 'Hosannah' and the emblematic 'Jesus Christ Superstar' fanfare, but the Judas character defines the piece. 'King Herod's Song', a comic drag number reminiscent of 'The Pharaoh's Song' in *Joseph*, provides humorous relief but is somewhat out of keeping with the mood sustained throughout the rest of the show. In the final moments of the controversial 1971 original Tom O'Horgan Broadway production, Christ appeared crucified on an inverted triangle some twenty feet in the air and was slowly projected forward from the back wall of the stage until he loomed over the orchestra as swirling, flickering light fragments flashed through the theatre to the musical accompaniment of the signature fanfare. The show won seven Tony Awards, including Best Musical and Best Score.

The diversity of musical styles in *Joseph* and *Superstar* suggests the genre of the revue, and is a significant aspect of Lloyd Webber's overall musical language. This character-defining treatment through music would reappear in *Cats*, where each cat has its own type of music, and even more so in *The Phantom of the Opera* and *Sunset Boulevard*, where the music of the protagonist is decidedly distinct from the remainder of the score.

It was the rock opera concept of *Jesus Christ Superstar* that Lloyd Webber maintained in *Evita*, his third collaboration with Tim Rice and his third musical on a religious-historical theme. The show begins with an inventive and forceful prologue – on 26 July 1952, in a Buenos Aires cinema, the death of Eva Perón is announced. Argentina weeps, for they have lost a woman whom they considered a saint. The opera documents Eva Perón from her lowly yet ambitious beginnings to her influential position as 'the woman behind the man' of Juan Perón, president of Argentina, and her untimely death. Eva's popularity grows to the point of deification, and her youthful death immortalises her beauty and strength in the operatic tradition of the dying heroine. The moral conscience challenging her rise to power appears in the persona of the revolutionary Che Guevara. *Evita* is cinematic and sweeping, a complex immersion into the political games of Argentina in the 1940s and the sexual politics of a passionate woman and her society. The libretto lends itself to the operatic formulation of Eva Perón as both an anti-heroine and the personified conscience of a nation.

Like *Superstar*, *Evita* began its life as a concept album. The show was a turning point in the careers of both its composer and lyricist. It gave 'the first real evidence that here was not simply a minor British talent with a knack for catching a pop wave, but a serious composer of depth, talent, and technique working in tandem with a lyricist of style and substance'.[6] In *Evita*, Lloyd Webber rendered a score in 'an original, vital melodic language that stamped his music as his own – and not as a collection of disparate influences'.[7] The show received numerous Tony Awards, including one for Patti LuPone as Best Actress. 'Don't Cry for Me, Argentina' became a signature tune for LuPone, whose arm-raised final pose is one of the classic images of the musical theatre. For the 1996 film starring Madonna and Antonio Banderas, Lloyd Webber wrote a new song, 'You Must Love Me', earning him an Academy Award. Even though *Evita* was the third and perhaps crowning jewel in the Lloyd Webber–Rice collaborations, it signalled the end of their working relationship. The show solidified the reputations of both creators, and in the case of Lloyd Webber, his post-Rice works, while maintaining the fundamental approach to theatrical music, would expand his conceptual and musical horizons.

Continuing the search for immortality sought by the Biblical and historical characters of his Tim Rice collaborations, two of Lloyd Webber's most popular shows, *The Phantom of the Opera* and *Sunset Boulevard*, explore the same idea through fictional models. Both musicals tell of an older, physically unattractive individual who searches for immortality through a younger, more beautiful one. A lush romantic operatic style with rock overtones pervades both shows. In many respects these are two versions of the same story – Norma is the Phantom in drag.

The Phantom of the Opera, Lloyd Webber's most popular score, is romantic and sweeping, dark yet seductive, and must be considered his signature composition. The 'Beauty and the Beast' tale based on the Gaston Leroux novel, set deep in the bowels of the Paris Opera House, gave Lloyd Webber the freest rein with his imagination and musical gifts. Mark Steyn asserts:

> And *Phantom* has made opera hip, after half a century of being outflanked by musical comedy and the musical play. Before the First World War, *The Merry Widow* was one of the few shows to approach internationally the scale of today's Lloyd Webber mega-smashes: at one point there were over one hundred productions around the world.[8]

In *Phantom*, Lloyd Webber fuses his pop/rock sensibility with the classical models of his youth. The half-masked, caped figure appearing and disappearing accentuates the duality, the mix of old and new, in the music, the rendition and the conception. Like *Evita*, the show opens with a prologue – an auction at the Paris Opera where items, including the chandelier, are visible. As the chandelier is lit (with modern electricity), the music begins and the chandelier rises above the stalls. The magic and mystery continue as the audience passes through the mirror with the virginal young heroine and are seduced by the Phantom's 'music of the night'. *Phantom* is a modern opera played on a classical stage. The theme of unrequited and inaccessible love is as elusive and poignant as any contemporary love ballad, as classical as any opera. The fantasy transports, the music invites, the theatre technology awes. The production in the hands of Harold Prince is complete and satisfying, if not mystifying. As the audience enters the doors of Her Majesty's Theatre in London, chosen specifically for *Phantom* because of its architectural features, to see the show, they pass through a portal to another world – a world of realised mystery and imagination. Michael Crawford and Sarah Brightman triumphed in the original production, the show marking a milestone in the careers of both performers.

Sunset Boulevard commences with a musical prologue worthy of a late 1940s Hollywood movie that prepares for the story to be told in a large flashback, as with *Evita* and *Phantom*. The fast-paced motoristic fervour of 'Sunset Boulevard' is an apt overture to Lloyd Webber's faithful musical treatment of the Billy Wilder film about the fading silent movie actress longing and determined to make a comeback. The House on Sunset, Paramount

Plate 18 Sarah Brightman and Michael Crawford in *The Phantom of the Opera*, Her Majesty's
Theatre, 1986

Studios, Schwab's Drugstore, the Paramount backlot are the locales; Norma
Desmond, Joe Gillis, Max von Mayerling, Betty Schaefer, Cecil B. DeMille
and a cast of Hollywood hopeful extras are the characters. The London
production starred Patti LuPone, while the Los Angeles and New York productions featured Glenn Close. Betty Buckley succeeded both LuPone and
Close in their respective runs.

In a departure from his through-composed musicals, *Sunset Boulevard*
adopts a more traditional Broadway musical structure with spoken scenes
advancing the narrative. Joe is a screenwriter, Norma an actress. The presence

of dialogue scenes anchors and supports the musical numbers. Norma invites Joe into her mansion and her bed proffering gifts and promises of work, success and contacts at Paramount. A phantom-like spectre, she haunts the Sunset House and fascinates the good-looking, down-on-his-luck young writer as she slowly weaves her web – she, a black widow and he, her prey. Her delusional hope for rejuvenation is based on the irrational belief that her conquest will assure her return to the silver screen. This is music of a much darker night. The jazzy swing and hip sounds of the Paramount people seem a world away from Norma's brooding, soulful, unresolved melodies and such telling lines as 'We taught the world new ways to dream' and her final 'I am ready for my close-up, Mr DeMille'. Her stare, her stance, her face and her eyes are etched into the lens of consciousness as she lights the darkness one last time.

The two shows, as mentioned above, have strong parallels both dramatically and musically. (See Table 14.2.) Both the Phantom and Norma are searching for immortality and hope to achieve this through a younger character, an apprentice of sorts. The Phantom teaches Christine to sing and star in his opera while Norma wants Joe to secure her return to the silver screen in her original version of *Salomé*. The chief protagonist is concerned about his or her physical appearance. The Phantom's facial disfigurement is covered by the iconic mask until he reveals himself to Christine. It is his physical appearance that is the root of his societal estrangement. Norma's faded physical appearance causes her great consternation, and her desire for corporeal beauty is the basis for the song 'Eternal Youth Is Worth a Little Suffering'. Both the Phantom and Norma look for youth and beauty in their apprentices.

Table 14.2 *Dramatic and musical parallels in* The Phantom of the Opera *and* Sunset Boulevard

Older/physically 'unattractive' character in search of immortality through a younger, beautiful one	
Phantom	Norma Desmond
Younger character	
Christine Daaé	Joe Gillis
Younger character's romantic interest	
Raoul	Betty Schaefer
Ending – release from reality	
Disappearance of Phantom	Madness of Norma
Introductory musical number for the principal character	
'Angel of Music'	'With One Look'
Subsequent musical number for the principal character	
'Music of the Night'	'As if We Never Said Goodbye'
Defining musical number for younger character	
'Think of Me'	'Sunset Boulevard'

Each of these apprentices has their own romantic interest with a young and vital person, resulting in love triangles. The ultimate result of the triangles differs in the two shows, however. In *Phantom*, Christine and Raoul are together at the final curtain while in *Sunset Boulevard*, Joe's death forbids a union with Betty.

The musicals end in a similar fashion with a release from reality. The mysterious disappearance of the Phantom into unknown regions contrasts with Norma's descent into madness at the end of *Sunset Boulevard* as she imagines herself on the set of Paramount Studios.

The dramatic parallels have musical implications that are realised by Lloyd Webber. The principal character in each show has two large-scale songs that define his or her demeanour and temperament. The first numbers, 'Angel of Music' and 'With One Look', are self-defining songs in which the characters assert their basic life views. A subsequent number illuminates their innermost desires. 'Music of the Night', a trunk song, reveals the deepest regions of the Phantom's soul through its ballad style, while 'As if We Never Said Goodbye' is an expression of Norma's sense of loss and her ardent desire to return to the world of Hollywood magic.

The younger character in each show has a solo number that defines his or her place in the drama. 'Think of Me' reveals Christine's innocence through its directness of musical expression; 'Sunset Boulevard' with its constant rhythmic underpinning depicts the angst that Joe experiences throughout his ultimately fatal relationship with Norma.

Other commonalities link the two works. A staircase figures prominently into the scenic design of both. The second act of *Phantom* opens with the New Year's Eve masquerade scene, set on a lavish staircase filled with live chorus members and mannequins. Norma Desmond's staircase in *Sunset Boulevard* is a central feature of the show.

A monkey also figures prominently into both musicals. In *Phantom*, a stuffed monkey is on the music box that is auctioned as the show opens. In *Sunset Boulevard*, Norma's recently deceased monkey is the subject of her mourning when Joe enters the mansion.

Murders take place in both shows. The Phantom threatens or kills those who attempt to thwart his plans to make Christine a star while Joe's murder by Norma frames the plot of *Sunset Boulevard*.

The concept of physical space is notable in both shows as well. In *Phantom*, the lair lies beneath the Paris Opera House. In order to escape the Phantom's influence, Christine and Raoul go to the roof of the building, a physically separate location. Most of the show takes place in the Opera House, between the roof and the lair. Likewise, in *Sunset Boulevard*, Norma makes her first appearance at the top of the immense staircase. Joe, by contrast, is seen first facedown in Norma's swimming pool – literally in the depths of her estate. Since the story is told in flashback, this is where Joe remains throughout the musical. The worlds of Joe and Norma are separate: the characters meet and interact on the ground floor of Norma's lavish palace – an intermediate domain between their two regions. The relationship between the physical spaces allocated to the principal characters is gender-based: female characters occupy the higher regions while male characters inhabit places physically beneath the setting of the central action.

This central mid-level dramatic location is the domain of the protagonist. Whether the Paris Opera House or Norma's mansion on Sunset Boulevard, the protagonists find security in their respective physical surroundings. They determine and dominate the events that take place in these domains, controlling through fear, intimidation or sheer willpower all who enter these realms that are every bit as private as the Countess's boudoir in *Le nozze di Figaro*.

Finally, the performing arts backgrounds to both shows are central to their concept. The Paris Opera House and its activities provide the backdrop for *Phantom*, but Lloyd Webber also alludes to various styles of opera in the musical. Scenes from three imaginary operas appear in *Phantom*: *Hannibal* by Chalumeau, *Il muto* by Albrizzio, and *Don Juan Triumphant* by the Phantom himself. In these 'operas within an opera', Lloyd Webber pays tribute to various European operatic traditions. *Hannibal* is a French Grand Opera, complete with a scenic elephant, while *Il muto* is modelled on Italian opera buffa. *Don Juan Triumphant* is a decidedly modern work that includes musical devices such as the whole-tone scale, setting it off from the other two works. The setting for the scene from *Don Juan Triumphant* is a banquet akin to that in Mozart's *Don Giovanni*. Likewise, *Sunset Boulevard* is not only a transformation of a cinematic paragon but also homage to the lost world of silent cinema, as was the original Billy Wilder film.

Whereas immortality is the goal of the protagonists in the above-mentioned shows, it also figures prominently in the plots of the second category, competition musicals, in which some sort of contest takes place. In *Cats*, the winner goes to the Heaviside Layer (cat heaven) and in *Starlight Express*, the various toy train engines try to win the race to the 'Light at the End of the Tunnel'. In both shows, it is the underdog who wins – the faded Grizabella defeats her fellow felines in *Cats* and the steam engine Rusty conquers newer technologies in *Starlight Express*.

In both shows, Lloyd Webber explores a variety of musical styles. *Cats* contains a wide range of songs, including an Elvis-style number. 'Memory', the show's climactic point, is a sentimental ballad that has been championed by the singers Elaine Paige and Barbra Streisand, among others. *Starlight Express* includes rock, blues and country music throughout, and concludes with a gospel finale, 'The Light at the End of the Tunnel'. In these shows, the mixture of musical styles and the search for a new life symbolised by light (a spaceship in *Cats* and the end of the tunnel in *Starlight Express*) is a shared feature, as is the transformation of the theatre into either a garbage dump (*Cats*) or a race track (*Starlight Express*).

'Cats: Now and Forever' – as the poster proclaims – proved to be more prophetic than might have been imagined by the Cameron Mackintosh team that coined it. Based on T. S. Eliot's *Old Possum's Book of Practical Cats*, this junkyard song and dance spectacle is a vaudeville/minstrel/burlesque populated by a company of colourful, dappled, tabby, be-whiskered and grizzly-coiffed felines. As a show it defies categorisation. *Cats* is an experience. The theatre itself is transformed into a junkyard, not just the stage but the house as well. Just as audiences enter the world of the Paris Opera House when they attend *Phantom*, they venture into the world of feline sub-culture in *Cats*. The popularity of the longest-running musical in both London and New York was further endorsed when the United States Postal Service honoured the show with a commemorative stamp in its 'Celebrate the Century' series. It was thus heralded as one of the fifteen most important events in 1980s American culture.

And if actors can be cats, why can't they be trains?

> Imagine yourself seated in a theatre which has been totally transformed into an incredible 'roller-coaster' race track. Against a background of stunning special effects, this track becomes the arena for an exciting and spectacular production. You will enjoy the thrills and spills of high speed races as they pass in front of you, behind you – and even over you! A ring-side seat at *Starlight Express* is a once-in-a-lifetime experience.[9]

Starlight Express capitalises on the formula experienced in *Cats*. The junkyard becomes a train yard and racing track. Actors on skates impersonate various types of trains – steam engines, diesels and electric engines and their coaches. Envisaged as a children's story, the production was an expensive technological spectacle. The technology of the stagecraft and the skating prowess of its athletic actors overshadowed the recorded music and over-amplified lyrics in performance except in the few quiet moments when the mayhem slowed. It has more in common with a roller-skating disco than with the musical theatre. Yet it is indeed original – another 'experience' created by the mind and music of Andrew Lloyd Webber, a 'theme park ride' of a musical. A ninety-minute version of *Starlight Express* opened in 1993 at the Las Vegas Hilton, the first major legitimate stage production to play in the famed gambling city.

The archetypal megamusical production includes lavish sets and a strong emphasis on choreography and other visual elements. In Lloyd Webber's intimate musicals, however, the lush musical style is maintained while some of the overt theatricality is eschewed.

Song and Dance represents a distinct departure from Lloyd Webber's large-scale work. It is an intimate two-part programme as literal as the title suggests – the first act is sung, the second is danced. Constructed from two earlier works – *Tell Me on a Sunday*, a 1979 song cycle, and *Variations for Cello and Rock Band* – it received its premiere on the BBC as a television special. In 'Song' a woman sings about her relationships with several men, her experiences and her thoughts as an English girl living alone in Manhattan. 'Song' is sung through, without spoken dialogue. 'Dance', a set of variations on Paganini's Twenty-fourth Caprice written for Andrew Lloyd Webber's cello-playing brother Julian, is a choreographic self-examination by one of the men mentioned in 'Song'. It consists solely of instrumental music, without either lyrics or spoken dialogue.

Aspects of Love is an adaptation of David Garnett's tale of intergenerational love. Here, as in *The Phantom of the Opera* and *Sunset Boulevard*, the central character uses the youth of another as a catalyst for personal transformation. Conceived as an intimate chamber piece in style and execution, it is a sung-through ballad of yearning and longing and the pains and penalties of love conquered and love lost. *Aspects* focuses on the human drama of a set of interrelated characters: Rose, an actress; Alex, a young Englishman; George, his uncle, an English painter; Giulietta, an Italian sculptress; Jenny, daughter of Rose and George; and Hugo, Rose's lover. The action takes place in France and Italy between 1947 and 1961, and is a virtual Rubik's Cube of love triangles. Michael Walsh says of the show that 'it displays Lloyd Webber's familiar melodic gifts, this time wedded to a solid technical foundation to produce moments of penetrating psychological insight and great emotional power . . . the score flows from one scene to the next, hardly stopping for breath . . . the penultimate scene . . . is the composer's finest dramatic creation'.[10] The show played for over three years in London, but its 1990 Broadway run lasted only 377 performances.

In *Whistle Down the Wind*, this idea of the transformative power of youth is combined with the religious messages of Lloyd Webber's early shows. The show opens as an electric neon billboard with the words 'Jesus Lives' hovers over a flyover where a church congregation gathers and intones a hymn, 'The Vaults of Heaven', cast in traditional Baptist mode. The minister then tells of an afterlife where there will be no more pain, loss or sorrow.

It is 1959 in a small Louisiana town and the music is that of a British composer. Lloyd Webber's adaptation of the novel and film of *Whistle Down the Wind* is a bucolic American gothic fable. The title song is a hopeful, simple anthem of hope and acceptance, and Lloyd Webber is deep in the American South, far away from Egypt, Paris and Argentina. When three siblings return home after their chores they are surprised to discover a longhaired, bleeding man hidden in the barn, sleeping in the hay. Swallow, the girl, startles the man, who, when she begins to ask who he is, responds with the expletive 'Jesus Christ'. She takes him literally, and the drama begins.

A slim premise at best, but with this *Whistle*, Lloyd Webber's imagination again takes flight. The Man is an escaped convict, an unlikely Jesus, yet the answer to months of unanswered prayers by the children. He is an object of hope and faith. The minister's exhortation is a reality in a town where racial tension, graft and passions smoulder. His appearance is a miracle of sorts, for the children, in their innocence and naiveté, protect, worship and love him. The plot meanders and is fed by the hypocrisy of fundamentalism, the restlessness of youth appearing like an insidious Southern stream. A collaboration with Jim Steinman, the score includes romantic love ballads, blues, country, gospel and rock music. The eclecticism chronicled throughout this essay is again apparent in *Whistle Down the Wind*.

The musical, while demonstrating the intimate, also includes some remarkable theatrical moments such as the hydraulically lifted flyover and the head-on approach of a train in a tunnel. These visual events are at least as powerful as they are in shows such as *Phantom* because of the intimacy of the overall setting and the tone of the musical. They are not part of an awe-inspiring aesthetic but rather accentuate moments in a show conceived in a much more private manner.

The Beautiful Game, a show about Belfast footballers in 1969, may appear at first glance to be a competition musical, but Ben Elton's book and lyrics prove it to be a logical continuation of themes addressed in *Whistle*: a search for peace and the responsibility of youth to achieve a better future. The intertwined stories of two couples – the men of whom are football players – address Northern Ireland issues: the Catholic–Protestant pair (Christine and Del) who leave for America and the inter-Catholic pair (Mary and John) who are separated after John's false imprisonment and subsequent IRA involvement. Mary's solo soliloquy 'If This Is What We're Fighting For' positions the political overtones of the show squarely in focus. Her unaccompanied singing for most of the song intensifies its heartfelt lyric, as does the critical line 'No child was ever born to hate'. Ireland is celebrated in the lyrical 'God's Own Country' and the energetic opening title number endorses football as a religion every bit as powerful as the faith of the Catholic priest who coaches the team.

Aspects, Whistle and *Game* all embrace themes of innocence and youth that are challenged by either carnal or spiritual forces. The principal characters are all searching for some sort of healing or catharsis. Because these shows lack the overwhelming set and costume designs that are generally associated with Lloyd Webber's work, the focus becomes more centred on issues within the stories themselves and how the music and the words work together (without fundamental reliance on overtly theatrical visual effects and sets) to deal with these dramatic points.

Like *Les Misérables*, the works of Lloyd Webber have enjoyed tremendous popularity outside the English-speaking world. Rebecca Sherburn, who played Carlotta in the Hamburg production of *Das Phantom der Oper* from 1993 to 1997, recalls the expansiveness of the German version. A theatre with a 2,000-seat capacity was built especially for the production. The stage, the sets and the costumes were all larger than in London and New York. The stage contained 160 trap doors and the medallion-covered hoop skirt worn by Carlotta in the *Hannibal* opera weighed 35 pounds. Many non-Germans were in the cast during the 1990s, and the theatre directors, realising the international aspects of the show, were not particularly concerned with uniform German accents among the performers. The show remains popular with German audiences: travel agencies include it as part of weekend holiday packages, and some audience members even dress up as characters in the musical when they attend the theatre.[11]

Capitalising on the high-tech staging associated with the European megamusicals are the Disney productions of the 1990s, appearing under the guise of Disney Theatricals. The live-theatre adaptations of *Beauty and the Beast* (1994) and *The Lion King* (1998) quickly became among the most popular shows in both New York and London. The transformation scene in *Beauty and the Beast* and the magical puppetry conceived by Julie Taymor for *The Lion King* took the remarkable staging and visual spectacle associated with the megamusical to new creative levels.

Like the European megamusicals, Disney productions have quickly become internationalised. In addition to English-language versions, *Beauty and the Beast* has been produced in translation in Stuttgart and Madrid and *The Lion King* has played in Tokyo and Osaka. Along these lines, the live theatrical version of *The Hunchback of Notre Dame* was first produced in Berlin in 1999 under the German title *Der Glöckner von Notre Dame*, bypassing an initial English-language version.

Disney Theatricals runs Hyperion Theatricals, whose first show was Elton John and Tim Rice's *Aida* (2000), a score that, like so many rock musicals, tried to expand the stereotypical Broadway sounds. Postmodern staging, including a vertical swimming pool, accentuated the theatrical experience.

The post-*Les Mis* megamusical model also includes shows such as *La Cava* (2000, London; music by Laurence O'Keefe and Stephen Keeling, lyrics by John Claflin and O'Keefe, book by Dana Broccoli based on her novel), *Jane Eyre* (2000, New York; music and lyrics by Paul Gordon) and *The Witches of Eastwick* (2000, London; music by Dana P. Rowe, book and lyrics by

John Dempsey). The first is a tale of love and betrayal set in eighth-century Spain, while the second is based on the Charlotte Brontë novel. *The Witches of Eastwick* includes the expected visual effects, complete with aerial acrobatics, as well as a convincing musical score.

But have megamusicals run their course? The shows themselves have become somewhat formulaic, and composers at the beginning of the twenty-first century have to find ways to break new ground. Three of the most prominent trends are: (1) dance-based shows; (2) pastiche scores; and (3) operatic approaches.

The Irish *Riverdance* phenomenon has created a demand for brilliant choreography in musical theatre productions since its first appearance in 1994. Allusions to the specific nature of *Riverdance* choreography as well as the general concept of dance has had a strong impact on musicals such as *Fosse* (1999, New York) and *Stomp* (2000, New York). *Notre Dame de Paris* (1999, Paris; 2000, London; music by Richard Cocciante, book and lyrics by Luc Plamondon, English lyrics by Will Jennings) relies heavily upon the creative choreography of Martino Muller, going so far as to list the names of twenty-four dancers and ten acrobats and breakdancers in the programme as equals to the seven singing principals. There is no chorus in the show – the choral sound is replaced by choreographic marvels.

Notre Dame de Paris also provides an excellent example of the impact of marketing upon the genre. The show was an unprecedented success in the French-speaking world, breaking box office records in France, Canada, Belgium and Switzerland. The French soundtrack album was released eight months before the opening of the show at the Palais de Congrès in Paris, and the single 'Belle' sold over three million copies. All of this contributed to the show being listed in the *Guinness Book of World Records* as having the most successful first year in the history of musical theatre.

Pastiche scores, those which invoke styles from the early twentieth century, are attempts to integrate the passion for nostalgia (so evident in the plethora of revivals on Broadway and in the West End) with forward-looking and innovative trends in the musical theatre. The revivals of John Kander and Fred Ebb's *Chicago* in black and white (1996) and the same team's *Cabaret* in black leather (1998) exemplify this trend. Furthermore, shows such as Cy Coleman, Betty Comden and Adolph Green's *The Will Rogers Follies* (1991), Lloyd Webber's *By Jeeves* (1996), Kander and Ebb's *Steel Pier* (1997) and Michael John LaChiusa's *The Wild Party* (2000) have scores that are modern incarnations of earlier popular music styles. *Steel Pier* concerns a dance marathon in the 1930s, combining pastiche with the choreographic focus described above.

Finally, many new composers of musicals take a more operatic approach to the genre. The relationship between opera and musical has been an on-going thread throughout this volume. At the beginning of the twenty-first century, yet another chapter opens. LaChiusa's *Marie Christine* (1999), a version of the Medea myth set in late nineteenth-century New Orleans and Chicago, includes musical complexities atypical of most Broadway musicals. Yet it appeared on a theatrical stage, not in an opera house. It was even suggested by a *New York Times* critic that had it appeared at Glimmerglass Opera, it might have gained a more appreciative audience.[12] But could this not also be a continuation of a more operatic approach to Broadway, seen in works such as *Porgy and Bess*, *Candide*, *The Most Happy Fella* and even *Evita*?

These are certainly not the only contemporary approaches to the genre. Adam Guettel's *Floyd Collins* (1995), Jeanine Tesori and Brian Crawley's *Violet* (1996) and Jason Robert Brown's *Parade* (1998) are but three shows that encapsulate the American regionalism pioneered earlier in the century and infuse it with plots of dramatic depth. Traditional book musicals such as Stephen Flaherty and Lynn Ahrens's *Ragtime* (1998) confirm that the approach is still viable – visual spectacle and choreography do not have to be the sole paramount qualities in contemporary musical theatre.

At the end of this volume celebrating the artistry, creativity, integrity, popularity and diversity of the English-language musical theatre, where are we? The rich traditions explored throughout the preceding chapters continue to be developed and transformed by creative artists who strive to combine music, words, dance and other theatrical elements into an art form that continues to entertain, edify and enchant audiences throughout the world.

Notes

The publisher has used its best endeavours to ensure that the URLs for external websites referred to in this book are correct and active at the time of going to press. However, the publisher has no responsibility for the websites and can make no guarantee that a site will remain live or that the content is or will remain appropriate.

1 American musical theatre before the twentieth century

1 Edith Borroff, 'Origin of Species: Conflicting Views of American Musical Theater History', *American Music*, 2/4 (1984), p. 102.

2 Susan L. Porter, 'English–American Interaction in American Musical Theatre at the Turn of the Nineteenth Century', *American Music*, 4/1 (1986), p. 6.; Anne Dhu Shapiro, 'Music in American Pantomime and Melodrama, 1730–1913', *American Music*, 2/4 (1984), p. 50.

3 Porter, 'English–American Interaction', p. 6.

4 Julian Mates, *America's Musical Stage: Two Hundred Years of Musical Theatre* (Westport, Connecticut, 1985), p. 22.

5 William Brooks, 'Good Musical Paste: Getting the Acts Together in the Eighteenth Century', in *Musical Theatre in America: Papers and Proceedings of the Conference on the Musical Theatre in America*, ed. Glenn Loney (Westport, Connecticut, 1984), p. 37.

6 Cynthia Adams Hoover, 'Music in Eighteenth-Century American Theater', *American Music*, 2/4 (1984), pp. 6–7; Brooks, 'Good Musical Paste', p. 37.

7 Shapiro, 'Music in American Pantomime', p. 56.

8 Porter, 'English–American Interaction', pp. 8–10.

9 *Ibid.*, p. 11.

10 H. Wiley Hitchcock and Stanley Sadie (eds.), *The New Grove Dictionary of American Music*, vol. III, *s.v.* 'Melodrama'.

11 Karl Kroeger and Victor Fell Yellin (eds.), *Early Melodrama in America: 'The Voice of Nature' and 'The Aethiop; or, The Child of the Desert'*, vol. II of *Nineteenth-Century American Musical Theater*, gen. ed. Deane L. Root (New York, 1994), p. xv.

12 *Ibid.*, p. xvi.

13 Shapiro, 'Music in American Pantomime', pp. 57–8.

14 H. Wiley Hitchcock, 'An Early American Melodrama: *The Indian Princess* of J. N. Barker and John Bray', *MLA Notes*, 12/3 (1955), p. 376.

15 Dunlap quoted in *ibid.*, p. 379; see also p. 381.

16 Anne Dhu McLucas (ed.), *Later Melodrama in America: 'Monte Cristo' (ca. 1883)*, vol. IV of *Nineteenth-Century American Musical Theater*, gen. ed. Deane L. Root (New York, 1994), p. xx.

17 *The New Grove Dictionary of American Music*, *s.v.* 'Melodrama'.

18 Mary Grace Swift, 'Celestial Queen of the Dumb Shows', *Musical Theatre in America: Papers and Proceedings of the Conference on the Musical Theatre in America*, ed. Glenn Loney (Westport, Connecticut, 1984), pp. 291–9.

19 Katherine K. Preston, *Opera on the Road: Traveling Opera Troupes in the United States, 1825–1860* (Urbana, 1993), p. 2.

20 *Ibid.*, Chapter 1.

21 *Ibid.*, pp. 101–6.

22 Sylvie Chevalley, 'Le Théâtre d'Orléans en Tournée dans les villes du nord, 1827–1833', in *Comptes rendus de l'athénée louisianais* (1955), pp. 27–71.

23 Preston, *Opera on the Road*, Chapter 3.

24 Katherine K. Preston, 'Art Music from 1800 to 1860', in *The Cambridge History of American Music*, ed. David Nicholls (Cambridge, 1998), p. 199.

25 For more information on the development of the American theatre during this period, see Alfred L. Bernheim, *The Business of the Theatre: An Economic History of the American Theatre, 1750–1932* (New York, 1932), pp. 12–25.

26 Shapiro, 'Music in American Pantomime', p. 61.

27 *The New Grove Dictionary of American Music*, *s.v.* 'Melodrama'.

28 Thomas Riis, 'The Music and Musicians in Nineteenth-Century Productions of *Uncle Tom's Cabin*', *American Music*, 4/3 (1986), pp. 268–9; Thomas Riis (ed.), *'Uncle Tom's Cabin' (1852) by George L. Aiken and George C. Howard*, vol. V of *Nineteenth-Century American Musical Theater*, gen. ed. Deane L. Root (New York, 1994), Introduction.

29 Dale Cockrell, *Demons of Disorder: Early Blackface Minstrels and Their World* (Cambridge, 1997).

30 Dale Cockrell, 'Nineteenth-Century Popular Music', in *The Cambridge History of American Music*, ed. David Nicholls (Cambridge, 1998), pp. 158–85.

31 *Ibid.*, p. 168. See also Renée Lapp Norris, '"Black Opera": Antebellum Blackface Minstrelsy and European Opera', Ph.D. dissertation, University of Maryland (2001).

32 Cockrell, 'Nineteenth-Century Popular Music', p. 174.

33 Gretchen Schneider, 'Gabriel Ravel and the Martinetti Family: The Popularity of Pantomime in 1855', in *American Popular Entertainment: Papers and Proceedings of the Conference on the History of American Popular Entertainment*, ed. Myron Matlaw (Westport, Connecticut, 1979), p. 242. This article by Schneider is almost the only source of information in this field.

34 *Ibid.*, p. 245. See also Cecil Smith and Glenn Litton, *Musical Comedy in America* (New York, 1950, 1981), pp. 5–6.

35 *The New Grove Dictionary of American Music*, vol. I, *s.v.* 'Dance, II. The Nineteenth Century, 2. Ballet'.

36 Deane L. Root, *American Popular Stage Music, 1860–1880* (Ann Arbor, Michigan, 1977), pp. 70–1.

37 *Ibid.*, p. 68.

38 Rita M. Plotnicki, 'John Brougham: The Aristophanes of American Burlesque', *Journal of Popular Culture*, 12/3 (1978), p. 422.

39 *The New Grove Dictionary of American Music*, vol. I, *s.v.* 'Burlesque'.

40 William C. Young, *Documents of American Theatre History*, vol. I: *Famous American Playhouses 1716–1899* (Chicago, 1973), pp. 102–3; William Brooks, 'Pocahontas, Her Life and Times', *American Music*, 2/4 (1984), pp. 19–48.

41 Preston, *Opera on the Road*, pp. 413–14, n. 9 and p. 417, n. 54.

42 See Bernheim, *Business of the Theatre*, pp. 46–63.

43 Root, *American Popular Stage Music, 1860–1880*, p. 37; Richard Kislan, *The Musical: A Look at the American Musical Theater* (Englewood Cliffs, New Jersey, 1980), p. 67; Ethan Mordden, *Better Foot Forward: The History of American Musical Theatre* (New York, 1976), p. 25.

44 Smith and Litton, *Musical Comedy*, pp. 8–10.

45 Root, *American Popular Stage Music, 1860–1880*, p. 92.

46 *Ibid.*, p. 113.

47 Smith and Litton, *Musical Comedy*, pp. 17–18.

48 Root, *American Popular Stage Music, 1860–1880*, p. 148; Smith and Litton, *Musical Comedy*, pp. 19–23.

49 Smith and Litton, *Musical Comedy*, pp. 20–1; Richard Jackson (ed.), *Early Burlesque in America: Evangeline (1877)*, vol. XIII of *Nineteenth-Century American Musical Theater*, gen. ed. Deane L. Root (New York, 1994), pp. xiii–xiv.

50 Smith and Litton, *Musical Comedy*, 32.

51 Root, *American Popular Stage Music, 1860–1880*, pp. 49–50.

52 Smith and Litton, *Musical Comedy*, p. 34.

53 McLucas (ed.), *Later Melodrama in America*, p. xv.

54 Shapiro, 'Music in American Pantomime', p. 65.

55 David Mayer, 'The Music of Melodrama', in *Performance and Politics in Popular Drama*, ed. David Bradby, Louis James and Bernard Sharratt (Cambridge, 1980), pp. 49–50.

56 McLucas (ed.), *Later Melodrama in America*, p. xvii.

57 *Ibid.*, p. xv; see also Katherine K. Preston, 'The Music of Toga Drama', introductory essay in *'Playing Out the Empire': 'Ben Hur' and Other Toga Plays and Films, 1883–1908: A Critical Anthology*, ed. David Mayer (Oxford, 1994).

58 Cockrell, 'Nineteenth-Century Popular Music', p. 174.

59 Eileen Southern, *The Music of Black Americans: A History*, 2nd edn (New York, 1983), pp. 229–30.

60 Allen L. Woll, *Black Musical Theatre: From 'Coontown' to 'Dreamgirls'* (Baton Rouge, 1989), p. 1.

61 Thomas Riis, *Just Before Jazz. Black Musical Theater in New York, 1890–1915* (Washington DC, 1989), pp. 9–11; Eileen Southern (ed.), *African American Theater: 'Out of Bondage' (1876) and 'Peculiar Sam, or the Underground Railroad' (1879)*, vol. IX of *Nineteenth-Century American Musical Theater*, gen. ed. Deane L. Root (New York, 1994), Introduction.

62 Woll, *Black Musical Theatre*, pp. 4–5.

63 Cockrell, 'Nineteenth-Century Popular Music', p. 175.

64 Root, *American Popular Stage Music, 1860–1880*, pp. 115–21.

65 *Ibid.*, p. 165; see also Gerald Bordman, *American Operetta: from 'H.M.S. Pinafore' to 'Sweeney Todd'* (New York and Oxford, 1981), pp. 15–16.

66 Bordman, *American Operetta*, p. 16.

67 Root, *American Popular Stage Music, 1860–1880*, pp. 136–44; see also Charlotte

Kauffman (ed.), *Early Operetta in America: 'The Doctor of Alcantara' (1879)*, vol. XII of *Nineteenth-Century American Musical Theater*, gen. ed. Deane L. Root (New York, 1994), p. xviii.
68 Paul Bierley, *The Works of John Philip Sousa* (Columbus, Ohio, 1984), p. 13.
69 Jane Stedman, '"Then Hey! For the Merry Greenwood!": Smith and de Koven and Robin Hood', *Journal of Popular Culture*, 12/3 (1978), p. 433.
70 Parker Zellers, *Tony Pastor: Dean of the Vaudeville Stage* (Ypsilanti, Michigan, 1971), pp. xiii–xix.
71 *Ibid.*, p. xix.
72 American Memory Webpage, Library of Congress: The American Variety Stage: Vaudeville and Popular Entertainment, 1870–1920.
http://memory.loc.gov/ammem/ammemhome.html.
73 Katherine K. Preston (ed.), *Irish American Theater: 'The Mulligan Guard Ball' (1879) and 'Reilly and the Four Hundred' (1891)*, vol. X of *Nineteenth-Century American Musical Theater*, gen. ed. Deane L. Root (New York, 1994), p. xvi.
74 *Ibid.*, pp. xvi–xvii.
75 *Ibid.*, p. xix.
76 Riis, *Just Before Jazz*, p. 13; Woll, *Black Musical Theatre*, pp. 68–9.
77 David Mayer, 'The Music of Melodrama', p. 49.
78 Joel H. Kaplan, 'Introduction', in *The Edwardian Theatre: Essays on Performance and the Stage*, ed. Michael R. Booth and Joel H. Kaplan (Cambridge, 1996), p. 1.

2 Birth pangs, growing pains and sibling rivalry: musical theatre in New York, 1900–1920
1 'The Decline of Comic Opera', *Musical America*, 4 (13 October 1906), p. 8.
2 '"The Red Feather", Reginald De Koven's Latest Comic Opera at the Lyric', *New York Times*, 10 November 1903.
3 Armond Fields and L. Marc Fields, *From the Bowery to Broadway: Lew Fields and the Roots of American Popular Theatre* (New York and Oxford, 1993), p. 214.
4 Rennold Wolf, *New York Telegraph*, 26 December 1906.
5 Some of the following material has previously appeared in the author's 'Wien, Women and Song: *The Merry Widow* in New York', *Sonneck Society Bulletin*, 22/1 (1996), pp. 1, 8–11.
6 Richard Traubner, *Operetta: A Theatrical History* (Garden City, New York, 1983), p. 243.

7 'All New York is "Merry Widow" Mad Now-A-Days', *Musical America*, 6 (2 November 1907), p. 21.
8 The *Oxford English Dictionary* credits the *Daily Chronicle* (9 July 1908) with the first written reference: 'The women in the galleries took off their "Merry Widow" hats, and waved them frantically.'
9 Danton Walker, unidentified clipping, c. 1945, *The Merry Widow* production folder no. 1, Museum of the City of New York.
10 Bernard Grun, *Gold and Silver: The Life and Times of Franz Lehár* (London, 1970), p. 128.
11 'London Amused by "The Merry Widow"', *Musical America*, 6 (15 June 1907), p. 7.
12 [W.J. Henderson], *New York Sun*, 22 October 1907.
13 [Richard Aldrich], *New York Times*, 22 October 1907.
14 Henry Krehbiel, *New York Tribune*, 22 October 1907.
15 *Musical Courier*, 30 October 1907, p. 22.
16 *Musical America*, 6 (26 October 1907), p. 21. The article quotes Reginald de Koven in the *New York World*, 22 October 1907.
17 *Musical America*, 6 (26 October 1907), p. 1.
18 Burns Mantle and Garrison P. Sherwood (eds.), *The Best Plays of 1899–1909* (New York, 1947), p. 554.
19 Acton Davies, unidentified clipping, Billy Rose Theatre Collection, New York Public Library.
20 Unidentified clipping, Billy Rose Theatre Collection, New York Public Library.
21 H. Wiley Hitchcock and Stanley Sadie (eds.), *The New Grove Dictionary of American Music*, vol. III, *s.v.* 'Musical Theater'.
22 Charles Hamm, *Irving Berlin: Songs from the Melting Pot: The Formative Years, 1907–1914* (New York and Oxford, 1997), p. 222.
23 Gerald Bordman, *American Musical Revue* (New York and Oxford, 1985), p. 79.

3 Romance, nostalgia and nevermore: American and British operetta in the 1920s
1 Vesna Goldsworthy discusses this phenomenon in the realm of literature in *Inventing Ruritania: The Imperialism of the Imagination* (New Haven and London, 1998).
2 For more on *The Merry Widow* and its New York reception, see Orly Leah Krasner, 'Wien, Women and Song: *The Merry Widow* in New York', *Sonneck Society Bulletin*, 22/1 (1996), pp. 1, 8–11.
3 Geoffrey Block, *Enchanted Evenings: The Broadway Musical from Show Boat to Sondheim* (New York and Oxford, 1997), p. 314.

4 Stephen Banfield, 'Popular Song and Popular Music on Stage and Film', in *The Cambridge History of American Music*, ed. David Nicholls (Cambridge, 1998), p. 333.

4 Images of African Americans: African-American musical theatre, *Show Boat* and *Porgy and Bess*

1 The early history of the Georgia Minstrels is discussed in Eileen Southern's article 'The Georgia Minstrels: The Early Years', *Inter-American Music Review*, 10/2 (1989), pp. 157–67.
2 Errol Hill's article 'The Hyers Sisters: Pioneers in Black Musical Comedy' is published in *The American Stage: Social and Economic Issues from the Colonial Period to the Present*, ed. Ron Engle and Tice C. Miller (Cambridge and New York, 1993).
3 For additional details on the many musicals presented during the years 1890 to 1910, see Thomas L. Riis, *Just Before Jazz: Black Musical Theater in New York, 1890–1915* (Washington DC, 1989).
4 See Eric Ledell Smith's *Bert Williams: A Biography of the Pioneer Black Comedian* (Jefferson, North Carolina, 1992) for an excellent overview of Bert Williams's career.
5 See Robert Kimball and William Bolcom's *Reminiscing with Sissle and Blake* (New York, 1973) for an informal biography of Sissle's and Blake's careers.
6 These 1920s gatherings were associated with indigent African Americans in Harlem, who held parties in their apartments at which invited guests contributed small amounts of cash to help pay their rent. These parties often included musical entertainment to attract guests.
7 For an overview of musicals seen during the Harlem Renaissance, see John Graziano's 'Black Musical Theater and the Harlem Renaissance' in *Black Music in the Harlem Renaissance: A Collection of Essays*, ed. Samuel A. Floyd Jr (Westport, Connecticut, 1990), pp. 87–110.

5 The melody (and the words) linger on: American musical comedies of the 1920s and 1930s

1 Frederick Lewis Allen, *Only Yesterday* (New York, 1931), chapter 5.
2 Malcolm Goldstein, *The Political Stage: American Drama and Theater of the Great Depression* (New York, 1974), pp. 313–15, 394–5; Ronald Sanders, *The Days Grow Short: The Life and Music of Kurt Weill* (New York, 1980), chapters 17 and 19.
3 *Cradle Will Rock*, written and directed by Tim Robbins, 1999. Tim Robbins, *Cradle Will Rock: The Movie and The Moment* (New York, 2000). See also Geoffrey Block, *Enchanted Evenings: The Broadway Musical from 'Show Boat' to Sondheim* (New York and Oxford, 1997), pp. 115–32.
4 Stanley Green (ed.), *Rodgers and Hammerstein Fact Book* (New York, 1980), pp. 12–13.
5 Stephen Banfield places *Girl Crazy* (1930) as a pivotal show that brought 'the dance-band viewpoint into the whole musical world of a stage show' (Stephen Banfield, 'Popular Song and Popular Music on Stage and Film', in *The Cambridge History of American Music*, ed. David Nicholls (Cambridge, 1998), p. 328).
6 Richard Rodgers, *Musical Stages: An Autobiography* (New York, 1995), p. 88.
7 Graham Wood, 'The Development of Song Forms in the Broadway and Hollywood Musicals of Richard Rodgers, 1919–1943', Ph.D. diss., University of Minnesota (2000), chapter 2.
8 Rodgers, *Musical Stages*, p. 80.
9 *Ibid.*, p. 45.
10 Philip Furia, *Poets of Tin Pan Alley: A History of America's Great Lyricists* (New York, 1990), p. 126.
11 John Clum, *Something for the Boys: Musical Theater and Gay Culture* (New York, 1999).
12 *Green Book Magazine*, February 1915. Quoted in L. Bergreen, *As Thousands Cheer: The Life of Irving Berlin* (New York, 1990), p. 57.
13 B. Sobel, 'Cole Porter Admits It Gladly: He Uses a Rhyming Dictionary', *New York Herald Tribune*, 20 December 1936; also quoted in David Ewen, *The Cole Porter Story* (New York, 1965), p. 114.
14 In the last years of his career with Hart, Rodgers was responsible for the opening of 'Too Many Girls' and an unidentified number of Hart's verses. After Hammerstein's death Rodgers wrote several new lyrics as well as the music for the remake of *State Fair* and the film version of *The Sound of Music*. He also successfully composed both lyrics and music for an entire show, *No Strings*.
15 Rodgers, *Musical Stages*, pp. 101 and 103.
16 For a detailed analysis of 'My Heart Stood Still' see Allen Forte, *The American Popular Ballad of the Golden Era: 1924–1950* (Princeton, 1995), pp. 82–8.
17 'Cleverest of Our Lyricists Are Seldom Big Hit Writers', *New York Herald Tribune*,

31 May 1925. Quoted without attribution in David Ewen, *Richard Rodgers* (New York, 1957), p. 119. See also Meryl Secrest, *Somewhere For Me: A Biography of Richard Rodgers* (New York, 2001), pp. 35–6.

18 In the film short *The Makers of Melody* (1929), Rodgers and Hart re-enact the compositional process that led to 'Here In My Arms' and other songs. The Paramount film is now available in a collection entitled *Jazz Cocktails* (Kino International, 1997). See Frederick Nolan, *Lorenz Hart* (New York, 1994), pp. 127–8.

19 Ira Gershwin, *Lyrics on Several Occasions* (New York, 1959), pp. 172–4; Edward Jablonski, *George Gershwin: A Biography* (New York, 1987), pp. 83–4.

20 Banfield, 'Popular Song', p. 315; *Sondheim's Broadway Musicals* (Ann Arbor, Michigan, 1993), pp. 107–21; and 'Sondheim and the Art That Has No Name', in *Approaches to the American Musical*, ed. R. Lawson-Peebles (Exeter, 1996), pp. 137–60.

21 According to Mordden, no fewer than fifteen (*recte* sixteen – he does not include *The Girl Friend*) of the twenty-six Broadway musicals exported to London were musical comedies. *Sally, The Blue Kitten, Lady, Be Good!, No, No, Nanette, Sunny, Tip-Toes, The Girl Friend, Oh, Kay!, Peggy-Ann, Hit the Deck, Good News!, A Connecticut Yankee, Funny Face, Hold Everything!, Heads Up!.* No musical comedies travelled in the other direction (Ethan Mordden, *Make Believe: The Broadway Musical in the 1920s* (New York and Oxford, 1997), p. 146). The only 1930s musical comedies to appear contemporaneously in London were *Gay Divorce, Anything Goes,* and *On Your Toes; DuBarry Was a Lady* arrived in 1942 and *The Boys from Syracuse* in 1963 (Stanley Green, *Broadway Musicals of the 1930s* (New York, 1971), p. 368).

22 Published musical comedy librettos: *I'd Rather Be Right, Johnny Johnson, Knickerbocker Holiday, Let' Em Eat Cake,* and *Of Thee I Sing;* published musical comedy scores: *Anything Goes, Babes in Arms, The Boys from Syracuse, Girl Crazy, Johnny Johnson, Knickerbocker Holiday, Of Thee I Sing, Red, Hot and Blue!, Roberta,* and *Strike Up the Band.* See Green, *Broadway Musicals of the 1930s,* pp. 372–3.

23 Allen L. Woll, *Black Musical Theater: From 'Coontown' to 'Dreamgirls'* (Baton Rouge, Louisiana, 1989), pp. 58–75. 'An archival re-creation of the 1921 production featuring members of the original cast' is available on New World Records 260 (1976) with notes by Robert Kimball. See also Robert Kimball and William Bolcom, *Reminiscing with Sissle and Blake* (New York, 1973).

24 Roy Hemming, *The Melody Lingers On: The Great Songwriters and Their Movie Musicals* (New York, 1986), pp. 113–15.

25 Notes to *Good News!*. Jay Productions Ltd. CDJay 1291 (1996), n. p.

26 In the 1963 off-Broadway revival *The Boys from Syracuse* all that was added to George Abbott's original book was a long list of excruciating jokes (Geoffrey Block, *Yale Broadway Masters: Richard Rodgers* (New Haven, forthcoming 2003)).

27 Block, *Enchanted Evenings*, pp. 41–59.

28 G. S. Kaufman, *The Cocoanuts*, in *By George: A Kaufman Collection*, comp. and ed. Donald Oliver (New York, 1979), pp. 202–58.

29 Among the *Babes in Arms* songs not included in the film are 'I Wish I Were in Love Again', 'My Funny Valentine', 'Johnny One-Note', 'Imagine' and 'The Lady Is a Tramp'.

30 Gerald Bordman, *Jerome Kern: His Life and Music* (New York, 1980), pp. 335–43; Arlene Croce, *The Fred Astaire and Ginger Rogers Book* (New York, 1972), pp. 44–53; Hemming, *The Melody Lingers On*, pp. 93–5.

31 *Anything Goes*, John McGlinn, conductor, EMI/Angel CDC 7-49848-2 (1989).

32 Tommy Krasker and Robert Kimball, *Catalog of the American Musical* (Washington DC, 1988), pp. 184–90; Tommy Krasker, notes to *Fifty Million Frenchmen*, New World Records 80417-2 (1991), pp. 11–17.

33 Tommy Krasker, 'It's Been Fun, But I Gotta Rumrun', notes to *Oh, Kay!*, Nonesuch 79361-2 (1995), pp. 19–23.

34 Leonard Bernstein, 'American Musical Comedy', in *The Joy of Music* (New York, 1959), p. 169. The lecture was originally telecast on 7 October 1956 for the *Omnibus* series.

35 Wayne Shirley also notices the loss of meaning that resulted from the relocation of 'Someone to Watch Over Me' to the second act, but views this as a positive dramatic change (Wayne Shirley, notes to *Oh, Kay!*, Smithsonian American Musical Theater Series, RCA Special Products (1978), n. p.).

36 Tommy Krasker, '*Pardon My English*: A Tale of Two Psyches', notes to *Pardon My English*, Elektra Nonesuch 79338-2 (1994), pp. 11–16.

6 'We said we wouldn't look back': British musical theatre, 1935–1960

1 For a brief narrative of the major British shows, their creators and performers see Andrew Lamb, *150 Years of Popular Musical Theatre* (New Haven, 2000).

2 For a study of Mayerl's significance more widely to British popular music see Peter

Dickinson, *Marigold: the Music of Billy Mayerl* (Oxford, 1999).

3 For a historical placing and explanation of the meaning of the monarchy to British society in this period see David Cannadine, 'The Context, Performing and Meaning of Ritual: the British Monarchy and the "Invention of Tradition", c1820–1977', in *The Invention of Tradition*, ed. Eric Hobsbawm and Thomas Ranger (Cambridge, 1983), pp. 101–64, esp. pp. 139–55; and Tom Nairn, 'Britain's Royal Romance', in *Patriotism: the Making and Unmaking of British National Identity*, vol. III: *National Fictions*, ed. Raphael Samuel (London, 1989), pp. 77–86.

4 For a thorough examination of the effects of rationing on Britain see Ina Zweiniger-Bargielowska, *Austerity in Britain: Rationing, Controls and Consumption 1939–55* (Oxford, 2000).

5 For Neagle's association with the role of Queen Victoria on film see Marcia Landy, *British Genres: Cinema and Society 1930–1960* (Princeton, 1991), pp. 68–9 and Jeffrey Richards, *The Age of the Dream Palace: Cinema and Society in Britain 1930–39* (London, 1984), pp. 116–17. For a brief assessment of the importance of Neagle in British film as a performing embodiment of the best of British womanhood (and hence as an appropriate candidate for the portrayal of royalty) see Jeffrey Richards, *Films and British National Identity: From Dickens to Dad's Army* (Manchester, 1997), p. 132.

6 British Library: Lord Chamberlain's Correspondence file (7 July 1953), report of visiting inspector R. J. Hill, 28 January 1954. (The apparent discrepancy in dates is due to the fact that each Lord Chamberlain's Correspondence file is dated from the issuing of the licence for performance. After a show had received its licence and opened, there was usually little additional correspondence; in this particular case, however, extra correspondence was occasioned by a complaint from a member of the public which thus had to be investigated.) Hill begins his report by stating that 'the entire theme is promiscuity, euphemized as "having fun" . . . [T]he theme as developed in dialogue is passable, but when translated into action occasionally goes a long way past the preliminaries of intercourse that ought to be acceptable for public presentation.' After a lengthy and remarkably detailed description of various actions and positions of the cast, Hill concludes 'that if anything could reconcile me to a life in Moscow, it would be

the prospect of an alternative life at "Camp Karefree" '.

7 The effects of censorship by the Lord Chamberlain's Office on musicals in particular has received little attention. For a general background to its effects on theatre in Britain in the twentieth century see Nicholas de Jongh, *Politics, Prudery and Perversions: The Censoring of the English Stage 1901–1968* (London, 2000).

8 Vivian Ellis, 'Give Us a Chance', *Plays and Players* (January 1956), p. 17.

7 The coming of the musical play: Rodgers and Hammerstein

1 William G. Hyland, *Richard Rodgers* (New Haven and London, 1998), p. 104; Hugh Fordin, *Getting to Know Him: A Biography of Oscar Hammerstein II* (New York, 1977, 1995), p. 138.

2 H. Wiley Hitchcock and Stanley Sadie (eds.), *New Grove Dictionary of American Music*, vol. II, s.v. 'Hammerstein, Oscar I'.

3 *Ibid.*, s.v. 'Hammerstein, Oscar II'.

4 Stanley Green (ed.), *The Rodgers and Hammerstein Fact Book* (New York, 1980), p. 502.

5 Fordin, *Getting to Know Him*, pp. 199–200.

6 For further information about various productions, tours, revivals and excerpts of reviews, see Green (ed.), *The Rodgers and Hammerstein Fact Book*; Fordin, *Getting to Know Him*, p. 202; and Richard Rodgers, *Musical Stages: An Autobiography* (New York, 1975; repr. with an introduction by Mary Rodgers, New York, 1995), p. 228.

7 Richard Rodgers and Oscar Hammerstein II, *Six Plays by Rodgers and Hammerstein* (New York, n.d.), p. 7.

8 For further discussion about the play and its Broadway run, see Hyland, *Richard Rodgers*, pp. 139–40.

9 Fordin, *Getting to Know Him*, p. 200.

10 See Geoffrey Block, *Enchanted Evenings: The Broadway Musical from 'Show Boat' to Sondheim* (New York and Oxford, 1997), pp. ix–x.

11 Philip Furia, *The Poets of Tin Pan Alley: A History of America's Great Lyricists* (London and New York, 1990), p. 181.

12 Ethan Mordden, *Rodgers and Hammerstein* (New York, 1992), p. 34.

13 Rodgers, *Musical Stages*, p. 238.

14 For a lengthy discussion of the complexity of 'The Carousel Waltz' as source material for songs in *Carousel*, see Joseph Swain, *The Broadway Musical: A Critical and Musical Survey* (New York and London, 1990), pp. 99–114.

15 Block, *Enchanted Evenings*, pp. 162–3.

16 Fordin, *Getting to Know Him*, p. 255.

17 Thomas Hischak, *Word Crazy: Broadway Lyricists from Cohan to Sondheim* (New York, 1991), p. 37.
18 Fordin, *Getting to Know Him*, p. 258.
19 *Ibid.*, p. 281.
20 Hischak, *Word Crazy*, p. 42.
21 Fordin, *Getting to Know Him*, p. 126.

8 The successors of Rodgers and Hammerstein from the 1940s to the 1960s

1 i.e. singing, dancing and acting.
2 Gerald Bordman, *American Musical Theatre: A Chronicle*, 3rd edn (New York and Oxford, 2001), p. 597.
3 Edward Jablonski, *Alan Jay Lerner: A Biography* (New York, 1996), p. 32.
4 Bordman, *American Musical Theatre*, p. 620.
5 Jablonski, *Alan Jay Lerner*, pp. 82–4.
6 *Ibid.*, pp. 101–2.
7 Alan Jay Lerner, *The Street Where I Live* (New York, 1978), pp. 43–4.
8 *Ibid.*, pp. 66–7.
9 *Ibid.*, p. 142.
10 Stanley Green, *Broadway Musicals Show by Show*, 5th edn, rev. Kay Green (Milwaukee, 1996), p. 168.
11 Bordman, *American Musical Theatre*, p. 661.
12 For more information about Arlen and his works, see Edward Jablonski, *Harold Arlen: Rhythm, Rainbows, and Blues* (Boston, 1996).
13 Lehman Engel, *The American Musical: A Consideration* (New York, 1967), pp. 76–9.
14 H. Wiley Hitchcock and Stanley Sadie (eds.), *The New Grove Dictionary of American Music*, vol. I, *s.v.* 'Bock, Jerry'.
15 Bordman, *American Musical Theatre*, p. 693.
16 Joseph P. Swain, *The Broadway Musical: A Musical and Critical Survey* (New York, 1990), p. 260.
17 For more details on the film and its background, see Tim Robbins, *Cradle Will Rock: The Movie and the Moment* (New York, 2000).
18 Punjab appears only in the film, and not the stage musical.
19 *Pearl Harbor* officially opened on 25 May, nearly two months after the broadcast of *South Pacific*. However, in March, trailers for *Pearl Harbor* and publicity for the film were widespread.

9 Musical sophistication on Broadway: Kurt Weill and Leonard Bernstein

1 Quoted in David Farneth (comp. and ed.), *Lenya the Legend: A Pictorial Autobiography* (Woodstock, New York and London, 1998), p. 130.
2 Kim H. Kowalke, '*The Threepenny Opera* in America', in *Kurt Weill: The Threepenny Opera*, ed. Stephen Hinton (Cambridge, 1990), p. 79.
3 Lotte Lenya interview with David Beams, 15 and 28 February 1962, transcript of audiotape in the Weill–Lenya Research Center, New York, quoted in Farneth, *Lenya the Legend*, p. 219.
4 Benjamin Welles, 'Lyricist of "The Saga of Jenny" et al.: A History of the Life and Some of the Works of Ira Gershwin', *New York Times*, 25 May 1941.
5 Paul Green, unpublished interview with Rhoda Wynn quoted in Larry L. Lash, 'Kurt Weill's Broadway Debut', liner notes for *Music for Johnny Johnson*, The Otaré Pit Band/Joel Cohen. Erato 0630-17870-2.
6 *New York Telegraph*, 4 December 1936. Quoted in Lash, 'Kurt Weill's Broadway Debut'.
7 Kurt Weill, 'Two Dreams-Come-True', undated (c. 1947), unpublished, and unpaginated essay, Box 68, folder 16, Weill/Lenya Archive, Beinecke Rare Book and Manuscript Library, Yale University.
8 *Life Magazine*, 25 October 1943.
9 Brooks Atkinson, 'Walter Huston in Maxwell Anderson's Musical Comedy, "Knickerbocker Holiday"', *New York Times*, 21 October 1938.
10 bruce d. mcclung, '*Psicosi per musica*: Re-examining *Lady in the Dark*', in *A Stranger Here Myself: Kurt Weill Studien*, ed. Horst Edler and Kim H. Kowalke (Hildesheim, 1993), pp. 235–65.
11 Brooks Atkinson, 'Struck By Stage Lightning: Comments on the Theater Wonders of *Lady in the Dark* with Special Reference to Kurt Weill and Gertrude Lawrence', *New York Times*, 7 September 1941.
12 Typescript letter dated 3 April 1944 from Kurt Weill to Ira Gershwin, Gershwin Collection, Library of Congress.
13 The renaissance included a new incarnation of Johann Strauss's *Die Fledermaus*, renamed *Rosalinda* (1942), a modern version of Offenbach's *La Belle Hélène* retitled *Helen Goes to Troy* (1944), and a romanticised stage biography of Edvard Grieg entitled *Song of Norway* (1944).
14 Weill, 'Two Dreams-Come-True'.
15 Kurt Weill, 'Score for a Play', *New York Times*, 5 January 1947.
16 *Ibid.*
17 Olin Downes, 'Opera on Broadway: Kurt Weill Takes Forward Step in Setting Idiomatic American to Music', *New York Times*, 26 January 1947.
18 Alan Jay Lerner, 'Lerner's Life and *Love Life*', *P.M.*, 14 November 1948.
19 Typescript letter dated 14 November [*recte* December] 1949 from Kurt Weill to Olin Downes, Weill/Lenya Archive, Yale University,

partially reprinted in David Farneth, with Elmar Juchem and Dave Stein, *Kurt Weill: A Life in Pictures and Documents* (Woodstock, New York and London, 2000), p. 268.

20 Virgil Thomson, 'Kurt Weill', *New York Herald Tribune*, 9 April 1950. After a memorial concert at Town Hall in New York, however, Thomson reversed himself: 'His American work was viable but not striking, thoroughly competent but essentially conformist' ('Kurt Weill Concert', *New York Herald Tribune*, 5 February 1951).

21 'Kurt Weill Dead; Composer, Was 50', *New York Times*, 4 April 1950.

22 Maxwell Anderson, 'Kurt Weill', *Theatre Arts*, December 1950, p. 58.

23 Olin Downes, 'Memorial to Weill: Program Honoring a Man Who Aided U.S. Opera', *New York Times*, 9 July 1950.

24 Denny Martin Flinn, *Musical! A Grand Tour* (New York, 1997), p. 247.

25 See the title page of the accompanying booklet for the compact disc *On the Town* conducted by Michael Tilson Thomas, Deutsche Grammophon 437 516-2, 1993.

26 Joan Peyser, *Bernstein: A Biography* (New York, 1987), p. 213.

27 Olin Downes, 'Wonderful Time: Bernstein's Musical Is Brilliant Achievement', *New York Times*, 10 May 1953.

28 Peyser, *Bernstein: A Biography*, p. 248.

29 Tyrone Guthrie, *A Life in the Theatre* (New York, Toronto and London, 1959), pp. 240–1.

30 See Geoffrey Block's essay on *West Side Story* in *Enchanted Evenings: The Broadway Musical from 'Show Boat' to Sondheim* (New York and Oxford, 1997), pp. 245–73.

31 Humphrey Burton, *Leonard Bernstein* (New York, 1994), pp. 343–7.

32 Ibid., pp. 374, 379.

33 Deutsche Grammophon 289 463 448-2, 2000.

10 Stephen Sondheim and the musical of the outsider

1 Frank Rich, 'Conversations with Stephen Sondheim', *The New York Times Magazine* (12 March 2000), p. 41.

2 *Ibid.*

3 *Ibid.*, p. 60.

4 *Ibid.*

5 Steven Robert Swayne, 'Hearing Sondheim's Voices', Ph.D. diss., University of California, Berkeley (1999), p. 27.

6 *Ibid.*

7 Joanne Gordon, *Art Isn't Easy: The Achievement of Stephen Sondheim* (Carbondale, Illinois, 1990), p. 7.

8 *Ibid.*

9 Stephen Banfield, *Sondheim's Broadway Musicals* (Ann Arbor, Michigan, 1993), p. 152.

10 Sondheim's first show as both composer and lyricist to open on Broadway was *A Funny Thing Happened on the Way to the Forum* (1962). An earlier effort, *Saturday Night*, was slated for a production in late 1955 or early 1956, but the death of the producer, Lemuel Ayers, resulted in the cancellation of the production. *Saturday Night* finally received a New York production in February 2000.

11 Craig Zadan, *Sondheim and Co.*, 2nd edn (New York, 1989), p. 82.

12 *Ibid.*, p. 88.

13 Harold Prince, *Contradictions: Notes on Twenty-Six Years in the Theatre* (New York, 1974), p. 158.

14 Gordon, *Art Isn't Easy*, p. 78.

15 The discussion of *Assassins* is drawn from two papers by the author. The first, 'Sondheim, Sousa, and the Electric Chair', was presented at the 1997 national conference of the Sonneck Society for American Music. The second, 'Propelling the Plotless Musical: The Sondheim Solution', was presented at the 2000 national conference of the Society for American Music. Similar observations and analyses, at the time unknown to the author, were made concurrently by Steven R. Swayne in his 1999 doctoral dissertation at the University of California, Berkeley.

16 Banfield, *Sondheim's Broadway Musicals*, p. 56.

17 The large acoustical 'shell' placed behind ensembles such as bands, orchestras or choruses when they perform outdoors.

18 'Transition', *Newsweek*, 1 (25 March 1933), p. 19.

19 Patrick Donovan, *The Assassins* (New York, 1955), p. 60.

20 *Ibid.*, p. 61.

21 See Sondheim's comments on harmony in Swayne, 'Hearing Sondheim's Voices', pp. 345–6.

22 Sondheim has often recounted the story of Sheldon Harnick's criticism of the lyrics to 'I Feel Pretty' from *West Side Story*. The inner rhymes, such as 'It's alarming how charming I feel', were too sophisticated for Maria, Harnick informed Sondheim. When Sondheim simplified them, however, they were rejected, and so 'there it is to this day embarrassing me every time it's sung' (Zadan, *Sondheim and Co.*, p. 22).

11 Choreographers, directors and the fully integrated musical

1 See Ethan Mordden, *Broadway Babies: The People Who Made the Broadway Musical* (New York and Oxford, 1983), pp. 12–13.

2 Hugh Fordin, *Getting to Know Him* (New York, 1995), p. 62.

3 Marian Monta Smith, 'Six Miles to Dawn: An Analysis of the Modern American Musical Comedy', Ph.D. diss., Cornell University (1971), p. 105.

4 Mordden, *Broadway Babies*, p. 133.

5 George Abbott, *'Mister Abbott'* (New York, 1963), pp. 177–8.

6 Smith, 'Six Miles to Dawn', p. 105.

7 Mordden, *Broadway Babies*, p. 133.

8 See Max Wilk, *The Story of 'Oklahoma'* (New York, 1993), pp. 127ff.

9 Smith, 'Six Miles to Dawn', p. 106.

10 Martin Gottfried, *Broadway Musicals* (New York, 1984), p. 112.

11 Sono Osato, *Distant Dances* (New York, 1980), pp. 230–47.

12 For a good overview of Robbins's career, see Gottfried, *Broadway Musicals*, pp. 101–9.

13 Abbott, *'Mister Abbott'*, p. 227.

14 For a good overview on the making of *West Side Story*, see Keith Garebian, *The Making of 'West Side Story'* (Toronto, 1995).

15 Materials on *West Side Story*'s conception exist in several archives. The folder of notes, draft scripts and draft lyrics for *West Side Story* in the Bernstein Collection at the Library of Congress is a treasure trove concerning the show's creation, but many documents are undated. Additional papers, considered by Stephen Banfield, exist in the Stephen Sondheim Papers at the Wisconsin State Historical Society. (See Stephen Banfield, *Sondheim's Broadway Musicals* (Ann Arbor, Michigan, 1993), pp. 31–8.) What seems an early outline and synopsis in the Bernstein Collection bears the title *Gang Bang* ('working title!') and dates from when the conflict was between Jews and Italians.

Most characters still carry their Shakespearean names and adults play a larger role in the story than in the final version. For example, in Act II, scene II, the boy's family sits down to their *seder*, but are interrupted by police with news of the death of 'Barnard'. No similar scene occurs in the final version. Bernstein's notes on *West Side Story* concerning the auditions, casting, and orchestra are found in Folder 75/5 of the Bernstein Collection at the Music Division of the Library of Congress. (For an overview of the Bernstein Collection at the Library of Congress, see Paul R. Laird, *Leonard Bernstein: A Guide to Research* (New York, 2002), pp. 230–42, and the collections website at the Library of Congress, http://memory.loc.gov/ammem/lbhtml/lbhome.html.)

The folder includes a letter of 18 October 1955 from Jerome Robbins to Bernstein and Arthur Laurents with reactions to a detailed outline they had sent. Robbins argues for two acts instead of three, objects to the description of Anita as an older and wiser, blues-singing second female lead, and insists that the audience must believe tragedy can be averted until the final moment. He states that the principals, except for the romantic leads, must be dancers. Along with this letter is the six-page synopsis to which Robbins reacts. There are other draft synopses and outlines as well. Another fascinating early document on the show in Bernstein's hand lists two acts and fifteen scenes and a short synopsis of the action in each.

16 William Westbrook Burton, *Conversations About Bernstein* (New York and Oxford, 1995), p. 171.

17 Mordden, *Broadway Babies*, p. 137.

18 Burton, *Conversations About Bernstein*, p. 179.

19 For an excellent consideration of the music of *West Side Story*, see Geoffrey Block, *Enchanted Evenings: The Broadway Musical from 'Show Boat' to Sondheim* (New York and Oxford, 1997), pp. 245–73.

20 For a good overview of Fosse's career, see Gottfried, *Broadway Musicals*, pp. 111–23.

21 Christine Colby Jacques, 'Bob Fosse' (unpublished paper), p. 6.

22 For more material on Hal Prince's Broadway career, see his autobiography, *Contradictions: Notes on Twenty-six Years in the Theatre* (New York, 1974), and Gottfried, *Broadway Musicals*, pp. 126–31.

23 Ken Mandelbaum, *A Chorus Line and the Musicals of Michael Bennett* (New York, 1989), p. 43.

24 *Ibid.*

25 *Ibid.*, p. 53.

26 Quoted in *ibid.*, p. 72.

27 *Ibid.*, pp. 93ff.

28 Two other fine sources on the making of *A Chorus Line* include: Denny Martin Flinn, *What They Did for Love: The Untold Story Behind the Making of 'A Chorus Line'* (New York, 1989); Robert Viagas, Baayork Lee, Thommie Walsh with the entire original cast, *On The Line: The Creation of 'A Chorus Line'* (New York, 1990).

29 Mandelbaum, *A Chorus Line and the Musicals of Michael Bennett*, p. 127.

30 Gottfried, *Broadway Musicals*, p. 35.

31 *Ibid.*, p. 36.

32 Mandelbaum, *A Chorus Line and the Musicals of Michael Bennett*, p. 164.

12 Distant cousin or fraternal twin? Analytical approaches to the film musical

I would like to thank the members of my graduate seminar on musical theatre and film

at the University of Minnesota in spring 2000
for providing me with inspiration and many
fruitful discussions relating to all aspects of
this repertoire: Meghan Allen, Enid Atkinson,
Alex Berglund, Beth Brandt, Phil Brown,
Stephen Carlson, Beth Denker, Gina Goettl,
Sara Keller, Ann Houck, Noë McKenna and
Lori-Anne Williams. I would also like to
thank Professors Phil Furia and Karal Ann
Marling for teaching me how to see and hear
musicals, Professor Geoffrey Block for his
encouragement and trust, and my colleagues
Preston Marx, Shawn Rowan, Sarah
Schmalenberger, Douglas Stetz and Jonas
Westover for invaluable additional comments.
1 If one can see beyond the political
incorrectness and scatological language of
South Park: Bigger, Longer and Uncut (1999),
this recent addition to the animated musical
catalogue is a brilliant pastiche of the entire
genre of musical theatre and film. Every song
is a parody of a particular musical and visual
style – from the *Oklahoma!*-style opening to
the monstrously over-the-top reprise-finale.
The deliberately crude animation style
(anti-Disney?), coupled with a highly
polished orchestral score, creates a visual and
musical disjunction that is both delightfully
horrifying and intoxicating.
2 Richard Fehr and Frederick G. Vogel,
*Lullabies of Hollywood: Movie Music and the
Movie Musical, 1915–1992* (Jefferson, North
Carolina, 1993), p. 48.
3 Gerald Mast, *Can't Help Singin': The
American Musical On Stage and Screen*
(New York, 1987), p. 2.
4 When two dates are listed, the first refers
the date of the original stage production, the
second to the movie version.
5 Mast, *Can't Help Singin'*, pp. 313, 309.
6 Geoffrey Block, *Enchanted Evenings: The
Broadway Musical from 'Show Boat' to Sondheim*
(New York and Oxford, 1997), p. 254.
7 See Mast, *Can't Help Singin'*, pp. 36–7 and
David Schiff, *Gershwin: 'Rhapsody in Blue'*
(Cambridge, 1997), pp. 94–100.
8 See John M. Clum, *Something For the Boys:
Musical Theater and Gay Culture* (New York,
1999), pp. 1–26. See also D. A. Miller, *Place for
Us* (Cambridge, Massachusetts, 1998).
9 See Richard Dyer, *Heavenly Bodies: Film Stars
and Society* (Basingstoke, 1986).
10 See Mast, *Can't Help Singin'*, pp. 37–8.
11 Fehr and Vogel, *Lullabies of Hollywood*,
p. 101.
12 See Jane Feuer, *The Hollywood Musical*, 2nd
edn (Bloomington, 1993), chapter 4: 'Dream
Worlds and Dream Stages'.
13 For a more detailed examination of the use
of these elements of songs for expressive and

dramatic purposes see Graham Wood, 'The
Development of Song Forms in the Broadway
and Hollywood Musicals of Richard Rodgers,
1919–1943', Ph.D. diss., University of
Minnesota (2000).
14 See Leonard Maltin, *The Disney Films*
(New York, 2000).
15 See, also, Jeffrey Magee, 'Irving Berlin's
"Blue Skies": Ethnic Affiliations and Musical
Transformations', *Musical Quarterly*, 84
(2000), pp. 537–80.
16 Miles Krueger, *Show Boat: The Story of a
Classic American Musical* (New York, 1977),
p. 117.
17 See Philip Furia, *The Poets of Tin Pan Alley:
A History of America's Great Lyricists* (New York,
1990), *Ira Gershwin: The Art of the Lyricist*
(New York, 1996) and *Irving Berlin: A Life in
Song* (New York, 1998). See also Stephen
Banfield, 'Sondheim and the Art That Has No
Name', in *Approaches to the American Musical*,
ed. Robert Lawson-Peebles (Exeter, 1996),
pp. 137–60.

**13 From *Hair* to *Rent*: is 'rock' a four-letter
word on Broadway?**

1 See, for example, Gerald Bordman,
American Musical Theatre: A Chronicle, 2nd
edn (New York and Oxford, 1992), p. 643;
Denny Martin Flinn, *Musical! A Grand Tour:
The Rise, Glory, and Fall of an American
Institution* (New York, 1997), chapter 18:
'The Rock Musical', pp. 315–22; and Mark
Steyn, *Broadway Babies Say Goodnight:
Musicals Then and Now* (New York, 1999),
pp. 213–27.
2 In describing the various strains of
popular music of the 1950s, 1960s and later
years, the term 'rock 'n' roll' identifies musical
styles that emerged in the 1950s out of the
American South, while 'rock' refers to the
modified pop styles that appeared in
the early 1960s and carry through to the
present. See H. Wiley Hitchcock and Stanley
Sadie (eds.), *The New Grove Dictionary of
American Music*, vol. IV, *s.v.* 'Rock, I. Rock and
Roll'.
3 Stanley Richards, *Great Rock Musicals*
(New York: Stein and Day, 1979).
4 For the definitive study of *Hair*, see Barbara
Lee Horn, *The Age of Hair: Evolution and Impact
of Broadway's First Rock Musical*, Contributions
in Drama and Theater Studies 42 (New York
and Westport, Connecticut, 1991).
5 The 1977 revival of *Hair*, ten years after its
premiere and just five years after the original
run closed, was panned as a period piece
whose time had passed. See Steven Suskin,
More Opening Nights on Broadway (New York,
1997), pp. 386–90.

6 Lewis Funke, 'News of the Rialto: Will B'way Rock?', *New York Times*, 10 December 1967, noted rock's appearance in several off-Broadway productions and the inevitability of its move 'north' to Broadway.

7 See the reviews of the original off-Broadway concert, *New York Times*, 13 March 1969, and of the Broadway production, *New York Times*, 25 September 1969.

8 Judy Klemesrud, 'She was the Perfect Grandmother for the Rock Musical Part', *New York Times*, 27 April 1971, and Clive Barnes's review, *New York Times*, 6 May 1971.

9 See the reviews of *Soon*, *New York Times*, 13 January 1971, and *Hard Job Being God*, *New York Times*, 18 May 1972.

10 *New York Times*, 2 December 1971.

11 Selected reviews in Suskin, *More Opening Nights on Broadway*, pp. 257–62, 949–53.

12 *New York Times*, 27 January 1970.

13 Selected reviews in Suskin, *More Opening Nights on Broadway*, pp. 325–9.

14 See Alan Hewitt, 'Why Can't Today's Actors Sing Out?', *New York Times*, 18 January 1970, for a description of the sound system used for *Promises, Promises* and for general commentary on the increasing use of amplification in Broadway musicals.

15 Even though its creators never labelled *Godspell* a 'rock musical', many critics clearly thought it was one, and the show's producers seemed willing to exploit this dichotomy. See, for instance, the display advertisement in the Sunday *New York Times*, 30 May 1971. About a quarter of the twenty-five quotations from various reviewers, which were undoubtedly chosen by the producers, specifically used the word 'rock' to describe *Godspell*'s music.

16 Selected reviews in Suskin, *More Opening Nights on Broadway*, pp. 334–7. *Godspell*'s Broadway run added 557 performances to make a grand total of 2,651.

17 For background on this new rock style and a descriptive analysis of one progressive rock classic, see John Covach, 'Progressive Rock, "Close to the Edge", and the Boundaries of Style', in John Covach and Graeme M. Boone, *Understanding Rock: Essays in Musical Analysis* (New York, 1997), pp. 3–32.

18 Louis Calta, 'Beset Queens Playhouse Shifts to Rock Musical', *New York Times*, 16 September 1974; review of the initial off-Broadway production, *New York Times*, 20 September 1974; 'Opening This Week' and display advertisement, *New York Times*, 9 March 1975; and 'Arts and Leisure Guide', *New York Times*, 16 March 1975.

19 Display advertisement for *The Wiz*, *New York Times*, 12 January 1975.

20 *New York Times*, 10 March 1978.

21 Quoted in Suskin, *More Opening Nights on Broadway*, p. 260; original review in *New York Times*, 22 October 1972.

22 See the reviews of the following productions, all of which were billed as 'rock musicals': *Soon* (*New York Times*, 13 January 1971); *Rockabye Hamlet* (*New York Times*, 18 February 1976); *Marlowe* (*New York Times*, 13 October 1981); *The News* (*New York Times*, 8 November 1985); *Platinum* (*New York Times*, 13 November 1978); and *Fallen Angels* (*New York Times*, 16 April 1994).

23 *New York Times*, 29 April 1988.

24 Because of significant differences between the London and Broadway versions of *Chess*, many individual numbers have different titles and lyrics, depending upon which recordings one consults. A number of websites have appeared, many of which contain guides to the multiple productions, the songs and their lyrics. See http://www.calpoly.edu/~bmarx/chess/chess_i.html for a representative site.

25 See Jon Pareles, 'Can Rock Play to the Broadway Crowd?', *New York Times*, 28 April 1996.

26 See *New York Times*, 24 September 1995 and 10 November 1995, for information on the album's planned release and a review. See Ben Brantley, 'Two Takes on the Devil: The Charms of the Seedy Give Way to Sunday Best', *New York Times*, 26 October 1996, for a review of the Chicago performance.

27 Ben Brantley, 'The Lure of Gang Violence to a Latin Beat', *New York Times*, 30 January 1998.

28 See the review in the *New York Times*, 23 April 1993.

29 http://www.mamma-mia.com/.

30 Ben Brantley, 'Broadway Doesn't Live There Anymore', *New York Times*, 7 November 1999.

31 Ben Brantley, 'Rock Opera À la "Bohème" And "Hair"', *New York Times*, 14 February 1996.

32 Anthony Tommasini, 'A Composer's Death Echoes in His Music', *New York Times*, 11 February 1996.

33 Margo Jefferson, '"Rent" is Brilliant and Messy All at Once', *New York Times*, 25 February 1996.

34 Kate Giel, ed., *Rent: Book, Music and Lyrics by Jonathan Larson*, interview and text by Evelyn McDonnell with Katherine Silberger (New York, 1997).

35 Laurel Graeber, 'Family Fare: Suffering and Survival', *New York Times*, 12 March 1999; and Anita Gates, 'Smells Like Teen Spirit,

Or Whatever', *New York Times*, 1 January 2000.

36 A preview article (*New York Times*, 8 March 1987) used the description 'rock opera'; and a review (*New York Times*, 13 March 1987) describes the music in these words: 'Mr. Schoenberg's profligately melodious score, sumptuously orchestrated by John Cameron to straddle the eras of harpsichord and synthesizer, mixes madrigal with rock and evokes composers as diverse as Bizet (for the laborers) and Weill (for their exploiters).'

14 The megamusical and beyond: the creation, internationalisation and impact of a genre
1 For further information on statistics regarding Andrew Lloyd Webber musicals, see www.tiretracks.co.uk/news/news.html.

2 Michael Walsh, *Andrew Lloyd Webber: His Life and Works, A Critical Biography* (New York, 1997), p. 14.

3 Mark Steyn, *Broadway Babies Say Goodnight: Musicals Then and Now* (New York, 1999), p. 286.

4 *Ibid.*, p. 280.

5 *Ibid.*, p. 276.

6 Walsh, *Lloyd Webber*, p. 97.

7 *Ibid.*

8 Steyn, *Broadway Babies*, p. 32.

9 From a booking advertisement for *Starlight Express*.

10 Walsh, *Lloyd Webber*, p. 224.

11 Interview by William A. Everett, 29 September 2000.

12 Terry Teachout, 'A "Musical" That's Really An Opera', *New York Times*, 2 January 2000.

Select bibliography

Allen, Frederick Lewis, *Only Yesterday* (New York, 1931).
  Since Yesterday (New York, 1940).
Alpert, Hollis, *The Life and Times of 'Porgy and Bess': the Story of an American
  Classic* (New York, 1990).
  Broadway!: 125 Years of Musical Theatre (New York, 1991).
Altman, Rick, *The American Film Musical* (Bloomington, 1987).
Aumack, Sheryl, *Song and Dance: An Encylopedia of Musicals* (Newport Beach,
  California, 1990).
Bach, Steven, *Dazzler: The Life and Times of Moss Hart* (New York, 2001).
Bailey, Peter (ed.), *Music Hall: The Business of Pleasure* (Milton Keynes and
  Philadelphia, 1986).
Banfield, Stephen, *Sondheim's Broadway Musicals* (Ann Arbor, Michigan, 1993).
  'Sondheim and the Art that Has No Name', in *Approaches to the American
  Musical*, ed. Robert Lawson-Peebles (Exeter, 1996), pp. 137–60.
  'Popular Song and Popular Music on Stage and Film', in *The Cambridge History
  of American Music*, ed. David Nicholls (Cambridge, 1998), pp. 309–44.
  'Stage and Screen Entertainers in the Twentieth Century', in *The Cambridge
  Companion to Singing*, ed. John Potter (Cambridge, 2000), pp. 63–82.
Barrett, Mary Ellin, *Irving Berlin: A Daughter's Memoir* (New York, 1994).
Barrios, Richard, *A Song in the Dark: The Birth of the Musical Film* (New York,
  1995).
Benjamin, Ruth, and Arthur Rosenblatt, *Movie Song Catalog: Performers and
  Supporting Crew for the Songs Sung in 1460 Musical and Nonmusical Films,
  1928–1988* (Jefferson, North Carolina, 1993).
Bennett, Robert Russell, *'The Broadway Sound': The Autobiography and Selected
  Essays of Robert Russell Bennett*, ed. George J. Ferencz (Rochester, New York,
  1999).
Bergreen, Laurence, *As Thousands Cheer: The Life of Irving Berlin* (New York, 1990).
Bernheim, Alfred L., *The Business of the Theatre: An Economic History of the
  American Theatre, 1750–1932* (New York, 1932).
Bierley, Paul, *The Works of John Philip Sousa* (Columbus, Ohio, 1984).
Block, Geoffrey, 'The Broadway Canon from *Show Boat* to *West Side Story* and the
  European Operatic Ideal', *Journal of Musicology*, 11/4 (1993), pp. 525–44.
  Enchanted Evenings: The Broadway Musical from 'Show Boat' to Sondheim
  (New York and Oxford, 1997).
  The Richard Rodgers Reader (New York and Oxford, 2002).
Bloom, Ken, *Hollywood Song: The Complete Film and Musical Companion*, 3 vols.
  (New York, 1995).
  American Song: The Complete Musical Theatre Companion, 2nd edn, 4 vols. (New
  York, 1996).

Bordman, Gerald, *American Musical Theatre: A Chronicle* (New York, 1978), 2nd edn (New York and Oxford, 1992), 3rd edn (New York and Oxford, 2001).

   Jerome Kern: His Life and Music (New York and Oxford, 1980).

   American Operetta: From 'H. M. S. Pinafore' to 'Sweeney Todd' (New York and Oxford, 1981).

   American Musical Comedy: From 'Adonis' to 'Dreamgirls' (New York and Oxford, 1982).

   Days to Be Happy, Years to Be Sad: The Life and Music of Vincent Youmans (New York and Oxford, 1982).

   American Musical Revue: From 'The Passing Show' to 'Sugar Babies' (New York and Oxford, 1985).

Borroff, Edith, 'Origin of Species: Conflicting Views of American Musical Theater History', *American Music*, 2/4 (1984), pp. 101–11.

Bradley, Edwin M., *The First Hollywood Musicals: A Critical Filmography of 171 Features, 1927 through 1932* (Jefferson, North Carolina, 1996).

Bristow, Eugene K., and J. Kevin Butler, '*Company*, About Face! The Show that Revolutionized the American Musical', *American Music*, 5/3 (1987), pp. 241–54.

Brockett, Oscar G., *History of the Theater*, 4th edn (Boston, 1986).

Brooks, Mel, and Tom Meehan, *The Producers* (New York, 2001).

Brooks, William, 'Good Musical Paste: Getting the Acts Together in the Eighteenth Century', in *Musical Theatre in America: Papers and Proceedings of the Conference on the Musical Theatre in America*, ed. Glenn Loney (Westport, Connecticut, 1984), pp. 37–58.

   '*Pocahontas*, Her Life and Times', *American Music*, 2/4 (1984), pp. 19–48.

Bowers, Dwight Blocker, *American Musical Theater: Shows, Songs, and Stars* (Washington DC, 1989).

Burton, Humphrey, *Leonard Bernstein* (New York, 1994).

Carnovale, Norbert, *George Gershwin: A Bio-Bibliography* (Westport, Connecticut, 2000).

Chevalley, Sylvie, 'La Première Saison théâtrale française de New York', *The French Review*, 24/6 (1951), pp. 471–9.

Citron, Stephen, *The Musical from the Inside Out* (Chicago, 1992).

   Noel and Cole: The Sophisticates (New York and Oxford, 1993).

   The Wordsmiths: Oscar Hammerstein 2nd and Alan Jay Lerner (New York and Oxford, 1995).

   Sondheim and Lloyd-Webber: The New Musical (New York and Oxford, 2001).

Clum, John M., *Something for the Boys: Musical Theater and Gay Culture* (New York, 1999).

Cockrell, Dale, *Demons of Disorder: Early Blackface Minstrels and Their World* (Cambridge, 1997).

   'Nineteenth-Century Popular Music', in *The Cambridge History of American Music*, ed. David Nicholls (Cambridge, 1998), pp. 158–85.

Comden, Betty, *Off Stage* (New York, 1995).

Croce, Arlene, *The Fred Astaire and Ginger Rogers Book* (New York, 1972).

Davis, Lee, *Scandals and Follies: The Rise and Fall of the Great Broadway Revue* (New York, 2000).

Dickinson, Peter, *Marigold: The Music of Billy Mayerl* (Oxford and New York, 1999).

Djedje, Jacqueline Cogdell, 'African American Music to 1900', in *The Cambridge History of American Music*, ed. David Nicholls (Cambridge, 1998), pp. 103–34.

Dyer, Richard, *Heavenly Bodies: Film Stars and Society* (Basingstoke, 1986).

Engel, Lehman, *The American Musical Theatre: A Consideration* (New York, 1967).
Words with Music: The Broadway Musical Libretto (New York, 1972).

Engle, Ron, and Tice C. Miller (eds.), *The American Stage: Social and Economic Issues from the Colonial Period to the Present* (Cambridge, 1993).

Everett, William A., 'Golden Days in Old Heidelberg: The First-act Finale of Romberg's *The Student Prince*', *American Music*, 12/3 (1994), pp. 255–82.
'Sigmund Romberg and the American Operetta of the 1920s', *Arti musices*, 26/1 (1995), pp. 49–64.
'King Arthur in Popular Musical Theatre and Musical Film', in *King Arthur in Music*, ed. Richard W. Barber (Woodbridge and Rochester, New York, 2002).

Ewen, David, *New Complete Book of the American Musical Theater* (New York, 1958), 2nd edn (New York, 1970).

Farneth, David, with Elmar Juchem and Dave Stein, *Kurt Weill: A Life in Pictures and Documents* (Woodstock, New York and London, 2000).

Fehr, Richard, and Frederick G.Vogel, *Lullabies of Hollywood: Movie Music and the Movie Musical, 1915–1992* (Jefferson, North Carolina, 1993).

Feuer, Jane, 'The Theme of Popular vs. Elite Art in the Hollywood Musical', *Journal of Popular Culture*, 12/3 (1978), pp. 491–9.
The Hollywood Musical, 2nd edn (Bloomington, 1993).

Fields, Armond, and L. Marc Fields, *From the Bowery to Broadway: Lew Fields and the Roots of American Popular Theater* (New York and Oxford, 1993).

Finson, Jon W. (ed.), *Edward Harrigan and David Braham: Collected Songs* (Madison, 1997).

Flinn, Denny Martin, *Musical! A Grand Tour* (New York, 1997).

Fordin, Hugh, *Getting to Know Him: A Biography of Oscar Hammerstein II* (New York, 1977, 1995).

Forte, Allen, *The American Popular Ballad of the Golden Era: 1924–1950* (Princeton, 1995).
Listening to Classic American Popular Songs (New Haven and London, 2001).

Furia, Philip, *The Poets of Tin Pan Alley: A History of America's Great Lyricists* (New York and Oxford, 1990).
Ira Gershwin: The Art of the Lyricist (New York, 1996).

Furia, Philip, with the assistance of Graham Wood, songography by Ken Bloom, *Irving Berlin: A Life in Song* (New York, 1998).

Gänzl, Kurt, *The British Musical Theatre*, 2 vols. (London, 1986).
Song and Dance: The Complete Story of Stage Musicals (London, 1995).
The Musical: A Concise History (Boston, 1997).
The Encyclopedia of the Musical Theatre, 2nd edn, 3 vols. (New York, 2000).

Garebian, Keith, *The Making of 'West Side Story'* (Toronto, 1995).

Gershwin, Ira, *Lyrics on Several Occasions* (New York, 1959).

Giel, Kate (ed.), *Rent: Book, Music and Lyrics by Jonathan Larson*, interview and text by Evelyn McDonnell with Katherine Silberger (New York, 1997).

Gilbert, Stephen, *The Music of Gershwin* (New Haven, 1995).

Goldstein, Malcolm, *The Political Stage: American Drama and Theater of the Great Depression* (New York and Oxford, 1974).

George S. Kaufman: His Life, His Theater (New York and Oxford, 1979).

Goodhart, Sandor (ed.), *Reading Stephen Sondheim: A Collection of Critical Essays* (New York, 2000).

Gordon, Eric A., *Mark the Music: The Life and Work of Marc Blitzstein* (New York, 1989).

Gordon, Joanne, *Art Isn't Easy: The Achievement of Stephen Sondheim* (Carbondale, Illinois, 1990).

Art Isn't Easy: The Theatre of Stephen Sondheim (New York, 1992).

Gottfried, Martin, *Broadway Musicals* (New York, 1979).

More Broadway Musicals: Since 1980 (New York, 1991).

Sondheim (New York, 1993).

Graziano, John, 'Sentimental Songs, Rags, and Transformations: The Emergence of the Black Musical, 1895–1910', in *Musical Theatre in America: Papers and Proceedings of the Conference on the Musical Theatre in America*, ed. Glenn Loney (Westport, Connecticut, 1984), pp. 211–32.

'Black Musical Theater and the Harlem Renaissance Movement', in *Black Music in the Harlem Renaissance: A Collection of Essays*, ed. Samuel A. Floyd Jr (Westport, Connecticut, 1990), pp. 87–110.

'The Early Life and Career of the "Black Patti": The Odyssey of an African American Singer in the Late Nineteenth Century', *Journal of the American Musicological Society*, 53/3 (2000), pp. 543–96.

'Vaudeville', in *The New Grove Dictionary of American Music*, ed. H. Wiley Hitchcock and Stanley Sadie.

Green, Stanley, *The Rodgers and Hammerstein Story* (New York, 1963).

Broadway Musicals of the 30s (New York, 1971).

The World of Musical Comedy, 4th edn (London, 1980).

Encyclopedia of the Musical Film (New York, 1981).

Hollywood Musicals Year by Year (Milwaukee, 1990).

Green, Stanley (ed.), *Rodgers and Hammerstein Fact Book* (New York, 1980).

Green, Stanley, rev. and updated by Kay Green, *Broadway Musicals Show by Show*, 5th edn (Milwaukee, 1996).

Grimsted, David, *Melodrama Unveiled: American Theater and Culture, 1800–1850* (Chicago, 1968).

Grubb, Kevin Boyd, *Razzle Dazzle: The Life and Works of Bob Fosse* (New York, 1989).

Hamm, Charles, *Yesterdays: Popular Song in America* (New York, 1979).

'The Theatre Guild Production of *Porgy and Bess*', *Journal of the American Musicological Society*, 40/3 (1987), pp. 495–532.

Irving Berlin: Songs from the Melting Pot: The Formative Years, 1907–1914 (New York and Oxford, 1997).

'Musical Theater, III. The Tin Pan Alley Era', in *The New Grove Dictionary of American Music*, ed. H. Wiley Hitchcock and Stanley Sadie.

Happy Talk: News of the Rodgers and Hammerstein Foundation, 1993–.

Hart, Dorothy, and Robert Kimball (eds.), *The Complete Lyrics of Lorenz Hart* (New York, 1986).

Hemming, Roy, *The Melody Lingers On: The Great Songwriters and Their Movie Musicals* (New York, 1986).

Henderson, Amy, and Dwight Blocker Bowers, *Red Hot and Blue: A Smithsonian Salute to the American Musical* (Washington DC and London, 1986).

Hill, Errol, 'The Hyers Sisters: Pioneers in Black Musical Comedy', in *The American Stage: Social and Economic Issues from the Colonial Period to the Present*, ed. Ron Engle and Tice L. Miller (Cambridge and New York, 1993), pp. 115–30.

Hirsch, Foster, *Hal Prince and the American Musical Theatre* (Cambridge and New York, 1989).

The Boys from Syracuse: The Shuberts' Theatrical Empire (Carbondale, Illinois, 1998).

Kurt Weill on Stage: From Berlin to Broadway (New York, 2002).

Hirschhorn, Clive, *The Hollywood Musical* (New York, 1981).

Hischak, Thomas S., *Say It with Music: An Encylopedic Guide to the American Musical Theatre* (Westport, Connecticut, 1993).

Film It with Music: An Encyclopedic Guide to the American Movie Musical (Westport, Connecticut and London, 2001).

Hitchcock, H. Wiley, 'An Early American Melodrama: *The Indian Princess* of J. N. Barker and John Bray', *MLA Notes*, 12/3 (1955), pp. 375–88.

Hoare, Philip, *Noël Coward: A Biography* (London, 1995).

Hoover, Cynthia Adams, 'Music in Eighteenth-Century American Theater', *American Music*, 2/4 (1984), pp. 6–18.

Horn, Barbara Lee, *The Age of 'Hair': Evolution and Impact of Broadway's First Rock Musical* (New York and Westport, Connecticut, 1991).

Hummel, David. *The Collector's Guide to the American Musical Theatre*, 2nd edn (Grawn, Michigan, 1978).

Hyland, William G., *The Song is Ended: Songwriters and American Music, 1900–1950* (New York and Oxford, 1995).

Richard Rodgers (New Haven, 1998).

Ilson, Carol, *Harold Prince: From 'Pajama Game' to 'Phantom of the Opera'* (Ann Arbor, Michigan, 1989).

Internet Movie Database, http://us.imdb.com

Jablonski, Edward, *Gershwin: A Biography* (New York, 1987).

Harold Arlen: Rhythm, Rainbows, and Blues (Boston, 1996).

Irving Berlin: American Troubadour (New York, 1999).

Jackson, Arthur, *The Best Musicals from 'Show Boat' to 'A Chorus Line': Broadway, Off-Broadway, London* (New York, 1977).

Jessel, George, *A Pictoral History of Vaudeville* (New York, 1961).

Jones, Tom, *Making Musicals: An Informal Introduction to the World of Musical Theatre* (New York, 1998).

Kaplan, Joel H., 'Introduction', in *The Edwardian Theatre: Essays on Performance and the Stage*, ed. Michael R. Booth and Joel H. Kaplan (Cambridge, 1996).

Kaufman, Gerald, *Meet Me in St. Louis* (London, 1994).

Kennedy, Michael Patrick, and John Muir, *Musicals* (Glasgow, 1997).

Kilroy, David Michael, 'Kurt Weill on Broadway: The Postwar Years (1945–1950)',
  Ph.D. diss., Harvard University, 1992.
Kimball, Robert (ed.), *The Complete Lyrics of Cole Porter* (New York, 1984).
  The Complete Lyrics of Ira Gershwin (New York, 1993).
Kislan, Richard, *The Musical: A Look at the American Theater* (Englewood Cliffs,
  New Jersey, 1980).
Kowalke, Kim, '*The Threepenny Opera* in America', in *Kurt Weill: The Threepenny
  Opera*, ed. Stephen Hinton (Cambridge, 1990), pp. 78–120.
  'Formerly German: Kurt Weill in America', in *A Stranger Here Myself: Kurt Weill
  Studien*, ed. Kim Kowalke and Horst Edler (Hildesheim, 1993), pp. 35–57.
  'Kurt Weill, Modernism, and Popular Culture: Öffentlichkeit als Stil',
  Modernism/Modernity, 2/1 (1995), pp. 27–69.
Kowalke, Kim H. (ed.), *A New Orpheus: Essays on Kurt Weill* (New Haven, 1986).
Kowalke, Kim H., and Horst Edler (eds.), *A Stranger Here Myself: Kurt Weill Studien*
  (Hildesheim, 1993).
Krasker, Tommy, *Catalog of the American Musical* (Washington DC, 1988).
  Notes to *Fifty Million Frenchmen*, New World Records 80417-2 (1991),
  pp. 11–17.
  'What Price Cheese?' and 'Two Strikes, Two Hits, and One Man Out', notes to
  Strike Up the Band, Elektra Nonesuch 79273-2 (1991), pp. 17–22 and 37–41.
  'A Wonderful Party: *Lady, Be Good!*', notes to *Lady, Be Good!*, Elektra Nonesuch
  79308-2 (1992), pp. 15–19.
  '*Pardon My English*: A Tale of Two Psyches', notes to *Pardon My English*, Elektra
  Nonesuch 79338-2 (1994), pp. 11–16.
  'It's Been Fun, But I Gotta Rumrun', notes to *Oh, Kay!*, Nonesuch 79361-2
  (1995), pp. 19–23.
Krasner, Orly Leah, 'Reginald de Koven (1859–1920) and American Comic Opera
  at the Turn of the Century', Ph.D. diss., City University of New York, 1995.
  'Wien, Women and Song: *The Merry Widow* in New York', *Sonneck Society
  Bulletin*, 22/1 (1996), pp. 1, 8–11.
Kreuger, Miles, *Show Boat: The Story of a Classic American Musical* (New York and
  Oxford, 1977).
  'Some Words About *Anything Goes*', notes to *Anything Goes*, EMI/Angel CDC
  7-49848-2 (1989), pp. 9–17.
  'Some Words About *Girl Crazy*', notes to *Girl Crazy*, Elektra Nonesuch
  75559-79250-2 (1990), pp. 15–24.
Laird, Paul R., *Leonard Bernstein: A Guide to Research* (New York, 2002).
Lamb, Andrew, *Jerome Kern in Edwardian London* (New York, 1985).
  150 Years of Popular Musical Theatre (New Haven and London, 2000).
Larkin, Colin (ed.), *The Guinness Who's Who of Stage Musicals* (Enfield, 1994).
Laufe, Abe, *Broadway's Greatest Musicals* (New York, 1973).
Lawrence, Greg, *Dance with Demons: The Life of Jerome Robbins* (New York,
  2001).
Lawson-Peebles, Robert (ed.), *Approaches to the American Musical* (Exeter, 1996).
Lee, Joanna, Edward Harsh, and Kim Kowalke (eds.), '*Street Scene*': *A Sourcebook*,
  2nd edn (New York, 1996).

Lerner, Alan Jay, *The Street Where I Live* (New York and London, 1978).
  The Musical Theatre: A Celebration (New York, 1986).
Levine, Lawrence W., *Highbrow/Lowbrow: The Emergence of Cultural Hierarchy in America* (Cambridge, Massachusetts, 1988).
Londré, Felicia Hardison, and Daniel J. Watermeier, *The History of North American Theater: The United States, Canada and Mexico: From Pre-Columbian Times to the Present* (New York and London, 2000).
Loney, Glenn (ed.), *Musical Theatre in America: Papers and Proceedings of the Conference on the Musical Theatre in America* (Westport, Connecticut, 1984).
Lott, Eric, *Love and Theft: Blackface Minstrelsy and the American Working Class* (New York, 1993).
Mahar, William J., *Behind the Burnt Cork Mask: Early Blackface Minstrelsy and Antebellum American Popular Culture* (Urbana, Illinois, 1999).
Maltin, Leonard, *The Disney Films*, 4th edn (New York, 2000).
Mandelbaum, Ken, *Not Since Carrie: 40 Years of Broadway Musical Flops* (New York, 1991).
Marmorstein, Gary, *Hollywood Rhapsody: Movie Music and its Makers, 1900–1975* (New York, 1997).
Mast, Gerald, *Can't Help Singin': The American Musical on Stage and Screen* (Woodstock, New York, 1987).
Mates, Julian, *The American Musical Stage before 1800* (New Brunswick, New Jersey, 1962).
  America's Musical Stage: Two Hundred Years of Musical Theatre (Westport, Connecticut, 1985).
Mayer, David, 'The Music of Melodrama', in *Performance and Politics in Popular Drama*, ed. David Bradby, Louis James and Bernard Sharratt (Cambridge, 1980), pp. 49–63.
Mayer, David, and Matthew Scott (eds.), *Four Bars of 'Agit': Incidental Music for Victorian and Edwardian Melodrama* (London, 1983).
McBrien, William, *Cole Porter: A Biography* (New York, 1998).
McCabe, John, *George M. Cohan: The Man Who Owned Broadway* (Garden City, New York, 1973).
mcclung, bruce d., 'American Dreams: Analyzing Moss Hart, Ira Gershwin, and Kurt Weill's *Lady in the Dark*', Ph.D. diss., University of Rochester, 1995.
  'Life after George: The Genesis of *Lady in the Dark*'s Circus Dream', *Kurt Weill Newsletter*, 14/2 (1996), pp. 4–8.
mcclung, bruce d., Joanna Lee, and Kim Kowalke (eds.), *'Lady in the Dark': A Sourcebook*, 2nd edn (New York, 1997).
McConachie, Bruce A., *Melodramatic Formations: American Theatre and Society, 1820–1870* (Iowa City, 1992).
McGlinn, John, 'The Original *Anything Goes* – A Classic Restored', notes to *Anything Goes*, EMI/Angel CDC 7-49848-2 (1989), pp. 29–34.
  'Finding the Bliss', notes to *Sitting Pretty*, New World Records 80387-2 (1990), pp. 10–16.
McNamara, Brooks, *The Shuberts of Broadway* (New York and Oxford, 1990).

Meyerson, Harold, and Ernie Harburg, *Who Put the Rainbow in 'The Wizard of Oz'?: Yip Harburg, Lyricist* (Ann Arbor, Michigan, 1993).

Miller, Scott, *From 'Assassins' to 'West Side Story': The Director's Guide to Musical Theatre* (Portsmouth, New Hampshire, 1996).

 Deconstructing Harold Hill: An Insider's Guide to Musical Theatre (Portsmouth, New Hampshire, 2000).

 Rebels with Applause: Broadway's Groundbreaking Musicals (Portsmouth, New Hampshire, 2001).

Moody, Richard, 'Introduction: *Po-ca-hon-tas; or, the Gentle Savage*', in *Dramas from the American Theatre,1762–1909*, ed. Richard Moody (New York, 1966), pp. 397–421.

Mordden, Ethan, *Better Foot Forward: The History of the American Musical Theatre* (New York, 1976).

 Broadway Babies: The People Who Made the American Musical (New York and Oxford, 1983).

 ' "Show Boat" Crosses Over', *New Yorker* (3 July 1989), pp. 79–94.

 Rodgers and Hammerstein (New York, 1992).

 Make Believe: The Broadway Musical in the 1920s (New York and Oxford, 1997).

 Coming Up Roses: The Broadway Musical in the 1950s (New York and Oxford, 1998).

 Beautiful Mornin': The Broadway Musical in the 1940s (New York and Oxford, 1999).

 Open a New Window: The Broadway Musical in the 1960s (New York, 2001).

Morley, Sheridan, *Spread a Little Happiness: The First Hundred Years of the British Musical* (London, 1986).

Morley, Sheridan, and Ruth Leon, *Hey Mr Producer! The Musical World of Cameron Mackintosh* (London, 1998).

Mundy, John, *Popular Music on Screen: From the Hollywood Musical to Music Video* (Manchester, 1999).

Myers, Paul, *Leonard Bernstein* (London, 1998).

Newsletter of the Stephen Sondheim Society, 1993–.

Noble, Peter, *Ivor Novello, Man of the Theatre* (London, 1951).

Nolan, Frederick, *Lorenz Hart* (New York and Oxford, 1994).

Norton, Elliot, *Broadway Down East: An Informal Account of the Plays, Players and Playhouses of Boston from Puritan Times to the Present* (Boston, 1978).

Oja, Carol, 'Marc Blitzstein's *The Cradle Will Rock* and Mass-Song Style of the 1930s', *Musical Quarterly*, 73/4 (1989), pp. 445–75.

Oland, Pamela Phillips, *The Art of Writing Great Lyrics* (New York, 2001).

Paskman, Dailey, and Sigmund Spaeth, *'Gentlemen, Be Seated!': A Parade of the Old-Time Minstrels* (Garden City, New York, 1928).

Peterson, Bernard L., Jr, *A Century of Musicals in Black and White* (Westport, Connecticut, 1993).

 Profiles of African American Stage Performers and Theatre People, 1816–1960 (Westport, Connecticut and London, 2001).

Peyser, Joan, *Bernstein: A Biography* (New York, 1987, 1998).
  The Memory of All That: The Life of George Gershwin (New York, 1993).
Plotnicki, Rita M., 'John Brougham: The Aristophanes of American Burlesque',
  Journal of Popular Culture, 12/3 (1978), pp. 422–31.
Porter, Susan L., 'English–American Interaction in American Musical Theater at
  the Turn of the Nineteenth Century', *American Music*, 4/1 (1986), pp. 6–19.
  With an Air Debonair: Musical Theatre in America, 1785–1815 (Washington DC,
  1991).
Preston, Katherine K., *Opera on the Road: Traveling Opera Troupes in the United
  States, 1825–1860* (Urbana, Illinois, 1993).
  'Art Music from 1800 to 1860', in *The Cambridge History of American Music*, ed.
  David Nicholls (Cambridge, 1998), pp. 186–213.
Rice, Tim, *Oh, What a Circus* (London, 1999).
Riis, Thomas L., 'The Music and Musicians in Nineteenth-Century Productions of
  Uncle Tom's Cabin', *American Music*, 4/3 (1986), pp. 268–86.
  Just Before Jazz: Black Musical Theater in New York, 1890–1915 (Washington DC,
  1989).
  *More Than Just Minstrel Shows: The Rise of Black Musical Theatre at the Turn of the
  Century* (New York, 1992).
Riis, Thomas L. (ed.), *The Music and Scripts of 'In Dahomey'* (Madison, 1996).
Robbins, Tim, *'Cradle Will Rock': The Movie and the Moment* (New York, 2000).
Rodgers, Richard, *Musical Stages: An Autobiography* (New York, 1975; repr. with an
  introduction by Mary Rodgers, New York, 1995).
Rogers, David A. II, 'Murder, Schtick, and Jazz: An Exploration of Realism in the
  Broadway Musical *Chicago*', M.M. thesis, University of Missouri–Kansas City,
  1998.
Root, Deane L., *American Popular Stage Music, 1860–1880* (Ann Arbor, Michigan
  1981).
Root, Deane L., and John Graziano, 'Burlesque', in *The New Grove Dictionary of
  American Music*, ed. H. Wiley Hitchcock and Stanley Sadie.
Root, Deane L. (gen. ed.), *Nineteenth-Century American Musical Theater*
  (New York).
  Vol. I. *British Opera in America: 'Children in the Wood' (1795) and 'Blue Beard'
  (1811)*, ed. Susan L. Porter (1994).
  Vol. II. *Early Melodrama in America: 'The Voice of Nature' (1803) and 'The
  Aethiop' (1813)*, ed. Karl Kroeger and Victor Fell Yellin (1994).
  Vol. III. *Italian Opera in English: 'Cinderella' (1831)*, ed. John Graziano (1994).
  Vol. IV. *Later Melodrama in America: 'Monte Cristo' (ca. 1883)*, ed. Anne Dhu
  McLucas (1995).
  Vol. V. *'Uncle Tom's Cabin' 1852 by George L. Aiken and George C. Howard*, ed.
  Thomas Riis (1994).
  Vol. VI. *The Collected Works of John Hill Hewitt*, ed. N. Lee Orr and Lynn Wood
  Bertrand (1994).
  Vol. VII. *The Collected Works of Alfred B. Sedgwick*, ed. Michael Meckna (1994).
  Vol. VIII. *Pasticcio and Temperance Plays in America: 'Il Pesceballo' (1862) and
  'Ten Nights in a Bar-Room' (1890)*, ed. Dale Cockrell (1994).

Vol. IX. *African American Theater: 'Out of Bondage' (1876) and 'Peculiar Sam, or The Underground Railroad' (1879)*, ed. Eileen Southern (1994).

Vol. X. *Irish American Theater: 'The Mulligan Guard Ball' (1879) and 'Reilly and the Four Hundred' (1891)*, ed. Katherine K. Preston (1994).

Vol. XI. *Yiddish Theater in America: 'David's Violin' (1897) and 'Shloyme Gorgl' (189–)*, ed. Mark Slobin (1994).

Vol. XII. *Early Operetta in America: 'The Doctor of Alcantara' (1879)*, ed. Charlotte Kaufman (1994).

Vol. XIII. *Early Burlesque in America: 'Evangeline' (1877)*, ed. Richard Jackson (1994).

Vol. XIV. *Later Operetta in America, Part I: 'El capitan' (1896)*, ed. Paul E. Bierley (1994).

Vol. XV. *Later Operetta in America, Part II: 'The Highwayman' (1897)*, ed. Orly Leah Krasner (1994).

Vol. XVI. *Grand Opera in America: 'The Scarlet Letter' (1896)*, ed. Elise K. Kirk (1994).

Rosenberg, Bernard, and Ernest Harburg, *The Broadway Musical: Collaboration in Commerce and Art* (New York, 1993).

Rosenberg, Deena, *Fascinating Rhythm: The Collaboration of George and Ira Gershwin* (New York, 1991).

Sanders, Ronald, *The Days Grow Short: The Life and Music of Kurt Weill* (New York, 1980).

Scheuer, Timothy E., 'The Beatles, The Brill Building, and the Persistence of Tin Pan Alley in the Age of Rock', *Popular Music and Society*, 20 (1996), pp. 89–102.

Schiff, David, *Gershwin: 'Rhapsody in Blue'* (Cambridge, 1997).

Schneider, Gretchen, 'Gabriel Ravel and the Martinetti Family: The Popularity of Pantomime in 1855', in *American Popular Entertainment: Papers and Proceedings of the Conference on the History of American Popular Entertainment*, ed. Myron Matlaw (Westport, Connecticut, 1979), pp. 241–58.

Schuster-Craig, John, 'Stravinsky's *Scènes de Ballet* and Billy Rose's *The Seven Lively Arts*: The Abravanel Account', in *Music in the Theater, Church, and Villa: Essays in Honor of Robert Lamar Weaver and Norma Wright Weaver*, ed. Susan Parisi (Warren, Michigan, 2000), pp. 285–90.

Secrest, Meryle, *Stephen Sondheim: A Life* (New York, 1998).

Seeley, Robert, and Rex Bunnett, *London Musical Shows on Record, 1889–1989* (Harrow, 1989).

Sennett, Ted, *Song and Dance: The Musicals of Broadway* (New York, 1998).

Shapiro, Anne Dhu, 'Melodrama', in *The New Grove Dictionary of American Music*, ed. H. Wiley Hitchcock and Stanley Sadie.

'Music in American Pantomime and Melodrama, 1730–1913', *American Music*, 2/4 (1984), pp. 49–72.

Sharland, Elizabeth, *The British on Broadway: Backstage and Beyond–The Early Years* (Watchet, 1999).

Sheppard, W. Anthony, *Revealing Masks: Exotic Influences and Ritualized Performance in Modernist Musical Theatre* (Berkeley, 2001).

Shirley, Wayne, Notes to *Oh, Kay!*, Smithsonian American Musical Theater Series, RCA Special Products (1978).

Shout, John D., 'The Musical Theater of Marc Blitzstein', *American Music*, 3 (1985), pp. 413–28.

Show Music, 1981–.

Shubert Archive, Staff of (Maryann Chach, Reagan Fletcher, Mark Swartz and Sylvia Wang), *The Shuberts Present: 100 Years of American Theater* (New York, 2001).

Smith, Cecil, and Glenn Litton, *Musical Comedy in America* (New York, 1950, 1981).

Smith, Marian Monta, 'Six Miles to Dawn: An Analysis of the Modern American Musical Comedy', Ph.D. diss., Cornell University, 1971.

Snyder, Linda June, 'Leonard Bernstein's Works for the Musical Theatre: How the Music Functions Dramatically', D.M.A. thesis, University of Illinois at Urbana–Champaign, 1982.

Southern, Eileen, *The Music of Black Americans: A History*, 2nd edn (New York, 1983).

'The Georgia Minstrels: the Early Years', *Inter-American Music Review*, 10/2 (1989), pp. 157–67.

Stedman, Jane, ' "Then Hey! For the Merry Greenwood!": Smith and de Koven and Robin Hood', *Journal of Popular Culture*, 12/3 (1978), pp. 432–45.

Stempel, Larry, 'The Musical Play Expands', *American Music*, 10 (1992), pp. 136–69.

Steyn, Mark, *Broadway Babies Say Goodnight: Musicals Then and Now* (New York, 1999).

Suskin, Steven, *Berlin, Kern, Rodgers, Hart, and Hammerstein: A Complete Song Catalogue* (Jefferson, North Carolina and London, 1990).

Opening Night on Broadway: A Critical Quotebook of the Golden Era of the Musical Theatre (New York, 1990).

More Opening Nights on Broadway: A Critical Quotebook of the Musical Theatre 1965 through 1981 (New York, 1997).

Show Tunes: The Songs, Shows, and Careers of Broadway's Major Composers, rev. and expanded 3rd edn (New York and Oxford, 2000).

Swain, Joseph P., *The Broadway Musical: A Critical and Musical Survey* (New York and Oxford, 1990).

Swartz, Mark Evan, *Oz Before the Rainbow* (Baltimore and London, 2000).

Swayne, Steven Robert, 'Hearing Sondheim's Voices', Ph.D. diss., University of California, Berkeley, 1999.

Swift, Mary Grace, 'Celestial Queen of the Dumb Shows', in *Musical Theatre in America: Papers and Proceedings of the Conference on the Musical Theatre in America*, ed. Glenn Loney (Westport, Connecticut, 1984), pp. 291–9.

Taymor, Julie, *The Lion King: Pride Rock on Broadway* (New York, 1997).

Thorne, Kathleen Hegarty, *The Story of Starlight Theatre: The History of Kansas City's Delightful Musical Theatre under the Stars* (Eugene, Oregon, 1993).

Thornhill, William, 'Kurt Weill's *Street Scene*', Ph.D. diss., University of North Carolina, Chapel Hill, 1990.

Traubner, Richard, *Operetta: A Theatrical History* (Garden City, New Jersey, 1983; 2nd edn, New York, 1989).

Turk, Edward Baron, *Hollywood Diva: A Biography of Jeanette MacDonald* (Berkeley, 1998).

Valance, Tom, *The American Musical* (London, 1970).

Walsh, Michael, *Andrew Lloyd Webber: His Life and Works, A Critical Biography* (rev. and enlarged edn, New York, 1997).

Waters, Edward N., *Victor Herbert: A Life in Music* (New York, 1955).

Webb, Paul, *Ivor Novello: A Portrait of a Star* (London, 1999).

Weill, Kurt, and Lotte Lenya, *Speak Low (When You Speak Love): The Letters of Kurt Weill and Lotte Lenya,* trans. and ed. Lys Symonette and Kim H. Kowalke (Berkeley and London, 1996).

Wilder, Alex, *American Popular Song: The Great Innovators 1900–1950* (New York and Oxford, 1972).

Wilk, Max, *OK!: The Story of 'Oklahoma!'* (New York, 1993).

Wilson, Sandy, *I Could Be Happy* (London, 1975).

Woll, Allen L. *Black Musical Theatre: From 'Coontown' to 'Dreamgirls'* (Baton Rouge, 1989).

Wood, Graham, 'The Development of Song Forms in the Broadway and Hollywood Musicals of Richard Rodgers, 1919–1943', Ph.D. diss., University of Minnesota, 2000.

Yellin, Victor Fell, 'Rayner Taylor's Music for *The Aethiop*, Part I: Performance History', *American Music,* 4 (1986), pp. 249–67.

Young, William C., *Documents of American Theatre History,* vol. I. *Famous American Playhouses 1716–1899* (Chicago, 1973).

Zadan, Craig, *Sondheim and Co.* (New York, 1986, 1989).

Zellers, Parker, *Tony Pastor: Dean of the Vaudeville Stage* (Ypsilanti, Michigan, 1971).

Index

Shows, sources of shows, songs, and dances are listed by title, not under authors' names.